SEWERO!
CHRISTIAN DRAMA AND THE DRAMA OF CHRISTIANITY IN AFRICA

Published by
Kachere Series
?.O. Box 1037, Zomba

3N 99908-76-26-6 (Kachere Monograph no. 20)
\N-13: 978-99908-76-26-0
Kachere Series is represented outside Africa by:
an Books Collective Oxford (orders@africanbookscollective.com)
ɟan State University Press East Lansing (msupress@msu.edu)

Martin Nthambo
ign: Mercy Chilunga

htning Source

SEWERO!
CHRISTIAN DRAMA AND THE DRAMA OF CHRISTIANITY IN AFRICA:

**On the Genesis and Genius of Chinyanja
Radio Plays in Malawi
With special reference to TransWorld Radio and
African Traditional Religion**

With a foreword by Patrick Semphere

Kachere Monograph no. 20

**Kachere Series
Zomba
2005**

Kachere Series,
P.O. Box 1037, Zomba, Malawi
email: kachere@globemw.net
www.sdnp.org.mw/kachereseries

This book is part of the Kachere Series, a range of books on religion, culture and society from Malawi. Other Kachere Monographs published are:

Ernst Wendland, *Buku Loyera. An Introduction to the New Chichewa Bible Translation*

Ernst Wendland, *Preaching that Grabs the Heart. A Rhetorical-Stylistic Study of the Chichewa Revival Sermons of Shadrack Wame*

Peter G. Forster, *T. Cullen Young: Missionary and Anthropologist*

Martin Ott, *African Theology in Images*

James N. Amanze, *African Traditional Religion in Malawi: The Case of the Bimbi Cult*

Silas Ncozana, *The Spirit Dimension in African Christianity. A Pastoral Study among the Tumbuka People of Northern Malawi*

J.W.M van Breugel, *Chewa Traditional Religion*

Pia Thielmann, *Hotbeds: Black-White Love in Novels from the United States, Africa, and the Caribbean*

The Kachere Series is the publications arm of the
Department of Theology and Religious Studies of the University of Malawi.

Series Editors: J.C. Chakanza, F.L. Chingota, Klaus Fiedler, P.A. Kalilombe,
S. Mohammad, Fulata L. Moyo, Martin Ott

DEDICATION

To

All my Lusaka Lutheran Seminary Students
(1968-*mpaka lero lomwe lino!*)

Who have indeed taught me much,
even as I have attempted to teach them
through the years,
by the grace of our mutual Teacher and Lord.

"And what you have heard from me through many witnesses entrust to faithful people who will be able to teach others as well."

"Mau amene udamva kwa ine pamaso pa mboni zambiri, uwasungitse anthu okhulupirika amene adzathe kuwaphunzitsanso kwa ena."

(2 Timothy 2:2—NRSV, *Buku Loyera*)

Table of Content

FOREWORD

Over the past decade, Malawi has seen the proliferation of drama groups. Although some of these have died a natural death, their popular emergence signifies the fact that in an oral culture like Malawi, drama is a powerful medium of communication. In this regard, the significance of vernacular radio drama in Malawi (and Africa in general) can not be over-emphasized given the low literacy rate of about 30%.

For over 12 years, the *Sewero* Christian drama programme has been on air on TransWorld Radio as a double-edged tool for evangelism and teaching. This program was aired weekly on shortwave from Manzini, Swaziland until 2002 when it was temporarily suspended due to financial constraints facing TWR Malawi. However, with an FM service currently covering the southern and central Malawi, we are still broadcasting archived editions of the program until a time when we can resume production of the play.

This book comes at a critical moment on the media landscape of Malawi. With many radio stations mushrooming in the country, TWR needs to take a critical look at its programs and redefine their purpose as well as relevance in order to remain true to its mission of preaching and teaching the gospel on the one hand while also being mindful of the times in which we broadcast. Under a political dispensation in which freedom of expression is the buzzword, *Sewero* provides TWR with an opportunity to be a mouthpiece of the church in addressing issues that are corroding our society.

Ernst Wendland makes an interesting analysis of the key subjects that feature in the *Sewero* productions. Scooping the top, the list looks like this— magic, witchcraft, sorcery, marriage and family life, sexual sins. If this is a reflection of the pressing needs of the Malawi society, the challenge for the church in Malawi is to go beyond mass evangelism and proceed to provide adequate teaching to its flock to ensure that the Christian life becomes a lifestyle amid all these challenges.

With radio technology evolving rapidly, Sewero, among other TWR programs needs to adapt and Ernst makes some plausible suggestions regarding making the program available on current technological platforms like the internet. With the TWR FM service expanding nationwide, the Malawi audience is currently enjoying the plays with a better signal than the shortwave.

In the closing pages, Ernst makes some potent recommendations regarding adaptation of *Sewero* to different media and modes of expression. This outline is helpful as it assists TWR management redefine the future of the program and take advantage of the many opportunities that avail themselves through radio drama and other audience-specific programmes. As I write this, TWR Africa has just embarked on a pan-African 52-episode children's radio drama, in Chichewa (Malawi), KiSwahili (Kenya), SiSwati (Swaziland) and Portuguese (Mozambique). For Chichewa, the program is titled *Madzi a Moyo*, aimed at sharing the gospel to rural 7 to 12 year olds. It is being aired on both shortwave (Swaziland) and FM (Malawi).

St Matthew records the words of Jesus in predicting the end times thus: "This gospel of the kingdom will be preached in the whole world as a testimony to all nations and then the end will come" (Matthew 24:14, NIV). The two-fold potential of radio drama to evangelise and teach the gospel goes a long way in helping fulfill this Great Commission of our Lord Jesus Christ.

Patrick Semphere, National Director
Trans World Radio (Malawi)

Series Editor's Preface

The Kachere tree is a local Malawian variety of the fig tree, and since it grows so big, that it provides much shade, it is a preferred tree for meetings. When Chief Kapeni in Blantyre welcomed the missionaries, they found many Kachere trees at his residence, and when Dr David Livingstone met the chiefs of Nkhota Kota, they met under a Kachere tree. When missionaries, black or white, opened their schools, they often chose to do so under a Kachere tree. That may not be the rule anymore, so we invite you to sit under our virtual Kachere tree and read dour real books and discuss with anyone who wants to share.

The Kachere Series is an initiative of the Department of Theology and Religious Studies at the University of Malawi. It was begun in 1995 with the aim of promoting the emergence of a body of literature to engage critically with religion in Malawi, its social and political impact and the theological questions it raises. By now the Kachere Series has over eighty publications, and while it still has its original aim, it has widened its remit to include fields other than religion like poetry, ecology, history or literary criticism. Most books deal *with* Malawi, but some just come *from* Malawi, but we believe that all may be useful both within Malawi and without.

In the beginning the Kachere Series had three sub-series: *Kachere Books* had a more general appeal, *Kachere Texts* were the mixed bag for smaller and unusual contributions, and the *Kachere Monographs* were the prestigious third branch, for which only full-length academic treatises based on solid primary research were accepted. Later the *Kachere Studies* were added, which provide room for works not necessarily dealing with Malawi, and the *Mvunguti Series* which mainly caters for books in Malawian languages other than English. Lately *Kachere Tools* (for teaching and learning) were added and the *Sorces for the Study of Religion in Malawi* were revived to provide an outlet for research results below the monograph level.

As editors we arehappy to present this Kachere Monograph (no. 20) as one of those which address the core intention of the Kachere Series: to critically engage with religion in Malawi. As radio is the most common medium for mass communication, a study of one type of Christian radio programme is worth a monograph, and so far it is the only one in the field.

Kachere Series Editors
November 2004

PREFACE

"Radio—a medium whose time has come…"
(Why so—now? Because we live "in a world where the number of people
who cannot read, or who choose not to do so, is growing" at an alarming rate.)[1]

0.1 Introduction: Explanation of the title to this book

SEWERO! ("A Play!") – That is title of the Chinyanja-language radio program that I will be reporting on in this book; it is also the word of identification that the announcer proclaims at the beginning of every show. The rest of
my title is rather long, and it might seem at first reading that by it I am simply playing with words. I trust that you will find that this is not the case. My
Preface provides a brief overview of the various interrelated subjects that
will be explored in greater detail during the course of the present study,
which stands as my partial and clearly imperfect attempt to describe one of
the most dynamic and creative examples of Christian communication that I
have experienced during my ministry in south-eastern Africa. In my title
then I try to summarize some of the chief elements of this highly significant
indigenous, vernacular phenomenon—designated by the simple noun *Sewero*
(plural: *ma-sewero*). The following is a short explanatory breakdown concerning what to expect in the chapters that follow.

0.1.1 "Christian Drama"

The weekly half-hour *Sewero* dramatic religious productions broadcast on
TransWorld Radio (TWR) are plays in terms of their literary genre, but this
is drama with a difference. These happen to be "*serious* plays" (an oxymo-
ron?) that deal with some of the most pressing issues and events of death and
life in daily Africa from a biblical Christian perspective. The dedicated pro-

---

[1] This quote is taken from a comment in the *UBS World Report* 356, December 2000, p. 9. The report
continues: "[R]adio offers Bible agencies an excellent alternative for effective Scripture communication.
New opportunities for radio are arising from a number of directions"—notably from new FM stations
throughout the world, "broadcasting" via the Internet and mobile phones, a greater openness on the part
of national radio stations to allow religious broadcasting, and cable systems that are being extended into
previously remote areas. An even more recent development of great significance is the development of
"satellite broadcasting", where a host of clear radio channels and stations can be accommodated. For
these, and many other, reasons many Christian communicators conclude: "We see radio as a robust tool
for the Gospel for the foreseeable future in spite of the massive technological changes that are taking
place" (Frank Gray & Eila Murphy, "The Unlikely Missionary" [i.e., radio broadcasting!], *Mission Frontiers* 22:5 (Dec. 2000), p. 21). The present monograph documents the story of a popular vernacular radio
program whose time too "has come"—namely, the Chinyanja *Sewero* dramatic plays currently being
broadcast on TransWorld Radio to south-central Africa.

ducer and cast of character "voices" aim to *educate* and *encourage* even as they also *entertain* countless listeners over space (the lower area of Africa) and time (for well over 12 years now).[2]

0.1.2 *"Drama of Christianity"*

The "Christian drama" of the *Sewero* radio plays seeks to explore and to elucidate the "drama of Christianity" as it is preached, taught, and lived by ordinary Christians who happen to be living, and listening, within the range of its broadcast voice. On this rugged continent, south of the Great Desert, everyday religion always involves a daily drama of potentially life and death issues—physical, social, moral, as well as spiritual issues. People come into conflict with ever-present malevolent forces, such as harmful magic, hostile witches/sorcerers, capricious evil spirits, secret oneiromancy and divination, dangerous social and familial taboos.

All these antagonistic powers and influences adversely affect the quality of daily life—these in addition to the many other serious struggles of human existence (e.g., drought-famine, the high cost of living, poor education, loss of jobs, corruption in high places, lack of adequate housing, AIDS and other diseases, conflicts in gender relations, rising radical Islamic influence, and many more). How should Christians react to such tests, trials, challenges, and uncertainties? These insightful Chinyanja plays document in dramatic fashion a great variety of typical responses as they might by given by Malawians living right next door to the listeners. They are excellent examples of popular "grassroots" biblical theology at work—and at play!

0.1.3 *"Genesis"*

I will attempt to describe, to the best of my ability as an informed outsider,[3] what goes on when a *Sewero* play is prepared, produced, and polished to perfection by its skilled cast of various character roles. The dramatic "genesis" begins with a central concept or theme—a colorful idea, current issue, prob-

---

[2]   In April, 2003 the *Sewero* programme was suspended as the TWR (Swaziland) management has undertaken a thorough re-evaluation of their entire schedule of programming for the southern region of Africa. We trust that this suspension will be only a temporary measure.

[3]   I have lived in Zambia (Northern Rhodesia) since 1962 and have been a guest-teacher here since 1968. Nevertheless, I do not consider myself to be either an "expert" or an "insider" with regard to the local Bantu culture—its world-view and way-of-life. For such essential insights, I have learned to depend on my successive classes of students at the Lutheran Seminary in Lusaka, on various Bible translation teams that I have guided as a UBS Translation Consultant, and on the many faithful urban and rural lay-Christians whom I have served as a weekend pastoral supervisor in the Lutheran Church of Central Africa. I wish to pay tribute in particular to seminary student *Bright Pembeleka*, who greatly assisted me with the transcription and translation of this *Sewero* corpus; without his help I would not have managed to cope in particular with the very idiomatic expressions that pervade these dynamic vernacular dialogues.

lem-area, or controversy that is often contributed by one of the key players themselves. This is followed by an informal brain-storming session involving all members of the cast, who dialogue together in order to flesh out the narrative "plot", assign the principal character voices, specify the central Christian message to be derived from the story, and supply key supporting Scripture passages. This communal, give-and-take compositional process proceeds through several stages of on-the-spot, spontaneous oral "scripting" and concludes with the finished recorded performance—one that sounds highly "professional" by any standards, even though it is produced by distinctly non-professional (unsalaried) players.

0.1.4 "Genius"

From the external "context" of *Sewero* production, I move to a closer examination of the texts themselves in an effort to describe and exemplify their manifest verbal artistry, rhetorical power, theological insight, and practical relevance for Bible believers (individuals and groups) living in central Africa. This is rather difficult to do since I thereby attempt to capture and display one dynamic medium of communication (dialogue—*sound*) within the necessarily restrictive confines of another (print—*sight*). But I hope that this attempt is better than nothing, and that my preliminary effort will be seriously followed up by all interested parties—that is, so that they are encouraged to actually listen to, benefit from, and then proceed to consider more carefully, a radio performance for themselves. These dramatic productions cannot fail to leave a positive impression on any audience, whether the listeners happen to understand Chinyanja or not.

0.1.5 "Chinyanja Radio Plays—TransWorld Radio"

Sewero plays are explicitly prepared for and transmitted by the mass-medium of shortwave (now also via FM) radio. They are not simply recorded at some outdoor public performance for a subsequent, second-hand broadcast. The venerable *medium* of radio has its own unique communicative possibilities as well as certain liabilities which need to be comparatively considered as one analyzes and evaluates these Chinyanja vernacular dramas. This necessitates an overview of the audio mode of artistic message expression and public transmission. I will include for the record a certain amount of background information on the history, nature, and purpose of TWR and its wide influence in south-central Africa, with particular reference to the *Sewero* program.

Part of the show's popularity derives from the fact that *Chinyanja* (formerly known as *Chichewa* in Malawi) is the major Bantu language of this

15

sub-region (Malawi, Zambia, Mozambique). It is spoken as a mother-tongue by over 7 million people, and as a second language by another 3-4 million more. Chinyanja is a specially-recognized, government promoted language in Malawi and, to a lesser extent also Zambia, e.g., in schools, radio broadcasting, television, official government publications, and so forth.

0.1.6 "African Traditional Religion"

African traditional religion (ATR) serves as the special subject and topical focus for this study of Christian intercultural communication. This in itself is a vast and very complicated subject, so I have further narrowed the scope of my investigation to the area of the *religious occult*, particularly its more malevolent, magical and mystic side.[4] Various aspects of this all-pervasive, life-governing belief system are dramatized and polemicized in the Chinyanja *Sewero* radio plays. How do these intimate public performances serve then to sensitize their large unseen audiences in an implicitly apologetic (defensive) manner to such controversial issues as the practice of sor-

---

[4] The adjective *occult*, here used as a generic noun, refers to phenomena that are "hidden, concealed, secret, esoteric, beyond human understanding, mysterious, or designating certain alleged mystic arts, such as magic..." (Webster's *New World* Dictionary). This is a Western definition of course and therefore it does not apply precisely to the Nyanja Bantu religious phenomena that will be the focus of my study. The designation will be retained, however, merely as a convenient English cover term to refer to the various practices associated with witchcraft, sorcery, magic, divination, and spiritism (ancestor veneration).

cery and witchcraft, recourse to the services of a diviner or traditional "doctor", or the periodic personal application of protective charms and magical potions?

There is no epistemological division between the sacred and secular either in African philosophy or its society—that is, between what is regarded as "religious" and the profane, or between the physical and psychological constitution of mankind. All created being (the initial activity of God is presupposed) is unified and its diverse aspects are intended to operate in harmony wherever life is manifested in the world. The *Sewero* dramas respect this traditional African perspective and work within its scope to proffer an alternative, biblically-based orientation and lifestyle. One of my main goals is to present a brief, perhaps also culturally beclouded (due to my alien background), glimpse of the great genius of this dynamic, locally-initiated Christian communicative endeavor.

0.2 Some practical aspects of this research project

I conclude this introductory Preface with a few additional comments concerning the research program that I have adopted with regard to the collection, analysis, and presentation of these Chinyanja radio plays.

0.2.1 Collection: Corpus and method

My collection of *Sewero* dramas consists of over 70 examples (cassette recordings) that were broadcast at different times on TransWorld Radio during a period that extends from the early 1990s to the present day.[5] They range in length from about 25 minutes to those productions that have been deliberately divided into two parts due to their duration, i.e., 45-55 minutes. I trained a succession of seminary students to transcribe, summarize, and in some cases also to annotate or translate roughly into English. I owe a great debt to these students (hence my opening Dedication), for they have acted as valuable co-collaborators on this project; without their assistance it could not have been completed.

I have also obtained some significant help from Mr. Patrick Semphere, National Director of TWR and long-time *Sewero* producer, Mr. Nyongani Chirwa (both based in Lilongwe, Malawi) in terms of background information and the provision of several studio-produced cassette tapes. I would

---

[5]   In the early years I collected these *Sewero* more or less on an ad hoc basis as part of an earlier research project that focused on Chichewa revival sermons broadcast on TWR (see Wendland 2000). More recently I have been able to record and have them transcribed and analyzed on a more systematic basis. Over the years I have encountered a number of duplicates and broadcasts that were simply too poor, transmission-wise, to record or to try and transcribe (e.g., static- and distortion-filled).

have liked to interact more with the radio staff in recent years (especially those who have succeeded Mr. Chirwa as program director) as well as with the *Sewero* players themselves and the technical recording team, but my work schedule and location, over 500 miles away in Lusaka, Zambia made closer contact impossible. With respect to production, I also owe a debt of thanks to Mr. Martin Ntambo of the Bible Society of Malawi for his expert help in the final typesetting of this book, which saved us much time in the overall publication process.

During the course of this investigation, I also benefited from observing several different audiences, individuals as well as groups, of typical Chinyanja speakers, both to observe their reactions during a play and later also to discuss certain aspects of its performance and message. To all these interested colleagues and fellow enthusiastic audience participants, including several classes of seminary students, I extend my heartfelt appreciation for their important contribution to this collaborative research effort.

0.2.2 Aims and limitations of this study

My principal goal is twofold; it is in short to reveal and describe as much as I can of the captivating verbal *artistry* as well as the engaging local *theology* of the Chinyanja *Sewero* radio programs. In these vernacular plays we have some excellent examples of Christian "contextualization" in vivid verbal action—that is, featuring a thoroughly localized (non-Western) treatment and application of some key Bible themes, teachings, concepts, and practices. This is accomplished by means of an expert welding together of an indigenous means of communication (dramatic performance) coupled with a modern mass medium (radio transmission).

The result is a novel (at least in a central African setting)[6] and highly effective method of confronting large audiences with the challenging message and mission of Jesus the Christ. How relevant are the Scriptures to everyday life and its various conflicts and crises? These plays not only suggest a solid biblical answer, but they also do this in a manner that fully captivates the listening audience, thus leading them to experience the message personally for themselves, both individually and as a group, which is the custom of ancient African oral tradition. I will thus endeavor through this study to provide readers with an initial exploratory insight into this dramatic art form—its power to persuade (rhetoric), the beauty of its language (artistry), and the

---

[6]   Other Christian drama groups produce and perform plays of course, in the various Bantu languages of the region, but only rarely or inconsistently is this done—and so well—for a specific radio audience. I may be wrong in this general blanket evaluation; readers are certainly invited to write and advise me otherwise—or to comment on any other aspect of these *Sewero* plays: Ernst Wendland, Lutheran Seminary, PO Box 310091, Lusaka, ZAMBIA; wendland@zamnet.zm .

penetrating, perceptive nature of its diverse religious and ethical messages (theology). Over and above this descriptive purpose, my aim is also one of encouragement—that is, to encourage the *Sewero* program staff to continue their excellent efforts in the field of contextualized biblical communication via the medium of radio,[7] and also to promote the development of this excellent model via other media (e.g., audio-cassette), languages (e.g., every Bantu language with two million speakers or more), and indeed neighboring countries as well. The audio channel of message transmission has not nearly reached its full potential for conveying the Word of God in south-central Africa.

Several of my glaring limitations in this effort have already been suggested. I am a non-mother-tongue-speaking cultural outsider. How accurate and reliable then can my observations and conclusions be as they are set forth in this monograph? In mitigation, I can only say that I have tried to "compensate" for my deficiencies by training and engaging a number of African colleagues—some of whom are expert oral performers, cultural analysts, and theologians in their own right. They have undoubtedly assisted me much more than I realize or can even acknowledge. On the other hand, they cannot be held responsible for any errors, omissions, or misinterpretations of fact that may appear in the pages that follow. The fact is that the present study merely lays a bare foundation for what is really required as a follow-up project—that is, a much more extensive, African-managed and composed analysis, interpretation, and evaluation of the *Sewero* phenomenon, both in Chinyanja and other Bantu languages.

0.2.3 Overview of previous research

I am not aware of any research that has been done in Malawi with a specific focus upon to the Chinyanja *masewero* program, or anywhere else for that matter with regard to Bantu vernacular dramatic plays. Some excellent general studies concerning the use of the radio medium in Christian communication are readily available in published form (e.g., Mitchell 1999, Smith 1992, Sogaard 1991, 1993, 2001, and a special edition of *Mission Frontiers* 2000). A more specific research project pertaining to the utility of radio transmission is Sundersingh's published dissertation that deals with "audio-

---

[7]   Dr. Lynell Zogbo, my UBS colleague in West Africa has come to a similar conclusion about the vast potential of radio communication. While acknowledging the growing influence of television throughout the country, she observes that "[i]n Ivory Coast, probably the best means of reaching people with the gospel is radio. People from every economic bracket and every social position, from illiterate immigrant workers to the highest officials in government have radios and listen regularly to them" (Zogbo 2002).

based translation" among the Tamil Nadu people of India (2001).[8] My own introduction to the vast communicative potential of radio broadcasting in Africa was my doctoral research on Nyanja radio narratives (1979). I am pleased now to have the opportunity of looking at my earlier study in the light of more recent developments in the style, structure, and strategy of communicating via this most accessible and widespread medium of transmission, with particular reference to the great success and excellence of the *Sewero* dramatic troupe as they continue to animate the airways of southern Africa via TWR.

0.2.4 Summary of contents

I begin with a general description of the large conceptual "stage" of radio, that is, a summary of the main characteristics as well as some important limiting features of this sometimes underrated mass medium of communication. Chapter two carries on with a brief historical introduction to and explanation of the informal *Sewero* production process as it has been carried out for broadcast on TransWorld Radio with little change now for over a decade (ch.1). In chapter three I present an overview of African traditional religion, with special reference to its occult beliefs and practices, which form the heart of my analysis of selected *Sewero* dramas. The plays themselves are then investigated, first in summary fashion with reference to their principal topics, biblical texts, and theological trends (ch.4), second, by means of a careful documentation and exemplification of seven outstanding stylistic-rhetorical techniques which they consistently manifest (ch.5). A complete radio play is presented (in translation) for examination in chapter 6, along with extensive annotation that is intended to provide a minimal, but hopefully adequate, "context for interpretation". My study concludes (ch.7) with some personal observations and ideas that pertain to the possible "future" of Christian vernacular radio drama in Africa. Following a selective Bibliography and preceding a final Index of topics are five Appendices that present, in turn, a TWR program report by Patrick Semphere (A), a TWR statement of ministry (B)[9], a sample questionnaire (in translation) (C), a

---

[8] For example, in his survey of the Tamilnadu people of India with respect to the most effective "mode" of audio-cassette production of a selected Scripture portion (Mark 1:21-28), Sundersingh found that a "dramatized format" (multi-voiced presentation) won out over both a "story-telling format" (single voice with modulated intonation) and a straight "reading format" (unmodulated reading voice) (2001:158-160).

[9] I wish to thank TWR National Director for Malawi, Mr. Patrick Semphere, for his support and encouragement during the course of this book's production. In addition, I owe a great debt of gratitude to Mr. Martin Ntambo, DTP Officer of the Bible Society of Malawi, for lending his expertise and time to the typesetting of this book, which made possible its publication sooner rather than later. Thanks also to the Executive Director of the BSM, Mr. Byson Nakutho, for allowing Mr. Ntambo to assist me in this way.

sample "sermon" included in a *Sewero* play (D), and a transcription and translation of part of an interview with the principal *Sewero* playwright, Rev. Josophat Banda (E), and a comparative reflection on the so-called "miracle-mystery plays" of the Middle Ages of Western Europe (F).

1. The Radio "Stage"—A Theatre of the Mind and Heart

1.0 The invisible *Sewero* "stage"

How can there be a "stage" in the case of an indiscernible medium of communication? In physical terms it is impossible; in another sense, however, this stage is very real, unlimited in fact. It is a "virtual" dramatic set, bounded conceptually only by the creativity of the minds of individual listeners. And where the minds of people are affected, it is just a short step to reach their hearts, emotively that is. Messages that influence the feelings as well as the thinking of an audience have a great capacity to achieve a significant overt behavioral impact as well.

In this opening chapter we will describe the principal features of the *radio* medium of message transmission, including a number of its limiting factors, i.e., situational influences that do restrict certain aspects of the effectiveness of radio communication. It is crucial to understand and appreciate the nature of the signal's channel before we attempt to delve into selected aspects of the artistry, rhetoric, and kerygma of the *Sewero* dramatic plays. While it is an overstatement to claim in the case of radio that "the medium is the message" (McLuhan), it is certainly correct to say that the chosen medium of communication greatly influences any text that it transmits. Therefore that same text must be formulated accordingly—that is, strategically composed beforehand with the intended medium, as well as the designated audience and their setting of reception, clearly in mind. How well does the *Sewero* program rate in this respect?

1.1 Characteristics of the radio medium

This section is based on the results of published as well as personal research concerning the effectiveness of radio (and/or audio-cassettes) in comparison with other popular mass media of communication, especially video (television), which reproduces a particular visual field but in the process also limits the imagination and conception to that specific contextual scene, sociocultural setting, and interpersonal situation (see Wendland 1979:87-110, 1989). My current interest stems from a professional involvement in projects that seek to utilize the *audio* medium as a special means of transmitting translations and adaptations of the Scriptures in the Bantu languages of south-central Africa, especially for a non- or low-literate audience. In this modern age which seems to be captured by video imagery and computer-generated graphics, the importance of the purely audio medium of communication for varied Scripture-use applications has recently been re-emphasized:

> In truth, audio has always been an essential element in our engaging in Scripture… it is arguable that audio is the most effective medium today to carry the Word of God to those who have yet to receive it (Fergus Macdonald, Foreword to Søgaard 2001).

I will briefly consider four closely interrelated and interactive aspects of a medium-oriented characterization of radio broadcasting—physical, conceptual, social, and economic—along with the effects that these have with regard to the production and/or reception of the *Sewero* plays. A radio message is created by a maximum of three possible constitutive elements—*speech, sound effects,* and *music*—mixed together in varied combinations depending on the nature of the program being created and its intended purpose. A more detailed and developed treatment of this subject may be found in the major works cited in the following sections.

1.1.1 Physical

Radio is a one-dimensional, single-sense medium. It features a total sound "event"—yet one that is invisible to its audience, who are thereby rendered "blind", that is, effectively deprived of all physical sight. This factor often necessitates a certain amount of additional explicit description on the part of the players during their speeches—at least enough to stimulate the minds of listeners to create an appropriate scene to "support" the dialogue. In any case, since oral-aural sound is completely in focus, radio producers must seek and creatively integrate voices, music, and background sounds of the highest possible quality (as determined by extensive survey research within the target community). Radio's augmentation of the audio channel sharply differentiates it from other common types of verbal communication, such as interpersonal dialogue, a public speech, writing/print, video, and television. On the other hand, radio is very similar and, as we shall see, also functionally complementary to the medium of cassette (or CD) recordings. Therefore, many of the characteristics of radio described in this section would apply also to audio cassettes as well (see 2.5).

One important difference is that a radio transmission is automatically directed towards the "masses"—that is, it is intended to reach very many people at once, wherever they happen to be, and inclusive of both rich and poor, literate or non-literate, rural or urban. It is able to cross all types of communication barriers (short wave in particular): geographical, political, social, religious, economic, and even cultural (i.e., in the case of a large lingua franca). This gives the radio "voice" a certain power of influence, prestige, and authority that cannot be matched by any other medium of interpersonal communication.[1]

Another distinctive physical feature of radio is its constant movement or temporal progression; its "sound" cannot be stopped without loss (as in the case of a cassette). In certain respects this may be regarded as a disadvantage (see below); on the other hand, the quality of "movement" contributes a great deal to the perceived naturalness of this medium. So it is that radio "voices" convey along with a sense of personal presence also a dynamic feeling for the present situation, thus placing listeners "in the middle of actuality" (Ong 1967:128) as if they were hearing a "live publication". This impression is magnified because it occurs alone, without any additional visual (or other) stimulation of the senses.

Thus the radio narrator or character (as in a drama) has but a single resource available to work with, though it is a very potent one, namely, that of *sound*—or its absence, significant silence. As noted above, this is normally manifested in three distinct audio forms: the human speaking *voice*, which is generally the most prominent, and two optional, variable adjuncts: diverse accompanying sound effects (see 1.3.2) and musical or vocal background (1.3.3). Some communication specialists have observed that despite the distance from which its signal emanates, the radio "voice" has a certain personal, "interiorizing" quality about it. Sound, as Ong puts it, "reveals interiors", that is, it gives the clearest, most reliable clues as to the mental and emotional state of the speaker (1967:118). Depending then on its vocal character (resonance, timbre, pitch, expressiveness, etc.) and the skill of the radio personage who happens to be speaking, her/his voice can communicate with a remote, invisible listener in a way that is psychologically as well as conceptually very close and attractive, even enticingly so.

Such "live", proximate personal contact can be achieved simply by the physical sound of a familiar human voice (see 1.1.2), upon which members of the audience must accordingly focus their complete attention. On the other hand, the opposite effect can also be easily evoked, whether by

---

[1] "Radio is the supreme medium of communication in Zambia, and the only one reaching a majority of the population" (Mytton 1978:207). Although this assertion may not be quite as completely applicable today as it was 25 years ago when this research was carried out, it is still valid and therefore a factor that bears great importance in the development of any comprehensive Christian communication strategy, either for Zambia or for neighboring Malawi where the *Sewero* broadcasts originate. It may be interesting to note that radio has not lost its former popularity even in highly technologized, so-called "first world" countries. In the United States, for example, a recent report states: "Americans love to tune in. More than 9 out of 10 people listen to radio every week, and 8 out of 10 do so every day according to Arbitron [a market research company]" (*U.S. News & World Report*, December 2, 2002, page 40).

accident or by deliberate dramatic design, that is, by means of a character voice that just as powerfully repels, antagonizes, angers, even disgusts listeners. In any case, in an oral-aural society interpersonal speech is highly valued, a feature that renders the dialogues of a *Sewero* play immediately interesting and attractive.

It needs to be pointed out however that this personally engaging sort of communication by verbal sound alone—or silence (which in the medium of radio is highly meaningful, at the very least as a generator of suspense and tension)—can be achieved only if there are no external distractions on the receiver's side of the transmission process. Here is where the physical characteristics of the setting of reception come into play, which is one of the crucial limiting factors that affect the quality of the message (see 1.2.1). The more conducive this setting, the more potentially effective the *Sewero* program, which, due to all the rapidly speaking voices involved, is not very easy to follow if the radio signal is weak or distorted in any way. This makes nighttime listening in rural areas, for example, relatively ideal, for there is not usually a lot of light around to bring competing images into view or many other disturbing activities going on in the village at that time. Since the qualities of sound are magnified in the process of radio transmission, physical modifications and modulations of the human voice (e.g., the use of volume, stress, intonation, tempo, etc.) can be very "meaning"-ful. The expert use of different backgrounded sound insertions too becomes essential in the evocation of local scenes and social situations (1.3.2).

1.1.2 Conceptual

Due to the complete absence of a physical, visible "set", the listener's mind must take over and actively create one—as well as providing a visualization of all characters, their physical attributes, actions, and other behavioral attributes. As in the case of a traditional vernacular oral narrative performance, the audience invariably plays a vital role in the dramatization of any radio play. For this reason radio drama has been commonly called a "theatre of the mind" and an "art of the imagination". What may at first be regarded as a deprivation or limitation thus turns out to be a significant asset, for as the narrator or characters provide the verbal images, the audience simultaneously actualizes these as current events and realistic scenes that are depicted on the stage of their individual conception. Such contextualized conceptualizations are distinct acts of their own creation, unbound either by an actual set and setting or the environment in which they happen to be perceiving the play. In the words of one radio commentator:

> From the author's clues the listener collects his (or her) materials and embodies them in a picture of his own experience—whether physical or psychological—and therefore more real to him than the ready-made pictures of the stage designer (Tyrone Guthrie, cited in Wendland *loc.cit.*).

Another analyst describes this conceptual process and "the power of radio" as follows:

> Having the space to draw their own images liberates listeners to participate or interact with what they are hearing. ... As a result, the pictures are better on radio: What you can imagine is almost always scarier, funnier, more real and more vivid than the explicit images of video and film (Mitchell 1999:55).

Thus the virtually unlimited resources of this vast scenic—and often subtly "seductive"! (Mitchell 1999:51)—storehouse of the mind allows much greater flexibility and a higher degree of local contextualization than is possible on any physical stage or even a movie screen. Swift temporal and spatial shifts can be accomplished, essential attributes of character given substance, the appropriate psychological atmosphere suggested, and any necessary prop or scenic detail supplied—each within the span of a sentence or two. An effective broadcast(er) can, as one radio playwright boasts, "build a house in three words and furnish it in five" (Paul Peters, cited in Wendland *loc.cit.*). The *Sewero* plays do not have a narrator available for this purpose; rather, the dynamic, picturesque, life-related dialogue itself fully suffices.

This particular quality is facilitated by the radio setting in Africa. In other words, mental creativity is effectively realized in a society whose members are experienced and often experts in the realm of vocal communication and who have inherited a vast oral storehouse of traditional art forms as evidence of this. As a result, they are past masters at processing language in sound along with the many indigenous scenes, situations, characters, events, and imagery that may be verbally evoked. This serves also to imbue the plot of any *Sewero* play with a pervasive unity and completeness, for there is never a defect, incongruity, or omission in one's own mental creation. Furthermore, due to the associative correlation of different faculties of the human sensorium, just about any sensory impression or image—even those of taste, smell, and touch—may be stimulated by means of a specific, well-chosen word or phrase that is placed within an appropriate imaginative setting.

Since every mind is different, however, and unique to its owner, each conceptual representation and psychological experience of a given radio drama will similarly be exclusive. What effect this factor has upon the overall message as intended by the radio author, producer, and cast needs to be tested for core similarities and differences with respect to a specified audience group. Obviously, the more disparate the audience—both from each other and also from the original sociological and cultural setting envisioned by the production team—the more diverse will be the "message" that is ultimately conveyed—that is, perceived, interpreted, reacted to, and applied to one's current thought and behavior. In the region served by TransWorld Radio, however, there is not too much danger of extreme sociocultural or religious diversity, certainly not among the mother-tongue or second-language speakers of Chinyanja (Chichewa) who constitute the principal audience of the *Sewero* program.

Another, related "conceptual" consideration is that of the "connotation" of radio messages, particularly in Africa. In this respect, there are certain indications, based on informal questioning, that radio is generally regarded as being a more "trustworthy" (i.e., authoritative, credible, reliable) medium of transmission than the other popular forms of mass communication. The use of television and the associated video medium for so much popular entertainment (especially that which originates from foreign, Western sources) greatly reduces its value in this regard. The credibility of newspapers, on the other hand, has been diminished in recent years due to their proliferation in the form of competing, often contradictory and overtly biased editions (e.g., pro-government, pro-opposition, denominational, ethnic oriented, NGO-supported, issue-driven, and so on). Although the number of radio stations is also increasing, these are regarded more as open, public forums, which are affected by a lesser degree of influence from private agendas and special interest groups. At least that seems to be the popular perception, one that has been strengthened by association, due to the introduction of local BBC broadcasts via FM (the BBC being regarded as the ultimate standard and source for news "objectivity", even more so than national government programs).

1.1.3 Social

The potential social function of radio and its constituent programs might at first seem to be very limited, but frequently the participation in a given broadcast is communal, especially in the rural areas of Africa where radio remains the primary medium of mass communication. In these situations, people do not usually listen to their radios in isolation;[2] in fact, there may

---

[2]   This is a major difference from the normal "scenario" of radio reception in Western societies nowadays. In the latter communications environment, "[r]adio has shifted from being an experience enjoyed in community, epitomized by the picture of a family clustering around the wireless, to a far more isolated experience enjoyed by listeners who can be mobile and active whilst listening. Broadcasters can assume even less than before that listeners are hanging on their every word or are 'sitting comfortably' eagerly listening to all their broadcasts" (Mitchell 1999:62). On the contrary, such a partially distracted or otherwise engaged audience would surely miss a lot that is being uttered within the rapid-fire *Sewero* dialogues, even if they were speakers of Chichewa.

well be a limited number of receivers in the local village or settlement area. Thus, like the expert local storyteller or folksinger, a larger-sized radio set (tuned in to a popular program) will normally attract an eager audience of people who live in the vicinity.

The relaxed and immediate "personalizing" effect of radio communication can be a very attractive socializing force in a rural community that may not have many other public or private outlets for people to avail themselves of:

> Radio is good for offering companionship and friendship in such contexts. A relaxed entreating program [therefore] builds up a large audience (Sundersingh 2001:69).

Furthermore, in such settings, radio listening tends to be very much a shared, interactive event, and so the contagious impact of a communal "crowd effect", whether major or minor, positive or negative, internal or vocal, can be just as great as that which typically occurs with a large audience-based medium, e.g., television and video to a certain extent, but especially in comparison with a public performance, such as a stage play. As they are listening then in the traditional communal manner to an exciting *Sewero* drama, one person can easily affect another with respect to their personal verbal and non-verbal reactions to the story that is actualized in their mutual hearing. As more listeners in the audience observe and imitate the vocal, emotional, gestural, and facial response of their colleagues, they may be similarly influenced, thus welding the group closer together socially in their common experience of the drama being played out in their individual minds.

> Whilst McLuhan [1987] stresses the intimate, person-to-person and private nature of radio [i.e., in Western society], his metaphors of 'tribal horns and antique drums' also point back to communication instruments of a former age, an oral culture. They evoke images of another kind of fireside chat, this time storytelling and informal conversations around the tribal campfire. McLuhan sees a parallel between radio and these traditional forms of communication. Both have the power to unify speakers and listeners…to instill a sense of 'shared life-world' (Mitchell 1999:65).

In Africa of course such a "shared life-world" does not need to be "instilled", for it is already a natural part of the comprehensive world-view and value system that people grow up with and according to which they both think and act in life (see chapter 3).

The overall effect of the public's generally positive view of radio programs (see 1.1.2) also has some important social implications. These admittedly subjective opinions and values with regard to the broadcasting of Christian drama have considerable impact, for it means that these plays are imbued by the medium itself with a greater amount of prestige, authority, and hence also the ability to shape or to influence public opinion on important theological as well as ethical and social issues. The *Sewero* program has generally avoided social criticism, especially with regard to any topic that might somehow be perceived and construed as being political or hyper-ethnic in nature. But the potential for stimulating social change and raising the public's awareness concerning such matters is certainly very great, though it will probably continue to remain untapped in keeping with current TWR production policy. Theological and hermeneutical controversies too will undoubtedly not play a large part in the programming, except those that bring anti-Christian or contra-Christological controversies and heresies to the fore. The main emphasis then is in the ethical-moral sphere—that is, in dramatizing behavior that either enhances or detracts from the biblically inspired model of the "ideal" Christian life-style, one that stands in conflict with many of the values, norms, and practices of contemporary living in south-central Africa.

1.1.4 Economic

Radio is a relatively inexpensive mass-medium, that is, on a total, per-capita/person-served basis (Søgaard 1993:131,134). Although an appreciable studio cost may be incurred when actually preparing a radio program and when transmitting it (Sundersingh 2001:67), the fact that the signal can reach so many people at once (especially S-W) greatly reduces the overall production figure. In addition, radio's dependence on the productive and creative powers of the listeners' minds also makes it the easiest, least complicated of the mass media to utilize, both from the point of view of program production and also audience processing. Elaborate and expensive sets or costumes are not needed, for everything is supplied and embellished by the human voice, while the same holds true on the receiving end of the drama, as long as the listeners' minds remain fully engaged and active in the vocal performance. Obviously, what is "programmed" by the players in their dialogue and what is "downloaded" in the imagination of the audience will differ, as noted above, but the relative social and cultural proximity of the two groups is close enough for an appreciable degree of correspondence and congruity to be achieved.

The economic factor must also be considered in relation to the cost of reception. In this respect, the price of a basic radio receiver is not very great, comparatively speaking. "As a technology, radio has become much more diverse and adaptable, making the radio set a most versatile, low-cost instrument of entertainment and information."[3] It was already pointed out

---

[3] Gray & Murphy, "The Unlikely Missionary", p. 18.

that people rarely listen to a radio alone in a non-western setting, whether rural or urban in location, and so a variably-sized group may be served by a single unit. Since the physical sonic quality of the signal, e.g., for musical purposes, is not a vital factor in any given broadcast, the purpose for which a program like *Sewero* drama is prepared can be satisfactorily accomplished in a very economical way by means of a simple short-wave radio transmission consisting of a sequence of varied character dialogues.

1.1.5 Summary

The various communicative possibilities of the especially "personal medium" of radio broadcasting may be summarized as follows (see Søgaard 2001:4/3; 1993:ch.7; Sundersingh 2001:68-69):

- Radio provides the widest possible coverage or range for a particular message, both spatially and situationally (e.g., potentially reaching many remote, inaccessible, or possibly even "prohibited" places).

- Popular radio programs have the potential to build a huge network of listening audiences, all of whom may be thus united and influenced in one way or another by the same source and perspective.

- Radio requires listening only and therefore can reach people who cannot read, due to non-literacy, blindness, the inability to access or afford glasses, or the non-availability of electricity at nights.

- Radio can engage people who are otherwise occupied, e.g., while working, playing a game, or driving a car.

- Radio is a powerful and current "knowledge conveyer"; it can easily disseminate new information and broaden conceptual horizons.

- Radio readily adapts to changing cultural conditions and diverse social systems, even sudden political changes.

- Local (i.e., FM) radio can focus attention on specific teachings and topics, especially those that are already known, thus making them the subject of intensive conversation in a society.

- Radio can raise aspirations for change; a positive climate for modifying certain beliefs, attitudes, and practices may be achieved through focused or targeted radio programming.

- Radio programs may be presented in a variety of relatively inexpensive formats, e.g., narrative, dialogue, interview, drama, preaching, instruction (more conversational), musical, recorded (public events), and so forth.

- When used with other media, radio can be used as an effective tool to directly or indirectly influence social values, norms, tastes, and opinions within a specific community or socio-religious sub-set.

- Radio is credible (believed) and therefore authoritative; thus the daily or recurrent broadcasting of popular programs can exert a significant influence on society.

- Radio gets into otherwise closed homes and even personal rooms; because of status and other social (or religious) barriers, radio is often the only way of reaching certain minority, outcast, conservative, or sensitive groups in a society.

- Radio works in the "mind" of the listener, and he or she provides the context for any type of communication through his or her imagination; this gives radio many more possibilities than most other media and is arguably its most powerful positive characteristic.

Some of these features are not exclusive to radio of course; but research and testing have shown that this is a pretty accurate description of the communication "package" that radio can deliver in a given situation, especially a setting where access to other forms of mass-media transmission are limited, as in many parts of rural Africa. Such qualities are also conducive to both the production and the reception of a Christian opinion-shaping, belief-reinforcing program like the *Sewero* dramatic plays.

1.2 Limitations of the radio medium

Like any other medium of communication, radio is characterized by a number of channel-related *limitations* in addition to the various possibilities that it presents to the author or originator of a given program. This discussion has been anticipated in varying degrees by that of the preceding section, so I will try not to repeat myself, but simply underscore those aspects of radio broadcasting that somehow restrict or limit the transmission and/or reception of its message. They must therefore be anticipated and compensated for, if at all possible, by both the composer (writer) and also the performers of a radio drama. In addition, such negative influences must be acknowledged and considered together with the positive features noted above as we comparatively evaluate the overall communicative achievement as well as the potential of the *Sewero* play corpus.

1.2.1 Physical

The quality of the radio signal is often less than optimal, in the case of both SW and also FM (the latter due to its limited range). Static, interference, and/or a weak, fading signal can block or distort key aspects of the story being transmitted, thus also reducing its impact, appeal, immediacy, and ultimate relevance to the audience. Such blockage is indeed a serious problem because it not only reduces radio's general quality of familiar "personal presence", but it also prevents the usual idiomacity and naturalness of the dialogue from being fully appreciated by listeners who must battle just to make out the words, let alone follow the plot line. In these cases, when the broadcast is especially difficult to perceive, it may be immediately terminated in frustration, simply with the twist of the dial.

To this degree then listeners monitor and control the communication process with absolute authority; if they are not pleased or sufficiently satisfied, they will quickly switch away and listen to something else. On the other hand, if a story captures the interest and imagination of a particular audience, they may be motivated to the point that they will not be deterred even by a relatively poor signal. It will simply force them to listen more attentively to the broadcast, perhaps also to depend more upon each other for clarification or explanation after an especially faint or imperceptible patch. However, a single radio set is also limited in the size of group that it can adequately serve, that is, unless the signal is amplified in some way within a larger venue.

Another physical limitation is a corollary of the dynamic, progressive quality of sound: A radio signal is ever in flight and cannot be recalled; having been registered upon one's hearing, it is gone, never to be heard again. The message then exists only in the memory, where its maintenance and accessibility depend on its relative importance, or relevance, its ease of decodability, and the strength of the impact that it registered upon reception. This swift mortality of the message is a product of its irreversibility; it cannot be reviewed or replayed and so listeners are at the mercy of the various speakers. Therefore, a radio audience must be able to immediately perceive, interpret, and assimilate what is being said. There is little opportunity to "catch up", ponder, or reflect upon the dialogue of a *Sewero* play, for example, except during the short interlude when one scene shifts to another.

The practical implication of this basic temporal quality is that the normal *Sewero* plot cannot be too complicated in either conception or progression. Its essential conflict and theme must be made abundantly apparent at the very start of a play, and these elements must be unfolded, with varied repetition, in a more or less straightforward manner through a limited number of "twists" or levels of complication, but always moving forward in the direction of a clear-cut climax and a satisfying explanatory (didactic) resolution. Similarly, the characterization and scene-setting cannot become too complex or copious, especially in view of the absence of an external "narrator" (who might be available to clarify certain points). Rather, a limited number of

32

central personages (no more than 4-6) must be given an obvious identification through their dialogue interaction as the story begins. These few voices must create an immediate and lasting impression on the listeners' minds, for that will have to serve as the foundation for all subsequent narrative development. The scenes too have to be set with a minimum of description, for that would sound quite unnatural coming from the character voices themselves. Rather, this essential function must be left largely to evocative sound effects and the familiar interpersonal situations that resonate with many similar life-scenarios in the listeners' minds.

The vivid naturalness and linguistic fluency of the dramatic dialogic exchanges of a typical *Sewero* drama (see ch. 4), while quickly capturing and firmly maintaining the interest and attention of the audience, do make such a radio play rather more difficult to grasp, certainly for non-mother tongue speakers of Chinyanja. Normally, however, the central design and message of most stories is simple enough so that if certain words, phrases, and even entire sentences are distorted or missed, one's overall comprehension of the action and associated thematic argument is not seriously affected, not unless the interference continues for a longer period, like five minutes or so. A break or gap of such magnitude becomes much more difficult to fill in by implication once the dialogue resumes again in a perceptible way. In any case, when the concluding resolution stage of the drama has been reached and the biblical lesson for the day is being imparted, a higher degree of deliberate redundancy, including an occasional bit of summarizing, is often built into the speeches of one or more of the lead characters.

1.2.2 Conceptual

Since there is no physical, face-to-face contact between a radio performer and his/her audience, a certain psychological barrier may be established that can prove to be a detriment to the communication event—*unless* the characters can vocally demonstrate themselves to be so realistic and believable that the audience can "identify" with them, either in a positive or negative way. This lack of a physical presence is accompanied by other aspects of sensory "deprivation," for example, non-verbal communicative aids such as costumes (or simply character-appropriate "dress"), make-up, gestures, facial expressions, eye-contact, and body movements.

It has been said that "a picture is worth a 1000 words." However, if this adage is true, and it does make an important albeit non-provable point about pictorial communication, then what happens in cases where no visual stimulation and imagery at all is possible or available? That is the case of radio. But as was noted above, the mind is thereby left unfettered and free to gen-

33

erate its own imagery—scenes that the listener views as being most relevant to the plot and purpose of the play being dramatized. This will normally involve a local contextualization of the text, one that is largely anticipated by the playwright as well as the dramatic players (voices). However, such mental engagement and personal involvement also presupposes an "active" hearer—someone who is closely following the dialogue and empathizing with the various character voices. Any external or internal distraction or lapse of attention can cut the picture being mentally screened, thus detracting from the intended effect. Luther Weaver describes this responsibility, along with the unique facility, of radio narrative as follows:

> In no medium can sound create mood or atmosphere, or set a stage as quickly as in radio. The reason: if the audience—one person or a million—is to get anything whatsoever from the radio, it must listen; that is all it can do: listen. It is not seeing at the same time it is listening. It is listening only (cited in Wendland 1979:95).

The operation of an audio-cassette transmission is similar, but not as focused or intense; one can always pause or stop the machine in order to review what has been missed.

1.2.3 Social

The most serious social limitation for radio performers (narrators, characters) is being completely separated in time and space from their audience. This is such an essential feature of any conventional African oral performance that it is amazing that the *Sewero* troupe can perform as easily and naturally in isolation as they do, since they most certainly grew up under the influence of their ancient traditions. In a typical oral narrative setting, the audience performs a crucial, supplementary role to the performance itself—in various ways, for example, by vocally responding immediately to the narrator's tale (e.g., laughter, gasps, cries, and other expressions of emotion), by their non-verbal responses (gestures, facial expressions, etc.), by filling in any voluntary or involuntary "gaps" in the presentation (included song choruses versus any forgotten elements of the story or dialogue), and by verbally stimulating the performer(s) with their exclamations of assent, pleasure, intensification, and encouragement to greater efforts.

It is obviously much more difficult to develop such a rapport or empathy between speaker(s) and hearer(s) when the communication event is both disjunctive (with a vast gulf separating performers and audience) thus unidirectional, and also purely vocal in character. Despite the separation, as noted earlier a shared or communal radio set can generate an appreciable degree of recompense in this respect, particularly when a realistic, closely interactive drama like the *Sewero* program is being broadcast. This is due to radio's constituent nature as pure sound which automatically forges a sense of human personality, proximity, and also community.

On the other hand, since radio is perhaps the most intimate, personalizing mass medium of communication, the optimal size of any given audience would seem to be limited. This is true whether or not the signal is augmented in any way to increase its volume (see 1.2.1). However, in most rural areas where radio is the predominant means of external information infusion, listeners will be more likely to take the time to discuss a given play with each other. Thus the program can serve a broader socializing function, in contrast to that which might be possible in the setting of a fast-paced modern urban audience which has many media options available to it. In other words, listeners in towns must often choose among many diverse stimuli and attractive messages, all competing with one another for the attention and consequent action of the people concerned. In towns, for example, sports events are much more likely to become the topic of casual conversation, at least for men, while women are more inclined to discuss major news events and local social functions, especially those of a political or religious nature.

1.2.4 Summary

The following points offer a summary of the principal limitations of the radio medium of communication (see Søgaard 2001:4/2; 1993:ch.7; Sundersingh 2001:67-68):

- Radio does not allow for natural face-to-face communication and personal interaction; thus the characters of a play, for example, cannot see the audience and the immediate evaluative reactions given by individual members of the audience, e.g., through exclamations and facial expressions.

- Narrators and other speakers are immediately "typed" or characterized, positively or negatively, largely by the phonic features of their voice, including their geographical and social dialect(s), which convey distinct connotations completely separate from personal appearance and individual behavior.

- Radio is greatly limited by the difficulties of providing adequate feedback, or any response at all, especially on the part of non-literate listeners or those who prefer oral communication.

- Radio is restricted to sound only, with no option of employing accompanying, supportive visuals or gestures; there is thus the possibility of some ambiguity or a lack of clarity in the introduction of purely phonic background effects.

- Radio conveys its messages in transient real time; the fast-paced dramatic dialogue can be heard only once—it cannot be repeated or replayed by the listener (unless it has been tape-recorded).

- Radio programs are aired at a specific time, and the listener has no control over this schedule, which may not be convenient or even appropriate (e.g., listening to a fictional, sometimes humorous drama on a religious "holy day").

- Many rural radio sets require batteries which may be too expensive for the poorest of society or simply unavailable locally. (The answer to this problem could be making arrangements for group listening.)

Except for the last characteristic, which they have no control over, the *Sewero* drama group seeks to compensate for the other limitations by means of a dynamic verbal performance style and topics that are highly captivating and relevant to their primary target audience.

1.3 Key production devices that capitalize on the medium

The *Sewero* players and their production team have developed a unique, combined strategy for dealing with the several limitations and restrictions mentioned above as being peculiar to the medium of radio. This technique centers in the completely natural and lively manner whereby they vocally perform their respective roles in harmonious, life-like conjunction with each other. Some of the main characteristics of their dynamic dialogic style will be described and exemplified in chapter five. In contrast to such textual, or "intrinsic", features, this section calls attention to several play-related "extrinsic", or studio-based, human and technical devices which the program "producer" and his/her colleagues may utilize in order to capitalize on the sonic, potentially *sonorous*, medium through which they are communicating to their large unseen audience.

It should be pointed out in this respect that a long-running program like that of *Sewero* drama naturally does vary in its quality from time to time depending on the personnel who happen to be available, both on the technical production side as well as the individual players themselves. The program announcer, for example (see below), may make more or less of a contribution to the day's play depending on who (how competent) s/he happens to be. Some character "voices" are less realistic, dynamic, and credible than others. The same goes for the producer: s/he may be more or less contextually creative, for example, in preparing suitable bridge or transitional music for a particular plot or theme. The following comments pertain to the "ideal" *Sewero* show—at least, in my opinion—when it is dramatized in terms of content, speech style, and special effects with the greatest amount of impact, appeal, and relevance for the average audience in central Africa.

1.3.1 Announcer

In addition to introducing the *Sewero* program in general, the announcer (especially skilled and experienced ones like Nyongani Chirwa) occasionally says a few words about the main topic to be considered in the drama for the day and the importance of this particular issue for the Christian community. S/he thus sets the tone for what is to come in the subsequent dialogues. More often, however, this relatively minor explanatory or didactic function (which might well be augmented on occasion in future productions) is performed at the end of the day's play, that is, after the story itself has come to an end. However, the program announcer never acts as an internal "narrator" for the drama; rather, s/he is a clearly a distinct, play-external "voice" that verbally sums up and underscores the story's central message and perhaps also adds a few additional implications for the listening audience to consider. Several examples of this personal device will be given in chapters 5 and 6.

1.3.2 Sound effects

The selective, judicious use of readily identifiable indigenous sound effects contributes a vital, naturalizing dimension to the dramatics of radio *Sewero* plays. Such supplementary sounds must be familiar and not too sophisticated (e.g., multiple and overlapping) or they might not be correctly perceived and interpreted by the target audience. A rather large inventory of these natural and mechanical phonic features has been noted, e.g., dogs barking, goats bleating, cattle mooing, doves cooing, rooster crowing, a baby crying, background thunder, blowing wind, rain falling, a roadside crowd "scene" or crowded market din, a car/motorbike engine running, a telephone ringing, and so forth—with rather surprising diversity (considering the radio broadcast location and a relatively low program budget). These important aural background devices have been obtained from several sources: from nearby Bunda agricultural college south of Lilongwe, the local BBC FM station in Malawi, and personal staff field recordings in order to obtain just the right sound for a particular dramatic scene. Alternatively, at times non-speaking members of the *Sewero* cast will provide spontaneous communal background noise (e.g., laughter, muffled conversation, shouting, work-related sounds, mourning as at a funeral) to contextualize the two or three characters who happen to be engaged in a dialogue.

The main purpose of sound effects is to suggest general "type scenes" as well as to evoke specific interpersonal sociocultural settings. In addition to setting the narrative scene or locale, certain sounds may be used selectively to achieve performance goals such as these: to project, clarify, qualify, or heighten the action that is occurring during character dialogue (e.g., a joint pounding of maize kernels at the women's village gathering ground [*pamtondo*]); to indicate certain physical character attributes (e.g., the sound of a limp-like walk or the shuffle of a heavy/aged person); to stimulate a particular atmosphere or mood (e.g., that of a mournful funeral or a joyous wedding); to help signal a point of transition in the play (i.e., fading drums either at an entrance or an exit); to suggest a particular time (e.g., the early morning crow of a rooster), or to mark the passage of time or space (e.g., the noise of an automobile engine that gradually fades from hearing). These varied foreground or background elements (according to their context) thus help to evoke that indispensable mental "stage" noted earlier, one that is restricted or conditioned only by one's imagination, experience, and degree of personal involvement in the drama that is being broadcast in the immediate present.

1.3.3 Music

Instrumental and/or vocal music is another essential aspect of dramatic radio broadcasting throughout the world. In this case, the medium most admirably matches the means, for like radio broadcasting itself, so also music emphasizes, enhances, and capitalizes upon the focused *audio* channel of communication. The use of musical (including drummed) interludes as well as special "mood" music functions both to begin and to end a given *Sewero* program and also to bridge an internal transition from one physical scene or dramatic situation to another.

Often verbal songs are carefully selected to reinforce the main theme or lesson for the day; these include occasional hymns or "choruses" sung by members of the radio cast, acting in the role of a small congregational choir (they are good singers!) or as a choral response group (see the example in 5.1.7). Music also serves to establish a particular mood, emotion, (happy, sad, serious, fearful, triumphant, etc.) or a specific setting (e.g., a tavern versus a church versus a traditional nyau ceremony), and sometimes as a reiterated leitmotif (e.g., to phonically "spotlight" a certain key character or critical activity).

In closing this section, it is important to note the need for carefully and harmoniously integrating these non-verbal resources with those of the dialogues of the drama that is being presented. Not just any music or background sounds or drumming will do; these effects must be crafted to fit the overall content, tone, and intent of the play within which they are incorporated. Perhaps more attention might be given to this resource and responsibility in future *Sewero* productions. When disregarded or downplayed, these essential supplementary features may detract from a play's impact and appeal. However, when used to enhance the overall oral-aural quality of the radio medium in general and a given play in particular, the whole effect becomes greater than the sum of its constituent parts, and a unique communicative potential is realized:

> Radio is not solely a word-based medium. ...[M]usic, sound effects, silence and audio montages can contribute to form a medium more 'visual' for the imagination than television (Mitchell 1999:55).

1.4 Contribution of the listening audience

Although there is a serious limitation in this respect (see 2.2.3), a willing, properly motivated radio audience is not completely cut off from the players of a *Sewero* program. As suggested above, their response must inevitably be indirect, subsequent, and dislocated in contrast to a traditional oral narrative performance, but it is a valuable reaction nevertheless. This normally takes the form of personal opinion letters sent in to TWR (eventually reaching a program producer), and it constitutes a vital contribution to any successful radio program. These reactions are very rarely overtly critical; usually they are highly complimentary, although some general suggestions for improvement may also be offered. Such audience response may also be positively "contributory" in the sense that they add something to the production itself through the skeleton plots and thematic ideas which are sent in. Since comments of this nature are limited to the literate among the audience, other means must be devised to elicit the opinions of the majority of those who either cannot or prefer not to write.

Listener letters (and occasionally personal visits to the TWR studio in Lilongwe) also perform a delayed but definite "enabling" and "encouraging" function. That is to say, if there is little or no positive public response, then the players may become discouraged, and the Sewero program itself might even be scrapped as being ineffective or irrelevant! Such a conclusion would be based on the broadcasting axiom that radio generates more receptor response than any other mass medium of communication; therefore, if there is little or none forthcoming, then something serious must be wrong with the program.

A "secondary" performance setting is created when a taped *Sewero* play (or even a live broadcast) is presented to a "live" listening audience, e.g., a gathering of seminary student families. This type of contribution is obviously external to the radio performance; there is absolutely no contact between the audience itself and the performing group. However, the recorded observations of such a response could be useful as a testing tool to enable the program producer to actually see what effect it is having (e.g., through facial expressions, hand gestures, etc.) as an aid the planning and production of future plays. For example, he (or a designated reporter/researcher) would note points at which the audience gets very excited or overtly reacts in an emotional manner, or where they seem to be confused or misunderstand what's going on, or where they appear to get bored or easily distracted.

In short, although radio drama depends on an intangible and ethereal mental stage, a live participating and contributing audience, albeit detached, is still essential to its current maintenance and ultimate success. In one way or another, therefore, the "communication cycle" (S ⇔ R) must be completed and the interaction further encouraged.

1.5 Using audio cassettes to complement radio programming

The audio cassette medium is similar to that of radio in many respects. For example, its mode of transmission is limited to sound alone, with no visual or any other sensory contact between the original performers and their listening audience. The implications of this characteristic, as noted above (1.2), are accordingly the same. However, cassette transmission also differs significantly in several other respects—in particular, since it has the capacity to be *stopped* (either for comments or to allow one's mind to pause and catch up) and/or *repeated* either immediately or at some other time (e.g., for clarification, as a reminder of what was said, or for pure enjoyment).

These latter features make it possible for a more complete, combined production and performance "package" to be prepared. The positive qualities of a radio broadcast may be retained (e.g., its wide, diverse, and simultaneous audience "outreach"), whereas several serious limitations of the radio medium may in turn be cancelled out and compensated for by means of audio cassettes. Thus selected radio programs can be easily tape- (or CD) recorded and then made available (for a reasonable price) to listeners who wish to (re) hear and experience a particular *Sewero* performance that captured their imagination, or powerfully moved them emotionally, or which conveyed a message that was of special importance and relevance to their Christian lives. The potential audience of a given dramatic play can thus also be extended to those who never heard it in the first place when broadcast or as an additional resource in the overall communications network of a particular Christian organization or some other para-church agency.

More about these possibilities will be said in chapter seven. They are noted here simply to call attention to the important similarities and differences, as well as the significant complementarity, of these two media—public radio and the more private audio-cassette (see Sundersingh 2001:70-71). A coordinated multi-media production strategy (e.g., radio drama => cassette reproduction => printed study guide) might make it possible for the *Sewero* program to become even more effective in communicating practical, life-related Christian theology to the masses in their mother-tongue.

2. History, Purpose, and Production of the TWR *Sewero* Program

2.1 Historical Background

In this chapter I give a short overview of TransWorld Radio (TWR), with particular reference to production of the *Sewero* program in Chinyanja. This information is derived from the TWR website (www.gospelcom.net/twr) as well as from personal tape-recorded interviews and correspondence that I have enjoyed with the National Director of TWR in Malawi (Mr. Patrick Semphere),[1] several of the *Sewero* program producers (Mr. Nyongani Chirwa, Mrs. Lilian Chikwenembe, Mr. Enos Kanduna), as well as its most prolific playwright to date (Pastor Josophat Banda).[2] I begin with the history.

2.1.1 TransWorld Radio

2002 marked the 50th anniversary of the broad-based TransWorld Radio ministry,[3] which was founded in 1952 (Cary, North Carolina, USA) by Dr. Paul Freed, a son who followed in the footsteps of his missionary father.[4] From its first Christian broadcasts to Spain in 1954, TWR has veritably proved its name by expanding its evangelical, gospel-centered outreach to encompass the entire world today—that is, some 1800 hours of weekly programming, in 160 countries, and in over 180 languages.[5] Africa has been a focal continent in TWR's plans from the very beginning (their first radio transmitter was located in Tangiers, Morocco), reaching out from two powerful broadcasting stations in Manzini, Swaziland and Johannesburg, South Africa. Virtually all of sub-Saharan Africa, a vast potential audience of some

---

[1]   See Appendix B for a written background paper on TWR that was presented orally by Mr. Semphere in 2002.
[2]   I am most indebted to these most helpful individuals and to the TWR staff as a whole for their great assistance in various ways during my research work in Lilongwe, Malawi. I sent a draft copy of the present chapter to them for review and correction as needed, and I am grateful for their comments. However, they are not responsible for any errors that may remain in the text, of which I was the final author.
[3]   "TWR is the most far-reaching Christian radio network in the world" (a quote from their website). "Where people cannot go, radio can go" (*ibid*). As for some specifics, according to the manifesto of its informative website, TWR is a "ministry" that is "experienced, partnering, proclaiming, discipling, training, pioneering, high-tech, connecting (interacting), and trustworthy" in character (see Appendix C).
[4]   Dr. Freed (1918-1996) was trained as a missionary at Wheaton College and later earned his Ph.D. in mass communications at New York University.
[5]   I have also included TWR's eight point evangelical "mission statement" in Appendix C (as provided on their website).

700 million listeners, lies within range of TransWorld's varied radio voice which is transmitted via medium wave, short wave, FM, and most recently, through a powerful satellite network (DSTV, which is popular in Zambia, for one). Programs in over 50 African languages are broadcast from Swaziland, including the following that will be familiar to listeners in south-central Africa: Bemba, Nyanja, Chokwe, Lomwe, Luchazi, Ndau, Ndebele, Sena, Shona, Tumbuka, and Yao.

In Malawi, where administrative offices and a fully-equipped recording studio are situated (Lilongwe), TWR has been operational for the past 17 years, largely on the shortwave frequency. A variety of vernacular programs have been produced in the country over these years and sent to Manzini, where they have been aired on the 49 meter wave band. In the year 2000, however, an exciting new development took place as an FM license was granted by the government to allow broadcasts via this "clear and cheap channel" medium.[6] To date, the TWR voice is already familiar to many listeners in the Blantyre area (southern region, 89.1 mHz), and plans are being made to extend this transmission to the other main regions of the country in the near future.

I turn next to the specific history of the *Sewero* show: How did this popular dramatic production originate and why—what were the aims of these locally set Chinyanja radio plays, and how, if any, have these changed over the years? What then is the foreseeable future of the *Sewero* program as it continues its second decade of existence, now in a new millennium?

2.1.2 Sewero

It is not clear exactly when the *Sewero* program was first prepared by the "TransWorld Radio Drama Group" for public shortwave broadcast, but sometime in 1990 seems to be the most likely date of origin. This was not too long after the Lilongwe studio began operating and was searching for some new and relevant programs to try out. Dramatic plays (*ma-sewero*) were an excellent idea, for this verbal art-form had its roots in the ancient oral narrative performing tradition (*nthano*) of the Nyanja-speaking peoples and was already familiar in its more modern (Western) form as a result of the local school system, where plays became a popular mode of entertainment and training among students at all levels of education.

---

[6] "Cheap" does not refer to the cost of program production, but to that of reception. FM receivers are relatively inexpensive, and added to the quality of the signal that is received (within range), this makes FM a most attractive local mode of Christian communication, especially for artistic, multi-voiced plays like those broadcast on the *Sewero* show.

The first *Sewero* producer was Mr. Pearson Chunga, who as TWR's first National Director was involved in just about every aspect of programming in those early years. This dramatic production work was soon taken over then by Mr. Nyongani Chirwa, a TWR-trained studio operator, who remained at the helm for the next seven years. This gave some much needed stability and guidance to the group and undoubtedly contributed to the high standard of excellence and wide listener-ship that this show has been able to achieve over the years. More recently, *Sewero* has been co-produced by Mrs. Lilian Chikwenembe, who oversees the content and biblical usage of the program, and Mr. Enos Kanduna, who takes care of the many technical aspects of production.

The *TransWorld Radio Drama Group* (TWDG) is a Lilongwe-based Gospel-outreach ministry (founded c.a. 1989) that has worked together now for over a decade under the leadership of their dynamic chairman and team-leader, Evangelist Gibson Kachaje. The group performs not only on radio, but they also act out their contextualized, life-challenging plays before live audiences—that is, at various church meetings and functions to which they are often invited (see Appendix E). Membership in this select troupe of Nyanja-speaking "players" has varied in its composition somewhat over the years (averaging 7-10 persons), but on the whole, the "team" (which is how they like to refer to themselves) has remained remarkably stable. This too is an important factor contributing to the group's artistic excellence and communicative effectiveness.

Some of the long-serving *TWDG* performers and familiar voices, in addition to Mr. Kachaje himself, are: Mr. Josophat Banda (the group's main playwright), Mr. Welis Banda, Mai Ligomeka, Mai Jairosi, Mai Saidi, Mai Tambala, and Mr. Nexon Mulela. These drama artists have not been formally trained and are non-"professional" in a secular sense (quality-wise, however, they are certainly "experts", *akatswiri*, in my opinion).[7] Thus, they do not receive any regular salary for their preparation or recording time, except for a small honorarium which they are granted after completing a quarterly cycle of productions. Rather, they regard this demanding activity simply as part of their willing service to the Lord. In the words of one of the group's current producers: "They are very committed—it is a matter of their hearts" (Kanduna).

---

[7]   The team's dramatist, Josophat Banda observes: "I never received any course of [drama] training, but it is just the grace of God" [i.e., with reference to the excellent artistic gift that he demonstrates in his plays].

2.2 Program Purpose

Why is the *Sewero* show produced and what do the producers and players hope to accomplish through their weekly dramatic performances? Instead of offering my own summary here, it may be better to indicate the team's manifold perspective (diverse in minor aims, but united in a common educative, evangelistic purpose) by allowing different members of the production staff to express this in their own words, that is, through citations from taped interviews [the words in brackets being implied]:

"[This program] addresses issues that affect people in rural areas [of Malawi]...things that affect the community in their day to day life, [especially] spiritual problems which unsophisticated folk encounter. ... We try by all means to be interdenominational, to avoid touching on [specific] doctrinal issues that [might] separate or bring controversy among Christians. ... We want to reach the common people, to give them proper [biblical] instruction...and to prevent teachings which may not be based on the Bible." (Nyongani Chirwa)

"It is a [Christian] teaching program—we also tackle difficult topics or areas, things having to do with magic, witchcraft, when people behave [badly]. The idea is to influence behavioral change through the Scriptures. ... We use the Scriptures to fit the situation that is being dramatized, to motivate the solution in keeping with the [main] problem of the play. ... [We focus on] cultural practices that have an adverse impact on how people think and behave. ... We present the Scriptures in such a way that the people will feel, 'Yes, that is correct!' [We do this] without rebuking them strongly, just applying the Scriptures so that they can learn by themselves that such [traditional religious] practices are evil. There are certain cultural practices that are difficult to preach against in the pulpit because the people will overreact...[so] we [*Sewero* players] do it in a very clever manner [i.e., implicitly, in the form of a dramatic presentation of the problem]." (Enos Kanduna)

"We preach the Word of God through plays... People are really attracted [to hear our message] through plays, more than anything else—even singing, dancing, choruses, personal testimonies—they pay attention to plays. ... Yes indeed, nowadays—and beginning long ago—this problem of witchcraft in the church has been very great, especially among those who have not been thoroughly taught about the power that is in the blood of Christ Jesus, those who do not know how to remain steadfast in faith and not to fear witchcraft. If there is anything that is retarding Christianity in the world, it is this witchcraft! ... So now, as things are, many people [listeners] are becoming very interested in the *Sewero* [program], and for this reason I will keep on helping them to reach the Lord through these plays." (Josophat Banda)

Mother-tongue, life-related, setting-specific, spiritually-relevant, biblically-informed, stylistically well-shaped, idiomatic and interesting—the *Sewero* dramas have great popular appeal for all of these reasons. The players' ultimate aim is to demonstrate how Jesus Christ may be manifested as Savior and Lord in the everyday experiences of ordinary people (mainly middle-aged, rural adults) and to illustrate how such a faith may be refined and reinforced through a careful study and application of the Word of God. This is shown to occur in a given play most often as a result of the concerned advice and personal intervention of believers to others in trouble, trial, or temptation. Occasionally such verbal help is offered by the local "pastor", but usually it comes from fellow church members and/or friends and neighbors—lay Christian men and women—who care enough to witness to and stand up for the truth of Scripture in a specific situation of theological or (more often) moral crisis and confrontation.

These plays are not perfect, and several possible improvements will be suggested below (2.3.4). However, given the very limited resources at hand and the great pressure to produce that the players must always work under, it is truly amazing—"a charismatic gift (*chisomo*) of God" (J. Banda)—that they are able to carry out their diverse evangelistic, didactic, hortatory, and apologetic purposes so effectively. In fact, the group simply must be heard to be believed, that is, with reference to the consistently high quality of their dramatic oral performances.

2.3 Production Procedure

How do the *Sewero* players go about preparing a drama for broadcast? In this section I will summarize the principal procedures as I have come to understand them from the program's producers. Naturally, not all plays follow the same general pattern, but the sequential overview given below should capture what happens in most cases.

It is interesting to observe at the outset some of the main differences that are found between the *Sewero* productions and the oral narrative (*nthano*) performances of ancient Nyanja tradition, which these drama players all grew up with. They may be contrastively summarized as follows (see 1.1-1.2; Wendland 1979:1181-1185,1316; 2000:41-44):

A comparison of key performance characteristics

Nthano vs. *Sewero*

Nthano:
a) face-to-face, homogeneous, immediate-present audience;
b) amateur, informal, periodic performers;
c) singular production (one narrator impersonates several characters);
d) depends on non-verbal elements (gestures, facial expressions, body movements);
e) much meaningful interaction with a relatively small, familiar live audience is possible;
f) traditional, secular, rural-set plots;
g) primarily a relational, entertaining communicative function, but often educative too
h) simpler and less diverse in terms of plot structure and use of stylistic features
i) varied mixture and proportion of narrator's and characters' speech (dialogue)
j) "interference" is mainly contextual in nature, a part of the local performance setting

Sewero:
a) mass-medium, heterogeneous, invisible radio audience;
b) practiced, educated, well-trained and experienced performers;
c) plural production (many character voices);
d) no non-verbal communication possible, but varied sound-effects are included;
e) completely cut off from a large, invisible, listening audience of strangers;
f) varied settings, non-traditional, with Christian application;
g) primarily a didactic, hortatory, and motivational function, but always entertaining
h) more complex with regard to structural organization and stylistic technique
i) the discourse consists entirely of dialogue, with no narration or "narrator"
j) "interference" is largely transmissional, such as static interference, a weak radio signal

Indeed, the difference as indicated above are considerable and hence also consequential; thus it is not a given that a good traditional teller of tales would be able to perform equally well on the radio as a member of the *Sewero* cast. On the other hand, both audiences typically reflect for the most part what anthropologists call a "high-context society", that is, people who tend to take a lot for granted when communicating verbally. In other words, they normally leave a great deal of contextual background information *implicit* in their discourse, e.g., that pertaining to geography, flora and fauna, social life and customs, traditions, communal institutions, and so forth (Wendland 2000:159-160). This is in contrast to "low-context societies", where most everything needs to be *explicitly* spelled out in the text, which, if literary in character, is usually printed out, not presented orally.

A Sewero drama naturally has to build more of the surrounding setting and interpersonal situation into the players' speech because its audience is much larger and more disparate in composition; in addition, there is no narrator on hand to perform this essential function. Nevertheless, these plays are very Malawi-specific in terms of theme, content, philosophy, and language (the dialect of Chinyanja spoken), with the result that non-indigenous listeners (like the present author) occasionally have a hard time following the rapid-fire dialogue—and what lies beneath the verbal surface of a given text. At such points, the essential help of cultural and linguistic "insiders" must be sought.

2.3.1 Selection

The presentation of dramatic plays for regularly scheduled radio transmission is a most rigorous, intense, and therefore also a challenging exercise in communication. It is easier to perform in a "live" public venue where the audience is present and the characters are able to interact with each other visually as well as orally (e.g., by means of gestures, facial expressions, etc.). On the invisible radio stage, however, the casting, arrangement, and blending of voices must be carefully programmed and practiced beforehand, and the players must learn to speak as unto the blind, that is, to people who cannot see them at all. Everything must therefore be concentrated into the words of a dialogue, and this requires demonstrated verbal experts. Such is the TransWorld Radio Drama Group.

As noted earlier, this group consists of a solid core of about ten players who have been performing together now for over five years, some for over a decade. This lends an important measure of constancy to the team that has both qualitative and quantitative implications. Thus *more* professional performances can be prepared in *less* time, with fewer costly edits required. Applications to join the group are regularly received, mostly from more youthful aspirants, but only a few are allowed an audition. This does not indicate a spirit of elitism on the part of the group, but rather their concern for excellence. It must be remembered that they are all unsalaried volunteers in this dramatic ministry, including team leader Gibson Kachaje, and so it is not possible for them to embark on any sort of large-scale testing and training program, much as they would like to do this. Therefore, new members are incorporated (after a thorough try-out period) only after one of the older members "retires" from the group, which is a relatively rare occurrence.

There are of course many other good drama troupes in Malawi, but it is not possible simply to invite even one of the more highly recommended of these to alternate with the *Sewero* group as a way of assisting them in this demanding weekly broadcasting effort. As already pointed out, a studio-manufactured radio presentation is quite different from a live performance on the stage; it is really a distinct as well as more difficult mode of artistic communication. Thus most groups would fail to meet the high production standards of TWR—again, with respect to both quantity and quality, that is, to prepare and present first-rate, entertaining and edificational plays lasting at least 25 minutes on a regular basis. There is an important moral requirement as well: the lives of members must match the message that they dramatize in their plays. Otherwise, the program may turn out to be offensive for including any locally-known "hypocrites" in the cast. Sad to say, this is not just a remote possibility, as the *Sewero* team discovered after a recent attempt to include the services of another drama group in the Lilongwe area.

2.3.2 Composition

The process of composing dramatic radio plays is one of the most fascinating aspects of *Sewero* team productions. This turns out to be a real interactive, cooperative effort once a given play has been drafted, which is the vital first step. Afterwards, all members of the group contribute to a story's development—that is, when preparing a revision or fleshing out the draft, selecting the characters (who should "play" whom), and finally, when recording the various voices in action, under the guidance and direction of the program's producers. From 1993-2000 the group's principal playwright was Josophat Banda,[8] but in recent years other members of the cast have also done some drafting of plays, mainly to fill in when Rev. Banda is away on some pastoral assignment.

---

[8]   Rev. Josophat Banda has been involved in Christian drama production for many years, though he has never received any formal, institutional training. During his younger years he was leader of a youth drama group in the Catholic Church. He was "converted", as he puts it, from a sinful life-style through a sermon that was preached on TWR by Evangelist Shadrack Wame (see Wendland 2000), and he later joined the African Assemblies of God. Rev. Banda is currently a preacher-leader of his own "New Jerusalem Church" which is located near Likuni (Lilongwe). After hearing the *Sewero* program on TWR, he appealed to team leader Gibson Kachaje to allow him to join, since he was already experienced in the art. He was given his chance and has taken advantage of this opportunity to utilize his gift from and for the Lord every since.

Each *Sewero* drama begins then with a draft version of the plot—the play's plan of action, as well as a specification of the characters that are to implement it, the different scenes or settings, and the main biblical message which the day's play is intended to convey. This last element, the "purpose" (*cholinga*), is crucial, for it serves to guide the rest of the production process. "The power of a play is in its purpose," says Rev. Banda. He derives his different plots and story lines from three main sources: from subjects that he hears being discussed "in the streets", from "interesting accounts that are found in the Bible", and occasionally, from dreams or visions that he experiences. He writes his plays "as if he were a (news) reporter" to give it human interest and personal relevance to the lives of his listeners, and he emphasizes his dependence on serious, ongoing Bible study.

Over the years and as he has gained experience, this compositional process has become less time-consuming for Rev. Banda. "In the past it used to take me over an hour (!) to script a play outline," he remarks, "but now I can draft one in 15 minutes or so." He normally writes up a set of plots at one time—time that he must set aside from his pressing pastoral duties. He carefully stores all his outlines in a file so that he can "avoid repeating the same topic and story." He also keeps notes on ideas that he will one day generate into a future *Sewero* drama.

When the team gets together then during their regular Thursday session, they begin by planning the day with their producers. This includes the goal of how many plays to record (two is the current average). After a reasonable schedule has been agreed upon, they carry on by discussing a certain play outline that they have already received in advance to study and critique. Each person takes crucial "performance notes" as they proceed to serve as cues during the actual recording. Sometimes they leave a given draft pretty much as is; at other times, they end up redoing it completely, often upon the advice of one or another of the producers, who act as joint "quality controllers" for the project. They agree among themselves about the various parts to impersonate, though this too must be cooperatively negotiated at times. Not everyone receives a character to play, for radio plots must be limited with respect to the size of a cast; too many voices become confusing for listeners, especially when the dialogue is rapid and sustained. Those who do not have a part do assist in a supporting role, for example, by providing the background chatter (or mourning, laughter, etc.) of a group of people, by singing a familiar chorus for a church setting, or by offering constructive criticism as their colleagues are performing.

Once the plot with its several scenes has been thoroughly discussed, debated, and "internalized" by the group, with the advice and assistance of their producers, they are ready to record. The characters' lines are not en-scripted in print at all and nothing is memorized beforehand; rather the play is generated spontaneously, as it were, on the spot and each player voices his/her part as if it were a real-live event. It is truly remarkable to hear how natural and life-like the drama turns out to sound; it is as if one were right there at some local setting, overhearing all the verbal action in person. The audience thus participates emotively in the action that is being dialogued, and hence they also experience the full force of its rhetoric as well as the moral or theological argument that is being made, all on the basis of a set of pertinent pre-selected Scripture passages.

2.3.3 Recording and editing

The recording process may proceed relatively smoothly, or there may be many interruptions, occasioned by the need for correction or further discussion on a critical point, then for redoing a particular segment or an entire scene. The team, at least the major players of a given drama, sits around a studio table on which have been placed four recording mikes. In fact, according to the producers, a few more of these are needed so that two players are not forced to share a mike, which can get a bit awkward or distracting at times as the pace of the verbal action picks up. A computerized, multi-track sound recorder captures the drama as it vocally unfolds, each voice taken at a different track. This is the "raw material" that the producers must later work with in order to put the play into broadcast-able shape.[9]

Editing work begins as soon as possible after a given play has been recorded in the rough. This is to ensure that the dynamics of interaction are still fresh in a producer's mind as s/he carries out what amounts to an elaborate process of dramatic fusion—that is, mixing together all the separate tracks that were recorded, inserting appropriate "break points" to provide a structural or provocative "pause" in the action, and incorporating all necessary sound effects and background noises to "naturalize" the play for the invisible radio stage. Sometimes the sound quality of a character's voice needs to be "mended", that is, made louder, softer, or in some other way acoustically modified so as to blend in better with the others. Certain material must also be edited out, for various reasons: because it might possibly (or even probably!) be offensive to some listeners, because it is redundant or relatively unimportant to the story, because a technical (e.g., an inadvertent pause) or a factual mistake has been detected, or simply because the raw play

---

[9]   Computerized technology has greatly increased the ultimate quality of the *Sewero* production process; the computer is able to cover-up and compensate for a multitude of errors, so that the final product sounds almost seamless as well as original.

is too long as it stands for a single program and too short to divide into a "part 1" and a "part 2" (to be broadcast the following week).

It usually takes Mr. Kanduna about 1-2 hours to complete his editorial process, that is, from raw footage to a fully polished play. More time is needed if there are a number of errors to deal with, or if some special audio effects are needed (in addition to the corpus that has already been catalogued and stored on the computer). In the latter case, he has to make a special field trip in order to procure the required sounds, for example, to a local school in order to record the buzz of a classroom in action, or downtown to capture the hurly-burly of the marketplace (or a certain area of it, e.g., where the hammering metal pot-makers beat out their wares). Any play would undoubtedly satisfy most listeners as it stands, without going to all the extra trouble, but the team aims to achieve the highest possible level of quality: "...we want something very natural for our plays—as if the radio audience were right there!"

2.3.4 Evaluation

As suggested above, the *Sewero* players critically evaluate their own work during the actual process of a play's production. Public criticism of a colleague during a performance is not easy either to give or to take, but the group has learned to do this effectively over time and with experience for the good of their joint project and the Christian message that they are proclaiming. Revisions (additions, deletions, corrections) are made on the spot as needed before they proceed. Two very capable and experienced program producers, Mrs. Chikwenembe and Mr. Kanduna, are always right there in the studio, guiding the team along the path to a quality-controlled, artistically satisfying conclusion. The former is very concerned too about the content, or subject matter of these dramas—that they "do not go off track" in terms of plot structure or along denominational lines; she wants to hear a play that will "connect" with the audience in a very meaningful, life-related manner.

Mrs. Chikwenembe, who has a degree in biblical studies and radio programming from Africa Bible College (Lilongwe), feels that although the *Sewero* program is quite polished and, indeed, very popular in Malawi, "there is still a lot to be done" in terms of making certain improvements where feasible. In her opinion:

> The group could use more training in the specifics of Christian drama. We are often too loose in the way we choose our themes—at times we even seem to be gossiping on the air about certain events that may have really happened somewhere. We must learn to dig deeper into the critical issues of the day, the things that are really affecting our society in a negative way. ... We also have to watch out that we do not just scratch the surface

as far as the Bible is concerned. We should be able to take particular texts and apply them in more detail to relevant social issues, for example, the manifold problems that are arising out of the AIDS crisis among us. Some verses are just mentioned [during a play] as if they are throwing stones. Therefore, some concentrated exegetical instruction is needed to remedy the situation. ... In the practical matter of production, the team needs to do more preparation before they come to the studio. More time for pre-recording program planning would also be helpful; at times it seems as if [the players] are going too fast, which also results in sameness and stereotyping—a cookie-cutter type of production. This could be helped if they had the opportunity to do some study and reflection with regard to a particular play before trying to perform and record it. Of course, this all takes time and, we must remember, they are not receiving any appropriate remuneration for their work; they are all strictly volunteers.

Surely that is quite an agenda to set as a goal, but it shows how serious the producers are about maintaining standards of quality that pertain also to Scriptural exposition and application. Some of these issues will be discussed further in the final chapter.

A limited amount of critical appraisal concerning the *Sewero* program comes from the letters of listeners who write into the station after a particular broadcast that strikes them. But since most people greatly appreciate the show, any sort of technical, not to speak of unfavorable, criticism is minimal, for their main concerns lie elsewhere (see below). A more valuable source of evaluation is the spouses of the team members, who are naturally much freer in their expression of something that they did not like. For example, in addition to suggesting some possible topics to her playwright husband, Mrs. Josophat Banda might also tell him something like, "Aah, you were not very helpful there [in that particular play]. You took only one side of the issue and left the other half; those others were disappointed."

Despite the length and eminence of their radio service, the *Sewero* group has surprisingly not seemed to stir up much of a reaction, whether good or bad, in the local news media, even in the vernacular religious press. This is surely a great oversight or omission, and it is rather unfortunate too because the show could certainly use a little PR promotion that might generate some form of sponsorship, even for the occasional program or two. According to TWR policy, however, this cannot be done directly on the air through any type of solicitation on the part of the actual presenters. Therefore, it is up to appreciative listeners themselves to take the initiative, that is, to demonstrate their positive assessment of these broadcasts in some concrete way—by means of financial as well as the expected prayer support.

A final, and very minor, agency of evaluation lies in the national "Programming Board", which consists of representatives of the Malawi Broadcasting Company, several church denominations, and some selected secular critics. However, this committee comes occasionally to prepare only a very general assessment of all the programs that are broadcast by a particular radio station in the country, and thus it does not focus on the *Sewero* show per se. Needless to say, no negative criticism of the program has ever arisen out of the periodic inquiries of this monitoring body.

One of the purposes of the present monograph then is to offer my own highly affirmative evaluation of the *Sewero* project along with my reasons for coming to this conclusion. The program's many regular listeners already know this of course, but it may be a source of encouragement to the group to put my assessment in writing and with sufficient descriptive exemplification to motivate others to lend their tangible support as well.

2.4 Listener Feedback

At the end of every *Sewero* broadcast, listeners are invited to write in to TWR (PO Box 49, Lilongwe, Malawi) with any questions that they may have about the program. Mr. Kanduna reports that an average of 5-10 letters a week are received from listeners all over southern Africa. As mentioned above, these are rarely critical in nature, but are rather sent in for a variety of different purposes, for example: to suggest a possible topic to dramatize in some future *Sewero* show; to submit an actual summary or a plot outline for a play; to offer a word of appreciation for a specific broadcast; to request the re-broadcast of a certain play; to give a testimony telling how the program has been of spiritual benefit; to inquire about how one might join the *Sewero* players; or to ask some question with regard to a particular play or concerning the Christian faith/life in general. The group does not have the time to deal with all this correspondence directly. Rather, a small "team of free-lancers" consisting of volunteers from local Christian churches has assumed this ministry on behalf of TWR. The members come in regularly to read all the letters, to sort them into categories of response required, and then to follow up with any necessary action, including writing letters in reply. The issues that specifically concern the *Sewero* program—concrete suggestions about subjects to dramatize in future and other pertinent advice—are convey to the two producers, who in turn pass the information along to the players at an appropriate time.

2.5 "Technical" Problems

I will close this chapter with a brief discussion of some of the main types of technical difficulties, mechanical and personal, that occur in connection with the *Sewero* project. These are quite diverse in nature and are combined in this section merely for the sake of convenience. One set of problems concerns the actual process of program production; the other set lists those that I encountered when attempting to analyze the results—the radio broadcasts as I received, recorded, transcribed, analyzed, translated, and now present in this book.

2.5.1 Production and transmission

Most of problems that can arise in this area are rather obvious and thus not unexpected. Personal *absence* is one of these. Since the TWR Drama Group is a volunteer, non-salaried ministry, it is not always possible for all of the *Sewero* members to be present at a regular Thursday recording session. The "critical-mass" for a performance is four, including the playwright for the day and at least one of the male voices; that is the bare minimum required for a play to materialize. If this quorum is not achieved, then the whole process aborts and must wait until the following week. Recording equipment malfunctions are rare, but they do happen and naturally cause an unwanted postponement. The present Lilongwe studio facilities are currently adequate, but could be improved by having a larger recording room to accommodate the entire team and by providing individualized supplies, such as a microphone for each character voice.

The *spontaneous* nature of the performance process sometimes presents some difficulties that can affect the program's quality. For example, the players do not always speak in turn, and the result is a certain amount of overlapping, hence obscurity, in the vocal expressions of the different characters. Occasionally, individual lines or utterances that turn out to be comparatively crucial in the context of the entire play were not highlighted or emphasized enough during the recording process. If this is not discovered in time and a repeat of that particular segment done, it may not be possible to correct at the later mixing and final preparation stage.

The key critical factor then is *time*: a lot of work must be done in a limited amount of time, and this requirement makes certain mistakes or infelicities hard to notice right away or to repair once the day's recording session is over. In addition, there is often not a sufficient opportunity for "working through" a play together before it must be actually recorded. The players are frequently left to perform by pure intuition, with little or no advance preparation. Most of the time this is good enough, and the play is produced in superb fashion. Occasionally, however, the team realizes at the end of a play that they could have used a bit more time to get it into shape conceptually among themselves beforehand. But it must also be said in this connection that only a trained critical ear would even notice, let alone be negatively affected by, such small imperfections. Anything major is of course detected and dealt with either by the players themselves or by the program's producers, who are there to monitor the entire recording process.

Mrs. Chikwenembe called my attention to another, in this case a relatively minor, technical difficulty, or better, incongruity, that may be heard in connection with the production of certain *Sewero* plays, in particular, those that are set in a rural location. This has to do with the fact that the various team members come from different districts of Malawi and thus speak different dialects of Chinyanja. This would not be very likely in a typical village setting, although it would be quite a normal occurrence in urban and peri-urban areas.

Finally, one can do very little about a large problem of communication which any radio program inevitably faces, namely, that involving the mode of transmission itself. Short wave broadcasts are good for reaching many listeners afar off, but their relatively poor signal quality frequently detracts a great deal from the enjoyment that one derives from an artistic drama program like *Sewero*. For example, the different character voices are often distorted or even obliterated by various types of medium-based interference. FM transmission is much better of course, but its geographical range is considerably less; outside of that limited area, the signal deteriorates rapidly, soon becoming worse than that of short wave. The TWR station management team is very aware of these problems and is actively trying to tackle them both—the first, by constantly adjusting the short wave frequency within the 49 meter band to accommodate to changing atmospheric conditions; the second, by endeavoring to add more FM stations to cover the country of Malawi at least.[10]

2.5.2 Reception and re-presentation

The many difficulties that I encountered in preparing this study also need to be set down for the record. This is not intended as an excuse on my part, but simply to note the limitations of what I have presented here. I was working closely with several advanced Seminary student assistants during the course of this exercise, especially in the task of text transcription and translation.[11] They learned quickly and did their best to make a contribution to the success of this project; however, they were not involved in the interpretation of this

---

[10] Perhaps this plan of development can be extended in the immediate future to cover also neighboring countries like Mozambique and Zambia.
[11] My main student assistants were: Philip Chikwatu, Faison Tarisayi, and in particular, Bright Pembeleka.

mass of data or the final write-up of results and therefore cannot be held responsible for any errors that remain in my presentation.

The process of accurately transcribing these *Sewero* plays was undoubtedly the most difficult aspect of the work. The cassette recordings that I made from my little short wave radio were not of the best quality; more often than not, the dialogue was distorted to a certain degree by static, fade-out, a weak signal, or some other type of interference.[12] Even when the recording was relatively clear, these dialogues were a real challenge to transcribe due to their dramatic rapidity, intensity, and idiomacity, coupled with the periodic overlapping of speakers. In addition, at times we could not find a convenient, conventional way to represent certain meaningful non-orthographic sounds—patterns of intonation, exclamations, emotive interjections, and paralinguistic vocal modification. My translations of the highly colloquial Chinyanja text are similarly flawed to say the least. Where the original recording and transcription were not clear, of course, a certain amount of reconstructive guess-work had to take place. Furthermore, the absence of any visual cues meant that the intended meaning of several ambiguous or unclear utterances could only be roughly conjectured.

I must conclude with this admission: My *Sewero* transcriptions, where they occur in subsequent chapters, are imperfect and cannot do justice to the artistic quality of these plays or to the impressive talents of the players. They constitute but a diminished reflection of the actual dialogue since the written words are a mere visual representation of full dimensional oral speech. This loss is considerable, and the result is a significant reduction in my intended representation of the creative excellence, vocal dynamism, and rhetorical power of the original discourse. My translations from the Chinyanja transcriptions suffer accordingly—as well as my critical interpretation of the data at hand upon which my conclusions are based. Constructive comments from readers are therefore invited with regard to any correction that may be felt advisable, or even necessary, with respect to each and every aspect of the following analysis and discussion.

---

[12] I was supplied with several studio tapes of the *Sewero* program by the TWR staff in Lilongwe; these were a real pleasure to work with—and, at the same time, to enjoy.

(L to R) Mrs Bezitta Mnthambala, Mrs Patricia Ligomeka, Pastor Yosofati Banda, Mr Gibson Kachaje, Mrs Mary Jailosi, Mrs Dorothy Saidi

(L to R) Pastor Yosofati Banda, Mr Gibson Kachaje, Mrs Mary Jailosi

(L to R) Mr Gibson Kachaje, Mrs Mary Jailosi

(L to R) Mrs Bezitta Mnthambala, Mrs Patricia Ligomeka, Pastor Yosofati Banda,

(L to R) Mrs Bezitta Mnthambala, Mrs Patricia Ligomeka,

(L to R) Mrs Bezitta Mnthambala, Mrs Patricia Ligomeka, Pastor Yosofati Banda,
Mr Gibson Kachaje, Mrs Mary Jailosi, Mrs Dorothy Saidi

(L to R) Mrs Patricia Ligomeka, Pastor Yosofati Banda,

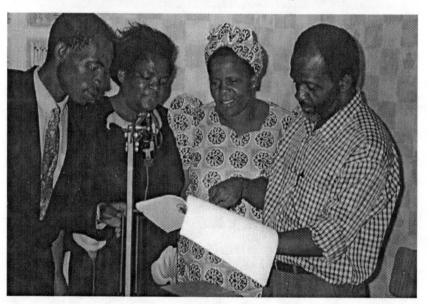

(L to R) Pastor Yosofati Banda, Mrs Dorothy Saidi, Mrs Mary Jailosi,
Mr Gibson Kachaje

(L to R) Mrs Mary Jailosi, Mrs Dorothy Saidi

(L to R) Pastor Yosofati Banda, Mrs Dorothy Saidi, Mrs Mary Jailosi,
Mr Gibson Kachaje

3. Aspects of a Traditional Chewa Religious World-View

3.0 The vibrant, persistent nature of African traditional religion

A people's religion constitutes an integral part of their ethnic ethos, especially in Africa where some would consider it to be the very core of everyday culture as it is believed and lived. Thus, the faith and practice of religion cannot be effectively analyzed and evaluated in isolation—that is, apart from that particular society's general world-view and life-style. I must therefore contextualize my study of the content, purpose, and indeed, the great success of these *Sewero* plays by presenting a little overview of this overarching cultural framework that underlies and motivates the thought and behavior of many, if not most people, including the dramatic world of the occult, which is the focus of our attention—namely, witchcraft, sorcery, magic, and spiritism.

Such a local Chewa point of view and religious value system may be partially summarized in terms of the seven core concepts that are elucidated below (3.1; see Wendland 1990:71-119, 1992; Mojola 1990:160-164).[1] These *etic* principles (i.e., a non-indigenous, alien perspective) are not original with me, but rather they are derived in various forms from the extensive published studies of recognized scholars in the field of south-central Bantu religious studies (e.g., Fiedler *et.al.* 1998; Gwengwe 1970; Kalilombe 1980, 1999; Ngulube 1989; Schoffeleers 1997),[2] and especially from personal conversations with indigenous experts, namely, my African colleagues for the past 35 years, including professional pastors, seminary students, and lay Christian participant-observers. The following summary, though inadequate, is offered merely to provide a general perspective that may assist cultural outsiders to understand certain important aspects of the rich indigenous philosophy which underlies and gives coherence to the different religious concepts that are discussed in this monograph.

It should be pointed out at the onset of this selective description that in reality there is no such thing as a discrete and uniform body of "traditional

---

[1] The Chewa people (*Achewa*) are an ethnic Bantu people who occupy the central plateau region of Malawi as well as certain areas of western Mozambique and eastern Zambia; they speak a major dialect of what constitutes the *Chinyanja* ('lake') language (alternatively called *Chichewa*).

[2] Unfortunately, the excellent study of van Bruegel (2001) did not become available to me until I had completed a full draft of the present work. It is interesting to see, however, how closely his research, which was conducted in Malawi in the 1970s, accords with my own results and conclusions.

Chewa religion". There does appear to be a common stratum, or deep structure, of assumptions, beliefs, and related values, but their overt manifestation in the form of explicit precepts and associated ritual practices may vary considerably—depending on the particular area concerned (e.g., central or southern Malawi, rural versus urban areas), the religious (including denominational Christian) background of the people involved, their age, and the specific life-situation that they are currently experiencing. Therefore, in many respects religion appears to be as disparate a phenomenon as it is prevalent among the national population.

Furthermore, ancient African ancestral religion is also becoming increasingly modified by some of the same pressures leading to intellectual stagnation, outward ritualism, and theological decay with respect to "doctrine", the cult, and an enveloping organizational structure that have rendered certain world religions, established Western Christianity in particular, more or less inactive and impotent as a significant force in the society at large. These factors include powerful alien secularizing influences (all sorts of "-isms") like humanism, rationalism, relativism, institutionalism, materialism, and globalization. Such enveloping forces are much more potent in cities than in rural areas, but because of the continual human movement between town and country, the latter, more remote areas are also becoming increasingly affected. For this reason then, the typical settings of *Sewero* plays are not static in their scope; rather, they tend to be as dynamic as the society that they are trying to reflect in dramatic form unto itself.

However, compared with the situation in the Western nations of Europe and America (where functional atheism is fast becoming the undeclared national "religion"), the fundamental philosophical setting in Africa remains more stable, conservative, and generally "spiritual" in outlook. Thus, for the majority of the latter population, religious beliefs as well as values tend to manifest a certain essential commonality and resiliency in the face of some strong pressures for corrosion and change. Accordingly, like the familiar chameleon, which is also a prominent figure in many local myths of origin, African traditional religion has the capacity to adapt and conform to the current external situation, in many cases blending in so completely with its sociocultural surroundings that it is virtually unnoticeable. Its overt forms (i.e., pertaining to ritual observance and the practice of worship) may vary considerably from one area to the next, and they may also be hidden or disguised by the formal cultus of Christianity. As a discrete, meaningful, and authoritative force, however, the underlying belief system of the past—the "faith of the fathers"—though modified through time in certain key respects, retains its essential influence for many modern adherents. This too, despite the tremendous social, economic, and political upheavals or crises that occur on every side due to disease, drought, deprivation, and the disaster of periodic warfare.

3.1 Seven principles of an African philosophy of life

The seven ideological principles that are described in this section represent just one interested observer's way of analyzing, organizing, and evaluating the mass of data that is available on the subject. Other valid ways of handling this material are certainly possible, for example, a more detailed, topical categorization instead of my broader thematic approach (e.g., Chakanza 2000).[3] My aim is simply to summarize some of the basic features of the central African belief system and to suggest some of their main areas of manifestation within contemporary society, with special reference to the various occult beliefs and practices that are the focus of my collection of *Sewero* dramas. Thus, I will not be dealing with some of the more ancient or localized strands of Chewa ancestral religion, such as the *Mbona* cult, the *nyau* male secret society, the territorial rain shrines, and practices relating to spirit possession or exorcism (see Kalilombe 1980; Schoeffeleers 1997; van Breugel 2001), since these topics do not figure prominently in my corpus of plays.

In any case it must be remembered that we are dealing here with a dynamic, flexible phenomenon, one that is composed of a multitude of different facets in many distinct local settings. These are all in a continual state of flux, of interaction and change, like that of a living organism, within the ongoing development of the culture as a whole. Thus, possible differences of perspective and formulation need not detract from the main ideas being presented or the more or less inductive, insider-informed methodology whereby they were arrived, for example: field research (Wendland 1974), formal and informal interviews and questionnaires, assigned essays from Malawian theological students, vernacular text analysis (sermons, radio programs, debates; see Wendland 2000), reading scholarly studies in the field, and my experience in Bible translation (Wendland 1998).

I will present a set of seven fundamental premises or presuppositions about reality, each of which appears to account for a significant dimension of the central African world-view complex. Together, they offer a summary of this ancient, and still active, system of belief and behavior. These principles are discussed in terms of their manifestation within traditional Chewa

---

[3] Chakanza's study, which I obtained after my initial draft of this chapter, pertains to Chinyanja proverbs, but it naturally includes many aspects of traditional religious belief and practice, which are organized in terms of his helpful topical "list of meanings" at the end of his book.

(Bantu) society, especially those areas that are of special religious relevance—that is, those which serve both to stimulate and also to stage "the drama of Christianity" in Malawi, Zambia, Mozambique, and surrounding countries. My emphasis will be upon those essential core values and affections to which a particular belief or conceptual system gives rise, and a corresponding attempt is made to provide some concrete illustrations of how the principle concerned is realized in actual behavior. This procedure is crucial for it demonstrates how the visible forms of a given cultural group may be analyzed with regard to their function, both as symbols which convey meanings or messages, to all members of the community, and also as indices that reflect some basic feature of the "common man's" ethical philosophy and associated way of life.

These seven principles should accordingly be viewed as broad, overlapping predilections rather than hard and fast rules or distinct conceptual categories—admittedly, to a great extent "the result of extrapolation and intellectual reconstruction" (Kalilombe 1980:39). Thus, they are hypothetical and hence also open to debate and, indeed, correction. Furthermore, while these generic notions are clearly interrelated, they do not seem to be equal in their dominance or level of importance and influence in society; some appear to be more fundamental to the central African world-view than others. In any case, my particular organization and interpretation of the data may be criticized and revised as the reader progresses.

I will begin then with the two concepts that are regarded as being basic to all the rest since they profoundly affect the average person's overall outlook on life, namely, a synthetic, dynamic perspective on the universe. These principles of *synthesis* and *dynamism* are crucial to one's understanding of the Bantu belief system as a whole. Five derivative, supplementary ideas follow; while still essential to the underlying world-view, they seem to be relatively subordinate in significance and import: *gradation, communalism, experientialism, humanism*, and *egalitarianism*. It will not be possible in the following overview to document, exemplify, and discuss these philosophical facets in detail. My presentation is much more modestly intended merely to provide some pertinent background information and a possible comparative framework that might serve to stimulate one's own investigation of such key cultural notions as they relate to one's observations of the occult's diverse manifestations within a given central African society—with particular reference to how they are dealt with both artistically and biblically by the *Sewero* dramatists.

3.1.1 Synthesis

Nkhuni imodzi siimanga mtolo.
"One piece of firewood does not make [bind up] a faggot."
This concept, like the very meaning to which it refers, seems to underlie and integrate all of the other principles of world-view orientation. Synthesis thus pertains to a predominant frame of mind, a consistent way of looking at the events, experiences, and entities of life from a *holistic* perspective. There is a general tendency to put things together rather than to take them apart, no matter how apparently dissimilar on the surface of immediate perception or sensation. The aim is to attain or ascribe an essential *wholeness* or *unity* to whatever is being examined, described, evaluated, or otherwise considered. There is accordingly a search for what is basically *similar* in human experience—the *common components* of life—and an effort is therefore made to link up all of the elements that occupy a given physical or conceptual space to create a communally oriented system (see 3.1.4) where everyone/thing has his/her/its designated purpose and place within the whole. An emphasis is placed on searching for the general "relatedness" of things, that is, to include rather than to exclude, in order to ensure that no one or thing is left out. The entire universe in fact, including its Creator (*Mulungu*), must function as an integrated unit, with all of the distinct, individual parts operating in smooth and harmonious interaction. *Apatsa mosiyana* "[God] gives out [distributes gifts and blessings] differently"—but for the good of community as a whole.

There are many examples that may be cited to illustrate the central unifying concept of synthesis, some of which will appear in my discussion of the six complementary principles below. Perhaps the most obvious instance is the elaborate African *kinship* system; within the clan, for example, everyone is either a mother, father, brother, sister, son, or daughter. Much more precise designations of a person's relationship can be given if needed, but in general conversation the more inclusive and proximate relational term is preferred. These familial references can be extended to encompass larger group relations, right on up to the tribe as a whole and even related tribes that are conventionally associated to the group on the basis of their virtual "cousinship". Relations and relatives, both human and otherwise, thus pervade the preferred synthetic logic of African thought. This is felt to be a distinctive feature of man's nature in particular. As the Chewa people themselves put it: *tili tawiri ntianthu—kali kokha nkanyama!* "When there's two of us we're people [i.e., human]—a person by himself is [like] an animal!" (a creature that is ontologically different).

The elaborate noun class and concordial copy system, which is such a prominent feature of all Bantu languages, reinforces this sense of a predilection towards inclusiveness. Every object and entity in the environment, new as well as old, has its designated place within the classification, and consequently the syntactic relations of every nominal within a connected piece of discourse are clearly marked. There is a general noun class into which all human beings are put, but this category is readily extended to include any creature that functions as a personalized character in traditional oral narratives—domestic animals, wild beasts, birds, even insects. Accurate semantic distinctions need to be made, of course, and to that end a certain measure of analytical processing is involved (one cannot have synthesis without as least some manner of prior analysis). But the primary emphasis is definitely upon amalgamation, on grouping together things that have a distinct familial resemblance, whether overt or attributed, so that a sense of wholeness and unity is either created, or confirmed—or indeed extended to include alien elements and newcomers.

A prominent synthetic inclusiveness is evident also in the various expressions of cultural life. Thus "religion" (for which there is not even a generic term in Chinyanja) is not regarded as being essentially distinct from the other major sociocultural institutions, such as the kinship system, political (royal) establishment, traditional education, arts and crafts, trades and occupations, or other economic pursuits. Rather, *religion* (the belief in, worship of, and/or attempted manipulation of higher spiritual powers) is seen to thoroughly infuse and energize all other social activities. It permeates, promotes, and propels all of life. It is therefore difficult, if not impossible, to fix a dividing line where religion leaves off in society and some other cultural practice begins. "Religion" in this more general sense includes the related belief systems of magic, sorcery, witchcraft, spiritism, and divination.

The same harmonizing, incorporative tendency holds true also for the specific social manifestations of religious belief. Take the practice of rain calling (*kuitanitsa mvula*), for example: whether the imitative or contagious variety of symbolic representation is applied during the prayer ceremony, the same basic synthetic principle is involved, namely, that a part of something can be employed to represent the whole—the former being mystically linked to the latter either by similarity or on the basis of some other relevant connection (e.g., the sprinkling of beer at a local shrine [*kachisi*], or the wearing of black clothes—the dark color being conventionally associated with rain clouds). The synthetic potency of such symbolic action can go so far as to effect a virtual identification of the metaphorical vehicle (image) and its tenor (referent), as happens, for example, when a witch (*mfiti*) attacks a victim by means of his or her secret personal name, or when people link the vital presence of an ancestral spirit (*mzimu*) with the blood of a living relative (cf. the saying *ubale ndi mwazi* "brotherhood [or sisterhood] is blood").

A synthetic conception of "reality" deeply influences one's perspective on the composition of the universe (*chilengedwe* "what was created", i.e., by God) and indeed life (*moyo*) itself. The latter, more precisely designating the existential "life-principle" of an animate being, is in essence undivided and cyclical, although it normally passes through a number of distinct stages and transitions during one's cycle of maturation and development. Life comes from God through the necessary mediation of the ancestors, is given bodily form at birth, grows, matures, reproduces, ages, and then finally returns again as an ancestor at the transition of "death", where it remains in varying degrees of contact with the living, depending on their continued remembrance of one's "name" (*dzina*), or personality (personhood).

As far as the cosmos is concerned, people do not distinguish formally between what analytical Westerners would designate as the "physical" and the "metaphysical" or the "material" and the "spiritual" (I continue to use these descriptive terms purely out of linguistic convenience). Furthermore, key traditional religious notions do not revolve around a central antagonistic moral dualism, good versus evil, certainly not in abstract impersonal terms. "Evil spirits" (*mizimu yoipa* the expression is not a natural, indigenous concept) as well as witches and sorcerers are all part of a single amoral conception of the "world" (*dziko* "land/country", where a given people, tribe, clan/matrilineage, family happen to reside). Thus what "analysts" would call the "natural" and the "supernatural" encompass for traditional thinkers but one integrated system of mutually interacting and influential life-forces in man's immediate environment, some being more prominent and powerful than others (see 3.1.3). The indigenous ideal was for the ancestors to promote and protect the central beliefs and values that upheld a harmonious communal society (as it was), that is, despite the presence of certain malevolent individuals (humans or spirits) who would work for the magnification of their own vitality of "life" to the detriment of others in the community.

It remained then for the heralds of Christianity to introduce an alternative, very alien, conception of the nature of man and his universe according to the teachings of a *written* holy book, the Bible. This new cosmos consists of an *immanent* (as distinct from a transcendent) deity and a host of *antithetical* non-human personalities—angels, under God, versus demons, following Satan—all vying to influence the morality of individual lives and their immortal "souls". The crucial moral component of human existence now also concerned the quality or state of one's inner personality or psyche (the

69

"heart", *mtima*), which invariably had also an external, good or evil behavioral manifestation ("righteousness" versus "sin"), as determined by a holy God and his perfect precepts, recorded in the Scriptures.

It falls to the *Sewero* group then to dramatize in a vivid contemporary Chinyanja all these profound conceptual differences (I have just mentioned a few) that derive from a biblical world-view and value system, but which concern the everyday faith and life of all real, potential, and as yet not fully committed followers of Jesus Christ within the current sociocultural and religious setting of south-central Africa. To be sure, there is a definite need for a rigorous moral and theological examination as well as a careful, analytical personal introspection that has to take place in orthodox Christian practice (as part of one's daily "repentance"). However, the players seek to *contextualize* this process meaningfully and forcefully within the synthetic, communal perspective that still governs the familiar cognitive and emotive framework of the vast majority of their listeners. This same hermeneutical challenge is confronted also in relation to the next fundamental notion as well as the five subsidiary principles that follow.

3.1.2 Dynamism

Dziti mafano, udzafa mano adakayera.

"[If you] say, '[It's just] superstition', you will die whilst your teeth are still white!" The concept of "dynamism", which concerns all the various and sundry manifestations of the vital "soul" or "life-force" (*moyo*) principle in society, dominates the traditional religious thought of central Africa. According to this personalization of the cosmos and the associated operation of cognitive "synthesis" (3.1.1), every living being, non-human as well as human, is believed to possess such an inner energy or force, even selected inanimate objects in the local environment that serve as a residence or habitat for certain spiritual beings. A person's life-force may be controlled—either enhanced or diminished—by specialists in the use of both natural and mystical powers (*wanga*), that is, for helpful or harmful purposes by the "healer" (*sing'anga*) and "sorcerer" (*wanyanga*) respectively (Ngulube 1989:29). In fact, the very same magical practice and its perceived effects may be regarded as being good or evil, depending on its specific purpose on the occasion and the personal perspective of the practitioner (or his/her "client").

One's life-force is neither a perceptible internal substance nor some tangible energy (such as Christ apparently was conscious of, e.g., Lk. 8:46). Rather it is believed to be an inherent vitality of being which is bestowed by God, the Creator and Preserver of life, through the mediation of one or more of his (her) ancestors. The latter is normally the spiritual personage which

70

whom s/he is closely associated by means of a common, inherited "name" (character) in what may be loosely described as a patron-client relationship. This life-principle (or "soul-power") is distinct from, yet integrally connected with (personal "synthesis" again!) the external manifestation of physical life, i.e., being "alive" in a physiological sense. The soul (life-force) thus activates a person's "life", which in turn reveals itself by means of such typical bodily functions as a breathing chest, blinking eyes, or a beating heart. Accordingly then, as one's *moyo* increases in vigor and vitality, being augmented either by natural process (physical growth) or supernatural intervention (e.g., magical means, spiritual empowerment), so also one's quality of life improves, increasing in health, strength, and productivity. Furthermore, one's standing in terms of social status and interpersonal influence within the community grows apace.

The problem is that it is also possible for one's enemies—"witches" (*mfiti*) and "sorcerers" (*vanyanga*)[4] in particular—to gain control of one's soul for iniquitous purposes, namely, to sustain and develop their life-force, that is, their own personal potency and physical well-being. As such human parasites mystically "eat" (in the case of witches) or magically "kill" (in the case of sorcerers) the life-force of their victim, s/he inevitably, sooner or later, becomes weaker and more infirm until at last the soul is no longer able to support physical life and the person "dies" (*kufa*, also "expire/be completely finished"). At other times, so the belief goes, a witch or sorcerer can "trap" and enslave one's soul, compelling it to do his/her own bidding, e.g., to steal the property of others. The victim is thus transformed into a zombie-like servile creature (*ndondocha*)—physically still alive, but spiritually (with regard to life-force) quite dead! When the individual finally does die in a physiological sense, whatever the human cause (no death is regarded as being just "natural"), the soul is thereby released to become an ancestral "spirit" (*mzimu*). The latter is potentially eternal, but in practice limited by the active memory of the living, i.e., relatives performing overt rites of remembrance, such as the brewing of a special, sacrificial batch of traditional beer (*mowa*).

If a person's soul-power can thus increase or decrease in vigor and potency due to the intervention of others, then it follows that the issue of spiritual "protection" as well as "promotion" will become quite crucial for the average individual. He (or she) must be able to defend himself against such external attack. Correspondingly, he also needs to reinforce or augment his own life-force, both qualitatively and quantitatively, in order to expand

---

[4] For a discussion of the difference between these two greatly-feared agents of evil, see Wendland 1992.

his familial posterity, personal prosperity, physical well-being, and influence in society. This critical task is accomplished by means of various kinds of "medicine" (*mankhwala*), that is, concoctions derived from selected inanimate and animate (including human) sources which are intended to tap and consolidate the energy inherent in their respective ingredients for specific defensive and self-promotional purposes.

Normally, the average person must obtain such magical potions and charms from a specialist in the field of the occult, namely, the *sing'anga*, the "medicine (wo)man" or "diviner-doctor". He (or she) is someone who possesses a spiritual (spirit-guided) insight into the detection and manipulation of natural forces through the preparation and application of medicines, either as a "GP" (general practitioner) or as a specialist in a certain area of human need (e.g., the healing of physical or psychological maladies, the enhancement of fertility, the production of wealth, job advancement, etc.). In certain more traditional communities, the qualitative state of one's being, selfhood, and/or situation in life is partially determined also by the vitality of one's relationship with his/her personal guardian spirit. If the latter is weak or estranged, it will not be able to effectively ward off the forces of evil and destruction that are continually directed against an individual in society.

In addition to such particular power boosters, a person can also increase the soundness of his (her) soul's dynamic condition by cultivating various general extensions of interpersonal association in the local community. This is accomplished by promoting social "solidarity" in the form of a sufficient number of dependency relations in life as well as in (before) death, for example, with individuals who are linked to that person by obligation (e.g., as inferior to superior in status), friendship, ritual (e.g., a common initiation ceremony), marriage (i.e., affinity), or more strongly, by blood (consanguinity), but especially through one's progeny. The different customs involving the practice of giving a mature or accomplished person honor and respecting his (her) authority naturally contributes to the maintenance of his soul-power, something that goes considerably beyond what in a Western setting might be termed one's "self-image".

In such a patriarchal society (though also matrilineal and matrilocal) this belief could also be adduced as a primary reason for polygamy, whether official or informal in nature, proximate or remote in setting. Such a practice naturally provided more offspring to care for one, both during this life and, more importantly, in the after-life, by sacrifices, libations, rituals, and naming ceremonies designed to memorialize the departed. This custom, which is not so common nowadays for economic reasons, thus had a definite religious intent in addition to its more obvious social and political functions.

The principle of dynamism, which is very much a "synthetic" concept in its holistic, integrative, all-permeating qualities, is also basic to the concepts mentioned below. It serves to establish the fundamental mind-set or notional framework within which the other principles operate in close conjunction with one another. Moreover, once the notion of a pervasive "soul-power" (technically, with reference to humans) or "life-force" (pertaining to nonhuman, animate beings) is correctly understood, it is not so difficult to recognize how the indigenous religious system of central Africa developed into the complex of complementary, coexisting, competing, and sometimes seemingly contradictory set of beliefs that it manifests today. This core idea of a divinely originated and spiritually sustained multitude of individual forces in continual flux and dynamic interaction with one another forms the hub, as it were, around which all of the other, subsidiary presuppositions about life, being, and reality revolve, like the connected spokes of a bicycle wheel. This key organizing principle also provides certain more dubious practices like divination, magic, and witchcraft, with a certain measure of popular validity and credibility by association, that is, through their common "religious" origin, relationship, and sanction.

The diverse precepts that pertain to dynamism, then, may be viewed as the generative nucleus that gives traditional African religion a distinctive vigorous vitality that continues to attract and to influence millions of overt and covert adherents on the continent today. Paradoxically, however, this same central belief system has also proved to be a serious, debilitating liability to the people's moral, spiritual, and psychological development since it condemns them to an endless round of existence living at the mercy of inscrutable powers which they can only attempt to partially control and ward off through magical methods. It has also led the masses to pin their hopes on familiar, local counter-agents who employ these same mystical means in order to procure the desired protection, healing, and personal empowerment.

A vicious, but also pathetic, cycle of dependency is therefore created and sustained, one that is firmly fixed on material concerns, human saviors, earthly cures, and spiritual intervention. Furthermore, there is seemingly no internal way to break the ever-present chain of causality and misfortune in life: *provocation* (whether real or imagined) => *retaliation* (e.g., an act of sorcery) => *divination* (mystical investigation) => *discernment* (discovery of the "guilty" party) => *retribution* (= "provocation" in reverse!). This is the vibrant, but conflict-ridden, socio-religious environment in which the *Sewero* plays seek to offer an alternative through a confident, equally

73

dynamic understanding of the power of the gospel and its personal application in life.

3.1.3 Gradation

Mulungu sampempha nyama, koma moyo
"From God one does not pray for meat, but for life."

This principle is closely related to the first two in that any dynamic system ("synthesis") of integrated, mutually influential forces will normally give evidence of a graded, or hierarchical, structure in which the individual constituent powers are explicitly or implicitly ranked according to some measure of "potency" (*mphamvu*). The main rungs of this culturally-defined ladder of authority and honor are established primarily on the basis of the esoteric as well as practical knowledge that is associated with age or seniority. That is the "natural order of things" (*dongosolo la chilengedwe*), which will always be manifested in a given community by a host of verbal conventions and non-verbal customs. Despite this recognized notion of social gradation, a synthetic concern for inclusiveness, unity, and harmony is never lost sight of. The hypothetical scale of spiritual dynamism may be outlined as follows:

GOD
⇧   (The transcendent Creator of all life on earth)

SPIRITS
| Clan Spirits (great originators, culture heroes, e.g., Banda, Phiri)
| Ancestral Spirits (those forgotten in name/personality)
| Living Dead ("named" ancestors, benevolent and malevolent)

MAN
| Paramount chief (and his council of sub-chiefs)
| Religious specialists (priests, diviners, prophets, sorcerers, etc.)
| "Headmen" and elders of the clan (including great "mothers")
| Adults (child-bearing age, esp. "uncles"—mothers' brothers)
| Youth (matured and initiated)
| Children (named after a personal ancestor)
| Infants (not yet under the protection of a guardian spirit)

NATURE
| Animals (also ranked or selected according to "potency")
| Plants (similarly selected)
| Locations (where nature spirits reside, e.g., great trees, rivers,

---

| high hills)
⇩   Objects, inert and impotent

I will not define this ladder of gradation any further (see Wendland 1992:88-91), except for the personal component, which is the focus of this study. Human society, being more perceptible in terms of actual behavior, naturally reveals the most clearly defined stratification in terms of life-force potential. This depends upon a combination of socially determined factors, all of which relate to the possession and control of more or less spiritual "energy", or soul-power, e.g., age, relationship to the chief, occupation, achievement, spiritual "endowment", and magically acquired wisdom or strength. Secular education or religious (Christian) education does not play into this mix. In other words, within the scope of such a traditional social organization, the principle of political equality and individual (e.g., gender) rights—so prized and sought after in Western nations—is neither valued or aspired to. Even modern scientific study or technological training advances do not necessarily give the young an advantage over their elders (unless there are political or economic implications). Instead, what really counts is not intellectual knowledge, but practical wisdom in the ways of the world—especially life-preservation (or the defenses against illness and death), whether based on personal experience and/or magical acquisition (e.g., "charms", *zithumwa*). Sooner or later, the advice of elders will prove to be true: *Mau a akulu akoma akagonera* "The words of the great ones are pleasant once they have slept the night".

The structured *hierarchical* organization of Chewa (Bantu) society, realized primarily in terms of seniority or status, manifests itself in a host of customary practices that pertain to the giving and upholding of deference, or "respect" (*ulemu*). "Shame" (*manyazi*), the reduction or depreciation of one's life-force, results when an elder, or "big person" (*wamkulu*), is not accorded the honor that tradition or convention dictates, and this negative emotion can in turn have a deleterious effect on the inner condition of his (her) soul. It can also result in a justifiable "curse" (*temberero*) being called down upon the offender to be inflicted by the ancestral guardians of clan morality, much like Elisha felt compelled to do when a group of unruly youths dared to mock his person and position (2 Kgs. 2:23).

This ladder of social status also contributes to the crucial importance of the *mediatorial* function in interpersonal relations. In the case of serious business or important issues, a person does not communicate immediately and directly with those who are situated on a higher rung. So it says in the opening proverb: people do not pray to God over the mundane matters of life, only when life itself is really threatened. Thus all sorts of "mediators" (*ankhala-pakati* "those who sit in-between" the parties concerned) are necessary to keep social relations running smoothly and appropriately, according to custom. These individuals are recognized by the community as having the insight and ability to perform this vital role, especially when dealing with questions of life and death. Such intermediaries are particularly essential then as leaders in the crucial rites-of-passage that mark important stages in the human life-cycle. The Chewa *nankungwi*, for example, is not only an experienced "instructor" in traditional wisdom and practice, but she (or he in the case of the *nyau* cult) also performs a prominent religious function as she brings her female charges, the *anamwali* "initiates", through an extremely dangerous liminal period as they mature from maiden- to woman-hood.

The gradation principle is probably most clearly revealed linguistically through a fairly elaborate system of "respect" terms and usages, which play such an important part in the daily conversation of a people like the Chewa. As the socially-determined distance between speakers increases, so also the terms of personal reference become increasingly oblique, moving from the second-person "familiar" to a second-person "honorific" plural to a third-person plural of "majestic" designation and reference. Such verbal conventions naturally have certain theological implications; for example, how is God—or Jesus Christ—to be addressed in prayer?

Deferential or *honorific* speech is usually accompanied during face-to-face conversation by corresponding actions that demonstrate one person's social position with respect to another. A young, unmarried woman, for example, in the presence of a respected elder would be expected to kneel down, clasp her hands together in her lap, look down at the ground, and speak only when spoken too—even then in the briefest, quietest manner possible. Similarly, one would never be so bold as to correct or overtly contradict what an elder has spoken, or directly refuse to do what one has been told. Rather, to avoid confrontation and a potentially shame-causing situation where a genuine and honest difference of opinion is concerned, a junior would make his (her) feelings known with great indirection, and proverbially if possible. *Kukana nsalu ya akulu n'kuviika m'madzi* "To refuse [to wash] the cloth[es] of the elders is to dip it [them] into the water" [instead of thoroughly scrubbing it, as asked to do]; in other words, rather than to bluntly say "no", one would at least go through the motions of what was wanted.

In a graded society then, everyone knows his/her place and how to maintain that position so that the underlying structure of interpersonal forces and relationships remains in its delicate *equilibrium*, for the ultimate benefit of all concerned. Any accidental or deliberate overturning of this time-sanctioned status-quo is likely to upset the balance of powers, an event that many would assume would have severe repercussions as far as the offender him-self is concerned, and possibly also with regard to the overall prosperity and welfare of the community at large. The ever-vigilant ancestors would see to that, for their position too is vitally affected by any such upset in terms of either speech or behavior. The *Sewero* players must remain cognizant of these time-honored customs, creeds, and conventions when they present their dramas, clearly confirming those that do not violate biblical values. How-ever, they are not afraid to confront any type of behavior that would contra-dict the higher biblical principle of the fellowship of all disciples in Christ, or detract from the consequent "synthetic" concept that we are *all* "brothers" and "sisters" by faith in the Lord (see Mt. 5:22, 12:50; Ac. 7:26; Ro. 14:10; Jas. 2:15-17).

3.1.4 Communalism

Ichi n'chiani n'kulinga muli awiri.
"There have to be two of you to ask, 'What's this?'"

The notion of hierarchy just described establishes a great number of implicit and explicit distinctions in a given human community, and indeed through-out the cosmos as a whole, on the basis of how much dynamism a particular being either possesses, controls, or is able to access in relation to others within the immediate environment. This may be viewed as the *vertical* dimension of human interaction in society, one that pertains to its diverse *power* and *authority* relationships. Obviously such a stratifying principle, if allowed to operate in isolation, would quickly fracture a group into many different and competing segments. But there is another prominent force that is active in the organization of central African peoples, one which serves to counteract the tendency towards fissure by working for the corporate unity of the group. This is the synthesizing, *horizontal* principle of communalism that builds social *solidarity* as well as a spirit of egalitarianism and justice on various levels within the clan and community at large. Such an attitude is colorfully caught by the proverb, *mnzako akapsa ndevu, mzimire*, "when your friend's beard catches fire, put it out for him" [implication: he may have occasion to do the same favor for you one day.]

The concept of *community*, together with the associated activities of mutual participation, cooperation, and sharing, is very strong in all African societies. Thus every individual, though valued in and of him/herself, is always viewed in relation to the corporate whole of which s/he constitutes a vital part, each with a definite role to play. This begins with the so-called "extended family", which is the fundamental kinship unit, and incorporates increasingly larger social units—throughout the clan complex and including finally the entire ethnic group ("tribe"). It is the familial body, including one's ancestors as well as descendants, which gives each person a sense of identity and purpose, for everyone has a functional niche in society with related obligations, responsibilities, as well as benefits: *chala chimodzi sichiswa nsabwe* "one finger does not smash a louse" (little though it may be). Rather, several fingers, along with the thumb, working together in close coordination are needed to get the job done. It is very important therefore for one to know his or her proper place in the group and to act accordingly, that is, cooperatively and harmoniously, in relation to others.

For every member of such a communally-oriented society then, all motives born purely out of self interest must normally give way to a group-sensitive perspective and cooperative operation. A competitive attitude, the drive to achieve success, a concern for personal rights and freedoms, or indeed, one's individual "self-image", tends to be suppressed in favor of an accommodating approach that stresses the need to stimulate and maintain harmony, uniformity, and conformity to the status quo. Blunt honesty is less important than one's ability to avoid shame and hard feelings in cases where the issue of "truth" is concerned. Friendliness, happiness, generosity ("open-handedness") and hospitality (which is part of the notion of "freedom" in Chinyanja) are virtues held in high regard, whereas all manifestations of anger, selfishness, envy, pride, and greed are strongly condemned and spoken against (e.g., *kunyada n'koipa* "pride is perverse"). These sorts of ill-humor will be punished too, if not by the living, then surely by the departed, ancestral members of the community, whose God-given job it is to maintain the mores and traditions that promote peace and concord within a group-living environment.

Mutual *sharing* ("African socialism") is a prominent expression of the principle of communalism. In older days, all property, for example, was held (not owned, but overseen) for the most part on a corporate basis, that is, by the larger family unit and not by an individual. Justice too was dispensed in a manner that was most beneficial to and supportive of the group. In addition, people tended to spend their leisure time as well as their working hours engaged in some form of communal activity whenever this could be arranged, and it usually was. This was especially true for the legitimate types of "religious" practice where public group participation was, and still is, the rule—for example, when appealing to the ancestral spirits in a time of crisis or disaster (drought, famine, floods, pestilence, etc.).

Where illegitimate, anti-social activities are involved, however, secrecy is essential, especially during the practice of divination, cursing, and sorcery (*kulodza*). Such covert expressions of unbounded egotism, individualism,

78

and selfishness are regarded as being the most despicable sins imaginable. This is because they directly promote the disruption of social concord and the consequent corruption of interpersonal relations at the most fundamental level—within the bonds of the immediate kinship group as well as the close circle of friends and neighbors. Sorcery promotes the deliberate use of vital force solely for personal ends and for private advantage at the serious expense of others. The diabolical practice of witchcraft (*ufiti*), on the other hand, does have its essential communal aspect in the "coven" concept—an ironic reversal of the righteous norm. Thus, witches (*mfiti*) are commonly believed to gather together at night for a mystical cannibalistic feast when they share the "meat" (corpse) of a recent victim.

In the face of such serious threats, the unity of the whole must be maintained at all costs and by any available measure. Accordingly, an elaborate system of protocols, avoidance taboos, purity-preserving regulations—and conversely, strictly observed periods of license—have been developed in order to release friction and to prevent pent-up social tensions from building up between closely related individuals, e.g., between a man and his mother-in-law, a woman and her maternal uncle, the husband and wives of a polygamous marriage, among cross-cousins, and so forth. Similarly, many of the restrictions that were designed to prevent "pollution" (*kudetsedwa* "to be darkened") served to establish and reinforce certain male-female roles and relationships in the community. These were further strengthened by means of spiritual sanction—that is, through the constant threat of punitive intervention in the case of blatant violations of custom.

Communalism was promoted too during the major decision-making process of the group where popular "consensus" was continually cultivated. The ability to find and effect a *compromise* where differences of opinion arose or to bring about a reconciliation in times of offense was highly regarded among the leadership of the community. Where a glaring wrong had been committed, the appropriate fines and punishments were levied mainly with the goal of repairing the break and restoring the interpersonal accord damaged by the antisocial action concerned (e.g., adultery, brawling, theft, and defamation). In this area too, as noted earlier, intermediaries such as the clan "coordinator" (*nkhoswe*) are required to help keep interpersonal relations—both human and ancestral—in good repair, especially again in times of social crisis, e.g., barrenness, a sudden or prolonged illness, crop failure, divorce, or the greatest of them all, death itself. In any case, "God" (*Mulungu*) is not usually viewed as being immediately concerned by the mundane matters of everyday human existence; in this sense then and from a traditional perspective, he is not really an active member of the community (due to his supremely high position on the scale of gradation, 3.1.3).

The *Sewero* dramas naturally seek to highlight those core African traditional values and social aims that reflect corresponding biblical principles, e.g., the need for politeness, modesty, honesty, respect, hard work, and a life-style that conforms to what we might term "natural morality". However, the ancient religious customs and rites intended to preserve the balance of mystical forces within a community (e.g., ancestral veneration and propitiation or the various protective measures taken against sorcery) must be decisively replaced by those principles that embody the radically changed world-view that the Bible demands—in, for, and through Christ.

3.1.5 Experientialism

Linda madzi apite, ndipo uziti ndadala!
"Just wait for the (flood) waters to go down before you say, 'I'm saved!'"

This principle, as it applies to central Africa (and to biblical Israel), reflects an approach to knowledge—and interpersonal communication—that is based primarily upon one's own past experience as well as on present sensation and observation, backed by an ancient tradition of wisdom lore. This contrasts in many respects to what has become known as the "scientific method", which depends on carefully controlled experimentation and theses that are derived from logical deduction and hypothesis formation. African empiricism, in contrast to the Western variety, is firmly founded upon a synthesizing impulse that begins with the world around man and relates that to one's subjective existential perspective and current purpose as influenced by the present time, space, and social setting. It lacks the continual and conscious striving to achieve a concrete "objectivity" which characterizes a rationalistic, analytical approach to life and thought. This is a viewpoint that regards the universe holistically—as a unified, integrated system in which man and nature live and interact in close harmony.

The environment is not simply a reservoir of inert resources to be exploited for commercial gain, that is, to be mechanically managed and manipulated in response to an overriding profit-making motivation. Rather, "nature" (*zolengedwa* "created things"—i.e., by God!), both animate and inanimate, is viewed as a complex living organism, one that manifests a distinct hierarchy of forces (see 3.1.2-3) with which human beings must seek to establish and maintain the appropriate relationships. Thus the traditional African desires to participate in or be harmoniously integrated with his eco-system in a balance that is ultimately controlled by God through the mediating ancestors. This is a communal, relational perspective that remains more or less the same whether one happens to be a farmer, hunter, herdsman, or artisan; in each case a person is obligated to make the appropriate sacrifice and prayer whenever an apparent problem develops in the natural realm, e.g., an invasion of devouring locusts, a prolonged drought, or unusual flooding.

So *time* in the indigenous central African scheme of things is not a commodity to be measured, bought, and sold as it is in the West. Life is experience-exercised, not clock-controlled. There is no such thing as "having no time" to do something, especially on behalf of someone who happens to be in need at the moment. God gave man life for a purpose—namely, to perpetuate his own by establishing various interpersonal relationships of provision and acquisition: *kupatsa ndi kuika* "to give [someone some help] is to set aside [for some future reimbursement]". Similarly, the annual calendar is governed not by hours, days, and months, but by the rhythmic round of natural progression—the seasons (arrival of the rains, planting, weeding, harvest, burning, a fallow period) and the various special events or ceremonies pertaining to the human life-cycle that are associated with them, the so-called "rites of passage" in particular (birth-maturation-marriage-death-spirit confirmation). Periodic seasonal rituals of renewal, traditionally associated with the royal establishment, are performed in order to ensure the continued vitality and harmony of man-in-nature (Schoffeleers 1997:ch.2).

This experiential, synthetic concept of time, promoted by an agriculturally-based economy, tends to be cyclical and continuous, or even repetitive, rather than being linear (beginning to ending), discontinuous (broken up into segments by the clock or calendar), and teleological (goal-oriented) as viewed by Western analysts. Thus another, more advantageous day will probably come when a task that had to be postponed for personal reasons can be undertaken. In other words, one can easily put off till tomorrow what some human need or circumstance prevents being done today: *Tsiku limodzi silioza mbewa* "one day does not cause a field mouse to rot" (i.e., one can always dry, cook, eat, and enjoy that same mouse on the morrow). There is, for all practical purposes, no beginning or ending of time to be concerned about, no pressing schedules to adhere to, no real advantage to planning too far ahead in the unknown. The future will be attended to by those who experience it at that time. Death, the great leveler, may intervene at any moment to initiate one's movement from this present state of existence ("world") to the next, from the visible community to the invisible "communion of spirits".

The past is also a very important consideration in the present—namely, time which has already been utilized, or experienced, and thus become a part of remembered tradition and the record of the ancestors. This is not to say that the average person has no notion of the future and no concern for what will happen tomorrow. It is simply that experience has taught him that the lessons of a history actually lived are more pertinent to his daily needs than anticipated events which have not yet taken place. The wisdom of custom and tradition reveals its relevance and utility with the very passage of time. The indistinct and uncertain future, on the other hand, is important only when it promises to be of certain practical benefit in contributing to one's protection and/or prosperity. It is then when past deeds of kindness will be repaid: *Chaona mnzako, mawa chili pa iwe* "what your friend has seen [today] will be upon you tomorrow" (i.e., help someone out of his misfortune and one day he will reciprocate).

Another important aspect of an experiential mode of relating to reality is of special concern to my study of the *Sewero* dramas. This has to do with a particular emphasis upon *sound* as a vital part of the human sensorium as opposed to a predominant focus upon the sense of sight. An intellectual, analytical approach to learning tends to stress the visual faculty, which is an individualizing, dissecting sense that concentrates on the external surface of persons, objects, places, and activities (Ong 1967:258). Thus knowledge, in a Western sense, continues to be evaluated largely in terms of information, that is, how many facts and figures pertaining to a given subject a person is able to store (either in the brain or a computer) and then retrieve and put to use, usually in some abstract visualizable form that is removed to a varied degree from one's everyday experiences in real life. As the performative power of the spoken word—to curse, bless, guarantee, testify, certify, ratify, and so forth—is gradually eroded in a predominantly oral-aural society, so also the traditional authority of the word-wielders—the elders, diviners, priests, and other wise men—is correspondingly diminished in favor of a growing class of young educated elite, who may "know it all" but regularly fail to put that to use in any practical, communally beneficial way.

In contrast to an educational process that is dominated by visual literacy and the printed or electronic word, knowledge as well as art is stored, managed, and applied quite differently in a more traditional, less-technological society. Sight is still crucial of course for one's perception of the world about him, but information about that world is conveyed primarily via the sense of sound in the oral instruction of the elders. There is also an underlying *symbolical* level of significance pertaining to deeper cultural, ethical, and relational issues that enriches the surface sense of most didactic or hortatory discourse. Thus sight, whether actual or verbally evoked, is utilized to complement sound, and the education of the young, for example, becomes a pleasant, ongoing discovery-motivated experience (not a rule-governed competitive activity like "school"). This is effected by means of verbal art forms—folktales, proverbs, riddles, songs, praise poetry, illustrations, and dramatic narratives—during which either calculated or spontaneous interaction between the speaker and his audience occurs. The learning process was, and still is in these situations, a highly participatory and a mutually reinforcing public media event. There is, however, a definite emphasis upon carefully listening to (and obeying) the precepts of ancient wisdom—*Gwada, umvetse!* "Squat down, pay attention!" (lest you miss what you are being directly, or more likely metaphorically, told).

The content of traditional education, then, is not a mere set of facts to be memorized by rote, but local case studies, figurative analogies, gnomic nuggets, dramatic accounts, poetic reflections, and various pieces of common sense and practical advice. All these wise words are intended to stimulate both the intellect as well as the imagination during the intended application of these concentrated bits of wisdom to the present and one's own personal situation in society. The *inductive* method of instruction and reinforcement is clearly preferred, as it was also in the ministry of Christ (e.g., Mt.13:34-35; see Wendland 2000:ch.2). There is thus a conceptual movement from the known to the unknown, specific to general, concrete to abstract, vehicle to tenor, question to answer, and problem to solution. Many life-focused examples are used in order to attract and compel the audience—to get them personally and emotionally involved with the message. They thus learn by doing; that is to say, by imagining and inserting themselves in the specific everyday situations that are called to mind by an experienced teacher, they experientially arrive at the desired conclusion or the thematic point that s/he is leading them towards: *Ziliko n'kulinga utatosa* "[you can say] '[The mice] are there!' only after you have already checked by poking a stick into their den" (notice how concise and concentrated the original Chinyanja proverb is).

Since most information storage in an oral-aural culture must take place in human memory (hence the obvious value of elders!), the verbal art forms of such groups like the Chewa people is characterized by a great depth and diversity of stylistic devices intended to facilitate the process of presentation, retention, and recall. Many of these sound-sensitive features are no longer appreciated in the sophisticated literary productions of the West, e.g., overt repetition, formulaic expressions, complex verbal rhythms, parallelisms on all levels of linguistic structure, standardized themes and traditional motifs, colorful character types, graphic down-to-earth imagery, and dynamic plots consisting of sharp contrasts treated in terms of exaggerated sets of virtues and vices. However, these are just the verbal techniques that best suit the radio medium, the biblically-based topics, and the dramatic productions of the *Sewero* players. As noted in chapter one, the vehicle of sound when employed in such a dramatization of the message operates as an experiential, synthetic means of communication. It thus actively personalizes the transmission and reception process while at the same time promoting a covert unity of the listening audience during what becomes in essence a common esthetic and emotional experience (see Ong 1967:ch.3). The written word, on the other hand, tends to divorce the message from the messenger and thus encourages more independent, analytical, and concentrated systems of thought or reasoning. This is because one always has the opportunity to read and evaluate a text again (and again) if one does not fully understand it or get the point the first time through.

This is not to suggest that "The Book"—written Scripture—is thereby diminished either in importance or value in the context of an oral-aural society, for this mode of text transmission remains the foundation of all Christian belief and behavior. The point is, however, that a more effective way, in both sensory and logical terms (i.e., than through silent reading and deduction), for packaging and conveying the Bible's diverse assortment of messages is needed. This is a mode of communication which capitalizes on a culturally more familiar, inductive and receptor-oriented strategy—like the radio dramas performed by the *Sewero* troupe, following the ancient path of the extremely popular mystery-morality-miracle public plays that were performed in medieval times. It remains to be seen whether such a more participant-centered, setting-sensitive, experiential and dramatic manner of presentation will be more seriously considered either as an alternative or a communicational complement for increasing the effectiveness of the church's evangelistic outreach and edificational ministry in Africa in this 21st century.

3.1.6 Humanism

Munthu m'munthu chifukwa cha anzake.
"A person is a person because of his/her companions."

It is not surprising that central African religious ideology, with its emphasis upon practical knowledge gained by both personal experience and from ancient tradition, manifests a strongly man-oriented perspective on life, being, truth, and reality. If religion is the heart and core of all cultural thought and behavior, then man (*munthu* "a human being, male or female") must be its measure. Accordingly, s/he is the center of all religious belief and practice—including that pertaining to "theology" and "spiritology", which is clearly conceptualized and carried out from a communal human reference point. The entire world thus revolves around man, and regular ritual activity is organized either around the human cycle of existence, as noted above, or with respect to those occasions when people find themselves experiencing serious difficulties in life, whether corporate (drought, plague, warfare) or individual (sickness, childlessness, poverty). This particular *humanistic* emphasis is of course typical of all natural religions in the world, no matter what the technological level of advancement or achievement of the culture concerned. Only the cultural forms of expressing this focus differ from one ethnic group to the next.

The traditional Supreme Deity of the Chewa people is believed to be the Creator of all things, human beings and nature in particular. "God" (*Mulungu*, more specifically *Chauta*)[5] is therefore regarded as being much greater than man, even the most powerful of the ancestors. He is nevertheless conceived of largely in vivid, contextually-colored anthropomorphic terms with respect to both his nature as well as his attributes.[6] Although God does possess superhuman qualities and abilities, he is still considered to manifest certain distinctly human foibles and failings such as anger, impatience, forgetfulness, favoritism, carelessness, even poor judgment and a relative impotence at times. These basic character flaws are patently revealed in the Chewa charter myths of origin and dispersal, the Kaphiri-ntiwa account in particular.

> According to this myth, one day *Chiuta* [sic] sent a man and a woman down to the earth with a hoe, a mortar and a winnowing basket. With them came pairs of animals as well as *Chiuta* himself who was accompanied by the first rains. They alighted on a flat-topped hill called Kaphiri-Ntiwa. Because of the rains the barren earth sprang to life and man began to cultivate his garden. During this time, *Chiuta*, men and animals lived together in peace. This condition was, however, completely destroyed when man invented fire. This set the grass alight and made the animals flee full of rage against man. *Chiuta* was rescued by the spider who spun a thread along which he climbed to the sky. Thus driven away from the earth by the wickedness of man, he [God] proclaimed that he [man] should die and after death join him in the sky (Schoffeleers 1997:60-61).

This widely-known story strongly suggests a rather diminished, creaturely conception of "God". Perhaps the greatest divine fault is his apparent antisocial attitude towards mankind. He has chosen to live afar off, both physically

---

[5] On the use and conception of these terms for the deity, see Wendland 1998:115-121.

[6] "God" is normally conceived of as being male in gender, but there are some prominent inconsistencies in this regard, for example, in "his" creative function, the Deity may be referred to by the praise name *Namalenga*—that is, with the female noun proper noun prefix *Na-*, i.e., "She-who-creates". Furthermore, in some traditions, the term *Chauta* may also be used to refer to the female consort, or "spirit wife", of God.

and psychologically, from his creation and original companions. This fact is further reflected in that all religious communication is initiated by man and formulated in accordance with his own needs and desires. A concept of divine revelation whereby the will of the Supreme Being was made known to man, whether for good or evil, is not very prominent, if it exists among most traditionalists at all. Rather, the departed spirits (*mizimu*) fill this vital gap; man thus appeals to his own human ancestors for help in dealing with all the major exigencies of everyday life. To be sure, the name of God is mentioned during crucial prayers, especially for rain, but the real agents for beneficial change in the environment and community are the mediating spirits.

These spirits, too, are noticeably human in their personal attributes and activities. Indeed, they are regarded as being extensions of human society, except that they are unseen and unlimited by the constraints of time and space. The ancestors, however, are believed to be rather unpredictable and fickle in their personality, hence difficult to deal with directly. Therefore, the appropriate intermediaries and spirit mediums are needed, once again to make effective communication possible. Furthermore, an individual must strive to remain on the good side of those spirits whom he is related to (e.g., by means of sacrifices, naming rituals, prayers, libations, etc.). Otherwise, one will most certainly provoke them to anger and thus invite retribution in the form of sickness, bad luck, or some other loss or affliction.

A humanistic perspective is demonstrated most clearly in the religious sphere by most people's interpretation of both their environment and also their experiences in life, especially if such phenomena happen to be abnormal or unexpected in any way.[7] The cosmos is personalized and thought to be responsive to the appropriate forms of symbolic behavior (e.g., ritual incantation, gestures, spells, sacrifices, magical procedures, etc.), which also depend for their efficacy upon some human agency in both a psychic as well as a physical capacity. On the other hand, the misfortunes and tragedies that one periodically encounters may in certain instances be viewed as the result of violating some social norm or taboo (*malaulo*), in particular, where the moral code of the clan or community is concerned (e.g., cases of incest or rape). In these instances an animatedly conceived nature itself acts automatically and in judicial fashion to inflict a prescribed punishment upon the offender(s).

---

[7]   African "humanism", such as that espoused by the former (and first) President of Zambia, Dr. Kenneth Kaunda, differs radically from the Western variety, which is non-theistic, rationalistic, and antisupernatural in character.

Most other accidents, illnesses, and deaths are supposed to be caused by the mean machinations of malevolent human agents, often aided by certain animal familiars ("misfits" like the hyena, bat, owl, or lizard) or harmful spirits. Specially endowed individuals thus have the power, or vital force (see 3.1.2), to influence and impinge on others for good or evil. Such potency may be theirs either innately or as a result of some magical infusion or inoculation carried out by a traditional mystic expert, such as a "medicine man" (*sing'anga*). "Even powers which are taken to be thoroughly impersonal are held to be reacting directly to the behavior of individual humans" (Douglas 1966:81). Traditional "medicine" (*mankhwala*) is believed to be mystically empowered and discriminating in its beneficial or harmful action since it is directed at, and hence will only affect, certain designated individuals and not others, for example, to protect one's spouse from an adulterer and to punish the wrongdoer (*ibid*:87). Similarly, a magical charm, amulet, potion, or activity operates according to the instructions and will of its owner or client, as long as the specific directions for use have been correctly followed under the right circumstances.

The humanization, or man-focused tendency, of traditional African religion appears to have progressed even more rapidly in recent years due to the diluting influence of such diverse factors as secular education, urbanization, Western individualism, improved medical care, intercultural contact, Christian doctrine, and a more materialistic attitude generally. For many people today, not only is the traditional Deity remote and out of touch—perhaps even replaced by the Christian God to be worshipped once a week in a church—but also the prestige, relevance, and authority of the ancestors is steadily declining. At times it seems as if they are completely disregarded, except during funeral ceremonies or in connection with the practice of *nyau* secret society rites as well as those involving indigenous cults of affliction ("spirit possession" and rites of "exorcism"; see Schoffeleers 1997:chs.5-6).

This spiritual void, even among many Christians, is presently being filled with beliefs and fears that are becoming increasingly man-centered in their orientation, specifically with regard to the threats of sorcery and witchcraft. After all, the witch, or sorcerer (this distinction is growing less significant as the original social and kinship functions of its practice diminish in importance) is a fellow human being. Thus for most people sorcerous activity poses by far the greatest danger to a person's well-being in life, and death (where the witches especially are concerned). It lies then within the province and power of man himself to provide the necessary protection from such malicious creatures—not with the help of God nor even so much the ancestral (guardian) spirits anymore—but through human methods and resources, namely, the insight, instructions, magical potions, and defensive charms of the diviner, the medicine-man, "African doctor", and related traditional practitioners.

This progressive movement towards a more man-centered religion embraces many modernized charismatic cults of possession and incorporates a growing emphasis upon magic as a means to attain, maintain, and augment one's prosperity in life. The development is not uniform and is taking place in diverse forms throughout south-central Africa (as elsewhere) among peoples of different ethnic backgrounds and socio-economic classes, but especially among the multitudes of (peri-)urban dwelling, semi-educated, semi-Christianized, lower income groups. One thing is certain: the humanistic, pragmatic, utilitarian nature of traditional religion, which was always a prominent part of the African world-view, is definitely being strengthened and extended into all forms of contemporary life. Obviously, religion exists, is viable, and is practiced to the degree that it is perceived to be of physical, psychological, and spiritual benefit to man. If the indigenous belief system appears to be deficient in any respect, then simply complement it by borrowing from others, whether Christianity or Islam.

This then is the utility of *syncretism*, whether overtly practiced (as in certain nativistic cults) or covertly so (by many so-called "Christians"). The notion that religion is there to serve man and take care of his needs goes back to the Garden (Gen.3:6), and this communication problem certainly affects other world regions, not only Africa. But given the prominent local inclination towards synthetic, holistic thought, a correspondingly syncretistic religion does seem to have more of an impact upon daily life in an African setting than in a Western one. In any case, the *Sewero* players have taken serious note of this corrupting tendency and are dealing with it both creatively and confrontationally within the theological and moral framework of Scripture and by means of a highly dramatic mode of mass communication. They are thus putting into practice the time-validated experiential wisdom of the proverb, *Konza kapansi kuti kam'mwamba katsike* "Prepare a little something down below so that which is up above will descend" (i.e., make careful preparations in advance and you will eventually succeed in your venture, no matter how seemingly difficult at the outset).

3.1.7 Circumscription

Ukalemera, umanenera m'chigulu.
"If you are wealthy, you tell about it within a gourd."

The preceding proverb, cited to illustrate the principle at hand, is semantically opaque without a bit of contextualized explanation. "The poor you always have with you", especially in a relatively poor society that depends upon a subsistence-based, agricultural economy (see Christ's words in Mt.26:11). The wealthy tend to stand out in such a community, and attention is therefore attracted to them—notably with respect to the particular manner in which they accumulated and/or are now utilizing their possessions. Those who selfishly seek to retain everything for personal use and greedily (so it appears) go looking for more will most certainly be accused of practicing sorcery against others (*kulodza anzao*); on the other hand, rich folk who freely dispense a portion of their goods to others in the community, especially in time of need, will be seen to exercise the quality of "communalism" for the common good. People won't worry then about how they became well-to-do because they put their "well-being" to work. Their deeds thus "speak out for" them (*-kunenera*), as the proverb above suggests, even if such largesse consists only in dispensing common (but essential) table salt from the little gourd (*chigulu*) in which it was stored (Kumakanga 1975:57). The converse is also true: *Ukasauka, usamagwira nyanga* "if you are poverty-stricken, do not lay hold of a horn"—that is, resort to sorcery to relieve your predicament.

A communal, humanistic, experience-oriented outlook on life contributes to this final, now rather specific principle among those that contribute to a central African world-view. This is "circumscription", or as it is more negatively termed by some social scientists, the concept of "limited good". While the basic notion of social equality among the various individuals that comprise the community is taken for granted as a fundamental "human right", nevertheless, in practice this is often superceded by the principles of "gradation" coupled with "dynamism". Thus, the dynamic, energetic rich keep getting richer, while the inert, inept, or incapacitated poor, so it seems, keep getting poorer. Why does this happen, and what can be done about it? These are some of the key questions of life, and they are not just philosophical in nature, that is, answerable only in the abstract. Rather, they are eminently practical issues in that they concern one's personhood (including his or her "life-force") and ultimate survival in this world; hence these are also deeply "religious" matters (again, in the wider ethical as well as numinous sense). They are also assumed to have some concrete answers, which may be discovered through the requisite divinatory techniques.

The members of any non-complex, low-level economic community, which is usually also a relatively small, relationally-controlled, hierarchically organized social group, frequently view the cosmos in terms of a closed circle of possibilities. The basic resources essential for life are seen to be limited in quantity and/or availability: *Fodya wako ndi yemwe ali pamphuno* "it's the snuff that's in your schnoz that's really yours" (i.e., you cannot take your possessions for granted). This includes everything that a person has need for or simply desires to have—material possessions, natural resources, social ties, physical characteristics, attributed qualities (e.g., honor, love, courage, fame), situational features (e.g., good weather, bounteous harvests, peace and security, and above all, an abundance of vital force, or soul power). All these possessions are considered to be finite in their availability or accessibility and, more often than not, in relatively short supply. The problem is that there is nothing that the average person (*munthu wamba*) can normally do about the situation through ordinary means; the crucial access and supply mechanism lies essentially outside of his (her) personal control or influence.

It stands to (experientially-based) reason that if there is just so much of this world's bounty and goodness to go around, then those who happen to accrue more than others must be accomplishing this somehow at the expense of the latter. S/he can only increase to the extent that somebody else decreases. But in the absence of actual robbery or theft (crimes of the highest magnitude in African society), how is such advantage believed to be effected? This question, though seemingly judicial or even economic on the outside, is fundamentally theological at heart, for if it was God who instituted and maintains the present world order (through the auspices of the ancestors), then any alteration from the established pattern must have some important religious implications for mankind. And so it does, for in this logic of limitation we are brought back to the iniquitous core of the central African belief system, namely, the operation of witchcraft/sorcery. Any augmentation or diminution either in the quantity or quality of "life"—that is, embracing now all of its present as well as any potential physical, psychological, social, or spiritual aspects—is directly related to one's soul-power (*moyo*), which is always at risk of being attacked.

That is to say, if person X suffers loss, whether real or supposed, with respect to any of the life-force indicators mentioned above, then, assuming that s/he has not broken a taboo or offended the spirits in any way, the inevitable conclusion will be that s/he is being be-witched or attacked by sorcery. Some enemy, rival, or jealous person either has already, or is attempting to, take control of his (her) soul power for personal gain. Conversely, if person Y begins to enjoy some unexpected success, for no apparent reason, then s/he must be practicing witchcraft in order to boost her/his vital force to the detriment of someone else (i.e., X). This conclusion would be inescapable if there were some hard feelings or bad blood between X and Y, whether overtly manifested in the community or revealed by divination.

The only remedy in such situations is to relieve the mystical "circumscription" that is choking out one's spiritual vitality and to try to restore the status quo. From a traditional religious perspective, this feat can be accomplished only by applying the appropriate counter-magic, that is, to oppose, reverse, and destroy the witch(craft) or sorcery that is waging the attack. The important thing in the larger sphere is to restore the dynamic harmony of individuals within the community and the equilibrium of their respective personal forces.

Any society that is founded on the assumption that the opportunities for advancement and blessing are predetermined or magically defined and consequently not normally open to adjustment and change will be characterized by certain viewpoints and values of a generally restrictive nature. First, there is automatically created an atmosphere where uncertainty, doubt, prejudice, jealousy, suspicion, and mistrust can thrive. A person must remain ever vigilant lest someone else succeed in high-jacking one's soul-power as well as the associated charisma or possessions that s/he has been blessed with. Ironically, and most diabolically, it is usually one's closest relatives that stand first in the line of mistrust when misfortune falls. But perhaps this is only to be expected because the potential for competition, envy, and strife would tend to be the greatest among the nearest of kin, including those incorporated by marriage, who happen to live in the closest proximity to one another in an ecological environment that so often turns out to be rather harsh and unreliable in terms of providing for one's life and well-being.

There is naturally a certain negative effect that such a limiting perspective may have on the traditionalist's personal initiative: Why should I work very hard to succeed in life only to encourage others to bewitch me (in order to tap my life-force and material possessions), or to become liable myself to the charges of witchcraft (by so distinguishing myself from others)? It is a clear case of the proverbial "Catch 22" situation, in which a person cannot win or feel safe unless s/he resorts to utilizing the same malevolent means that s/he presently fears. One's primary goal therefore is to cultivate and to reinforce various power as well as solidarity relationships with others in the community. The point is personal protection, not to gain prestige that would cause one to stand out in terms of success—not unless one is prepared to pay the price, the price of engaging in magic to ensure self-preservation. Thus the person who is truly progressive, or even ambitious, by nature is almost channeled, as it were, whether physically or psychically into the practice of sorcery because that is the standard social expectation. The same applies to others who do not fit the usual pattern due to some deficiency, departure, or defect, e.g., any person who happens to be an isolationist, iconoclast, spinster, or scrooge.

Kalilombe puts the nefarious practice of witchcraft and the principle of circumscription together in a wider existential and religious framework with the following observation:

> Any abnormal departure from the established ways is seen as a threat, just like any excess even in things that are good and desirable in themselves. A person who in any way outdistances fellow humans is suspect. He is disrupting cosmic balance. The symbolic accusation of witchcraft will be thrown on such a person, and witchcraft is the worst evil in Chewa society. It is the seed of destruction for the community and the cosmos (1980:49).

The trouble is that such an accusation of witchcraft (or sorcery) is "symbolic" only in the sense that it has several levels of significance and repercussion in society. These are not only psychic or psychological in nature, but are all too often also deeply physical and personal as well. This fact is highlighted in a most specific and dramatic manner in many of the *Sewero* plays.

Because of the special topic that I am exploring in relation to the *Sewero* program, I have focused on the potentially detrimental, antisocial aspects of the principle of circumscription. There are, however, a number of positive, redeeming or beneficial features as well. These represent the ideal, of course, and are not always, or even usually, realized nowadays because of the prevalence of sorcery and its offshoots within contemporary Chewa society. In any case, it should also be noted that a relatively circumscribed worldview serves in a general way to promote a spirit of contentment in the community, especially among the closely related members of a particular kinship group. There is a certain security that comes from the knowledge that one's current affairs and future developments are an issue of the clan as a whole, including the protective and providing ancestral spirits. One need not, in fact should not, depend on one's own efforts, resources, or powers. It does not pay to rush to get things done: *Fulumira anadya gaga* "Speedy ate the husks [not the maize meal]".

Furthermore, from a traditional perspective, if one's place or status within the clan depends more on natural endowment (a gift of the ancestors) with respect to wisdom, strength, or some ability and on the passage of time (i.e., age), then why should one get overly concerned about trying to change what has already been ordained? There's always some talent that a person has to help him/her fit into society at some level: *Ukaipa, dziwa nyimbo* "If you're ugly, learn how to sing songs" (i.e., you will be attractive, at least functional, even with that seemingly minor capability or facility). It is also well-known that *wopusa anaomba ng'oma, ochenjera navina* "while the fool was playing the drum, [all] the clever folk were dancing away". You never know how influential you will be, insignificant as an individual, but playing a role of great communal importance—that is, within the great circle of human possibility that is circumscribed by the larger society in which you live, move, and have your being.

3.2 Interaction and integration of these seven principles

The following is one, admittedly rather crude and artificial, attempt to visually depict certain aspects of the interaction among the seven world-view principles discussed above. Humanism is, as suggested, in the middle, while Circumscription constitutes the outside, bounding concept. The other principles move towards the center in a roughly decreasing cline of generality or scope, beginning with the tendency towards Synthesis:

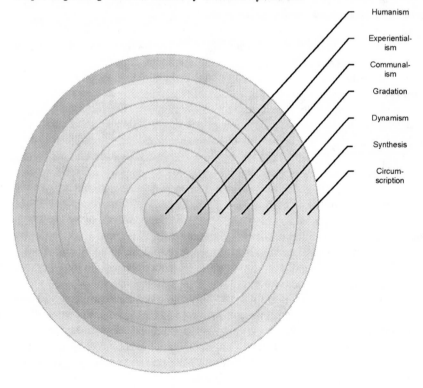

Humanism

Experiential-
ism

Communal-
ism

Gradation

Dynamism

Synthesis

Circum-
scription

As was noted earlier, the preceding overview represents just one way in which some of the critical aspects of a dynamically dramatic central African outlook on life might be described and organized as a holistic framework of reality in which all personal and communal experiences are perceived, interpreted, evaluated, and acted upon. The relevant data could certainly be analyzed and assessed differently. Other significant distinctions might require inclusion or additional treatment. We might reiterate, for example, the two important sub-principles that are also frequently manifested in this hypothetical nuclear complex of closely interacting philosophical and religious concepts.

First, there is the vital activity of *mediation* on the part of the leaders of human society, the kinship elders and ritual specialists in particular. Such intervening, often intercessory action is necessary in order to maintain the essential balance in the community between competing as well as coexisting forces, between power and solidarity, bane and blessing, the sacred and profane, excess and lack. So it is said, *kalulu adatuma njovu* "hare sent the elephant" (i.e., on an important personal mission). In other words, when you happen to be in a serious situation, send the most effective representative available to act and speak on your behalf, even if that happens to be the "trickster" himself!

Secondly, the preceding discussion has brought out the fact that a pervasive and pragmatic *reciprocity* is promoted on all levels of social and religious organization and behavior. This is a *do ut des* "I give that you may give [me in return]" mindset—or, as they say in Chinyanja: *chifundo chiitana chifundo* "kindness [or, mercy] calls for kindness"; in other words, when you do a good deed for someone, you may expect that s/he will do the same for you one day when you happen to need a favor in return. Thus mutual sharing and assistance coupled with the cultivation of personal dependencies, both on a horizontal, interpersonal plane and also vertically between humans and God/the ancestors, is essential for keeping social relationships in good repair and the community functioning smoothly for the ultimate welfare of all concerned.

Finally, it is necessary to take care lest one over-idealize the traditional setting, which of course no longer exists any more as it once did in modern, contemporary Africa, except perhaps in the remotest rural villages. These seven governing principles and related values or attitudes not only interact in the everyday practice of life and religion, but they may also vie with one another to varying degrees in a certain set of social circumstances, particularly in situations of human tension and conflict. Thus one principle, taken to extreme, may upset the balance in relation to another, and one may take

94

precedence over another as people work out or attempt to resolve the difficulties that have arisen.

One example of what appears to involve primary religious tenets in conflict may be seen in the oft-noted tendency for African Independent (Instituted) Churches (AICs) to split, resulting in one or more splinter groups. Why should this happen, given the fundamental synthetic, communal orientation that we noted as being manifested in so many ways within a traditional Bantu society? While it is necessary to avoid simplistic explanations for what are usually rather complex interpersonal and situation-specific phenomena, it is probably correct to view such corporate breaks as instances of the serious dysfunctional nature of human society in general ever since the Fall. Things simply do not always operate as intended, readily or without friction, no matter how ideal and well-established the principles upon which the community has been founded, whether formally (as in a political "constitution") or implicitly by way of a set of presuppositions and values inherited in the oral traditions passed down from the ancestors. *Matako saleka kuperesana* "the buttocks never cease rubbing against each other"—thus, where people live together in contact, there will always be arguments and other forms of discord.

So in the case of a fractured religious body, the interpersonal forces that normally complement one another to keep the group together, i.e., power and solidarity, now work in overt or covert opposition to one another. This results in a fissure within, rather than a consolidation and reinforcement of, the organization concerned. It is basically an issue of negative dynamics, where rivalry over position and status on the social hierarchy of authority overrides the need for unity and harmony within the association at large. Although the value of cooperation and concord is recognized and often appealed to in order to save the situation, the man-centered, now individualistic, power principle almost always prevails. *Atambala awiri salira m'khola limodzi* "two roosters do not crow in the same chicken pen". This is because the motivation is itself often based upon an argument for the ultimate benefit of the group—or that portion of it that remains after the split. In other words, the authority figure (pastor, prophet, healer, protector) who wishes to take control of or to lead a faction out from an established larger religious body does this in the belief (or delusion) that s/he has access to a greater measure of the life-force or spiritual charisma (along with accompanying charismatic "gifts") that is so vital for maintaining or augmenting the well-being (*shalom*) of all those whom s/he represents and is responsible for.

To summarize: The basic orientation of the central African perspective on reality is *synthesis*, the preeminent desire and determination to preserve the essential unity of society within all the other aspects of a given culture, despite the multifaceted diversity of these individual components. This outlook is reinforced by an active *experientialism* which sets the established wisdom tradition, the patterns of nature, and human experience as the primary criterion for deciding what constitutes knowledge and how to interpret or evaluate what goes on in the universe. Man himself thus serves as the fundamental measure and central reference point of this *humanistic* epistemological system and religious philosophy. An individual never stands alone, however, but s/he is always conceived of in relation to several *communal* groups within society (age/sex-based, work-related, kinship, locative, tribal), composed of the living as well as the departed. Each person, young and old, therefore contributes as a vital member of each of these groups, which in turn give meaning, purpose, and a certain sense of existential solidarity to her/his life. Although everyone has a place to occupy and a role to play in this inclusive community, all are not equal in terms of their social status or authority. Instead, there is a *gradation* of potency and influence which is profoundly religious in nature. This is because it is founded on a firm belief in the existence of a great host of vital forces which comprise every living being and control the destiny of all people under the ultimate supervision of the Creator-Deity and the practical administration of the ancestors. This *dynamic* constellation of interacting principalities and powers does not operate in an individualistic, open-ended, and unrestrained manner. It is rather closely *circumscribed* by a principle of relative limitation, which ensures that a critical balance in blessing is effected whereby a stable and harmonious status-quo might be maintained for the benefit of the corporate whole.

The main enemies of man-in-community, on the other hand, are precisely those mischievous and malicious people who deny or disregard these seven focal features of the well-ordered whole—those egotistical, selfish, iconoclastic, overly progressive, capitalistic, anti-social, irreverent, and impious individuals who have regard for neither God nor their fellow man. Since these negative attitudes and attributes are epitomized in the person of the "witch/sorcerer" (*mfiti*), it is only natural that people should consider the primary defender of the indigenous world-view and customary way-of-life to be the "witch doctor" (*sing'anga*). This traditional "psychiatrist", healer, and protector thus turns out to be regarded as the savior of all threatened and afflicted individuals in a given local setting, despite often being labeled as "demonic" in Christian, especially missionary, messages. The battle for control of one's "soul", or life-force, is indeed believed to take place during a person's earthly existence; however, the implications and consequences are likewise thought to concern life as it is *now* lived—not in some indistinct future age when the dead will rise again. What need is there for a "resurrection", so conventional logic goes, if the deceased have already been transformed and are currently living among us (as ancestral spirits)? The preceding has been just a glimpse of the complex world of thought, reality, and behavior that the *Sewero* group enters and engages with their creative polemic that aims to counter by means of their dramatization of a life-related but manifestly biblical perspective.

I turn now to survey some of the main topics that are included in my general corpus of tape recorded radio plays (ch. 4); these are described within the framework of a dramatic perspective on the main "powers and principalities" of a traditional society. This overview provides some additional background in preparation for a more detailed analysis and illustration of the principal stylistic features that are displayed in the performances that have been selected for special attention, namely, those which deal in one way or another with the African occult (ch. 5). In order to provide a closer look at the *Sewero* team's mastery of their message in its medium of communication, an outstanding example of this dramatic-religious art-form will be presented in its entirety (ch. 6); this is accompanied by a sequence of explanatory footnotes that will hopefully contextualize the text sufficiently for an alien readership. Finally, I will discuss several of the major implications of my study, along with a personal evaluation and a proposal for some possible future developments in the field of Christian radio drama (ch. 7).

4. The Topics, Texts, and Contexts of *Sewero* Dramatic Performances

4.0 Overview

This chapter gives an overview of the content and themes that are found in my corpus of over 80 *Sewero* dramas. In addition to this general topical survey, I present plot summaries of 20 plays that deal specifically with the African occult. In order to appreciate this ethnographically rich material, readers must of course be aware of some of the chief aspects of the dynamic worldview that underlies these beliefs and practices, many of which are common or similar to those of related Bantu-speaking peoples in central Africa. I therefore describe this belief and behavioral system in somewhat greater detail, as a follow up to the sociocultural overview of the preceding chapter, but now focusing on the *occult*—that is, witchcraft, sorcery, spiritism, divination, and taboo.

I have adopted a dramatic conceptual framework in order to more closely examine this existential heart of the "drama" of customary religion as it is currently being professed, promoted, and practiced, to a greater or lesser extent, within the region, and indeed, throughout the continent as a whole. In other words, these occult beliefs form the vibrant conceptual "context" that constitutes both the "raw material" from which the *Sewero* plays are fashioned and also the referential background within which they must be understood, interpreted, and then either applied to or repudiated in the lives of listeners. The present chapter is an attempt to provide a model to assist in this essential hermeneutical exercise.

The Scriptures, whether considered in part or as a whole, provide a completely changed, or at least a significantly different, Christocentric perspective on life and death. This biblical point of view is utilized by the *Sewero* plays to dramatically demonstrate what it means to be an "African Christian" when living in a contemporary setting that is still heavily influenced by a traditional world view and value system. This is the perspective that comes to the fore towards the end of each play, as a small selection of Bible passages is normally applied in practical terms to the issue or problem at hand. The current chapter ends with some concluding observations from a theological-polemical standpoint: How do these engaging indigenous dramas enable ordinary Christians, not only to confront but also to combat, where necessary, some of the most secret, sensitive, and controversial aspects of their culture?

4.1 Survey of subjects in *Sewero* dramas

The summary material of this section is based upon the research that my student assistants and I carried out on the entire active corpus of 80 recorded *Sewero* plays.[1] The students used the questionnaire found in Appendix C to initially explore the general topical and biblical (textual) landscape of each drama. Their feedback gave me an idea of the program's main subject areas, themes, plots, biblical teachings, and array of supporting Scripture references. I also asked the students to offer their own personal opinion of every play's relative quality in terms of form (style) and content (message). This survey provided me with a rationale for my selection of 20 plays treating the occult that I gave special attention to, including a complete transcription and translation into English of ten examples. Plot synopses of this select corpus are supplied below; they offer some idea of the range of occult topics that are dealt with in these plays, that is, with respect to their cultural and religious *content*. I will examine their distinctive aspects of verbal *form* by means of a more detailed descriptive stylistic analysis in chapters 5 and 6.

4.1.1 General topical survey

The questionnaire that was applied to each *Sewero* play included the following major clusters of information: any available performance details (e.g., *Sewero* title, name of drama group, date of broadcast, place of performance), an English summary of a given play (what was the story about; who were its main characters and what were the main events), the principal lesson or Christian teaching of this play, a qualitative evaluation or "grade" (*excellent, good, fair, poor*) with reasons, an indication of which aspects of African traditional religion were mentioned as a major or minor element in the story, a note as to whether the analyst felt any contra-biblical teaching were present, and an inventory of that play's principal stylistic devices (e.g., ideophones,[2] idioms, figures of speech, proverbs, dramatic/forceful language).

To be sure, this type of survey expected quite a lot from theological students who did not have much training or experience in literary analysis, least

---

[1]   I actually have closer to 100 plays in my collection; some of these, however, have not been sufficiently analyzed to include their data in my exposition.
[2]   An *ideophone* is a dramatic form of predication that may occur with or without a normal finite verb, e.g., *anagwa/iye ali pansi* khu! "he fell/ he is down (to the ground) *plop!* (i.e., a heavy or violent fall is implied).

of all in their own mother tongue. Accordingly, the quality of their answers and summaries varies quite considerably; some analysts demonstrated in their comments noticeably more accuracy and insight than others. But the overall results of this questionnaire at least gave me a place to begin my own detailed analysis of the material. That not only saved some time, but more important, these African student evaluations also provided me with an initial indigenous entry point and perspective to lessen the degree of my own alien bias with respect to the complex cultural and religious world being explored by these dramatic productions. Students were naturally also very closely involved in the transcription, annotation, and to some extent even the translation of these *Sewero* plays. My presentation thus owes a great deal to their insightful input into this project as a whole.

A summary of *Sewero* subjects is shown below; these are listed in order of preference. Most plays manifested an average of two major topics; a few dealt only with a single problem, while 12 of the 80 were considered to dramatize three (or more) important biblical and/or life-related issues.[3]

Major topics found in *Sewero* plays	No. of Occurrences
Magic, witchcraft, sorcery	22
Problems in marriage and family life	19
Sexual sins (adultery, prostitution, incest)	18
The need for personal/corporate witness and evangelism	10
The need for repentance and confession	8
Crucial social problems and the responsibility of parents	8
Violation of pastoral responsibility or authority	8
Stealing and cheating	7
False witness, lying, slander, evil talk	7
Sins against parents and authorities	5
The church in opposition to unbiblical teachings	5
The second coming of Christ, last days, final judgment	5
Sickness, death, and other physical trials	4
Coveting, greed, envy, jealousy, selfishness	3
Hatred and murder, including suicide	3
Unbiblical customs and taboos (*mdulo, nyau, fisi*)	3
Nature and purpose of prayer	3
The fruit of the Holy Spirit, e.g., forgiveness	3
Personal stewardship/offerings or the lack	3
Drunkenness and drugs	2
The Law of God and Christian education	2

---

[3] For a comparison with the main topics of a selection of Chichewa revival-type sermons, see Wendland 2000:20-23. It may be noted that this survey was made several months before my *Sewero* collection was complete—that is to say, several other plays were subsequently analyzed.

It may be apparent that this is just an approximate survey since there are different ways of determining what might constitute a "major topic"; furthermore, the categories themselves are perhaps not as clearly defined as they might or should be. It would be more accurate and revealing to establish another grouping of "minor topics" in order to more fully represent the various subjects considered in the corpus. Finally, the fact that several persons were involved in this assessment also complicated the overall process (although I made the final categorization). Be that as it may, the listing above does indicate several interesting features about the content of *Sewero* dramatic plays.

We note first of all the general popularity of certain compelling and/or controversial subjects. "Magic, witchcraft, and sorcery" was a clear favorite, although no special attempt was made to single these plays out for inclusion within the overall corpus during the recording process. The topics of "spiritism" and "unbiblical customs" could also be fit into this chief grouping of *occult* beliefs and practices. The next two principal categories may also be considered together, namely, "problems in marriage and family life" along with "sexual sins", thus revealing another major contemporary social-religious crisis that these dramas attempt to address and provide biblical counsel for. The crucial issue of AIDS came up several times during the presentation of this set of plays, but it was not made the dominant problem in any individual performance, except one (see ch.6).

As is evident from the preceding preference listing, the *Sewero* shows clearly favor practical as distinct from strictly theological themes, which is not surprising in view of the strongly life-related nature of African religion, whether traditional or Christian. Biblical teachings do appear, of course, but they do not usually become the central topic of discussion; one may note several exceptions at the bottom of the table, e.g., "the Law of God", "salvation by grace through faith", "the nature and work of the Holy Spirit", and "the Holy Scriptures". Perhaps in future the *Sewero* team might like to consider some of these more didactic, instructional subjects as they pertain to particular biblical texts (see 7.2). I will not discuss the general content of these plays any further but will instead zero in on the focal set in which traditional religious beliefs and practices appear as an important element of a drama's plot (nearly a quarter of the corpus). This key topic thus also features prominently in the didactic message or exhortation that these plays conclude with, namely, in a problem-resolving dialogue which features an assortment of Scripture passages.

4.1.2 Plot summaries of plays on the occult

The special "corpus of the occult" constitutes over a quarter of my larger collection of *Sewero* plays. 20 of these are summarized below in terms of general theme and content simply to provide an overview of their subject matter. Such abstracts of course cannot do justice to the rhetorical argument, the interpersonal dynamics, and the compositional quality of these dramatic productions, but at least they give an idea of what sort of socio-religious issues the drama team are dealing with in relation to a Malawian life-setting.

- "The evil of medicine for making one rich" (*Kuipa kwa mankhwala olemeretsa*):[4] A young man complains to his parents about their low economic status. He desires to rise above his current circumstances. They try to give him some advice—about working hard, being content, etc.—but he does not want to listen. He finally turns to the village "medicine man", "healer" or "witchdoctor" (*sing'anga*), who assures him that he can supply him with the magical solution, or "medicine" (*mankhwala*), that will make him rich. But in order for this concoction to become effective, the young man is told that he must sleep with either his mother or his sister. The greedy fellow agrees and drinks the noxious fluid down. Since he is afraid to sleep with his own mother (a terrible taboo), he begins to work on his sister, bribing her with the promise of part of his future wealth. Finally she agrees and they plan together for the adulterous deed to be done one night when her husband is away and while her children are sleeping. However, the young man has waited too long; the potent medicine inside him begins to make him very ill. This sickness quickly gets worse and he dies before he is able to meet his sister as agreed. Instead of buying wealth, he has bought death, and the sister remains to bury her brother!

- "Wealth comes from God" (*Chuma chichokera kwa Mulungu*):[5] There was a certain man who wanted to become rich in order to escape his current poverty-stricken lifestyle. He goes to the local medicine man for help in his endeavor. The medicine man gives him a cup of magical liquid to drink. Then he informs the eager man of

---

[4]   The italicized words in parentheses are the Chinyanja title of the radio play, as given by the program announcer at the beginning of each performance.

[5]   These first two plays illustrate how the same basic theme and religious problem may be handled through the use of similar plots; the narrative surface dialogues of course, as well as individual character developments, are very different from one another.

several additional requirements necessary to "activate" this powerful potion. He is told to obtain the hair of a dead person as well as the water used to wash the corpse and also to sleep with his sister. After hearing these drastic requirements, the man changes his mind, but the doctor tells him that since he has already drunk that medicine, he will have to go through with the rest of the instructions or lose his mind on account of the toxic substance that is now circulating within his body. Reluctantly, but in fear for himself, the man kills his brother and thus is able to acquire two of his needs—the funeral hair and water. However, his sister absolutely refuses to sleep with him because she is a Christian. The man goes back to the medicine man to try to find a way out of his predicament, but is told that there is no way; it is too late to back out. As he was warned then, the young man gradually goes mad and has to be cared for by the very sister whom he had wanted to sin with (and against).

- "My, but this one is a real healer!" (*Uuuh! Ndiyetu sing'angatu uyu!*): The central character is a renowned healer called *Masamba-asiyana* ('Leaves/healing substances-differ'). People flock to her, and she even attempts to cure the dreaded AIDS disease. One day a couple who are chronically sick go to her for treatment. They had already gone to the hospital, but were told that they were suffering from AIDS. No, the healer reassures them, they have only been bewitched, and she can heal them. They pay a big price for some medicine and happily return home. However, the medicine does not work, and their health soon begins to deteriorate. Not long thereafter, the sister of a local pastor goes to the medicine woman with her daughter who has become pregnant out of wedlock. She wants the healer to perform an abortion so that the girl will not get expelled from school. Surprisingly, they arrive only to find that the healer herself is very sick, unable to do anything to help. Meanwhile, the sister's brother, the pastor, has heard where they have gone. He rushes there to prevent any "treatment" from being administered. He sends his wife and niece home, and begins to "treat" the healer spiritually. She tries to defend herself by saying that this is her only means of support. He refuses all excuses and finally leads her to repentance, which is signified as genuine when she allows him to burn all her ritual apparatus and medicines.

- "Call out to him, but he cannot protect you!" (*Mufuulireni, sangakuchinjirizeni ayi!*): Dr. Luka is a famous medicine man who has deceived many people into believing that he can cure any disease. But his specialty is property protection—guarding the kraal (corral) from cattle thieves who are rampant in the area. A rich widow lives in his village, the owner of over 200 cows. In order to protect them, she goes to Dr. Luka along with her only child, a daughter. The good doctor assures them that he has just the medicine to do the job; however, its potency depends on an equally powerful activating agent—his having sex with the beneficiary! They are reluctant, but he convinces them through a misuse of Scripture (that everything is possible, if you only believe!). Afraid for her huge herd, the woman relents and allows her daughter to sleep with Luka. She also has to pay the fee of three head of cattle. Several months later, all her cattle are stolen at night. She runs to her neighbors for help and bitterly complains about Dr. Luka's poor protective medicine. They tell her that he had passed away the day before—another victim of AIDS! The mother now mourns her double loss: all her wealth and her daughter as well, who had surely become HIV infected by the (now) dead doctor.

103

- "Mother, you have caused me great pain!" (*Amayi, mwandipweteketsa!*): A young couple has been happily married for several years, even though they have no children; they live in town. The girl's mother, a widow, is very concerned about this unhappy situation, especially about the future of her bloodline. One day she comes in from the village and fills her daughter's head with all sorts of complaints. The daughter passes these on along to her husband and tells him that she is going back home with her mother to seek traditional help from a medicine man. He protests, but cannot convince her to stay. So the mother and her daughter go to visit the local healer. He divines and reveals that the woman's childlessness is not her fault, but her husband's. Nevertheless, he has just the medicine to help her conceive; however, it will only "work" if she agrees to sleep with him. She refuses, but her mother convinces her to go through with the prescribed "treatment". The daughter now does get pregnant, but her husband does not know that he is not the father. This happens on two more occasions. Finally, the man suspects foul-play because his children do not resemble him at all. He confronts his wife about the matter, and she reveals what had happened. He becomes very upset and goes to live elsewhere. She must return in poverty and shame to her mother in the village. They then take up this matter with the medicine man and tell him to marry the daughter because he is the father of her three children. He refuses saying that he already has five wives and cannot afford to support any more! In great grief, they go to see a local pastor for advice. He encourages them first to repent of their sinful behavior, which they do. He then promises to go visit the husband to see if he can reconcile him with his wayward wife.

- "You must always pray before you eat!" (*Muzipemphera musanadye!*): A certain butcher goes to find some cattle to supply his business. He buys two fine-looking animals from a local farmer. He does not realize that these are actually his two relatives whom he had sent on a mission to steal some cattle for him. They had been magically transformed into dumb beasts by the seller, a sorcerer, who had previously applied some powerful protective "medicine" to his kraal. The seller warns the butcher not to slaughter these cattle and sell their meat until he gives his permission. This sounds like strange advice, and so the butcher ignores it; he kills both cows and begins selling the meat. The man who sold him the cows hears about this and comes to reprove the butcher for his hasty decision. A former medicine man in the community who had repented and is now a Christian discovers what has happened. He publicly reveals this dastardly deed of witchcraft and how it was carried out. All the people who had bought meat from the butcher now have to throw it away. They are very angry about the matter and want to call the police. The new Christian, on the other hand, goes to the man who used the potent protective medicine and tries to persuade him to repent of his use of magic. The outcome is left open—but all the people in that community now pray very seriously before eating, lest they happen to ingest something that has been infected with witchcraft!

- "About old customs" (*Za miyambo yakale*): An older woman has three daughters who had married and moved away from their village to live in town where their husbands had jobs. One day the mother decides to pay them a visit. She is assisted in this effort by her brother who then bids her farewell. The woman arrives at the house of one daughter, and they enjoy a nice visit before the latter goes into the kitchen to prepare some food for her mother. When the meal is ready, the mother asks who salted the traditional stew that they are about to eat. The daughter replies that she did this herself. The mother becomes very angry because such action broke a dangerous taboo; she should have gotten her child or allowed the mother to do this lest she risk passing on a serious disease. The mother leaves in a huff without eating a thing. She proceeds to the second daughter's house. She is happy to see that her daughter's new baby girl is very healthy. However, she gets offended again when she notices that the baby is not wearing the protective charm that the mother had sent to tie about her neck. She becomes very angry at this disregard and rushes off to her third daughter, who also had recently given birth to a child. The daughter welcomes her with a cup of tea, but this too offends her visitor because a new mother is not supposed to prepare any sort of food at all. They get into an argument over the matter, and the mother leaves, this time back to her home in the village. She reports to her brother how she had not been received in a respectable way by all three daughters, but without going into details. The brother summons his three nieces so that they can explain their various un-social actions towards their mother. First she is given the chance to explain what happened, and then her daughters are asked to respond. They all say that after moving to town they became Christians and now no longer follow such customs which require the belief in and adherence to mystical forces. Her brother tries to mediate by saying that the old ways may have had a purpose in the past, but now that people have been educated and know the truth of God's Word, they are freed from all these powers which Satan simply uses to confuse them.

- "Being freed from witchcraft" (*Kumasulidwa za ufiti*): This is the story about a son, Josophat, who inherits the practice of witchcraft from his father, Banda. Banda teaches his son all the tricks of the trade as well as the various potions and spells that go with it, but warns him that if he fails or leaves this "calling", he will become mad. Banda suddenly dies one day (his magical powers are unable to save him!), and Josophat naturally requests that his father be given an honorable Christian burial in the local church. The chairlady of the congregation strongly opposes this plan because those who practice witchcraft, she says, have died in sin and therefore must be repudiated also at the time of their death. Because of this Josophat promises to kill this strong Christian lady with witchcraft. She casts all his threats aside and claims that God will protect her from his diabolical powers. Josophat starts to practice his father's trade but fails to keep all the instructions; as a result, he begins to lose his mind and threatens to bewitch everyone in the village. This makes people worried, and some even begin to consult local medicine men for protection. A church council is called at the urging of Josophat's aunt (Banda's sister), and the chairman, Mr. Gulupa, decides to take some leaders to confront Josophat. They do so and lead the young man to repentance and a confession of sins. This impresses the entire congregation and they too renounce their former beliefs in witchcraft.

- "The evil of love magic" (*Kuipa kwa mankhwala a chikondi*): A middle-aged man and his wife are having troubles in their marriage simply because the man thinks that she is old-fashioned and so he is tired of her. Finally he divorces her on the false accusation that she was practicing witchcraft at night. All his relatives oppose his foolish plan because his wife is truly a good person, but he refuses to listen. They then counsel her to be patient because they are convinced that their in-law will come to realize the error of his action and eventually return to her. The man soon marries a beautiful young woman and thinks that now he is set for the rest of his life. She, however, does not want him to repeat what he did to his first wife, so she begins to introduce a special "love potion" into his food. The purpose is to keep him faithful to her alone. Unfortunately, this medicine is toxic, and it causes his stomach swell up with the result that he becomes very sick. He suspects what has happened and realizes that he has made a serious mistake that he is now paying for with suffering. His former wife hears that he is sick and comes to visit him along with several of his relatives. They rebuke him for divorcing his first wife, and tell him that he is now being punished for that sin. He publicly repents, saying that he is like the fool who "looks only on the outside of the fig, without considering all the ants on the inside" (*cikome-kome cha mkuyu, mkati muli nyerere*). He agrees then to send his young second partner back to her parents and receive back his first wife. He promises that he will be faithful to her for the rest of his life; he has learned his lesson the hard way!

- "Please don't do that!" (*Musamatero ayi!*): This play is about two contrasting couples; one man is a local pastor, the other is a leader of a coven of wizards in the same village—but he is also a member of the pastor's congregation. The pastor's wife fears witchcraft herself and tries to persuade her husband not to oppose it in his sermons, but he refuses on the basis of Scripture. The wizard's wife tries to persuade her husband to repent of his sin of practicing witchcraft, but he stubbornly refuses. The pastor organizes a little crusade in the village to try to win converts, especially those who are engaged in magical activities. The wizard tells his followers that he will secretly go to the prayer meeting in order to disrupt it. He is jealous of the pastor because he thinks that his Christian powers are stronger and because the pastor is having some success in gaining new members. So the two "congregations" come into secret conflict during that crusade. While the pastor is preaching from the Bible the witch is mysteriously (or miraculously) exposed and his black magic is turned against him, seriously injuring him in the process. The wizard realizes that Christ has defeated him so he begs the pastor for help. The pastor gets him to openly confess his sin of witchcraft and to become a genuine disciple of the Lord. The former wizard now promises that he will seek to convert his former colleagues in occult crime.

- "It takes two to make a family" (*Banja ndi awiri*): A newly married couple is happy despite the fact that two years have passed and they have not had a child. Some of the man's relatives come for a visit and advise him to try some other women in order to prove his manhood. He considers the idea but his pastor persuades him against such sin. The young wife too has her advisers; among them is a traditional healer called the "Prophetess Joel" (*Mneneri Yoweri*). The prophetess gives her many charms and medicines, including some to help her bear children and others to cause her husband to love her no matter what. The wife faithfully applies all these ancient aids, but nothing happens. Meanwhile, the husband's aunt comes for a visit and says that he is foolish for remaining faithful to a woman who cannot bear him any children. His attitude towards his wife now changes and he becomes very rude and disrespectful. One day the wife meets a female evangelist and they have a good talk about her family problems. The evangelist encourages her not to trust in magical charms but in the Lord alone, who will one day help her like Hannah. She makes an appointment to visit the couple at home to follow up on their learning about God's will from the Bible. On that very day the Prophetess Joel comes to give them some more instruction about the use of traditional devices for childbearing. The woman evangelist interrupts this discussion and chases "Joel" from the premises by trying to persuade her to repent of her spiritism and become a follower of Christ. The evangelist then turns to the married couple and teaches them about the truth of God as opposed to the deceit of traditional idolatrous beliefs and practices.

- "If it had been you, what would you have done?" (*Mukadakhala inu, mukadatani?*): The play opens at the scene of a celebration at which the master of ceremonies is praising the Lord for his many blessings. He tells his life history (a dramatized flashback): This man was very wealthy; he owned many commercial vehicles, farms, houses, and had a large family as well. One day things started going badly for him: his vehicles were destroyed in accidents, his livestock died of diseases, his crops burned in the fields—even his children all died under mysterious circumstances. While all this misfortune was happening, the man's wife kept urging him to seek help from a diviner-medicine man—that is, to discover why all this was happening and to obtain protection for what was left. Like Job, the man steadfastly refused to disobey God by resorting to any traditional occult practice. Instead, he promises to remain faithful to God who had given him everything in the first place. Later, after he has lost everything, the man himself is stricken with severe boils all over his body. Finally, his wife can take it no longer; she leaves her husband rotting in pain and returns to her home village. But there she starts to have some strange dreams which give her a guilty conscience, so she returns to help her suffering husband. She repents of her sin of deserting him in his misery. Then all of a sudden the man recovers, and God now blesses him with much more than he ever possessed before. He is so thankful that he organizes a little praise and testimony service in order to tell what the Lord has done for him. He warns his guests not to trust in witchcraft and medicine men if they ever face severe troubles like he did. The play ends with them all singing a hymn of praise.

- "Evil follows its doer" (*Choipa chitsata mwini*): This is the story of a certain merchant whose business was not progressing very well. He became jealous as he saw his colleagues prospering while he did not seem to be moving forward at all. He finally decided to resort to magical means to make some advancement. He consulted his wife about this matter because it is believed that in order for such ventures to succeed, both the man and his wife must agree and work together in the traditional manner. The man's wife, who is a Christian lady, refuses to participate at first because she says that God knows what he is planning and will punish him for it in the end. But the man goes ahead and consults several medicine men from whom he obtains charms that are supposed to increase his business by attracting customers and giving them the urge to buy his merchandise. However, after a number of attempts, there is still no success. His store remains virtually empty while people flock to his competitors. At last the man wins his wife over to his occult venture and she agrees to help him. A certain medicine man advises him that his charms have not been powerful enough; only "medicine" that has been energized by a human life (death) will do. So the couple plans a big party to which they will invite many people. At that time they will target one of their guests, a relative (as specified by the medicine man), and give him a fatal dose of poison by secretly applying it to his food. After he dies at home, they will be in the clear and the charm will begin working for them. As they are carrying out this diabolical plot, however, the child who is supposed to deliver the poisoned food gives it to the wrong person. Since the charm's instructions were not correctly followed, its power rebounds to the detriment of the one who applied it. In this case, the man goes mad, his business fails completely, and his wife is left destitute.

- "You really must not eat again!" (*Musadyensotu inu!*): A poor rural couple would desperately like to improve their status and condition in life. The husband decides that the only way is to go to town to seek their fortune there. The wife opposes this plan because she knows of the various other temptations that can destroy family life in urban areas, but according to tradition, she dutifully follows him to the nearest town. Immediately the man turns to theft in order to make a living, and he eventually joins a band of notorious thieves. These rogues depend on traditional magic for protection and to increase their success, so this man obtains a certain powerful charm that is supposed to make him strong as well as fast of foot, to escape from any vengeful pursuers. His wife keeps this charm safe for him at home while he goes out on his nocturnal missions. The man becomes rich by means of his stealing and because of this he begins to get proud as well. One night he plots with his friend to go and steal some goats from the kraal of a local farmer whom he has a grudge against. His wife warns him not to attempt this because if his friend gets caught, they might reveal that he was with them. The boastful thief, however, refuses to listen. The pair is caught in the act and the owner chases them with a spear. He happens to stab the wayward husband, and he dies on the spot. His wife is left a poor widow who can barely make ends meet by selling small foodstuffs along the street. One day she is approach by some Christian women who befriend her. She later reveals to them how and why her husband died, and they lead her to repent of her own passive involvement in his sinful activities.

- "The evil of polygamy" (*Kuipa kwa mitala*): A polygamist is causing domestic anxiety, jealousy, and suspicion because he does not remain satisfied at home; instead, he is out running with even more women. His wives begin to compete for his little remaining attention; they do this by seeking various love potions from local medicine men. It turns into a destructive competition for increasingly stronger stuff to do the job. The senior (first) wife feels that her position as the head lady of the household is especially in danger. In her effort to find the ultimate solution, she gets some medicine that is highly toxic to the system. She realizes the danger, as even the "doctor" warns her, but she wants to risk everything in the belief that if she fails, her husband will no longer be good for any of her rivals either. So she secretly applies it to his food, and the damage is immediately done. His brain is destroyed by the poisonous substance, and he becomes completely retarded. Indeed, now he no longer chases after other women and in his childish way he loves all his wives. But he can no longer provide for them, and the whole family is forced to suffer in poverty and sickness. The village pastor comes to minister to them, encouraging them to work together for their common good, and to rely no more on traditional means to change their situation one way or the other.

- "Medicine for bringing childbirth" (*Mankhwala obereketsa*): A young couple is in love and they promise to marry in order to raise a family together. After the wedding, they are quite happy for several years simply enjoying the company of one another. However, when the wife does not become pregnant, they begin to quarrel, and each accuses the other for being at fault (barren). One day when the wife is visiting her mother-in-law she receives some traditional advice: she is given a string of amulets which she must continually wear around her waist in order to induce pregnancy. The wife is a faithful Christian and at first she refuses to do this, but when she reports the matter to her husband, he forces her to go along with the plan. The next Sunday, while they are worshiping together in church, one of the women leaders publicly condemns the use of such charms to promote childbirth and reveals that some of her colleagues are currently resorting to these tactics. The woman feels guilty and wants to remove that magical string from her waist. Again he refuses, saying that they must give it some time to do its work. His wife goes back to the church leadership to plead her plight. The chairman of the congregation comes to visit the couple in an effort to persuade the husband to relent—and repent. Still the man will not listen, not even to the Word of God, and threatens to divorce his wife if she removes those charms. The chairman counsels them to continue to discuss and pray about this matter and that he would return once they had both agreed to stop this traditional religious practice.

- "Have you forgotten?" (*Kodi mwaiwala?*): This play is about the problems that develop when an extended family is divided in their worship—one side preferring to continue with traditional religious beliefs and practices, the other following a strict form of Christianity that prohibits syncretism. The matriarch of the family was in poor health and so she often had to be taken into town where she could get treatment at the hospital. She stayed with her daughter in town during these times, and it so happened that on one of these visits she was introduced to Christianity and became a strong believer. Finally the old lady passed away and was taken to her home village for burial. A Christian service was conducted there, but later her brother wanted to include some prayers to the ancestors along with a beer-drinking celebration of remembrance in their honor. This was not allowed by local Christians. Now however, a number of other deaths occur in this village and some people begin to worry that the ancestral spirits have been offended and are now punishing the people for neglecting to observe the traditions correctly. The dead lady's brother organizes a special beer-brewing celebration in order to placate the angry spirits. The daughter in town hears about this so she returns to the village and a big argument ensues with her uncle. The daughter finally prevails when she convinces all the participants that the old lady had indeed become a strong Christian and would herself have been offended by what they were planning to do. They finally agree and the traditional worship ceremony is summarily aborted.

- "Have you really been sent?" (*Kodi mwatumidwadi*): A certain pastor was assigned to work at a parish with a vacancy. He went there with his whole family and was well received by the congregation. The parishioners were so happy that they decided to hold a special celebration in honor of their new pastor and his family on the day of his installation. During these festivities both the pastor and his wife stand up to speak about the responsibilities that the congregation has to support them in the right way. Their list of duties and obligations is rather legalistically presented, and the people are not too pleased about this. Their demands were also unrealistic for a rural parish, for example, that they must buy him a car and pay all the school fees for his children. As time goes by, the congregation fails to do everything that they agreed to. So the pastor in turn starts neglecting some of his duties, like visiting the sick and serving at the funerals of small children. As a result the church elders decide to pay him a visit to give him a reprimand. An argument develops and he rudely chases them out of his house. The leaders then write a letter to their synod officials to complain about their pastor's behavior. These superiors respond positively and set a date when a meeting to investigate these matters will be held. The pastor now begins to fear the outcome of that case; he could lose his job. So he goes to consult a medicine man in order to obtain some magical assistance. He purchases a number of charms to help him win his case. That night the pastor had a terrifying dream. In it a deep voice tells him to get rid of the magic that he had just procured and to repent of his behavior. Soon thereafter, another small child dies and the pastor again refuses to officiate at the burial. When the congregational elders come to visit him about this, he chases them off. That is the last straw. The synodical meeting of inquiry is held and the pastor is found guilty of misconduct. The church leaders lead him to repentance and he promises to change his pastoral ways.

- "God is our help" (*Mulungu ndiye thandizo*): Mr. and Mrs. Banda are living an unhappy domestic life together. He likes to go out drinking at the local tavern and then beats his wife while in a drunken state. He complains about the untidy nature of their house and about his wife's disrespect. His drinking buddies encourage Banda to beat his wife some more to teach her a good lesson. He does so and seriously hurts her this time. The next day two neighbors come by for a visit and to see what happened; they had heard her cries and weeping the previous night. At first Mrs. Banda denies what had happened out of shame, but finally she reveals the story and tells them that she is going to leave Banda and return to her village. The neighbor ladies tell her that they have come to help her with some traditional charms that will cause her husband to stop beating her but to love her instead. They gave her an assortment of magical substances and instructions as to how to use or apply them. Mrs. Banda faithfully does all this, but to her surprise, there is no change at all in her husband's behavior; in fact, he treats her worse than before. She decides now to go home for sure, but on the way she meets the pastor's wife, who on learning of her plight, encourages her to stay with Banda and to pray for him rather than to use traditional devices that cannot help. She begins to go to church regularly now, but this change has no affect on her husband's violent treatment of her. One day the two neighbors come for another visit and inquire how the charms that they gave her are working. She tells them that she threw all that material away because she was now a Christian and would depend on God alone for help. The two neighbors try to convince her to give these medicines another try, but at that moment the pastor's wife arrives. She chases the others away because she knows why they are there. She then investigates Mrs. Banda's situation a bit more and discovers that her response to her husband's ill treatment is still too hostile in word and deed. She counsels her to win him over with a soft response and good works. By the power of God, that plan works and the pair are reconciled, now as a true Christian couple.

- "Let us judge one another!" (*Tiyeni tiweruzane!*): This is the story of a pastor and his wife who are ministering in a peri-urban village that is filled with sinful activities, all stemming in one way or another from beliefs in witchcraft. One day the pastor's wife is on her way to town to buy some things at the market. At the bus stop she overhears two young women from her husband's congregation who are planning to go to town to engage in prostitution in order to obtain some extra money. The woman waits till she has a captive audience in the bus to begin witnessing to these woman—and to anyone else who will listen, for she speaks loudly so that everyone can hear. The two women start to mock and insult her to try to get her to shut up, but she carries on with her message. Finally, one of the young

110

women is touched and she publicly repents on that bus. She returns home and tells her husband the whole story, and he too resolves to live a genuine Christian life. The second part of this play tells of how the pastor was suddenly summoned one day to conduct the funeral service for one of his members. He uses the occasion to make a general appeal to all those present to repent of their sins, for their village life is being destroyed by such activities, especially by the practice of sorcery and witchcraft, which may have led to the death of the person being buried. After the funeral, a number of people who were present come to the pastor to confess their sins. As an overt sign of their repentance, they produce all of their charms, medicines, magical potions, and tools for use in sorcery so that they may be destroyed. The pastor and his wife now have a very dynamic and committed congregation of Christians to minister to.

4.1.3 Concluding observations

The basic biblical principle that is reiterated by the TWR dramatic group throughout the topical subset synopsized above centers on the dichotomy involving God versus demonology, truth versus error—the folly of beliefs in witchcraft as opposed to the wisdom of seeking help (healing, forgiveness, protection, peace) from Christ alone. The apparent success of traditional healers and diviners is dramatically shown to be just that—a mirage that is not genuine and cannot last. It leads inevitably to dissention, discord, damage, and all too often even to one's personal demise, which is, ironically, what people are seeking to avoid by resorting to such practices. According to "*Sewero* theology", accommodation and compromise with respect to one's religion is not an option: a person must choose either-or. In favor of Christ means life—for the ancient occult tradition, which derives from Satan, means death, sooner or later, and ultimately for eternity. The choice is clear, and it is supported by a variety of Scripture passages which are effectively blended into the dialogue as it works towards its thematic and narrative resolution. A diverse range of plots, characters, settings, speeches, and lessons renders the essential message as captivating as it is confrontational. The semantic array that characterizes the narrative surface of these plays has the effect of rendering their singular rhetorical argument and its Scripture-based polemic and apologetic all the more powerful and convincing as it recurs in each new setting, and as one dramatic situation is reflected off of another from a unified biblical perspective.

As we observed in 2.2.1, due to the transitory, irreversible nature of the radio signal, the *Sewero* dramas cannot be constructed in a very complex manner. Because of the large potential audience, the program's themes and teachings too must remain at a more general level—while retaining a broad popular appeal, with topics that cater for the needs, values, interests, problems, concerns, and experiences of average rural (Protestant) Christians.

Radio broadcasting, via short-wave in particular, is not a very efficient medium for communicating with minority audiences or special interest groups, unless such audiences can be catered for within the framework of a story having a larger scope and a wider appeal. Most of the specific subjects listed above as found on our survey sheets would fall into this more generic category as this relates to the Christian life and testimony. This includes our focus of attention, namely, those plays that explicitly treat the African occult—e.g., witchcraft, sorcery, magic, taboo, and spiritism.

One might note the apparently "sparse" nature of these radio plots. On the whole, there is not a great deal of embedded description devoted to setting the scene or to the characterization of the individual dramatis personae. Neither can much action be recorded, simply because there is no "narrator" present to recount it. This is "reality radio"—consisting almost entirely of a sequence of "slice of life" conversations that are typical of "high context" oral-aural societies (see 4.4.2), both in their everyday communication and also in their conventional verbal art forms (e.g., their oral narrative tradition). That is to say, the various physical and social settings that underlie these radio dramas are largely presupposed and assumed to be accessed by the speakers during their dialogues. On the other hand, it is not really fair to make a critical literary judgment on the basis of the topical summaries of works that are designed for oral-aural production and reception. A clearer picture of the amount of essential presumed information that is incorporated into these dramatic performances may be gained from the presentation of a complete play in chapter 6. In any case, while the plots per se may be rather general, the way in which they are encoded into dialogue form is socio-culturally very specific, and that includes the dynamic psychological development of the leading speech characters as they are given "voice" by the members of cast.

Thus the plot summaries found in our corpus also show a definite preference for *melodrama*, a type of narrative composition that features relatively stereotyped characters who manifest exaggerated feelings and reactions to the crucial events of life, which tend to bunch together in a close succession of crises, problems, tests, challenges, and enigmas. Melodrama is frequently (not always) distinguished by thrilling action, powerful emotive expression, bold verbal rhetoric, and a plot that may border on sensationalism—at least up until the crisis has past and one or more "strong" Christians put things into their proper biblical perspective. The stories are not really intended for children; at best, they could be given a "PG" rating due to their often controversial content involving various "sins of the flesh". In other words, the issues taken up are rather clearly "adult" in character, and they are typically discussed in a very frank and forceful manner, including the appropriate figurative language, idioms, proverbs, symbolism, and euphemism (see 5.1.2), in order to make the particular theological or moral point for the day as pertinent, potent, and persuasive as possible.

In the rest of this chapter, a conceptual overview of the occult is presented in order to provide a more detailed framework for interpreting the diverse facets that appear, either explicitly or implicitly, in the *Sewero* dramas. Such a "systematic occultology", as we might call it, may serve to give at least some idea of how pervasive and persistent it is in contemporary central African society—at all levels and in virtually every respect.

4.2 The sociocultural setting: An ancient African "axis of evil"

The characteristics of a Bantu "world view" as outlined in the preceding chapter and reflected in many *Sewero* plays (section 4.1), demonstrate a decided focus upon the *occult*, especially its malevolent and malicious dimension. The term "occult", we recall, has reference to all "supernatural influences, agencies, or phenomena…beyond the realm of human comprehension, inscrutable" (*American Heritage* dictionary). Although as noted earlier, a dictionary definition like this considers such phenomena from a Western point of view, which is quite different from an African perspective on the world's cosmology, ontology, and epistemology, it can serve in a practical way to sort out the data and the metaphysical phenomena under consideration here. The topical survey of the preceding section served to indicate how important this subject is to the *Sewero* playwrights due to its multiple manifestations at all levels and in every area of contemporary society. These diverse aspects of the occult must therefore be confronted in Christian ministry as it was in the days of Christ and later by the Apostles Peter and Paul—now by means of these dramatic performances of the Scriptures applied in and to everyday life. The crucial relevance of this topical complex requires a little closer look.

What we might term the "African axis of evil" involves prominent anti-personal destructive forces such as these: witchcraft (*ufiti*), sorcery (*zanyanga, zolodza*), magic (*mankhwala*), "evil" spirits (*ziwanda*), hostile curses (*matemberero*), and dangerous taboos (*zolaula, mpingu*).[6] This is a multifarious force-field so potent and ubiquitous that it cannot fail to impinge upon

---

[6] This focus on the *negative* aspects of traditional religious beliefs and practice corresponds to a similar emphasis that is manifested in the selection of main topics in the *Sewero* plays. It is supported by van Breugel's observation that "it could be true, as J.M. Schoffeleers declares, that the centre of interest is shifting from the traditional religious practices (such as offerings to the ancestral spirits) towards a type of pseudo-religion dominated by magic and belief in witchcraft" (2001:211).

daily life as a regular occurrence; hence people are gripped with a constant worry that borders on outright fear and the ever-present desire to obtain protection, both for themselves and their loved ones.[7] This personalization of evil is so prevalent, enigmatic, and interactive in essence and manifestation that it really requires a full treatise of exposition as well as pointed sermons concerning its diverse aspects that have been composed by cultural insiders (e.g., Nyirongo 1997, 1999; Wame in Wendland 2000). Their lack of such an authentic indigenous perspective in the present description obviously marks a great deficiency in my offering. However, I have tried to compensate by reflecting as much as possible the beliefs and opinions of national African co-workers and acquaintances with respect to the various subjects being treated.

The highly pervasive and invasive nature of traditional ancestral religion may be symbolized by the ancient, but familiar yin-yang figure [☯] representing the continual dynamic interaction between the living and the ("living") dead, man and nature, good and evil in an African setting. Birth and death, as indicated by the small included circles, are the key points of transition in the human life-cycle and therefore liable to special manifestations of spiritual and mystical influence for good or evil. Life is a continual struggle, a constant battle in fact, to maintain the equilibrium and well-being of one's personal life-force ("soul"), which is under constant threat of attack from closely related occultic powers (*bwanga*/witch-craft ⇔ *ung'anga*/witch-finding; Wendland 1992; see Wendland & Hachibamba 2000). The clear prominence and centrality of this aspect of ATR led to the decision to limit my study to a consideration of those *Sewero* plays that foreground this particular topical field, namely, the African occult, as a prominent feature of their dramatic plot and performance. This subject, though familiar to all participants in the program as well as their listeners, is summarized below as an extension of the overview of chapter 3 to provide some additional information that may be helpful, even necessary, for creating a conceptual context for the uninitiated or foreign reader.

4.2.1 A "natural" religion with traditional *man* in the middle

As was observed during the course of our survey of a central African world view (3.1.6), the most important being from a traditional perspective in reli-

---

[7]   In a recent article on this subject, Kisilu Kombo observes: "In spite of the many efforts to eradicate it, [witchcraft] continues to haunt the destiny or spells fear, death and destruction to its victims. The voluntary and repeated confessions and lynchings of witches prove that witchcraft exists [and thrives!] in Africa. Even within the church, some adherents strongly believe in witchcraft. Consequently, the belief in this vice is a reality in Africa. Africans who do not openly admit its existence, do so in their hearts" (Kombo 2003:73; implied material in brackets added).

gious terms is not God, but man (*munthu* m/f). Indeed, it is quite clear from a study of typical patterns of behavior within the established patterns of social organization as well as from various types of personal testimony, both formal and informal in nature, that human beings form the heart and core of this indigenous philosophy and natural science (and others like it all over the world). Man is thus defined, situated, and evaluated in life objectively as well as subjectively by virtue of his relationship to others—to his own family and clan first of all, and then to the surrounding community at large.[8]

The universe, in turn, is completely humanized; that is to say, the diverse beings and forces of which it is composed are perceived, interpreted, and reacted to largely in anthropomorphic and anthropopathic terms. The interaction of two prominent dimensions of power in society, namely, vertical *status* and horizontal *solidarity*, as manifested by the structure of interpersonal relationships in the traditional community, may be illustrated by the following figure:

Model of Social Forces

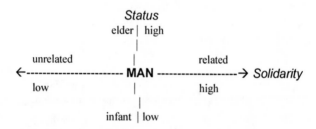

The dichotomy of the preceding diagram roughly reflects two of the principal values of African life. On the one hand, the power hierarchy of *status*, in which each member of the matrilineal clan and associated kinship groups has a recognized place and an associated role to place, gives every individual, no matter how lowly in the eyes of an outsider, an important sense of *security*. On the other hand, the cohesive force of *solidarity*, which focuses more on the group as a whole, creates a feeling of *harmony* that is crucial to the preservation of such a close-knit, often interrelated, face-to-face community.

It is at the center then of this essentially "religious" force field that the various hostile or helpful powers which envelop a person in his individual

---

[8]   Simply for the sake of convenience, I will refer to "man" in the generic sense by a masculine third person pronoun. This difficulty does not arise in Chinyanja where the corresponding pronouns are not marked for gender.

existence converge to interact with his own personal life-potency and potential, whether for good or evil. It is here too where the process of communication is initiated as an individual seeks through varied means to relate to these different personal and impersonal forces. The aim is to preserve himself in a state of animated equilibrium with respect to his total situational context, which of course includes the surrounding natural environment. This man-centered focus may be viewed as extending in possible influence and interaction along each of the two planes of power manifestation, as well as on several distinct levels of operation, to delineate the principal aspects of religious belief and behavior as they are realized in a typical central African setting.

There are two common negative, or personally detrimental, dimensions of this phenomenon—that is, as conceived of by the overt traditional adherents in a given community, which is a gradually decreasing number. This ancient world-view is essentially shared, however, by a host of semi-traditionalists, or "para-Christians", that is, recognized or certified "members" who are involved in different levels of syncretism, observing ancestral beliefs and practices that may be both overt and covert in nature. These activities concern primarily the medial or horizontal axis of "solidarity", where we find a prominent, distinctly human perversion of religious symbolism. Two distinct manifestations of this facet may be noted. First, there is "witchcraft" (*ufiti*), which in its most dangerous or lethal form, is typically thought to be worked immediately or telepathically, through pure psychically controlled malevolent energy, by women against those who are related by blood. "Wizardry", or sorcery (*zanyanga*), on the other hand, is practiced mediately, through various magical means, mainly by males and for the most part against those who are unrelated to them, but including affines (Wendland 1992; see Marwick 1965:98-103; van Breugel 2001:212-213).

In popular thinking (as reflected for example in most daily newspapers), however, especially in more recent times, the distinction between these two anti-social types of behavior is often blurred, and they are thus often used interchangeably or in a generic-specific relationship. In other words, although the characteristics of the pure necrophagous witch (*mfiti yeniyeni*) and the practitioner of so-called "African magic" (*wamankhwala*) are recognized and applied in specific cases, all such hostile action is commonly referred to in general terms simply as "witchcraft" (*ufiti*). But depending on the situation of use, more specific (and colorful) designations may be employed, for example, the *mpheranjiru* "someone who kills out of malicious envy". In any case, we are dealing with a flexible continuum of adverse, highly feared mystical activities that work insidiously to destroy cohesion, cooperation, and concord in the community at large and any of its sub-groups, including, sadly, certain church bodies or individual congregations. Such practices inevitably weaken the internal fabric of the group, whether the members happen to be related to one another or not, in effect stimulating or exacerbating feelings of jealously, mistrust, suspicion, fear, and hatred, which may arise from repressed social and economic tensions, particularly in periods of rapid culture change or external calamity (e.g., drought, pestilence, joblessness, high cost of living).

Some social anthropologists have interpreted witchcraft and/or sorcery as being beneficial to a community by providing a ready psychological safety valve, as it were, for the release and externalization of pent-up interpersonal conflicts in society. This may be valid to a certain extent, but such behavior is certainly not viewed in a positive light by the people themselves. Furthermore, any release or reprieve that comes after one set of accusations erupts and is dealt with is generally maintained only for a short time, for the antagonistic attitudes which these practices generate never die out completely. Instead, the malignant feelings simply feed on themselves, festering away beneath the surface of community awareness until another combination of suspicious and provocative circumstances appears to bring them back out into the open again. Thus if they are not checked and totally eliminated by a decided world-view shift—such as that effected by a genuine Christian conversion—they continue to reproduce and bear bitter fruit in a hostile social environment where divisions, arguments, separation, and even murder (i.e., of the unjustly accused) recur with debilitating regularity.[9]

The traditionalist does have recourse, however, to a pair of potentially positive, beneficial forces—personal as well as impersonal—on the vertical scale of "status" (see 3.1.1). These can give him protection against the many malicious agents seeking to control, corrupt, and consume his life (soul-power). Thus a plaintiff may appeal to those with increased rank in terms of power and influence, namely, the ancestral spirits—in particular, his own personal guardian spirit and the ones who are most closely related to him—

---

[9] "[The belief in witchcraft] brings about a dichotomy and a divided loyalty, especially of the Christian believers who are supposed to embrace Christianity fully. However, such people in times of social problems resort to traditional practices and explanations. It is in his light that witchcraft is considered as a permanent feature in the lives of many. Consequently, witchcraft will continue to dominate the minds of many people for a long time unless a traditional alternative for the vice is found" (Kombo 2003:84). But one wonders whether the hope in such a "traditional alternative" is well-placed. It would seem that in the case of a key socioculturally-ingrained proclivity towards evil—whether it be African witchcraft or, for another example, American materialism—only a radical cognitive and emotive transformation in and through Christ will serve as a lasting solution.

to defend him from his adversaries and, if so desired, also to take vengeance upon them. We might term this religious activity *"spiritism"*. It is the sacred duty of these ancestors to uphold the moral order of society and to preserve its ancient traditions. In some cases, so it is believed, this will involve a disciplinary chastisement in the form of a personal accident or illness, but such misfortune will usually be seen (and confirmed through divination) as having the constructive purpose of correcting some human failing or fault within the community. Of course, there are also certain alien (as opposed to family-related) and antagonistic spirits which, under the direction of a sorcerer, can seriously harm or even kill a person. But even these are normally viewed as having been provoked or originated by an actual physical or psychological transgression (e.g., murder or inveterate hatred) on the part of man, including the very practice of witchcraft itself.

On the other hand and more often nowadays, a person might turn to the readily available (at any local market) impersonal means of *magic* to provide him with the desired protection or to retaliate against supposed enemies. The effectiveness of such "medicine" (*mankhwala*) is believed to be dependent both upon the reliability and potency of the source, the "medicine-man" (*sing'anga*), as well as on the correct usage of the substance(s) supplied. This normally involves a manipulation of certain symbolic media and a utilization of the natural potency believed to be inherent in select materials of the environment. The powers concerned are lower on the scale of status/vitality, but they are augmented by the force of human will (+ faith?) in order to either defend or develop one's own life-force, which is the source of a person's physical, mental, and spiritual well-being in life (hence similar to the Hebrew notion of *shalom*).

In actual practice, therefore, magic turns out to be a rather ambiguous source of strength from the point of view of a given individual. He (or she) definitely requires it in various forms and on different occasions throughout life as a defensive measure in order to counter its iniquitous use by others, i.e., sorcerers. From the opposite perspective, however, such magical practice, either with or without the involvement of potent spiritual agencies, may also be employed egocentrically—offensively, as it were—in order to enhance a person's public standing and/or material position in the community. But inevitably this must happen at the expense of someone else's status and "spirituality" (life-force), and hence it is not publicly sanctioned or approved. The key religious concepts and practices discussed above invariably impinge upon the lives of traditionally-minded folk, for better or for worse from their perspective, on a day-to-day basis. They may be related to each other schematically as shown on the following diagram:

Positive-Negative Vectors of Dynamism in ATR

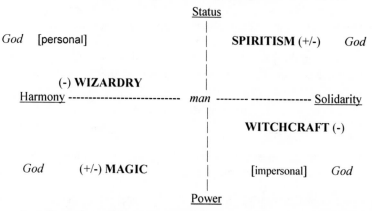

Status

God   [personal]   SPIRITISM (+/-)   God

(-) WIZARDRY

Harmony -------------------------- *man* ------- --------------- Solidarity

                                   WITCHCRAFT (-)

God   (+/-) MAGIC   [impersonal]   God

Power

Any discussion of the *impersonal* forces unlocked or unleashed through the application of magical practices must at some point consider the operation of taboos in society. A *taboo* is a socially oriented and sanctioned rule, usually a prohibition—against incest, for example—which entails a clearly specified and inexorably enforced punishment in the event of its transgression. While an overt violation of such a stricture may result in ostracization by the family, clan, or larger community, a more feared consequence is a certain mystical affliction which sooner or later is believed to occur. This may be a particular sickness, deformity, debility, or even death that strikes either the offender him/herself or, more likely, a close relative. For example, some believe that a man who commits adultery while his wife is pregnant will automatically cause her to abort the fetus and perhaps die when he returns home and crosses the threshold. He is thus said to have "cut" (*-dula*) his wife by violating a taboo of the same name (i.e., *mdulo* "cutting disease"). Many view the ancestral spirits as being involved in such adversity, at least in a passive way, by allowing it to happen as punishment for the grave offense that was committed. Proscriptive and prescriptive taboos like this function to maintain social equilibrium and the balance of nature within a traditional belief system by keeping what is regarded to be ritually pure separate from the impure, and the mystically powerful away from the impotent (see Wendland 1990:34).

The practice of religion in central Africa engages man in various attempts to maintain a positive, advantageous relationship (i.e., solidarity) with respect to personal beings (i.e., spirits) whose power and status he clearly recognizes as being considerably greater than his own. A much more critical pragmatic objective, however, is negative—evasive—in nature. In other words, the overriding concern of most people (*all* traditionalists and syncretists) is to defend themselves from the host of hostile entities with which they share their living environment. The major reasons and remedies for misfortune—

such as death, illness, spirit possession, infertility, job loss, crop failure, flooding, and so forth—to which one might fall prey at any unguarded moment or point of weakness are summarized on the chart below. In most cases, especially the serious, life-threatening ones, the specific cause of the threat or attack would be sought, and usually determined, through the process of divination (*kuombeza maula*) of one sort or another, including the use of spirit mediums (see Schoffeleers 1997:chs. 5-6).

Aspects of Misfortune		
Type	*Cause*	*Remedy*
Deserved	-provoke an ancestral **spirit**	sacrifice +/- compensation
	-violate an ancient **taboo**	[same]
Undeserved	-mystical attack by a **witch**	counter-magic: curative,
	-magical attack by a **sorcerer**	defensive, +/- offensive

It is quite natural then that most people, all conservatively-minded individuals at any rate, regularly seek out a variety of precautionary, prophylactic, and preemptive measures in order to try and insulate themselves from such pressing everyday calamities and crises. Often this is done with the help of the local medicine-man (*sing'anga*—or the one with the greatest reputation in the community). The practice of "religion" in this lower, self- or man-centered dimension obviously requires a great deal of time, effort, expense, and mental commitment. Simply put, it is a matter of both *power* (who/what is in control here?) and also *solidarity* (with whom do I need to be allied for sufficient security in life?). Sad to say, the intellectual, dogmatic brand of Christianity that many have been exposed to—or have misinterpreted—all too often fails to provide the necessary relevant answers to practical life-related issues such as these. This is the crucial task that the *Sewero* group has set for themselves—namely, to dramatize appropriate responses that are firmly based on the Bible, but flexibly geared for an African setting.

For a majority of African Christians today, the ancient dynamic nucleus of traditional beliefs and practices remains very much at the center of their present thoughts and lives. The distinctive faith and rites of their respective denominations may be reflected quite strongly on the outside, especially when times are good. But when times get tough, no matter how much modern sophistication a person might exhibit otherwise, there is a great, almost overwhelming, temptation for him (her) to revert to the religious principles and precepts of the past—to those that pertain to spiritism, magic, sorcery, and witchcraft in particular. This is because all too often, as far as Western theology (and medicine) is concerned, such beliefs have no basis in empirical fact—hence no reality or credibility. Theoretically, then, since such nefarious phenomena do not exist, there is no concrete way to deal with the life-threatening problems which they pose, except perhaps to perfunctorily ascribe them along with all evils to the wicked workings of Satan and his diabolical agents in the world.

This vital core within the hierarchy of personal as well as cosmic forces represents what Hiebert terms "the excluded middle" (1982:43). This is the (usually) unseen mode of existence that stands between the visible natural world managed by man and the vast unseen realm of God (on the outer fringes), non-human spirit beings (angels, demons), and the many impersonal mystical powers of the universe. It is this world that is often avoided in the practice of foreign-based ecclesiastical preaching, teaching, and other forms of Christian proclamation (e.g., writing, singing). For all practical purposes, like the concept of "God" in the typical secularized, scientifically-oriented Western world-view, so also orthodox denominational Christianity in an African context often remains—when religion really counts in life—on the outside, looking away (not even "in"!). It is frequently left then for one of the semi-Christian syncretistic sects in the area to provide some sort of a bridge between biblical teachings and indigenous beliefs or practices with regard to answers and solutions that people urgently seek as they attempt to deal with their life-death crises, both as individuals and as larger associations within the community. The *Sewero* drama group offers another, more Scripture centered alternative.

4.2.2 A dramatic model to depict the drama of traditional religion

We might further explore the vibrant and vigorous nature of central African traditional religion in relation to the *Sewero* plays by viewing the former, the indigenous field of metaphysical forces in terms of a *narrative drama*. A "narrative" in the literary sense is some form of historical (chronologically-based) account, either oral or written, in prose or in poetry. A "story" is a narrative with a "plot" built in—that is, a sequence of events that proceeds from some crucial *problem* (e.g., a need, lack, task, obstacle, disability, or crisis) in the lives of the chief participants through a situation of *climax*, when the conflict is confronted head-on, to a final state of *resolution* one way or another. At the final stage of the story, either the conflict is ended (e.g., the need supplied, the lack liquidated, the task accomplished, the obstacle overcome, the crisis settled)—or it is not, and the tension is left unresolved. A "drama" is a serious (non-comic) story that is normally performed orally, either in public or for the purposes of recording, the various character roles of the plot being impersonated and performed by one, or usually several, different persons (or "voices" in the case of radio).

For the purposes of formal analysis, six "universal" (regularly found) role relationships may be distinguished in dramatic narrative, that is, according to the so-called "actantial model" proposed by the French Structuralist A.J. Greimas (see Calloud 1976:29-32; Patte 1976:42-43). These may be schematically depicted in their characteristic dramatic interaction according to the diagram below:

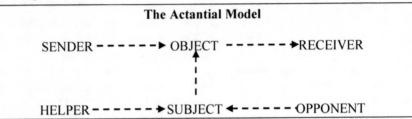

The Actantial Model

SENDER – – – – – – ▶ OBJECT – – – – – – ▶RECEIVER

HELPER – – – – – – ▶SUBJECT ◀ – – – – – OPPONENT

These six roles may be defined as follows: The "Sender" is the overall architect or originator of the narrative's primary sequence of plot-related "events". He (rarely "she") desires to fulfill some lack or to supply a vital need in the life of the "Receiver", or receptor group (which the Receiver may represent). The Sender is generally a rather remote figure who, if he is present at all, usually appears only at the beginning and/or the ending of the story. The "Object" in turn is some essential item which must be conveyed, transmitted, or communicated in some way to the Receiver by the "Subject", who is normally the "hero" (or "heroine") of the plot as a whole.

Dramatic conflict is introduced into the account by the "Opponent", that is, *what*ever (in the case of some inanimate "obstacle") stands in the way of the Subject or *who*ever (the "villain") actively seeks to prevent him from carrying out his noble task or accomplishing his beneficial goal. Any personal Opponent thus maliciously endeavors by whatever means possible to keep the Receiver(s) in a state of weakness, need, deprivation, or oppression. The Helper, like the Opponent, may be either human or non-human, and in the latter instance, animate or inanimate. He/she/it either works to assist, or is utilized by, the Subject in his efforts to complete the difficult mission that he has undertaken. It is possible in this dramatic scheme for the same personage in the narrative to play more than one functional role; for example, the Helper and the Sender may be one and the same person. Furthermore, there are a variety of ways in which the different "actants" may be manifested and interrelated with one another within a given story, accordingly producing a diversity of plots.

How does an abstract literary scheme like this apply to the study of African traditional religion? A thorough sociological examination and analysis of a large number of case-studies, reviewed and corrected by indigenous experts, suggests the following hypothesis. In a majority of pertinent situations, i.e., social contexts in which traditional religion is practiced, there is a fundamental interpersonal conflict of some sort—whether overt or implicit, real (verifiable) or supposed (asserted), with respect to some serious problem, lack, or need in life. The devotee, who never acts in isolation but always as part of a larger social unit, naturally seeks a resolution that would eliminate the source of the discord, which clearly troubles, or worse, threatens his very existence, and probably that of the entire community as well. It is in this sense then that we might characterize or describe such an individual or corporate effort in "dramatic" terms. Thus one could view life in general terms or better, a particular localized situation of conflict or crisis, as being a cosmic (or communal) religious drama involving positive and negative personalities and powers. These are all arrayed in forceful opposition to one another and playing out their various roles on the stage of human history, or more likely, some small segment of time.

How would the six generic roles noted above be filled in this vast scenario, if it were set in Africa? The following is one arrangement that seems to typify most of the possibilities:

An "Africanized" Actantial Model

GOD - - - - - - - - ▶ LIFE/*MOYO* - - - - - - ▶ MANKIND

⬆
┊
SPIRITS/MAGIC - - - ▶*SING'ANGA* ◀ - - SORCERER/WITCH

To explain: "God" (*Mulungu*) is universally acknowledged in central Africa to be the great Sender of every good and perfect gift to the human Receivers whom he also created, that is, all "mankind" (*anthu*). God's greatest gift, that Object which is most needful from an anthropocentric perspective, is the dynamic *force* of "life" itself (*moyo*). As already observed, this is a wide-ranging concept which is not only *physical* in nature (i.e., the animating principle of a living body, thus endowing it with "life"—also *moyo*), but one that in the case of the mature adult ideally also has many other culturally-specific dimensions: *material* (freedom from want), *physiological* (health), *psychological* (mental stability), *social* (fertility, many descendants), *mystical* (immunity from attack by witches, sorcerers, and evil spirits), and *spiritual* (transformed into the essence of an ancestral spirit at death).

Throughout one's earthly existence, however, certain powerful Opponents, or agents of evil, in the person of witches, sorcerers, and malevolent spirits continually seek to either trap or destroy one's life-force, or soul, so that they can access its essential vitality or energy for their own iniquitous purposes. People therefore invariably turn to the hero or Subject of this great drama, the diviner/psychiatrist/ medicine-man (*sing'anga*), for protection so that the gift of life is not cut off or diminished, either from themselves or from their offspring, through whom their own lives are perpetuated and their future existence thus guaranteed. The *sing'anga* in turn depends on various Helpers, both animate (e.g., spirits of possession that enable his/her profession) and/or inanimate (i.e., defensive, offensive, augmentative magic) in order to supply him with the insight and power to carry out his vital task and service to the community.

In a slight modification of the actantial model, we note that as far as the central African situation is concerned, it is necessary to posit an additional set of Helpers for the category of Opponents as well. The unique development here is that this assemblage of agents and objects turns out to be the same in character as that specified for the Helper group. That is to say, sorcerers and witches are also believed to employ the services of either spirits or magic in their attempts to snatch away a person's soul or to frustrate the efforts of a medicine man to protect the same. The difference is that in the case of such Opponents, alien, aggrieved, and aggressive spirits (i.e., *ziwanda*, not *mizimu*), high-jacked souls or "gremlins" (*ndondocha*), and noxious magic (*zolodza*, not *mankhwala*) are engaged. The primary antagonists, then, in the drama of human life and death may be represented as follows:

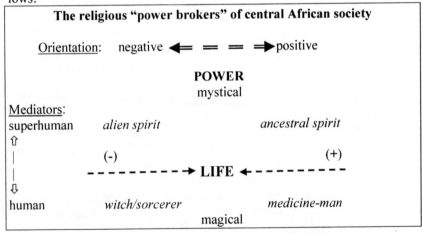

| The religious "power brokers" of central African society |

Orientation: negative ⬅ = = ➡ positive

POWER
mystical

Mediators:
superhuman   *alien spirit*   *ancestral spirit*
⇧
| (-)   (+)
| - - - - - - - ➔ LIFE ⬅ - - - - - - - -
|
⇩
human   *witch/sorcerer*   *medicine-man*
                              magical

Viewing this volatile state of *spirit*-ual affairs from a sociological perspective, we might say that during one's earthly bodily existence one is engaged in a ceaseless battle over "life", that is, with respect to one's inherent, personal soul-power (*moyo*). The struggle progresses in varied, cyclical fashion from one conflict and resolution to another. Social strife, resulting from an otherwise inexplicable deprivation or disaster, whether prolonged or brief, predictable or unexpected, may be attributed by experienced intuition or, more likely, divination to the unseen activity of hostile forces arising from within the in-group itself (close relatives) or from some external source, the out-group (non-relatives, neighbors). Such disharmony, which often breaks out in overt conflict, may be the product of latent tensions within the community and/or may be attributed to some form of overt anti-social behavior. In either case, the crisis is believed to manifest itself through two basic types of personal affliction: alien spirit *possession*, which is associated with a certain physical ailment or infirmity, or more commonly, the *assault* of witches (if the enemy is related) or wizards/sorcerers (i.e., unrelated individuals).

Once the diagnosis has been made through the insights of a diviner and/or medium, a psycho-religious specialist (who may be one and the same person) must then deal with the matter. This is the *sing'anga*—the medicine-man/diviner-doctor/psychiatrist (sometimes misleadingly termed a "witch-doctor")—who is consulted in order to determine and procure healing, protection, or both, depending on the situation. In the event of a spirit-caused illness, the afflicted being is either exorcised, if it happens to be a foreign spirit, or if an angry ancestor is involved, it is allowed to express its will (e.g., through therapeutic dancing or a trance) and placated (e.g., by means of a stipulated offering or the observance of certain designated ritual taboos).

Where witchcraft/sorcery is diagnosed, on the other hand, some appropriate counter-magic is required in order to undo the spell and neutralize its injurious, potentially fatal effects. In either case, some sort of a resolution is brought about, with varying degrees of success, to re-establish social harmony and restore the balance of opposing forces in the community at large. This resolution of the interpersonal drama may be either superficial and temporary in nature or more substantial and long-lasting. But inevitably, underlying conflicts are again generated, and the cycle of aggression repeats itself, perhaps in a different form and on a different level of seriousness, specificity, and scope within a given social group. A summary of the possibilities with respect to this conflict-prone state of affairs is charted below:

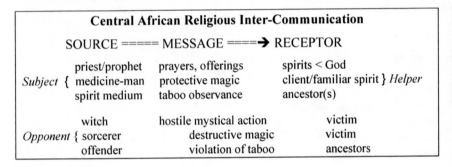

The Socio-Religious Drama of Life ⇔ Death

	Diagnosis	Treatment
Spiritual	spirit possession	exorcism/appeasement
Magical	sorcery/witchcraft	counter-magic
Mystical	taboo affliction	acts of expiation

CONFLICT ←==================➔ RESOLUTION

This dramatic perspective may be combined with a simple "communications model" to depict the dynamic core of the central African religious experience as follows:

Central African Religious Inter-Communication

SOURCE ===== MESSAGE ====➔ RECEPTOR

Subject {	priest/prophet medicine-man spirit medium	prayers, offerings protective magic taboo observance	spirits < God client/familiar spirit } *Helper* ancestor(s)
Opponent {	witch sorcerer offender	hostile mystical action destructive magic violation of taboo	victim victim ancestors

If the symbolic or ritual communication carried out by a traditional ritual practitioner has been efficacious—and there are many participant-related failures and foibles that can derail the process—a positive outcome for the client/victim will be forthcoming (or subsequent events will at least be divined to be optimistic). Thus the locus of *power*, whether a personal being or a humanly mediated impersonal force, conveys what is desired by the "source", e.g., [+] rain, healing, provision, protection // [-] drought, disease, deprivation, injury. Such intervention will either benefit those whom the specialist is representing (clients, victims, constituents), or it will harm those whom the former is attacking (opponents, enemies). In the case of a taboo violation, however, the process is somewhat different since it may be presumed that that victim (offender) did not deliberately commit the offense in order to be punished (though s/he may have known that s/he was taking a chance—"tempting fate"—by carrying out a certain prohibited activity, e.g., illicit sexual relations). The "receptors" are thus implicit, namely, the ancestral guardians of traditional customs, mores, and values, who are at the same time preservers of the time-hallowed status quo.

It is important to note once again the prominent, in fact essential *mediatorial* part that is played by the traditional religious specialist in these activities. This refers to the *sing'anga* "diviner-doctor" in particular, but to a lesser degree also to these three roles: that of the spirit medium (*wamizimu* "the [person] of spirits"), who functions as a prophetic voice; the ritual priest (*wansembe* "the [person] of sacrifices"), who is often the local "chief" (*mfumu*); and in a certain antithetical sense also to the "sorcerer" (*wanyanga* "the [person] of horns/magic). There is in actual practice (or public perception) only a very fine line that separates the personality and profession of the sorcerer from the generally positive role that is attributed to the medicine man. In a sense, it all depends on who you are working for and why.

In any case, as the "subject" of the dramatic action, the ritual specialist (at times also the traditional worship leader) is believed to control the very power of life and death on behalf of ordinary mortals and members of society. S/he is supposedly able to preserve, even to enhance, a client's well-being in several respects: by revealing the cause (or the impending threat) of particular misfortunes and dangers; by providing both medicinal (natural) as well as metaphysical charms, potions, amulets, etc. for the purpose of protection; by attacking, neutralizing, or reversing the influence of all types of enemies; by offering "inspired" advice about how to avoid such problems in the future; and in a rather more questionable practice, by selling to people specifically concocted "medicines" that are intended to augment her/his possessions and prosperity in life, both physical and mental. These would include such desirable blessings as a bumper harvest, success in business, social prominence, a productive wife, many children, surpassing abilities in various skills, crafts, trades, and occupations.

So it is that the "witchdoctor"—the individual (or profession) whom Christianity has condemned as being the epitome and principal exponent of Satanic activity in African society—turns out to be the "hero" of the religious drama of everyday existence. It is he who defends people from danger and delivers them in the time of trouble. He answers their "prayers" for help for one thing or another—at least it is assumed that s/he will succeed more often than not. It is no wonder then that this socially strategic and ever adaptable profession continues to thrive in the midst of great cultural, economic, educational, political, and technological change (whether positive or negative) and in the face of the tremendous growth of the Christian church on the continent during the past century.

For many people, it seems, the two religious systems are able to coexist happily in their minds and lives, each having its own specific sphere of influence and area of specialized activity. A rather fuzzy dichotomy thus emerges: Christianity takes care of preparing one for a better life beyond the grave (usually conceived of in earthly, material terms), while traditional religion assumes primary responsibility for the here-and-now—for life as it transpires from day to day in an electric, but essentially hostile world that is filled with powers which can be manipulated by a person's enemies to control, gain possession of, or to extinguish his/her life-force, hence also the essence of one's being. Such a cognitive split or *separation* is most likely to occur for those who happen to be members of the longer-established, Western-originated, mainline, dogmatically-oriented denominations, where all too often there is an over-emphasis upon correct instruction at the expense of a genuine personal and relational application of biblical teaching to encounter the current challenges of daily life in a dynamic, but demonic socio-religious environment.

For a rapidly increasing number of other adherents, on the other hand, especially those of the charismatic persuasion, whether traditional African or of modern, Western origin, the potential danger comes from a different direction. In this setting, overt and covert assimilation or *syncretism* appears to be the major problem, as indigenous beliefs are simply absorbed into the church with little or no change in substance, but clothed in a new ecclesiastical form—that is, a relatively superficially taught and understood evangelical terminology (or jargon). In such a scenario, God the Father easily assumes the role of the remote, mythic Creator-Deity, while Jesus the Christ becomes in effect the second Law-giver, analogous to Moses. The Holy Spirit then occupies center stage as the Distributor of diverse gifts of power, which enable selected "helpers", or "anointed" individuals, namely, those who have been magically (so it seems) "born again", to deal proactively with the hostile attacks and machinations of evil spirits, witches, or sorcerers, plus all types of other threatening and debilitating situations in life.

In either case, whether conceptual separation or syncretism is the motivating force, indigenous beliefs, values, and practices remain the animating nucleus of the world-view of a majority of the population, whether they happen to be overtly "Christianized" or not. This manner of thinking naturally has consequences; there are various behavioral manifestations, which cannot be dealt with by merely denying its presence or downplaying its relevance in the "modern world". Any such avoidance or repudiation, or any exercise of the confrontational "power-encounter" approach, if unaccompanied by substantial and sustained biblical teaching, only serves to force the traditional ideological system underground. There, undetected by casual, uncritical observation, it continues to flourish and operate freely whenever a personal crisis develops that cannot be handled either by a Western-biased, rationalistic theological method or a superficial charismatic healing attempt. Situations vary, of course, and the pastor or evangelist needs to have a variety of intensive, Scripture-based strategies available for application in a given set of circumstances.

In this endeavor, it would be a good idea to emulate the irenic-polemical methodology of the New Testament writers.[10] These expert cross-cultural communicators did not shirk from making a confrontational, culturally-relevant, but also a situationally sensitive, attempt to bring about a significant *paradigm-shift* whereby the presuppositions of an unregenerate world-view, whether traditional or modern, are directly challenged, and ideally—by the power of the Holy Spirit—transformed through a biblical perspective. This is intended to produce an immediate (but in practice, usually more gradual) displacement of the ancient, resistant conceptual core to the periphery of a person's faith, where it will eventually disappear due to the influence of sound, contextualized Scripture-centered instruction, coupled with progressive spiritual growth and maturity, again under the Spirit's guidance and enablement.

Following the Apostle John and the writer to the Hebrews, for example, a perceptive, provocative, and polemical pedagogy will focus upon the total *superiority* of Jesus Christ as Savior and Lord over all beliefs, traditions, and practices of the past. Indeed, he is the very *Son of God*, the divinely appointed heir and ruler of the universe (Heb. 1:2-3), who has destroyed the power of the Devil and all the demonic forces of hell (Heb. 2:14-18). As the God-Man and appointed "MEDIATOR" (μεσίτης) of the new covenant of grace,[11] established through his sacrificial and redemptive death on the cross (Heb. 8:6, 9:15, 12:24; see 1 Tim. 2:5-6), Jesus Christ now integrates all of the familiar dramatic roles perfectly in himself. He personally intercedes with the SENDER, his heavenly Father, to communicate LIFE (*moyo*) to his people in all its fullness, both now in this world and forever in the next (a theme strongly emphasized throughout John's gospel, e.g., 1:3-4, 3:16, 11:25-26, 14:19, 20:31). Christ also supplies the necessary *power* by sending a divine HELPER, the Holy Spirit, to lead and instruct his disciples in the Word of God so that they can withstand all the attacks of their chief OPPONENT, Satan, and any other enemy, human or otherwise (see Jn. 14:16,26; 15:26; 16:7; 1 Jn. 2:18).

---

[10] For a good model to follow, see Fernando 1999:chs. 10-12.
[11] As in the days of the early Christian Church, false teachings abound today in Africa too with regard to Christ's essential deity as well as his true humanity (see Wendland 1991).

Furthermore, Jesus is himself the perfect SUBJECT—Prophet (God's "Medium", the eternal Word; Jn. 1:1-3; Acts 3:19-22; Heb. 1:1-2), Priest (and the all-sufficient Sacrifice as well; Heb. 7:27), King (the great "Chief"; Rev. 17:14), Healer (God's own "Medicine-Man"; Lk. 5:24,31-32; Acts 10:38), Judge (Jn. 5:22), Warrior (Rev. 19:11-21), and many more. He is the (only) One who makes it possible for all people everywhere to be victorious in their daily struggle with the various physical and spiritual, magical and mystical powers of this world (Jn. 16:33), thereby fulfilling God's purpose and achieving the glorious end for which they were created (Rom. 8:37-39).

But Jesus Christ is much more than just a divine power figure. He also humbled himself to become like one of us—the perfect Munthu (humanity personified; Phil. 2:7-8; Heb. 2:14). Thus in complete *solidarity* with all people, he lived the life that we failed to live—perfect in the sight of a holy and righteous God (Heb. 4:15; 5:8-9; 7:27-28; 9:14,25-28). Christ also became a "curse" for us on the cross, someone who was completely taboo (Gal. 3:13), so that we might be redeemed from all spiritual, religious, and cultural "slavery" (Gal. 4:1-11) and thereby reunited by faith into the extended family of God the Father (Gal. 3:26). Being led, therefore, by the purifying Spirit Representative of this great Ancestor of ours (Rom. 8:14-17; Heb. 2:10-18), we are empowered to resist temptation and do the things that demonstrate our personal relationship with Christ—whether as a "brother, sister, or mother" (Mk. 3:35). Through this oneness with our Lord, everything that is his becomes ours (2 Tim. 2:12; Heb. 2:10)—that is, all those who trust and obey him (Heb. 5:9) and who remain faithful to his principles (Heb. 6:1-12). Christ's blessings for his family of faith include abundant provision for those needs in particular that happen to be most relevant to the society and culture concerned—in central Africa: life (Jn. 10:10) and power (Acts 1:8).

The following diagram illustrates this contextualized theological position in terms of the earlier diagram of the paradigm of power and solidarity:

Christ is our divine, sacred *Sing'anga*

This representation is obviously a simplification, but it at least suggests a conceptual goal that contemporary evangelists might aim to achieve in their communicative efforts. It also serves as a handy summary of the strategy that the *Sewero* group has adopted in their dramatized mode of message transmission. Once a person becomes convinced, through the workings of the Spirit, that Christ is the Key—that he, God's *Man in the middle*, is in addition also the omnipotent Savior, Provider, and Lord of his/her life, both in this world and the next, then there will be no need for him/her to return to the partial and imperfect religion of the past (Hebrews 6,10,12). Such a progressive, step-by-step (as opposed to an "either-or"), people-specific (rather than some "universal"), and culturally-sensitive (but not an ethnocentric) program of "searching [and sharing] the Scriptures" (Acts 17:11) combines serious biblical instruction with a more realistic and relevant approach with respect to the indigenous religious system on the one hand and a vibrant indigenized Christianity on the other. This must be a receptor-group oriented method which honestly and openly seeks to understand the traditional mindset, even as it tactfully endeavors to expose the many failings of any anthropomorphically-based faith by comparing it to the supreme preeminence of Jesus, the all-sufficient Savior for all (Col. 1:15-20; 2:13-15; Heb. 1:1-4).

In the preceding discussion, I focused upon passages from John and Hebrews in developing my argument for a more culture-specific approach in Christian education and edification. What then are the particular texts that the *Sewero* players find most helpful in their dramatic depiction of the supremacy of Christ, the Great Ancestor who has defeated all powers of the occult in their midst? That is the next stage in our survey of their apologetic (defensive), but also artistic, narrative strategy.

4.3 Primary Scripture texts employed in this dramatized polemic

A prominent aspect of my analysis was to ascertain the manner in which Scripture is selected, interpreted, and applied by non-professional dramatists and performers—that is, with specific reference now to educating and equipping the radio audience regarding the manner in which biblical Christians may confidently and competently confront the occult in their lives. Obviously, the *Sewero* players bring their own unique ideas, viewpoints, opinions, and goals, which are continually reflected in their artistic work, whether overtly or more subtly. To what extent does this represent a significant "local" or "lay" theology, as distinct from that of the regular clergy? Which denominational background seems to be most prominent in these plays? What hermeneutical techniques do the players manifest in their narrative-dramatic treatment of a particular religious topic? These are some of the key issues that I also needed to investigate as I reviewed my select corpus of plays in the process of analyzing and assessing them.

4.3.1 General survey of passages

To begin with, I made a general survey to determine which Scripture books, pericopes, and individual passages are preferred within the corpus as a whole.[12] In this exercise I originally wanted to distinguish among several different types of biblical reference, that is, to have my student research assistants record whether specific texts are quoted exactly (i.e., from the vernacular KJV equivalent, the *Buku Lopatulika*, "Sacred Book" [Bible Society of Malawi, 1923])[13] as distinct from being summarized, paraphrased, or alluded to, either with or without an explicit citation of the exact Scripture passage concerned. However, given a number of time constraints, I abandoned this effort and simply had all significant biblical usages recorded. The following table summarizes our results:

Book of the Bible (OT)	Number of Citations	Book of the Bible (NT)	Number of Citations
Isaiah	8	Matthew	13
Genesis	7	John	13
Psalms	7	Romans	13
Proverbs	7	Hebrew	10
Exodus	4	Mark	8
Jeremiah	4	Luke	8
Deuteronomy	3	Revelation	8
Job	3	James	7
Numbers	2	Acts	5
Esther	2	Ephesians	5
Ecclesiastes	2	1 Timothy	5
Ezekiel	2	1 Corinthians	4
Malachi	2	1 Peter	4
1 Samuel	1	1 John	4
2 Samuel	1	Galatians	3

[12] The following results may be compared with the preferred texts of a popular revivalist preacher in Malawi, Evangelist Shadrack Wame (Wendland 2000:23-25).

[13] A modern, more idiomatic translation of the Bible in Chinyanja has been available for several years (NT—1977, OT—1998), but the *Sewero* team does not seem to be very familiar with this text (see Wendland 1998), since we did not notice any citations of it in their plays. It might be an interesting subject for the group to dramatize sometime, namely, the issues that may arise for lay Christians (and pastors too!) from the different renderings of these two translations. The point would not be to promote one version over or at the expense of the other, but simply to illustrate in a practical way how their diverse styles and purposes might be used to complement each other in a more thorough program of Bible study.

2 Kings	1	2 Thessalonians	3
2 Chronicles	1	2 Timothy	3
Nehemiah	1	1 Thessalonians	2
Lamentations	1	2 Peter	2
Hosea	1	2 Corinthians	1
Amos	1	Philippians	1
		Colossians	1
Total OT	**61**	**Total NT**	**123**

What can these raw figures tell us? Clearly the New Testament is more popular in terms of serving as a source of supply for passages than the Old Testament, though the latter is roughly three times longer. On average, any given *Sewero* drama may be expected to make use of at least two Bible passages (more exactly, 2.3/play) when dealing with the specific Christian issue under consideration. It is not surprising that Genesis, Psalms, and Proverbs are among the top OT source texts, but the appearance of Isaiah is more noteworthy in this respect. However, it would require a much more detailed text-contextual study in order to investigate the possible reasons for this prominence.

The gospels provide the most passages of all for application, which is not really strange since these books are probably the most familiar to ordinary Christians and, after all, Christ is the ultimate authority when it comes to governing one's faith and life principles. The relatively high number of citations from the "doctrinal" book of Romans is a bit unexpected, but we must remember that the latter half of this epistle does contain a great deal of practical advice too—as does the letter to the Hebrews, which is especially relevant for Christians who happen to be living in a situation of testing and trial. James is helpful for the same reason. But more important than quantity is quality—that is, not only how many Bible passages are used, but how effectively they are integrated and applied in the dramatic context of a particular play. The latter aspect of usage may be evaluated as readers consider the various segments from the *Sewero* plays that are cited in the pages that follow.

4.3.2 Examples of local applications

In order to specify the overview found in the preceding section, I will summarize a number of examples that give a representative selection of Bible texts and their local dramatic application within certain *Sewero* plays. As already noted, these context-specific usages normally occur towards the end of the drama during the closing "moral" portion of a given story. Again, I have chosen these excerpts from the sub-set of plays that highlight traditional religious/occult practices.

I have also included below several typical instances of what may be termed a *"catena"* of texts, that is, a series of Bible passages which the speaker(s) string(s) together in close proximity to supply the rhetorical "proof" with regard to a particular dramatic issue, personal crisis, or interpersonal confrontation. In addition, I have recorded an example or two of what would appear to be a "mis-quote"—in other words, a Bible passage that seems to have been either misunderstood in the original biblical context or misapplied within the local context. This critical assessment could be debated of course, depending on how loosely one is allowed to understand and/or "interpret" the original text.

But my primary concern in this section is to indicate how far the practice of unsophisticated (i.e., laity-generated), local "theologizing" goes in these dramas and to offer several fascinating examples of such hermeneutical creativity and insight. The communicative significance of this interpretive practice is considered further in the next section (4.4), and additional examples will also be given in the text portions that are cited in chapters 5 and 6. It is especially interesting to observe how the original intent and implication of a given Bible passage may be creatively re-contextualized, more often than not by female characters (especially "the pastor's wife"), to fit into a modern Malawian setting—but with the basic content and essential theological or moral thrust of the passage largely retained.

- **1 Corinthians 9:7** would normally be cited in cases where a congregation needs some encouragement to support their pastor properly. In the play *Kodi mwatumidwadi?* ("Have you really been sent?"), however, the application receives an interesting reversal. Here a concerned lady of the parish uses these words with reference to a "shepherd" who has not been very reliable in carrying out his pastoral responsibilities; he has thus been getting the "milk" (i.e., support from his people) without faithfully "tending the flock".

- **Isaiah 3:7** is referred to in summary fashion by a pastor's wife in *Kodi mwatumidwadi?* ("Have you really been sent?") to testify to her belief that in the "last days" when Christ comes for judgment all the medicine men (*asing'anga*) will try to repudiate all their magical potions and charms in an effort to escape the punishment that is due them. This shifts the focus of the original Hebrew text somewhat, but it certainly is an interesting localized interpretation of this passage.

- **Proverbs 15:1** fits most appropriately in the play "God is [my] help" (*Mulungu ndiye thandizo*) as a group of Christian women seek to counsel a fellow wife who is being mistreated by her husband. The problem is being made worse because she responds harshly in bitter words back at him after he has injured her. Soften his anger and evil behavior with a gentle reply, they advise, and see what happens. She does so, and this policy (plus prayer) works wonders for their marriage.

- **Ezekiel 3:18** is a crucial verse in the play "You should not be affected by these things" (*Inu zisamakhudzeni izi!*) which is quoted by a Christian lady who has accompanied the church chairman during a visit to their local pastor. They have come to complain over the fact that in his sermons he fails to speak out against polygamy because the village headman happens to be a polygamist. The pastor must not fail to reprove this practice, she warns, otherwise he will be guilty of the sin that is specified in this passage. God "will hold him (the pastor) accountable" for the polygamist's condemnation to hell if he does not repent and change his life. On the other hand, the pastor need not fear those in power, for God will protect him according to **Jeremiah 1:8**.

- **Ecclesiastes 8:8** is the passage that is used by a pastor who confronts a medicine man at the conclusion of the play "Ah, what a wonderful medicine man he is!" (*Uuh! Ndiyetu sing'anga uyu!*): The devious "doctor" is about to prescribe some magical potion to abort the unwanted child of the pastor's niece. The pastor persuades her not to go through with it and then confronts the medicine man with his sinful practice. No one must try to determine the "day of his death"—or the death of any human being, even an unborn child! Furthermore, "wicked actions cannot rescue wicked people"—i.e., the ungodly deeds of witchcraft will not save those who are committing a sin, in this case, attempting to kill this baby who has not wronged them in any way.

- **Mark 2:17** is uttered by a medicine man in his effort to convince a female client to obtain some protective "medicine" from him. He feels that the Bible, this passage in particular, gives him the authority and the ability to heal and help people according to the will of Christ. His practice, he claims, is specifically mentioned there—i.e., he is the *sing'anga* 'healer' that Jesus is referring to in this passage. He is thus the healer who is able to help all the "sinners" who come to him in their time of need. In this instance we see how the Scriptures may also be mis-used for nefarious purposes, and the *Sewero* group dramatizes such cases of religious "interference" as well.

- **1 Timothy 4:4-5** is utilized in a novel manner in a play about witchcraft ("Pray before you eat" *Muzipemphera musanadye!*) which dramatizes the story about some cattle thieves who have been caught and magically transformed into cows by the owner; they were later slaughtered and their flesh sold publicly as meat. This practice was subsequently exposed by a former medicine-man turned Christian and now a local evangelist. He cites this passage to encourage people to pray, seriously, before they eat—or even before they go to the market to buy food—asking that God would lead them to purchase and consume only the proper goods that are on sale there. A female parishioner on the scene of this concluding conversation adds a reference to **Mark 16:18** and claims that when Christians pray in the name of Jesus before eating, no harm will befall them even if they happen to consume some poisonous substance, or something that has been corrupted by witchcraft, as in the present case. This is certainly a creative application of the Markan passage, which is itself in dispute as to its textual validity.

- **Isaiah 54:17** is cited in the play "Freed from witchcraft" (*Kumasulidwa ku ufiti*) by a staunchly Christian woman, the chairlady of a certain village congregation, to refute the threats of a local healer. He had come to her husband, the congregation's lay minister, to try and persuade him to conduct a funeral service for his father, a pagan "witchdoctor", who has just died. She encourages her husband to refuse this request, thus provoking the young man's wrath and promise to kill her by means of his sorcery. "No weapon will succeed" against the Lord's "servants", she says, for God himself will protect them. She also employs **Mark 16:18** in support of her faith-stance.

- **Hosea 4:6** is applied by one of the relatives of a man who has divorced his faithful first wife in order to marry a younger woman (in "The evil of medicine [used in] polygamy" – *Kuipa kwa mankhwala a mitala*). In this instance, a general reference in the original text, i.e., to "the law of your God", is made pointedly specific in the play—that is, to rebuke the sin of divorce. Another relative gives a second instance of such a situationally specified, and locally contextualized, usage when he adds **2 Peter 2:20b** to the words of condemnation; thus the "second state" of the divorcer will turn out to be much "worse than the first".

- **Lamentations 5:16** is figuratively transformed by a lady school evangelist to refer to a female student who has become pregnant (in "What childishness!" – *Chibwanatu ichi!*). Thus the lost "crown" originally applied to the former honor and glory of the wicked city of Jerusalem is here applied to the "honor" of a woman's virginity, which has been foolishly lost. The girl, who was a professing Christian, should have "resisted the devil" in the form of sexual temptation according to the words of **James 4:7**. The girl's foster parents, on the other hand, should adopt the attitude of God towards all sinners and in this case "blot out" from their memory this great misdeed on the part of their daughter (**Isaiah 43:25**). Thus they are encouraged to continue to "do good" as they "sacrifice" (**James 13:16**) on behalf of this wayward girl whom they have adopted as their own. In this case we have the example of a closely linked *catena* of Scripture passages that are used in a particular dramatic situation to reveal God's will to one or more of the dramatis personae.

- **John 14:27** is given an unusual application in the play "A family [consists of] two [people]" (*Banja ndi awiri*). At the close of the drama, a childless Christian husband and wife console themselves with these words of Jesus concerning the special "peace" which he gives—a serenity that is so different from worldly peace. Thus even though they do not have children, which normally is a cause for warfare in families, they can still take comfort and courage in Christ's spiritual rest. They are led to this conclusion, along with the warning to avoid traditional magical charms, by a lady counselor who also encourages them further with the stories of Elkanah and Hannah (**1 Samuel 1**) and Zechariah and Elisabeth (**Luke 1**).

- **Psalm 127:1** is used by a pastor when counseling some wealthy parents who do not want to allow their daughter to marry the poor young man whom she loves ("Cast you worries upon God" – *Tulani nkhawa pa Mulungu*). It is God who "builds the house" of a believer's family, and one's parents should not interfere in this building process. On the other hand, the young woman is advised by the pastor not to get impatient because of her parents' opposition. Even though their "hearts were hardened" (like Pharaoh's) against her marriage, God will still allow his will to be done to deliver his people (**Exodus 14**). Her dreams, like those of Joseph in relation to his family (**Genesis 37**), will one day be fulfilled according to God's plan for her life, even though this may take some time. Like Joseph, she too must patiently await the Lord's time to do things.

- **2 Thessalonians 3:10-12** is summarized by some Christian women who have come to discipline a female member of their congregation, a lady who has been supporting her husband in using magic to steal the property of others at night ("You must not 'eat' [i.e., through the practice of sorcery] again" – *Musadyensotu inu!*). The use of witchcraft is not acceptable "work" in the eyes of God; instead, it is "meddling in the labor of others" by means of theft. God will punish such sinful behavior. Therefore, all Christians must work hard in order "to provide their own food to eat".

- **Revelation 22:14** becomes the basis for an analogy in which a pastor's wife compares the bus that she and her fellow passengers are traveling on to the Christian church which is taking believers on the road to their heavenly destination (in "Let us judge one another!" – *Tiyeni tiweruzane!*). All "passengers" must be wearing the proper clothes, however—that is, "robes that have been washed in the blood of the Lamb of God". A decision must be made, she urges, because death may come at any time, and then one must face "God's judgment" (**Hebrews 9:27**), which will indeed be serious for those whose "names have not been written in the book of life" (**Revelation 20:15**). On the other hand, God loves all people and has sent his Son to die for sinners and to prepare a place for the penitent in heaven (**John 14:2**). Christ's invitation is there for all the passengers to receive: "Come to me" (**Matthew 11:28**); when they trust in him and confess "that Jesus is Lord", they will be saved (**Romans 10:9**). Their sins will be washed away and they will become "as white as snow" before their heavenly Father (**Isaiah 1:18**). This was an impressive string of passages that the women put together in her biblical testimony to all the riders on that bus.

- **Jeremiah 33:3** is the reply of the same pastor's wife (see above) when a visiting parishioner asks where her husband is; he is praying and requesting that God reveal to him how he can deal with his troublesome congregation, for he is at a loss. When the visitor announces that a member has died and the pastor must come and bury him, his wife encourages him to take the opportunity to rebuke those in attendance for their sinful life-style; this death should be a warning to them! She then applies **2 Thessalonians 2:3** to the current situation: The time of their "deception" was over; the people were living in "rebellion". The pastor (her husband) had to take action now since these "lawless" folk needed to repent lest they face God's "destruction". She thus contextualizes a Pauline eschatological text and applies it to the present time and a local setting of church conflict.

- **John 8:44** is used by a pastor's wife to condemn the practices of a certain medicine man in the play "Wealth comes from God [alone]" (*Chuma chimachokera kwa Mulungu*). This "witchdoctor" is doing the works of "his father, the Devil" and they are nothing but "lies" and deceit. She and her husband, the pastor (who says very little), are in a heated conversation with the medicine man and a pair of his current clients, one of whom is a member of the pastor's congregation. The good lady then warns these young people that they are in danger of death according to **Isaiah 30:1** because they are making their plans to get rich "without consulting or consorting with God". In fact, God is the only "Helper" we need "in times of trouble" (**Psalm 46:1**). The work of the witchdoctor, Christ says (**John 10:10**), is that of a "thief"—

to "steal, kill, and destroy" God's work. In the present case, the "doctor" wanted to involve the couple in a sexual sin in order to get his magic to work, which was contrary to God's will as stated in **Exodus 20:14**. Only the word of Christ "is able to set them free" from such sin (**John 8:32**), and it can even liberate the medicine man from his bondage to Satan's works. Jesus is the only "way" to real "life" (**John 14:6**), but they must repent of their evil activities and trust in him alone for deliverance. In the end, the woman fails to convince the witchdoctor and the young man who wants to become wealthy through the way of wicked magic, but she does persuade his sister to reject that method and remain faithful to Christ.

4.4 To what extent are the *Sewero* plays "contextualized"?

In this section I will briefly discuss the popular missiological concept of "contextualization" as well as the anthropological distinctions of "high-context" and "low-context" socio-cultural settings in relation to the *Sewero* broadcasts. In the light of these notions, I will conclude with a few thoughts regarding the nature and purpose of this crucial process whereby these dramatic radio plays are contextualized, or localized, in terms of their theology and praxis.

4.4.1 What is "contextualization"?

In brief, to "contextualize" a biblical message is to communicate it via translation (with or without supplementary extra-textual helps), paraphrase, adaptation, recreation (as in a dramatized performance) or through some form of application (in the case of specific pericopes and passages) in such a way that it becomes more clear, meaningful, and relevant to a specific, envisioned audience (readership) in their current sociocultural environment and immediate religious circumstances. Whether or not they agree on the details of this rather broad definition, most Christian communicators undoubtedly affirm its overall importance to the worldwide mission of the Church, with particular reference now to ecclesiastical growth and development in Africa.

No text (that is, any meaningful combination of significant signs)—oral or written, verbal or nonverbal—ever occurs in isolation. It is always contextualized (modified in form, content, and/or function) to a greater or lesser extent by means of other texts. This essential process occurs both "intertextually" by means of other instances of oral and written communication, and also "extra-textually" due to the influence of the particular situational context and communication setting, or occasion, within which it takes place. This includes of course the medium of message transfer, for example, shortwave radio as distinct from a printed publication. These are important circumstantial factors that greatly complicate the process of human communication whereby a Source/Author interacts with his Receptors/Audience by means of a Text/Message. The relative degree of success (or failure) of any given attempt at textual transmission may be affected for better or for worse at any point along the way. For this reason, such features must all be carefully analyzed and assessed when planning and evaluating any enterprise that aims to achieve a greater measure of communicability with respect to a specific set of goals and objectives, for example, in terms of intelligibility, relevance, and utility in the case of the *Sewero* dramatic radio plays.

The great difficulty that one faces when trying to communicate by means of a written message alone concerns the relative amount of essential information that may be left unexpressed, that is, presupposed or "implicit", without serious loss to the intended message.

This "unwritten part" includes the things an author presumes the audience knows about how the world works, which he or she can leave between the lines of a text, so to speak, yet which are crucial to its understanding (Malina & Rohrbaugh 1992:9).

Not only "how the world works" must be taken into consideration, but more important perhaps is how a particular society "thinks" and "feels", that is, its so-called "world-view" (beliefs, assumptions, values, desires, fears, felt needs, etc). On the one hand, a speaker or writer cannot state overtly, or "explicitly", everything of possible significance in and to his/her message, for such a mass of detail would undoubtedly leave the target group confused, frustrated, or just plain bored with it all. It would probably also prove far too expensive to publish or broadcast such a composition. On the other hand, if s/he leaves too much essential information implicit, it is highly likely that readers or hearers will either not fully understand what is being said, or they will simply give up on the message as being too difficult to carry on with.

The key is to achieve a relative *balance*—that is, allowing enough implicit material to challenge the audience and to encourage them to play a participatory role in the process of conceptualizing the message—yet also including a sufficient amount of explicit detail to keep the communication moving smoothly along from point to point, event to event, or scene to scene. Not everything needs to be said for adequate communication to take place. To a greater or lesser degree the intended receptors normally participate in a common cognitive, sociocultural, experiential-sensory world and a relatively familiar literary framework that enables them to "read/listen between the lines" of any verbal discourse and supply the required background information for a correct interpretation of the message to occur.

One way of describing this vital conceptualizing process is the so-called "scenario model" of communication:

> We understand a written [and presumably also an oral] text as setting forth a succession of implicit and explicit mental pictures consisting of culturally specific scenes or schemes sketched by an author. These in turn evoke corresponding scenes or schemes in the mind of the reader [hearer] that are drawn from the reader's own experience in the culture. With the scenarios suggested by the author as a starting point, the reader then carries out appropriate alterations to the settings or episodes as directed by clues in the text. In this way an author begins with the familiar and directs the reader to what is new (Malina & Rohrbaugh 1992:10).

This interpretive model is rather oversimplified in that it appears to be formulated in favor a straightforward narrative-type discourse and thus ignores other possible interpretive strategies, such as dialogic drama or the use of certain "logical" or analogical patterns of hortatory text development that vary in accordance with extant genres of accepted oral or written argumentation. Furthermore, we frequently find associated with such visual "scenarios" various verbal-based "scripts" which model, outline, or summarize conventionalized discourses appropriate to particular cultural settings and social situations (e.g., a typical revival "sermon" and subsequent "altar call", a "testimony" of deliverance, or an evangelism "witness" talk). Thus the briefest textual mention or allusion to familiar occasions like these can conceptually "trigger", or cue, for listeners most of the details that they need to know in order to interpret the utterance in which they are embedded. Problems quickly develop, however, when receptors do not have such a cognitive reservoir of common experience or shared instruction pertaining to events that are characteristic of the culture and society concerned. This inevitably happens in the case of the Scriptures, where the intended message must cross the additional communication barriers of language, space and time.

4.4.2 "High context" versus "low context" societies

Another important factor for consideration and possible action during the communication process is the distinction between what Malina and Rohrbaugh (following Robert Hall) term "high-context" and "low-context" societies. High-context peoples tend to presuppose a great deal more of the situational setting in their oral and written discourse (the latter being much rarer in occurrence). A relatively large amount of information is normally left implicit in the text—material that is expected to be accessed on the basis of common experience or which is conveyed either para-linguistically (e.g., by intonation) or non-verbally in a dramatized oral presentation (the communicative norm, e.g., gesticulation, facial expressions, etc.).

> Thus, writers in such societies usually produce sketchy and impressionistic texts, leaving much to the reader's or hearer's imagination. They

encode much information in widely known symbolic or stereotypical statements. In this way, they require the reader to fill in large gaps in the unwritten portion of the text (1992:11).

The ancient Mediterranean (biblical) world, like most parts of Africa today, was characterized by high-context societies, and this fact is reflected in the literature of the age, narrative in particular, such as we have in Genesis or the four gospels. Thus, only the major details of a given episode are usually provided in the text, with very little extended explanation or supplementary description of characters, scenes, settings, and situations.

In contrast, much of the Western world consists of societies that are "low-context" in nature. This means that writers, narrative authors in particular, tend to produce very detailed texts that require relatively little of readers to supply by way of background information. Therefore, when an author knows that he will be dealing with a subject that is new or unfamiliar to his audience, he will make explicit in his text all the supplementary content that is needed to correctly understand it. A serious problem may develop, however, when modern Western readers encounter a document such as the Bible that was initially composed for a high-context audience. They often assume that the written form itself includes all the information needed for its own interpretation, like the literature that they are used to. They then proceed to construe this text from the perspective of their own built-in world-view, value system, and way of life, which is very different indeed from that implicitly encoded by the biblical authors.

African hearers and readers, on the other hand, not only exemplify cultures that are much closer to those of the Bible (especially Jewish society), but they also prefer to communicate for the most part in a "high-context" manner. However, a number of significant differences in respective ethos and outlook remain (e.g., with regard to the nature of "God" or the vast unseen spiritual "world" of existence and its relationship to the land of the living). Hence, not recognizing many of the pertinent signals in the biblical (translated) text that establish the intended cultural context, and lacking the explanatory resources necessary for understanding these variations and discrepancies, local receptors, a listening audience in particular, may misunderstand or misinterpret the text of Scripture on the basis of their own conceptual and behavioral framework.

Generally speaking, based on their overall consistency, quality, and reliability of performance, the *Sewero* team is an excellent group of vernacular communicators. They are able to adapt, or contextualize, their dramas to fit a wide variety of contemporary venues and life situations in Malawi, traditional and modern, rural and urban. They depend on the fact that their listeners, as members of a typical "high-context" culture, will be largely familiar

141

with these different local settings and interpersonal circumstances and will not expect a great deal of description, exposition, explanation, or illustration. Therefore, the players do not expend many words to "set the scene" by providing such supplementary background information. Neither is there an external "narrator" to serve this common narrative function. The necessary dramatic set is assumed to exist complete and ready-made in the minds of the audience. A typical play thus tends to move straight to the verbal action of the plot dialogue and the "message", or thematic point, develops more or less directly out of that—more often than not, with great success (based on the individual and group evaluation of both pastoral as well as lay listeners).

However, if there is any criticism to be noted or a suggestion to be offered (see section 7.2), it lies on the other side of the overall communicative context, namely, that which pertains to the biblical text(s) that serve as a foundation for the "moral" or teaching of a given play. Thus when the players cite a certain Scripture passage during the resolution portion of a particular drama, they seem to assume that not only that it is (well) known to the radio audience, but also correctly understood in relation to its textual context as well. I suspect that such an assumption cannot always be taken for granted and that often a bit of biblical "contextualizing" might prove to be helpful to make the relevant moral (rarely doctrinal) point clear(er) for the average listener. Further testing with various audiences is needed, however, to substantiate or to disprove this hypothesis. Of course, one cannot go overboard in the provision of such supplementary material either, lest a play become "dogmatized" and turn out to sound like a multi-voiced radio Sunday school lesson or Bible study. But it may be that some pertinent, unobtrusive, concisely and naturally expressed background information could go a long way to point listeners in a reliable hermeneutical direction, thus rendering any given drama that much more instructive in terms of Scripture knowledge enrichment and more insightful with respect to a personal life application.

4.4.3 Conclusion: An ideological evaluation of the Sewero dramas

The term "ideology" refers to the specific set of doctrines, ideals, values, and beliefs that are consciously held by a particular group of people in society or even the society as a whole and passed on to others, either formally (e.g., though a class of religious instruction) or informally (e.g., by observing the typical words and actions of members of the group). A variety of general and specific ideologies tend to co-occur, complement, or conflict with each other in any large community, some being more widespread, influential, and strongly held or controversial than others (e.g., cultural, political, religious, ecclesiastical—even economic or art/craft-related). Religion then, at least in its cognitive dimension, is one ideology among others, and, as noted earlier, in Africa it is normally predominant. In Africa too, the ideology of religion tends to be more accommodative than in other parts of the world; in other words, one set of religious beliefs and practices (rites) may happily coexist or even merge with a completely different set, with each being applied or activated either as a mixture (syncretism) or else with specific reference to a particular sociocultural setting or need. This is the great challenge that Christianity, with all its popularity, faces in Africa: how far can biblical faith be modified before it becomes crippled or fatally compromised?

The *Sewero* group carefully explores such issues of custom and culture in their plays. What is the acceptable, Scripturally-defensible, relationship between tradition and theology, between contemporary context and biblical content? Any ideology, if sincerely believed and adhered to, needs to be effectively presented, justified, and defended. That is what these dramas endeavor to do—not in the form of a discursive, logically reasoned treatise or even a powerfully preached hortatory sermon—but artistically in traditional narrative fashion in the form of a multi-person performance. But an "apologetic" defense is put forward, none-the-less, one that is forcefully and uncompromisingly argued. But the ideology, let alone the practice, of "Christianity", is very diverse throughout the world; there are so many different brands and clones with regard to "denomination". Where do the *Sewero* plays stand in this respect, and how strongly, or polemically, is any particular ecclesiastical heritage or background expressed? These two issues—the theology and praxis of *Sewero* drama—are briefly described and evaluated below, in anticipation of a fuller discussion and exemplification in chapter seven.

4.4.3.1 Theologically conservative and selective

My comments here must not be considered to be a definitive theological characterization or assessment of these *Sewero* performances. These observations merely summarize my own subjective perspective on the corpus that I have selected for special consideration, which may not adequately reflect the majority or the norm of all *Sewero* programs that have ever been broadcast on TWR. What "brand" of Christian doctrine seems to be most prevalent in the complete plays and specific examples that have been examined? How thoroughly are the basic tenets of biblical theology covered? Which key teachings are not represented, and is there any possible reason for this? Do any significant departures from a "mainstream" Protestant perspective manifest themselves at one time or another? These and similar questions

143

certainly need to be investigated to a fuller degree than I have time for in this introductory study of the *Sewero* group. What follows will hopefully encourage greater efforts toward this end.

I will summarize first of all the fundamental set of beliefs that governs all programming on TWR (see Appendix B for the detailed confessional statement).

- The Trinity of the Deity—Father, Son, and Holy Spirit—three coequal persons but one God.

- The verbal and plenary inspiration of an infallible, inerrant, and authoritative Holy Scriptures.

- The incarnation, virgin birth, sinless nature, vicarious atonement, resurrection, glorification, and second coming of the Son of God, the Lord Jesus Christ.

- The divine personality of the Holy Spirit, who regenerates, indwells, preserves, and guides all believers in faith and life.

- The cause of original sin leading to a complete corruption of human nature which results in the total condemnation of all people.

- Salvation as a gift of God by grace through faith in the redemptive work of Christ.

- The bodily resurrection of all people—the righteous to eternal life, the wicked to eternal punishment.

- The presence with Christ of the souls of all believers while they await the resurrection of their bodies.

- The spiritual, universal nature of the Church universal, which is composed of all the redeemed and regenerated, no matter what visible local church they may belong to.

- The obligation of believers, as members of the Body of Christ, to promote fellowship, edification, and the world-wide propagation of the Gospel of Jesus Christ.

This listing of chief teachings would no doubt be acceptable to most, if not all, church members who would consider themselves to belong to the "evangelical" side of the denominational divide. However, it may be observed that certain potentially contentious doctrines are largely avoided, for example, regarding the nature and purpose of the so-called "sacraments" (i.e., Baptism and the Lord's Supper), the function of the "Law" of God, the nature and timing of the "millennium", the operation of personal faith versus divine sovereignty in conversion, and so forth. There are occasional lapses, in my opinion, when a certain character exhorts or advises concerning some issue that may be debated, especially when the subject matter touches upon eschatology and some apocalyptic passage or another (e.g., in Ezekiel or

Revelation). But for the most part, such potential controversies are avoided, thanks to the guidance and oversight of the experienced production editors of the *Sewero* program (see 2.3).

It must also be said that most of the other major evangelical doctrines do not receive much attention in the *Sewero* corpus at my disposal, with two general exceptions. The first concerns God's moral Law, that is, various aspects of the Ten Commandments that happen to be violated and subsequently corrected in certain dramas, especially the 6/7th concerning adultery. The second principal biblical teaching that is emphasized is the need for personal repentance and a public confession of one's gross sins, coupled with a call for faith in the Jesus the Savior in order to receive forgiveness and the assurance of salvation. This second dimension of instruction and exhortation normally comes towards the close of a given play, when the previously dramatized "problem" is resolved in one way or another, usually with a positive outcome (i.e., blessing), but often enough too with an unhappy, even tragic conclusion (i.e., punishment, sometimes death). Other doctrines come into prominence only occasionally (e.g., one play that featured a preacher who was promoting an obvious aberration of the Trinity), if at all, because that is not the program's main area of emphasis, which is more pragmatic in nature. It thus deals mainly with "practical" theology—that is, Christianity (the basic precepts of which are presupposed) as it is lived in conflict with traditional beliefs and practices on the one hand and many modern temptations to licentious living on the other.

4.4.3.2 Pragmatically radical and comprehensive

If doctrinal theology is treated lightly in the *Sewero* corpus, practical theology is applied very pointedly and persuasively, especially with regard to the principal besetting sins of contemporary society, including the prevalent syncretistic tendency to retain a "fail-safe" sort of adherence to African traditional religious beliefs and practices. The earlier overview of ATR (4.2) would suggest that, as in the case of any of the world's "natural" or indigenous belief systems, there are a number of critical foundational features that do not jibe with a biblical world-view and way-of-life. This deep conceptual contradiction and conflict may be overt and obvious, but all too often it lies covert and unrecognized or is merely ignored by many present-day, "fair-weather" believers and churches.

This is the root problem that confronts the Church in general in Africa: Despite the prevalence and widespread influence of Christianity, in the southern regions at least, ATR is not dead or even dying at all. In the mainline and offline (AIC) churches as well, the deep-seated religious ideology of the ancients has all too often simply gone "underground" or out of sight, sometimes just barely so. Then, when the difficulties and dilemmas of everyday life arise, so do the traditional religious practitioners and their standard solutions. The result is that for many nominal "Christians" the unwritten framework of ATR forms an essential and integral part of their normal thought processes and behavioral responses.

There are various strategies and degrees of engagement possible for churches to adopt when dealing with this crisis, as suggested on the following continuum of choice:

Standard policy of the church with respect to ATR

denial – avoidance – compartmentalization – *confrontation* – accommodation – syncretism

◀ == ▶

While "denial" was often the policy of many older missionary dominated churches, "syncretism" is the standard procedure for the adherents of many contemporary AICs (African Independent Churches). This is not an evaluation or condemnation of the genuineness or quality of their faith; it is simply my evaluation of their primary stance vis-à-vis ATR.[14] In contrast to both of these extremes (and everything else in-between), I would describe the dominant strategy of the *Sewero* program as being strongly within the area of "confrontation". Whereas many well-known, well-attended churches prefer to "avoid" the salient issues concerned, the *Sewero* dramatists vigorously and explicitly oppose such indigenous, anti-Scriptural interpretations and customs, as noted above and exemplified further in chapter six.

This policy of open "confrontation" may also be described as being "apologetic", even polemic" in nature. "Apologetics" has to do with providing a reasoned, systematic, biblical defense of the Christian faith against any false religion, whether its teachings or its practices, while "polemics" adds the dynamic component of creating a confrontation in the process, one that often involves a controversial sort of public engagement. Such a no-holds-barred, no-compromise policy revives a Christian theological discipline that has fallen on hard times in recent years, particularly in the present age of "postmodernism", which much prefers to take the easy way out by promot-

---

[14]   My conclusions here are based on periodic primary research projects carried out by my seminary students over the past 20 years. For one semester they are each given the assignment to investigate the teachings and practices of a single AIC in the Lusaka area. They interview church leaders as well as ordinary members and attend at least one worship service. They must finally write up their findings in a detailed report. I therefore have quite a body of such independent "case studies" to refer to.

ing the laissez-faire approach of "accommodation" with regard to virtually all controversial issues, no matter how important or diametrically opposed to biblical theology.

The producers and players of the *Sewero* programs clearly recognize the critical conflict that most African Christians experience when living out their faith in cases where a life-changing choice must be made (which is also contrary to conventional Bantu ideology, see 3.1.1). They thus seek to utilize their creative artistic expertise and practical theological insights to deal with such challenges, trials, and difficulties head-on. How do these emotively-charged, experience-based plays confront the chief areas of dispute involving cultural and religious "interference" or outright contradiction? They choose to polemically engage the traditional religious system through the "drama" of participation, that is, capturing the audience through a down-to-earth, life-like performance to sense a vicarious personal involvement in a play's plot, one that usually deals with some familiar everyday topic or local situation. The goal is to get listeners to empathize and adopt a more biblical perspective with respect to this fictitious crisis or problem by means of direct reference to selected passages of Scripture. The hope is that they will then be in a better position to apply the recommended solution realistically to similar issues of conflict or controversy that occur in their own lives. This is a "natural", narrative-oriented, inductive method, much like that of their own oral didactic tradition, which is therefore highly effective from both a rhetorical as well as a religious perspective.

We will take a closer look at this imaginative strategy of dramatic biblical engagement in the next two chapters, first from the standpoint of its inventory of key artistic techniques (ch.5) and then from the perspective of a complete *Sewero* example, given in an liberally annotated translation (ch.6).

5. The Dynamic Stylistic-Rhetorical Features of *Sewero* Drama

5.0 Style and rhetoric

From the preceding overview of the subject matter, or content, of the *Sewero* dramas (chapter 4), we turn now to a consideration of their dramatic form or "style". *Style* may be generally defined as a characteristic way of *doing* something (see Wendland 1979:ch.3 2000:ch.3). With reference to an oral or written verbal composition, style refers to a particular method or manner of speaking or writing, whether this happens to be typical or distinctive (extraordinary) in relation to some comparable corpus of texts. In other words, the technique of formulating a given oral or written discourse, that is, with regard to the whole work or any of its parts, may be analyzed as being either common or conventional in terms of the norms of that language; alternatively, it may be characteristic of a certain author in one or more definable respects. The same principle applies to a certain text that is transmitted by means of a different medium of communication; there will always be at least some important differences in the composition due to the influence of the channel that is used to convey it. As was pointed out in chapter 2, the *Sewero* group pays careful attention to the radio broadcasting medium when presenting their dramas for their invisible and widely dispersed audience of the air.

After a description and exemplification of seven principal forms or techniques typically used when composing these plays, I will briefly discuss their performative *function*—that is, the so-called "rhetoric" of these *Sewero* performances. *Rhetoric* deals with the communicative dimension of oral or literary composition, the aspect of *persuasion* in particular. In other words, how do the prominent formal and semantic features that have been identified for a certain *Sewero* play, for example, pertain to the general and specific pragmatic goals of this radio program. Such communicative features become especially evident in face-to-face dialogic interaction (character conversation). In the case of our *Sewero* corpus, on the other hand, the actual oral/aural performance is both restricted and unrestrained. Thus there is no live, interactive audience to perform in front of or get feedback from, whether critical or supportive. Instead, the story must be dramatized using only the imagination-stimulating and evoking medium (vocal "stage") of radio. This makes any attempt to identify functions and goals a rather hypothetical exercise. Nevertheless, I will offer a few observations in this respect simply to stimulate those who may wish to explore this important subject further in relation to the different media and modes of message transmission that are available for Christian communication outreach in Africa.

5.1 Aspects of stylistic form

Why do thousands of listeners continue to tune into the *Sewero* program on a weekly, monthly, even yearly basis? In other words, what is it about the verbal style of these radio plays that so strongly attracts listeners and keeps them coming back for more? In this chapter I describe seven overlapping and interrelated stylistic devices that seem especially characteristic of these Chinyanja plays: *idiomatic dialogue, rhetorical vigor, local color, dramatic action, emotive realism, subdued humor,* and *audio effects.* This inventory of typical techniques is of course rather arbitrary, for the corpus could have been categorized and analyzed quite differently. Even though interaction is the norm in their operation within a given drama, I am treating them separately here in order to highlight the distinctive impact and appeal of each particular feature.

After a summary description of one of these primary devices, I illustrate it by means of an annotated representative selection from a particular *Sewero* drama, especially one of those that focus upon the religious occult. I have usually chosen to employ a few longer examples for this purpose rather than many smaller ones so that a better overall contextual impression of the team's dramatic art might be conveyed. Thus each distinctive feature is exemplified by means of a different passage, taken from another play in order to demonstrate the diversity of usage that the entire corpus manifests as well as the unifying force that each technique contributes to a complete drama. These excerpts are cited in English, which obviously dulls the original effect a great deal; however, certain key terms and idiomatic vernacular expressions are supplied for reference in parentheses, both to add a little spice to the presentation and to serve as an original reference point for readers who do happen to understand Chinyanja. These stylistic devices constitute the overall norm for the *Sewero* plays that I have collected. Within the corpus as a whole there are of course instances of unevenness in quality, and occasionally some lackluster passages do occur. But my observation of several actual live audiences indicates that most if not all vernacular listeners are genuinely impressed, even amazed, by the virtuosity and the consistently high quality of these dynamic radio performances.

5.1.1 Idiomatic dialogue

This is perhaps the most prominent and exceptional of the primary *Sewero* stylistic characteristics. All plays feature a sequence of exceptionally vibrant, yet also remarkably natural (that is, colloquially expressed) conversations, including occasional soliloquies by the chief characters. A given play therefore consists entirely of direct discourse, thus clearly making this the most prominent stylistic and rhetorical technique in terms of its potential for conveying not only semantic "meaning", but also pragmatic significance, such as psychological mood, connotation, attitude, emotion, empathy, impact, and appeal. There is little, if any, use of a third-person "narrator", except for the external producer/announcer who introduces and closes each group performance. A play's dialogue sequence is normally segmented by some extra-narrative device (e.g., music, drumming, a song verse) into a variable number of "scenes", usually about 5-7 in number which constitute the drama as a whole.

This character speech is not only colloquial in quality, it is also highly "dramatic" discourse (see 5.1.7), for the skilled *Sewero* radio performers are able to re-produce a veritable life-like verbal interaction and to ad-lib appropriately on the spot in such a way as to preserve a complete illusion of sociocultural realism (see 5.1.4). Their effective use of imitative intonation patterns and varied paralinguistic modification manifests a range of conversational styles that is extremely diverse when viewed in relation to the small size of the regular corps of performers, for example: drunken slurs, sickness-weakened voicing (including the appropriate coughs and wheezes), deep mourning (with sorrowful weeping and a grief-stricken tone), the laughter of rejoicing or ridicule, the panting of advanced old age, the vitality of youth, the simplicity of child speakers, and so forth.

The *Sewero* dialogues present the typical speech patterns of a variety of characters as naturally and idiomatically as if they were being recorded in the towns and villages of Malawi today. To be sure, not every possible ethnic, social, or regional dialect is represented, but enough diversity is included from one play to the next to stimulate a credible impression of verisimilitude. It is very difficult, if not impossible, however, to verbally describe or represent in writing the many different facets and the full dramatic force of this outstanding vernacular characteristic. This is especially true with respect to the many different paralinguistic features that are normally manifested, such as: vocal pitch, stress, volume, tempo, length, special modification (e.g., a high "head voice", guttural grunts, an overtone of weeping—or laughter, anger, frustration, excitement, etc.). In order to fully appreciate this stylistic feature, therefore, one must be able to actually hear—and understand—the text in the original Chinyanja. The best I can do at present is to cite the following extended example as it is artfully and persuasively represented in the play entitled "The evil of enrichment magic" (*Za kuipa kwa mankhwala olemeretsa*), a portion of which is set out below:

(Setting: A man recently went to visit his rural friend to ask him how he has managed to become so wealthy. He has been advised to carry out certain magical procedures that will enable him too to prosper. In this scene then the man is explaining to his eager wife what he has learned and what they too need to do in order to duplicate their friend's example of good fortune [M = the man, W = his wife].)

M: He-he-he-he! (excited laughter), iiiih! (exclamation of wonder)[1] Really, my wife...Oo-ooh, iih! (more excitement), let's go into the house.
W: What's up? (*Bwanji?* 'How?')
M: Eh, let's first get into the house. Then after we have entered (I'll let you know what I have to tell you)—ha ha haa! (laughter)
W: Now you are really rejoicing (*mwasangalalatu*) E-eeh! (exclamation of surprise)
M: Right here and now I'm so very happy! (*chimwemwe chidzala tsaya* 'joy has filled up my cheek' – an emphatic idiom)
W: What is it then?! (*Bwanji nanga?!* 'how now'— spoken with a bit of skepticism)
M: There is—there is something to tell (*Chilipo, chilipo*)! But let's wait till we get inside (i.e., for the sake of secrecy—one never knows who may be listening on the outside!).
W: Now you are making me rejoice! (i.e., your joy is infectious)
M: Ah-ya-ya-ya-ya! Mmmm! (amazement, i.e., over what he has been told)
W: Well, how about letting me know then?! (*Ayi, timvetu nanga!*)
M: Iiih! (exclamation of amazement) My wife, I went to that friend of mine... [she interrupts him]
W: Alright (i.e., go on with your story).
M: I went to pay him a visit (ndidakawayendera).
W: Oh, that friend of yours [who lives] up on the hill? (note the specific detail)
M: [Yes], that very wealthy fellow.
W: Eeh, carry on...

---

[1] I will observe the following conventions when citing such translated excerpts, both here and in future: Material in (*parentheses*) is either explanatory or it cites the original Chinyanja expression and its literal translation, given in single quote marks. English loanwords found in the Chinyanja text and reproduced in the translation will also appear in single quotes. Material in [*brackets*] is directly implied by what is being said in the vernacular; it is therefore required to give a more complete sense to what has been said. Three periods indicate a pause or interruption in an utterance.

I will try also to give an approximate semantic value or connotative (emotive) implication for each of the many *interjections* (conveying deeply personal attitudes) or *exclamations* (emotions) that are heard in idiomatic discourse. These short, non-dictionary, but vitally important expressions are a stock in trade of normal Chinyanja oral dramatic discourse, artistic and/or rhetorical. They may be spelled the same (my representations are only rough approximations, not phonetic transcriptions), but they often have a different intonation—hence a different implication, as suggested by the immediately following words in parentheses. It is quite probable that a number of these mini-words were missed out during the process of transcribing the *Sewero* radio recordings, especially in cases where the audio quality was poor.

M: I-ih! [I'm telling] you! (*Iiinuu!* – i.e., an emphatic pronoun represents a complete predication)

W: Eeeh? (what?)

M: If we are foolish… (*tikapusa*, i.e., if we don't seize this opportunity)

W: Completely so… (*Mpaka pamenepo* – lit. 'right up to that very point').

M: I found him, I mean my good buddy (*ayise*), sorry! (*pepa* – rhetorically meaning just the opposite here, I have news of such great importance to tell you).[2]

W: O.K.

M: [You know how] I have tried this and that (*apa ndi apa*) to become wealthy…

W: Hmmm (i.e., yes, I know).

M: …so that I might reach the point where he is at (*kuti ndifike monga pamene adafika iyepa*'). But it's been difficult for me. I've even gone and slept at the graveyard [already].[3]

W: Eeeh! M-mm! (i.e., that's correct, with a bit of a laugh)

M: I've tried this and that, this and that—to arrive there (i.e., to get rich). Don't you laugh now!

W: Yes, I'm listening.

M: Because this matter is very problematic (*ndi yovuta imeneyi*)—so you better not laugh!

W: O.K. Keep going…

M: What sort of impudence (*chibwana*) is this—you'd better listen, c'mon now![4]

W: Yes, I'm listening [now]. (i.e., she is more serious in tone)

M: So he began by telling me, "Aah! (a negative assessment), to be quite honest, when you went to sleep out there at the graveyard, and to do all those other things, you were just troubling yourself [for nothing] (*mumavutika*)!"[5] But now if you want to get rich, just look at my example. I am going to tell you the [proper] way [to prosper].

W: Eeeh! (affirmation)

M: That is, he mentioned three ways…

W: Alright![6]

M: But [first] it's important to take courage (*kulimba mtima* 'to be strong in the heart'),[7] but there are also some other things…

---

[2] The man's discourse is rather redundant due to his excitement. Such natural speech patterns might have been edited out of a Western oriented production. But they are uttered, and retained, in the *Sewero* plays because this is dialogue as it is actually spoken by everyday folk, who are the ones being characterized.

[3] A common "get-rich" scheme stipulated by medicine men is for their clients to "empower themselves" magically by so sleeping among the dead (spirits).

[4] This is a rather humorous exchange (except from the man's perspective). He has obviously tried to "sell" his wife on his "get-rich" schemes in the past—but they have all failed to produce anything for them.

[5] To underscore his past failures, the man actually quotes what this new medicine man, his "friend", told him. Cited speech is always more impressive in support of one's argument. One "doctor" often tries to depreciate the competence and results of his/her competitors.

[6] The wife keeps interrupting her husband in her eagerness to find out the "secret" he wishes to reveal to her.

[7] This is a typical requirement pronounced by a medicine man because it gives him a ready excuse should his magic fail to perform. In such cases he can simply tell his disappointed client(s) that they did not manifest enough "courage" when carrying out his characteristically bizarre and disgusting instructions.

W: Tell me—let me hear it! Just tell me, husband (*bambo*)! (i.e., she too is getting excited now)

M: He-he-heeh! (i.e., laughing at her excitement and happy at his anticipated good fortune)

W: Just tell me!

M: "So my friend says (i.e., he is quoting his sorcerer instructor now), "If you want to get rich so that you possess maize grinding mills and motor cars and 'restaurants' (i.e., eating places)—it's not difficult at all. Just do this...[8]

W: Eeh!

M: He mentioned three things... (i.e., repetition to playfully heighten the rising expectation of his wife)

W: Alright!

M: The first requirement (*mfundo*), he said, [is that] you and I must fully agree (i.e., with the plan and its specified details), so that when you are like that (*otere* – i.e., a euphemism for being pregnant), when you are expecting (*woyembekezera* – a more direct reference now, but a calque), we will really try [to do what is necessary] (*tidzachite moyesa* 'we will do by trying'). So that means to get rid of it (*choncho ndiye n'kuchotsa* i.e., to have an abortion).

W: A-aaah! (shock) What are you saying we must do?! (*Ndiye titani?!*)

M: Aaah! (frustration with her hesitancy) You, you—to get rich, to get rich! (i.e., he tries to encourage her) You won't have to do any more farming (*sudzalimansotu* i.e., manual labor [a metonym], in order to earn a living).

W: Don't start that [subject] now! (*Musayambepotu* – i.e., she suspect that he is about to get her involved more deeply in the practice of witchcraft, which as it turns out is very true.)

M: You won't have to farm [anymore]!

W: That is some hard work (*Ndi nchitotu imeneyiyi*)!

M: A-aah! (agreement)

W: You well know that you used me to sleep at the graveyard there (i.e., so you could get rich)! Another time you gave me a charm to wash clean with some [magical] potion—'daily' (*deyli*) at a cross roads (*pa mphambano*)![9] And there's not a thing that I gained by doing that!

M: So I'm saying... (he is interrupted by her)

W: And so (i.e., despite all our past efforts) right up till today the shoes that I have to wear everyday are made of 'plastic', and I own just a single torn up cloth for wearing [publicly] (*kachitenje kamodzi kong'ambikang'ambika* i.e., no doubt spoken with some hyperbole here)!

M: [But] today is our day for rejoicing! (i.e., with just as much hyperbole on his side)

W: Aah! (i.e., doubtful) All this has been just too tiring for me (lit. 'you' – *Inutu, n'zolemetsa zimenezi*)!

M: Just let me tell you that today we're in luck because I've found the way! Those other methods were just useless (*mpadera*)—but [now I have] the real way for getting rich! (*Koma njira yeniyeni yolemera* – an exclamatory verbless predication)

---

[8] Three popular examples of local prosperity—pluralized—are mentioned here. The implication is that he would be very rich indeed, well above the norm for being considered "wealthy" in fact.

[9] Any place where roads or paths cross is believed to be particularly potent or active with magical forces and spiritual powers since so many people happen to step there during their travels.

W: So now you [really] know?! (i.e., she is a bit skeptical now, having recalled all their past failures)

M: How can you say that—ooh! (exclamation of reproof)

W: Well, let me hear it then! Anyway, you mentioned three ways, so tell me the others now. Yes, just tell me! (i.e., the repetition and tone of her voice indicates her impatience)

M: I've heard (*ndinakaona* lit. 'seen') some awful things (i.e., to make the magic work)!

W: Eeh (yes), tell me.

M: So when we have taken out that energizing agent (*mochotsa chizimba* – i.e., done the abortion)...[10]

W: Yes...

M: ...the second way then is that I must sleep either with my sister or my mother—I must choose [which one]![11]

W: Well, do you think that they'll agree?

M: Aah! (i.e., confidence) Nowadays they can agree, 'darling' (*ada* – a colloquialism)!

W: Ooooh! (with considerable doubt)

M: Nowadays it's the money (i.e., that the soon-to-be wealthy person will bribe them with).

W: Alright, carry on!

M: All I must say is, "You'll be the 'cashier' (i.e., the person who manages all the newly gained wealth)!"—no, she won't refuse.

W: You think so (*eti*)?

M: Yaah! (correct) Now the last way...is perhaps for you to go and...like to finish [things] off (*kukonza*)...perhaps that you kill your younger sister, the young girl![12]

W: My own sister?!

M: The one who draws water for you (*amakutungira madzi*).[13]

W: Who will go and draw water for me then?!

M: Aaah! (disappointed at her protest)

W: Because that one is the one whom I depend on, I do!

M: So what can you suggest instead , ah! tell me (*M'malo mwake, aah, iwe!*)? We'll just go and kill her, that younger sister of yours—then I will hire a servant (i.e., to replace her)—to draw water, to [go to] the maize mill... You will simply relax and take your ease (*muzidzangokhala phee!* – an ideophone)!!

W: Eeeh? (is that so?)

M: Everything!

W: So will it really happen (i.e., that this will make us rich)—tell me!

---

[10] The 'energizing agent' (*chizimba*) is a certain object to be acquired or some action to be performed that is very problematic in nature, often because it conflicts with cultural norms or social mores either to handle or to carry out. In this case, it is to cause the abortion of one's own child (a metomymic usage here as a euphemism). But if this is not done according to specification, the magic will not operate correctly; in fact, it normally backfires, with dire results for the intended user, e.g., injury, madness, even death.

[11] This is a very familiar condition for success (*chizimba*) since it involves such a gross taboo; the murder of a family member or close relative is also common.

[12] This requirement is so terrible that the husband cannot tell his wife directly—he hems and haws and finally refers to the victim using traditional honorific terms.

[13] This must be a younger sister who, in accordance with custom, is living with her older sister to learn how to manage a household by helping out with the domestic duties. Hence the wife's next question.

M: Yes, there's no other way. So now you have to choose (i.e., whether you are willing to go through with this plan)!

W: Oooh? (is that so?)

M: This method will make us rich, [but] you must choose. This is the only way to get rich!

W: Oooh? (is that so?)

M: Do you promise (i.e., to go through with it)?

W: Well, I am tired of wearing these rags (*nsanzazi*)![14]

M: Yaah! (that's right)

W: Alright, I agree.

M: You will be wearing [real] shoes—and many other things as well!

W: You're telling me (*Inuu*), I am [now] ashamed when I visit my friends.

M: And so this is what we're going to do, right?

W: Indeed (*eti*)!

M: It's settled then (*basi*)!

W: Well, if it's possible, alright, I do agree.

M: Just do those very things (*Chita, zimenezozo*)!

W: I fully agree.

M: I praise the Lord (*Ambuye*) that [he has allowed] us to know this way (i.e., to get rich).

W: Yes, it's so true—he's a God of mercy (*Mulungudi wachifundo*)![15]

M: Aah! (with mock wonder)—he's a God of peace![16]

W: You said it (*Ndipo inu*)!

M: May he be praised (*Alemekezeke*)!

W: You are so right (*Ah, zedi*)!

M: So how about giving some water for me to drink? (i.e., he's thirsty after speaking so many words to try and persuade her!)

W: Ah, you just sit right down here—not just mere water, I've prepared some 'tea'!

M: Eeh (yes), that's what I really need! (The scene comes to an end here.)

The dialogue of a typical *Sewero* play turns out to sound so smoothly articulated because it is completely spontaneous, not scripted at all. These experienced players "imagine themselves" deeply into the psyche and personal circumstances of the individual characters whom they are representing and converse just as if they had taken their place in actual time and in a particular dramatic situation. A story's dialogue is thus extremely convincing and captivating, as the preceding example would suggest. The characters' utterances readily evoke a scenario that the radio audience can easily visualize and identify with, especially when some sort of tension or strong feeling is involved. No manner of speech act, rhetorical motivation, heartfelt emotion, or human attitude is beyond the range of their creative vocalization—

---

[14] The wife is beginning to weaken; her desire for wealth is growing greater than her abhorrence for what she will have to do to obtain it.

[15] Here is a major stroke of ironic *paradox*—to praise God for assisting them to break the first commandment through the practice of magic!

[16] "Peace"?—here perhaps in the sense of the Hebrew *shalom*, i.e., general well-being in life.

from the fiercest reprimand to the most fulsome praise, from the most intimate expressions of love to the most bitter articulation of disgust or animosity.

The stimulation of such a verbal "illusion of authenticity" is never gratuitous, but it rather serves some pertinent dramatic and/or didactic function, with the ultimate aim of making the thematic message both memorable and immediately applicable to the spiritual life of the listener—whether directly, or with reference to some needy acquaintance. The concluding speeches of a given play are especially important, for they normally serve to reveal the immediate relevance of the Scriptures to all committed Christians living in contemporary south-central Africa (see example below).

5.1.2 Rhetorical vigor

The language of the *Sewero* dramas features a powerfully persuasive appeal simply by virtue of the fact that it is consists entirely of direct discourse, as already illustrated in general terms by the example of the preceding section (5.1.1). This lifelike style of conversation is always heightened by language that is filled with memorable imagery (see 5.1.3 "local color" below) and a dynamic manner of appropriate idiomatic expression. The latter feature is what we wish to focus on more specifically in this section. How does the natural dialogue of these didactic stories serve both to enhance and to augment the credibility, reliability, immediacy, and potency of the extended "argument" of the narrative plot? This is usually manifested in the form of a particular problem or dilemma involving the Christian faith/life that is dramatized "either for or against" by the verbal action of the play.

A survey of the corpus at hand indicates that the animated speeches of the *Sewero* characters are punctuated by additional rhetorically motivated stylistic devices such as these, to list some of the more prominent features: irony, hyperbole, exclamations, diverse repetition, deliberate questions, many verbal intensifiers (especially particles and affixes), and connotatively flavored vocal modulations (e.g., tempo, pitch, volume, tone, etc.). We hear an overall vigor of verbal expression and a variety of voices that sound to the radio audience almost as if the words could be emanating from the outside veranda or the sitting room next door. This power expressed in and through the dialogue makes it difficult, if not impossible to mentally "rest" or "wander" during a performance. On the contrary, the listener's mind must remain constantly engaged with the story just to keep up with the action and thus to remain, as it were, an actual eavesdropper on the stage. On the other hand, the familiar, idiomatic utterances also strongly attract and hold listeners to the program; they represent a verbal "slice of life" experience that appeals to virtually everyone out there in the radio audience.

In the following example, special attention will be given by means of footnotes to the particular rhetorical devices that serve as prominent "points of persuasion" in the words of their speakers. This selection can illustrate only a small number of the vernacular devices that are available for this purpose in idiomatic discourse, but their importance to a powerful, convincing argument can at least be suggested. Other examples will be found in the other selections that have been included in my description. The following excerpt is taken from the play entitled "M-mm! This fellow is really a [wonderful] medicine man!" (*Mmmm! Ndiyetu sing'anga uyu!*):

(Setting: A man and his wife are showing the symptoms of different illnesses. They have now gone to the "office" [home] of a well-know medicine woman named "Masamba-asiyana" ['leaves/medicines differ'] in order to seek help. The three have just exchanged greetings and the "doctor" is about to begin her diagnosis and prescription. [D = the traditional doctor, M = the man, W = his wife].)

D: Eeeh! (affirmation) You have arrived! Tell me your complaint.
M: Aaah! (frustration) As for me, I've been having diarrhea for two months now.
D: Well (*Ayi*), I just want you to speak freely for yourselves. (gentle laughter, to put them at ease)
M: Then there's also these sores (*zironda*)...
D: Eeeeh heeeh! (I see!)
M: They are all over my legs here...
D: Eeh-eeeh! (affirmation)[17]
M: This is now the third month [that I've had them]...
D: Aa-aaah! (interjection of sympathetic empathy)
M: They never heal up at all!
D: Aaaah! (sorry about that)
M: So people are telling me...
D: You are [my] children![18]
M: ...[to come see] *Masamba-asiyana*.
D: You are [my] children!

---

[17] In typical fashion, as part of her plan of persuasion, this "doctor" keeps interrupting the man with exclamations of affirmation, thereby suggesting that she already knows what's wrong and what cure to prescribe. Traditional medicine (wo)men are expert psychologists who have a knack for instilling and building confidence in their clients, even in the most dire of circumstances when dealing with cases that seem to be quite hopeless. That is why these non-Western practitioners are so popular: they exude optimism, and patients always feel better, at least mentally, knowing that something, albeit small and unseen, is being done to remedy their adverse situation.
[18] The doctor portrays herself as a loving parent (mother), who will do her very best for "her children". This usage also suggests that they would not have the power/magic to solve their problems on their own, but she will help them out. She thus creates a positive atmosphere and a high level of credibility from the very beginning. She will need this because of some of the fantastic claims and observations that she later makes when doing her "diagnosis". Again, notice the *repetition* used here to emphasize both her *ethos* and her *logos* in the minds of her clients.

157

M: My wife here too is sick—coughing (*chifuwa*).
D. You are [my] children!
M: Haah! Eeh! (affirmation)
W: I just never feel good! (*osapeza bwinoyi*)
D: Ee-eeeh! (that's obvious!)
W: Right, I just keep on coughing.
D: Ahaa-haaa!
W: My body aches all over (*M'thupi kumangophwanya*)!
D: Mmmm
W: And my lungs are in pain (*zibayo* – i.e., pneumonia).
D: Ha-haah! I suspect (*ndikuona* 'I see' – i.e., by means of her divinatory powers) that you have gone to many other medicine (wo)men.
M: A-aaah! (surprise, i.e., how did you know that?!)
D: But [by doing so] you were going astray (*mumapita m'mbali*).
M: Eeh! (recognition) Do you hear that, Nagama (i.e., the name of his wife)?
W: Mmmm. (affirmation)
D: The one who is making you weak is a very difficult person indeed![19]
M: Aaah! (chagrin)
D: One day did not the uncle of the lady here (*amaiwa*, lit. 'these mothers', i.e., an honorific plural form of indirect reference) come to your home and revile you (*kudzalalata*)?[20]
M: Oh-ooh-ooh! (gradual recognition) And not only once (*ngati kamodzi ngati*)![21]
D: [I am] someone who knows everything (*zozidziwadziwa*, i.e., a self-praise name)! He-heeh!
M: [But] very often! (*kambirimbiri*, i.e., unbridled exaggeration has taken over now)
D: There—he cast *katsipa* there, on your sore[s]![22]
M: Oo-ooh! (exclamation of rising anger)[23] Do you hear that, Nagama?!
W: Mmmm. (affirmation)

---

[19] "Make you weak" is a weak translation of the original verb –*pikisula* a Chinyanja technical term from the vocabulary of the occult that refers to a sorcerer or a witch who has the power to overcome any defensive magic that you may have applied in advance specifically to ward off such attacks.

[20] Such suggestions are so general that they could apply to any number of situations, especially in the minds of those, like these clients, who are seeking a cause or explanation for their present misery. The "doctor" thus plants the spark of suspicion that s/he will normally be able to fan into the full flame of a dangerous witchcraft accusation.

[21] The doctor's "bait" has been taken, and suspicious minds readily supply further evidence to incriminate the "guilty" party who has been suggested.

[22] *Katsipa* is a swelling disease (usually in the legs) that is believed to be "cast" (-*ponya*) by sorcerers at their victim(s); some say that a small mouse-like creature (by the same name) is the animal "familiar" which carries it on behalf of the sorcerer. One bacterial sore quickly gives birth to another until the whole lower part of the body is covered. This malady, i.e., a form of elephantiasis (?), can be fatal if the sores become infected and remain untreated with the proper antibiotic. From a rhetorical perspective, notice the specific detail that is introduced here in the dialogue, to give it greater impact and verisimilitude.

[23] This expression, like the other exclamations, carries a great deal of expressive force that cannot be easily represented orthographically. For example, *Oo-oooh!* is spoken with a rising pitch, loudness, stress, and an elongated final vowel—all paralinguistic modifications that here convey along with the normal strong emotion a specific attitude of anger that is rising with each apparent revelation. Such features constitute a powerful rhetorical device in the vernacular that is unfortunately discernable only on a good audio tape. I am calling attention to it here simply to indicate that this is yet another important dimension of the Sewero group's artistry that has to remain largely unrecorded and unrecognized, for the time being.

D: Yaaah! (success—i.e., I've demonstrated my diagnosis)

M: He cast *kasipa* on this sore here!

D: Mother here can bear me witness [now]—she feels a strong burning pain (*pakumaocha*) on her chest there...

W: Eeeh! (affirmation)

D: [It's a] frog (*chule*)![24]

W: Ee-eeeh! (shock and fright—with affirmation)

D: Ahaa! (affirmation) He cast a *namchidwe* frog [upon you]![25]

W: It feels heavy there! (*Pamalemera!*)

D: A certain heaviness in the chest?[26]

W: Iiiih! (shock) It's true (*zoona*)!

M: Do you mean to say that you can take a frog and cast it upon the chest (lit. 'heart' *mtima*) of a person (*munthu*)?![27]

D: Right upon the heart (*Pamtimaaah* another exaggerated final vowel for emphasis)!!

M: Nagama, [there's] a frog in your chest—a frog!

D: Now the purpose (*cholinga*) was that mother here would die, and then you'd go back home.[28]

M: Now I want to know—this person, what's his/her problem (*nkhani yache* 'his/her story')?!

D: Because you are too hard of a worker (*kugwiragwira inuyo* 'you [are] grab-grabbing [work]' – i.e., an idiom)!

M: So do I have to die (*ndiferako*) because of that garden plot (*dimba*)?! I'm telling you [my wife], that garden [of mine]!

D: Ahaa-haa! (affirmation)

W: You work too hard![29]

D: But that's why you've come here—it's finished! (*koma m'mene mwafika kuno, zatha!* – another idiomatic expression, i.e., in order to get healed/protected by me).

W: You work too hard! (i.e., repetition with incredulity, as if she cannot believe that this is why they are being be-witched).

D: And Mother here was thinking that [she has] 'AIDS' (*henzi*)!

---

[24] First a *mouse*, now a *frog*—these are well-known mystical familiars or "secret agents" of sorcerers (*vanyanga*) and witches (*mfiti*) in the local community. In this case, it is probably "witchcraft" since close relatives are involved.

[25] *Namchidwe* is a particular type of harmful magic, or sorcery, that attacks the victim's chest in the form of a mystical "frog"; the symptoms (e.g., coughing) are varied, but always painful and the outcome often fatal.

[26] Notice the implied elements here (and elsewhere). *Ellipsis* is not only idiomatic in terms of style, it is also yet another rhetorical tool in the verbal artist's repertory. It maintains the excitement level of the dialogue and involves the audience by requiring them to "fill in the gaps" as they eagerly follow along.

[27] Such *rhetorical questions* do not ask for information, but rather, forcefully give it—along with associated emotions and attitudes (here: surprise, and probably also a certain measure of disgust as well).

[28] The *Achewa* and related peoples are matrilineal and traditionally matrilocal. Thus a new husband would normally reside at the village of his wife's parents and in the vicinity of her maternal uncle, the head of the clan (*mwini-mbumba*). If the marriage would fail (divorce) or if she would die, the man would usually return to his home village. Such customs are still observed in rural areas, but not in urban locations.

[29] Literally, 'to hoe very much'—a verbless predication used emphatically as an exclamation here. 'Working hard' is used metaphorically here to mean that he is prospering in his labor. His prosperity has attracted the attention of sorcerers who wish to tap into his wealth by attacking his well-being.

W: [She begins to cough repeatedly…]
D: Ayiii! (strong negative)
M: Haaah! (surprise—i.e., at this terrible subject being brought up)
D: It's not 'AIDS' (*si heenzi* –an emphatic pronunciation) at all![30]
M: You are a real 'doctor' (*adokotaladi*)!
D: Ahaa-haaa! (self-affirmation)
M: They told Mother here that it is (i.e., she had) 'AIDS'.
D: 'No-no-no-nooo!' (*English*-isms!), it's not 'AIDS'!
M: We were quarreling (*kumangokangana*) [about the fact that] she has 'AIDS'.
D: No—it's not 'AIDS', it's not 'AIDS'!
M: Aaah! (wonder) Now a 'doctor' like this (*dokotala ngati uyu!*) is a real medi-
    cine (wo)man (*sing'anga weniweni*)!!
D: Indeed, I can reveal everything [you need] (i.e., to treat your illnesses)! I am a
    healer of everything—a medicine woman who is famous in every local area and
    [even] in [other] countries![31]
M: In all these places indeed (*Koma muzonsedi*)![32] Surely we have found some very
    good fortune (*mwaitu*) here!
D: Medicine… [she is interrupted periodically during this utterance of self-praise]
M: Yes! Yes! (*Ayi, ayi!* lit. 'No, no' – i.e., negatives used rhetorically with positive
    force)
D: …for any type of illness…
M: Haaa! (affirmation)
D: …whether diarrhea, or pleurisy…
M: Haaa!
D: …when you step on a magical mine (*zopondetsedwa* 'things stamped upon') …
M: Haaa!
D: …when your charm is disarmed (*zochesulidwa*)…
M: Yes (*Ayi*), real luck!
D: …when your magic is reversed (*zopidigulidwa*)[33]—whatever, I can easily put an
    end to it (*ndimathana nazo*)![34]

---

[30] Here we see an instance of the great danger of such traditional diagnoses—the real medical cause is
concealed and therefore can keep spreading. This is not the main "lesson" of the present play, but it is
subtly taught as a secondary theme. The instruction is effected in this case indirectly, by the suggestive
method of negative dramatic (narrative) exemplification, rather than by some explicit didactic condemnation.
[31] The couple's praise goes to the medicine woman's head and she starts boasting beyond measure—
hyperbole with humorous effect. Humor (see 5.1.6) is another important rhetorical technique, not only to
give a weighty theme some "comic relief", but also to reinforce an aspect of this play's main message—
namely, that the wild claims and often bizarre methods of traditional "healers" must not be taken seriously by listeners. In fact, such potentially dangerous practitioners ought to be strictly avoided by Christians.
[32] Another example of the persuasive force of exclamatory utterances; this is a verbless predication
consisting simply of an initial adversative conjunction followed by a [locative concord + adjective +
emphatic suffix] compound word. This patient is obviously impressed by the doctor's boasts and acts as
her praise-responder. Her rhetoric has worked—in fact, 100% better than her actual treatments!
[33] Notice the highly specific terms used to refer to different types of indigenous magic here—the language (argot) of traditional specialists! The last verb (*-pidigulidwa*) is a metaphor with the image being
that of a tin, bottle, or some other container which one must struggle with in order to open it up. This too
is a powerful persuasive tool in the argument structure of a captivating speaker, the rhetoric of local
imagery, employed in this case, for nefarious ends.

M: We have surely found some good fortune here, Nagama!

W: Eeeh! (affirmation)

M: We were almost too late [in finding you] (*Tinkachedwatu ife*)!

W: That's for sure! (*Zeeedi* – with vowel elongation for emphasis)

D: So now since you have just come into the sitting room (*pa alendo* '[place] of visitors') here...

M: Mmmm. [affirmative interruption]

D: Why not enter the big room![35]

M: Eeeh! (Yesss!)

D: Enter the big room!

M: Yes, indeed!

D: When you come out from there, you'll be O.K.

M: Haaah! (excitement and joy)

D: Here you are at the well [of healing] (*chitsime* – a "medical" metaphor)![36]

M: Nagama, we were almost too late, wouldn't you say?!

D: No person ever comes in here and leaves with his/her illness, no way!

W: (She coughs—perhaps in expectation of soon having it healed.)

M: Nagama, this coughing [of yours] (*chifuwa ichi* 'this chest' – a metonym) is about to end!

W: Mmmm! (affirmation)

D: When a person comes to the well, s/he leaves with all body dirt (*litsiro*) gone![37]

M: Yes, that frog is gone now!! (*Achoka chule uyu!* – i.e., spoken with hopeful anticipation) Haa!

D: Eyaaa! (you're so right!)

M: Aah! (affirmation) Thank you very much!

W: (She goes into a bout of heavy coughing—is this a positive or negative sign? The audience will soon find out the answer, if they did not already know it in advance.)

M: Thank you very much!

D: Yaaah! (affirmation) I am the very one [who can help you]! (*Ifee ameneyo* 'we are the ones' – honorific plurals, here rather conceitedly applied to oneself!)

Masamba-asiyana, the medicine woman, has completely convinced these poor clients of her claims by means of her expert psychological insight and rhetorically persuasive verbal technique. This scene is so realistically performed by the equally masterful *Sewero* players that the radio audience must surely imagine themselves sitting right there in the dubious doctor's waiting room. They are thus able to listen along there with those two unfortunate

---

[34] The doctor claims, in typical boastful fashion, that she can cure or correct any ailment or problem with ease. In response, the man can simply sing her praises in mantra-like fashion.

[35] This 'big room' (*chipinda chachikulu*) is most likely a non-literal (figurative) reference to the doctor's special "treatment room", where the actual magical substances and their directions for use will be given to her willing clients.

[36] As Mr. Pembeleka explained this metaphor: "[The 'well' is] where thirsty [sick] people drink their cures [medicine], and their thirst is quenched [their diseases healed]."

[37] Here is another effective metaphor that simply reinforces the impression that she has already made on her clients. Therefore, they enter into her treatment with the utmost confidence of being completely healed.

patients—perhaps themselves being rather favorably impressed, even enticed, by her elaborate sales pitch!

5.1.3 Local color

The *Sewero* dialogues are delightfully decorated with many colorful local descriptions, well-known allusions, concrete details, sensual vocabulary, proverbial sayings, and varied sorts of figurative expressions (especially similes and metaphors). All this familiar pictorial language is harmonized and narratively focused to accurately reflect the Malawian situational and sociocultural setting of specific performances, especially those that depict a rural-based environment and interpersonal milieu. In the fast-moving dialogic interchange of a dramatic plot, such evocative imagery is not allowed to retard the verbal action that is taking place, or to eclipse the events and issues being discussed. Rather, this reservoir of "Malawianized" imagery, whether expressed explicitly or only by allusive suggestion, serves as essential local coloring agent to contextualize the characters' speeches by calling to mind well-known background scenery and common countryside vistas. Such "pictorial" depiction and "multi-sensory language" is thus able to create corresponding "images on the screen of the listeners' imaginations" (Michell 1999:38-39, 54).

In addition to being memorable (hence reminding people of a particular drama and its lesson), these everyday descriptive pictures and figures of speech constitute a vital part of the play's realistic representation of Christian lives in conflict with the powerful negative forces of indigenous mystical tradition and the universal human inclination towards evil. Taken together (their effect is cumulative), they also function to contribute an added measure of both credibility and immediacy to the aural performance, giving any listening audience the added visualizable impression that these dramatic events, as represented in a play's dialogic progression, are transpiring in the proximate vicinity of their radio receiver. This localized significance of the *Sewero* plays is a characteristic that enhances their dramatic impact, their artistic value, as well as their religious relevance.

In the following selection (from *E-eh! Munthu ameneyu sangakuchinjirizeni, ayi!* "E-eh! This person cannot protect you, not at all!"), we hear—and see, via the stimulating descriptive dialogue—a medicine man teaching his wife how to be a good "office assistant" for his business. We again seem to be sitting right there in the traditional "doctor's office", as he instructs her as to the proper distinction and use of his various potions, charms, and other "medicines". The details that emerge in this dialogue enable the audience to imagine a very specific setting—"colored" of course with the shades of their own local environment, surrounding circumstances, and personal experiences.

(Setting: The play begins at this point—that is, with the medicine man and his wife quietly conversing together in his supply room, which is obviously crammed with bottles and other containers filled with all sorts of exotic concoctions and supposed curative potions, salves, drinks, and other charms. [D = the traditional doctor, W = his wife].)

D: Well, now we must be very thankful, Nabanda (i.e., his wife's name)... (she interrupts him)

W: Right (*Eeeti*)!

D: ...because it is God who is helping us (i.e., perform our traditional "healing" practice), and because he has allowed us to keep loving each other...[38]

W: Aaah! (exclamation of wonder, perhaps at her husband's great mystical knowledge)

D: ...but also because he has enabled us to be a 'doctor' (*dokotala*).[39]

W: Aah! (strong affirmation) Yes—'doctor'—yes! (i.e., she seems a bit awed at this notion)

D: And so God is here! (i.e., with us – *Ndipo Mulungu alipo!*)

W: Iiih! (amazement) You said it! (*kwabasi!*)

D: Therefore, I think that it is a good idea for us to do this:

W: Mmmm. (mild affirmation)

D: Clients [who arrive] here, you must give them a warm welcome (*muziwalandira*)...

W: Mmmm.

D: ...with great joy.

W: Certainly! (*Zeedi!*)

D: Because we are here to help people.

W: That's for sure! (*Basitu!*)

D: That is why you must not simply take medicines and give them to patients just anyhow, no!

W: Is that so? (*Eeti?*)

D: But dispense [them with caution]—I have put all the medicines in their proper order.

W: I see! (*Inde!*)

D: For example, there is this medicine in the shell (*mkomechiwo*)...

W: Yes? (i.e., carry on—I'm listening)

D: ...right here.

W: Yes, you've written a label on it (*mwalembalemba kadzina*).

D: Right! (*Ehede!*) This one is for [curing] AIDS (*edzi*).[40]

---

[38] There is an interesting syncretistic religious mix in the doctor's call for a prayer of thanks: both their magical practice (wrong) and their married love (right) is attributed to God.

[39] The singular noun "doctor" (here referring to a traditional magical practitioner, a *sing'anga*) is here applied to them both, in recognition of Nabanda's contribution to his work. Most medicine men are not so gracious or generous in attributing any assistance from others in their practice.

[40] Most traditional doctors claim to be able to cure AIDS, perhaps because its symptoms develop relatively slowly.

W: (she laughs) Really! (*Ndithudi!*)
D: If a person comes in who has constant diarrhea (*kutsegulatsegula*)...
W: Yesss?
D: ...indicating that [s/he has] AIDS...
W: Diarrhea like that?
D: ...its medicine, its cure (*mtela wake*), is this very one.
W: Alright!
D: Just break off a bit (i.e., as if it were a root or stem of some kind)...
W: Right.
D: ...and just give him (her) a little piece like this.
W: Right.
D: He's [as good as] cured! (*Wachira!*)
W: Completely cured? (*Wachiriratu?*)
D: Eeya! (strong affirmation)
W: (she laughs and claps her hands in satisfaction)
D: As for paralysis or rheumatism (*choyala kapena nyamakazi*)...
W: Right.
D: ...here it is (i.e., the medicinal cure). Yes indeed!
W: Alright.
D: Right! Now, ah, this one is for back pain (*amsana*).
W: [What about] that whitish stuff (*otuwirira*)?
D: [Also] for backache.
W: Alright!
D: Now these roots here (*amizuwo*)...
W: Yes?
D: These are to bind a family together (*omanga banja*).[41]
W: The family?
D: [Yes], for binding the family.
W: For binding the family tightly together?
D: Right!
W: Just like you bound...
D: Yes?
W: Just like you bound our [family] together (*Monga mwamangirira lathu lino*)?
D: Aaah! (concern—i.e., don't start talking about personal matters!) Hey, that could not be true, could it? (*Eeh, bodzanso eti?*)[42]
W: (she laughs) Absolutely! (*Zedi!*)
D: So when dealing with such cases (i.e., marriage problems)...
W: Yes?
D: ...that is to say, in this area, [we are engaged in] the matter of helping (i.e., without making a profit).
W: That's true.
D: For that reason, even where the deposit is concerned (*chiponda-m'thengo* 'that which steps in the bush' – i.e., to procure a particular medicinal substance), do not charge too much—not at all! (*nh-nhaah!*)

---

[41] There are various types of such "family-binding" medicines for different problems that arise between a husband and a wife in the home; basically, they are all intended to increase their mutual love so that neither becomes "untied" and gets attached to another partner.

[42] The medicine man and his wife have great affection for each other, so the conclusion would be that he has applied some of that same magic to them—but he does not want to discuss such personal issues.

W: Nooo!

D: Because we are helpers of the people...

W: Right.

D: ...who represent God (*tikuimira Mulungu*) in this matter.[43]

W: Right!

D: So as from today I [want to be known as] 'Doctor Luke' (*Dokotala Luka*).

W: Indeed!

D: So when people come here [for help], it would not be good if you get angry with them...

W: Nooo!

D: ...[and] don't entertain them (*osamawasangalatsa*)!

W: [But] it is necessary to show happiness to them—[share your] joy, yes!

D: [To reveal] how a medicine man really lives (i.e., for the people)...

W: Mmm.

D: ...and how we dispense all our medicines. However, that medicine there has just come in—yes indeed. You may recall that this medicine we have to procure from afar...

W: Oooh! (with wonder)

D: ...[water] used to bathe dead bodies (lit. 'accidents' *otsukira ngozi aja*).[44]

W: Eeh (weak affirmation), alright.

D: All of that, all of that [medicine], has just arrived (i.e., he seems to be quite proud of this latest "delivery").

W: Oooh? (wonder—i.e., she may not have known these dark details of her husband's "practice")

D: It came in last night.[45]

W: Alright.

D: So there's no more difficulty at all (i.e., in procuring this particular noxious ingredient).[46]

W: That's good.

D: If it gets finished again, he says (i.e., quoting his "supplier", most likely a night witch), "If you see that the water for bathing corpses is [about to] run out..."

W: Yes?

D: "...I'll go and get you some more!"

---

[43] Many "Christian" healers clearly view their role as being "ministerial" in a practical way; indeed, "Luke's" instructions to his wife sound very pastoral. The problem is that their proposed "cures" in many cases (as illustrated later in this same drama) do not work, but rather often cause serious medical, psychological, and spiritual harm.

[44] All of a sudden, the activity of witchcraft enters the picture: these seemingly benign "healers" seek mystical power from the dead! Whether they actually cause the deaths of the persons involved is not yet apparent at this stage; at the very least though, they are somehow engaged in using corpses for nefarious purposes in the attempt to increase the potency of their curative charms as well as their magical practice in general. This water, which had been used by mourners to wash the bodies of their departed relatives provided the liquid substance for many of their powerful potions.

[45] This is a further intimation that genuine witchcraft is involved; it seems like Dr. Luke "orders" this specially potent medicine from certain witches that are operating in their vicinity during the night. Whether he actually goes out with them on their nocturnal forays to the local graveyard is not immediately clear—not yet!

[46] There must have been some recent temporary shortage in the availability of this crucial commodity—burial water! But now Dr. Luke reassures his wife that his sorcerer-suppliers are very confident that things are back to normal.

W: Alright!

D: He says that those whom he contracts with (*amagwirizana nawo* lit. 'he makes and an agreement with them' – i.e., other witches)...

W: Yes?

D: ...because the supply of water can be erratic at times (*avutavuta* – i.e., either because the water was in high demand from other medicine men or due to the low local mortality rate!)...

W: Yes?

D: ...[but] it will no longer be a problem (*sadzavutanso ayi*).

W: It will no longer be a problem! (i.e., that's good!)

D: You remember (*Pajatu*), we must tell [people] that this water comes from the lake (i.e., Lake Malawi—about 60 miles from Lilongwe area, where the play is set).[47]

W: You don't say! (*Inuu!*)

D: Don't forget that we must deceive them!

W: We do deceive them (she laughs).

D: Ehe-heee! (strong affirmation).

W: Ih-ih-ih! (mock surprise) Is this not what we always tell them?

D: But you must keep the secret!

W: Yes—aah! (i.e., how could you doubt me, even playfully?)

D: For this reason, when people are ready to quaff [this water], really...Iiih—yaah! (fear + disgust – i.e., even the doctor shudders that the thought of drinking this sort of polluted liquid!)

W: So if we reveal [what it is] to them, will they die? Iih! Nooo!

D: Well, people really like to drink this water![48]

W: Iiih! (repulsion) They really gulp it down! (*Amwereratu!*)

D: I even have to pour it into this drum (*m'golomu* – i.e., since so much of that water is required)!

W: This one right here? (i.e., as if she is pointing right at it in their medicine room)

D: Iyaa, haha! They do drink a lot! (i.e., thus a whole drum is needed to store this water).[49]

W: Haah! (affirmation) And it does help them (to recover from their illnesses)!

D: Yes, they drink it!

W: (she laughs)

D: Well (*Iyayi* 'No'), let us just praise heaven (i.e., God, a metonym) indeed!

W: He surely helps [heal] them (i.e., our patients)![50]

D: That's right!

---

[47] People believe that if the medicine man must obtain some of his ingredients from far away, they tend to be more impressed and to put greater trust in its potency.

[48] The physical act of "drinking" this "corpse water" is highlighted here in the dialogue through lexical repetition coupled with gross exaggeration as a thematic counter-motif and a subtle de-familiarization technique to work implicitly on the minds of the radio audience. It would make a special impression upon any listeners who have already received such "medicine" from a traditional healer—or who may have contemplated doing so. Do they really realize the sort of abhorrent activity that they thereby engage in?!

[49] Obviously, magical activity must be involved in order to provide so plentiful a supply of this toxic liquid—a traditional African WMD, "weapon of magical destruction"! The water used to clean a corpse is not very plentiful, and it is normally very carefully disposed of by designated relatives—in order to prevent just such tapping of the supply by witches to use for their evil purposes.

[50] What a horribly contrastive utterance—that God would empower the most polluted water possible to heal people! This is syncretism at its worst.

W: Our God is most loving!

D: Eeeh! (affirmation) Indeed, that's for sure (*kwabasi, ndithu!*), aah! (wonder)

W: So loving—He really loves us!

D: That's that then! (*Zateremu tsopano!*) So let me go then to find some of that other medicine—the stuff that makes people mad (*ozunguza mutu* 'it causes one's head to spin'—i.e., causes hallucinations). We need that in order to bewitch someone (*munthu timulodze*)![51]

W: That's right!

D: That very medicine [is needed]!

W: Yes, it really causes a person some pretty severe pain! (*kungompwetekeratu!*)

D: I can see (i.e., he must be holding up a bottle) that this here (remaining) is not enough.

W: You're so right! (*Zeedi, eeh!*)

D: It's just a little, not enough!

W: No, it's not enough—you remember, that little amount that remained we gave to that young man?

D: Eeeh! (affirmation) This here just won't do, it's not enough.

W: You said it! (*Aati!*)

D: All I can do is to go and find some more.

W: Ahaaa! (agreement)

D: Go bring me that hoe.

W: Alright.

D: Eeh. (thanks)

W: O.K. Here it is, here it is!

D: So, I'll be seeing you then (*Iyayi, ndikupezani*).

W: You'll find me, yes, I must receive [some more] clients.

D: That's right.

W: Yes, just like a house-wife (*mai wapakhomo* 'mother of the doorway') — awaiting some guests.[52]

D: Do everything carefully!

W: Eeh (affirmation), yes, I'll do it all.

D: And take the necessary precautions (*ndi moopa nchito* – i.e., because of the hazardous nature of some of their noxious magical ingredients)!

W: Aah! (agreed) In everything!

D: I'll see you then.

W: [You'll find] everything in order (*Mwa dongosolo*).

D: Thank you very much (i.e., for being such a good assistant)!

What a wonderfully loving and mutually cooperative couple! Too bad that they are sorcerers—directing their unified efforts towards such harmful, antisocial purposes. To be sure, some of their "clients" may be assisted in gaining their selfish ends, but many, as dramatized later in the play, are not, and the result is untold misery as well as unmitigated suspicion. Consequently,

---

[51] At last the dark secret is revealed—the suspense has been carefully built up in the dialogue to the present climactic point: This husband-wife team are no innocent herbalists; they are bona-fide sorcerers—traditional practitioners who employ magic for harmful purposes, including murder!

[52] The ordinary, casual style of their conversation belies the diabolical nature of their occupation.

the entire community is seriously retarded in both its secular and also its spiritual development as a consequence of such beliefs and practices. The "local color" of the *Sewero* dramas paints that message large and most vividly for all to hear and learn a lesson from.

5.1.4 Emotive realism

What do we mean by "realism"? In general terms, this quality is a compositional feature that permeates all of the *Sewero* stylistic devices that are being discussed in this chapter, the rhetorical vigor (5.1.2) and the local color (5.1.3), for example, even the varied sound effects (see 5.1.7) that create a vivid vocal background to every production. Realism also applies to the interlocking plot and purpose of any given play considered as a whole—that is, as a dramatic "slice of life", or an "excerpt from experience", which is here viewed differently, that is, from a biblically-informed, contemporary Christian perspective. The plots are thus stylistically distinguished by natural, true-to-life, everyday contemporary characters, scenes, and situations (5.1.5); the lively dialogues dramatize events that could easily happen in the lives of the listeners or to someone whom they know (5.1.1). These happenings are carefully focused however upon their lives as believers and the temptations, trials, controversies, and challenges that any one of them could easily face in their lifetime. It is this immediacy and relevance—the impression that "this could happen to me (or it already has)!"—that keeps the radio audience attentive and brings them back week after week in order to hear, as it were, the next episode in the history of their very own community.

An important aspect of this pervading "realism" is the complex of strong emotions that is characteristically expressed during the dramatization of any *Sewero* play. Every story arouses a great deal of tension that also raises some serious questions in the listeners' minds (e.g., how are things going to turn out in the end?—how can so-and-so get out of the predicament s/he is in?—or, why did s/he give in to that temptation?). Accordingly, at one or more points in a play the level of passion expressed reaches a peak of intensity. The full range of human feelings, sentiments, and attitudes may potentially be manifested in one way or another (the cast commands quite a diverse inventory of possibilities)—whether exultant joy, grief-stricken lamentation, bitter jealousy, raging anger, hopeless frustration, or hope-filled expectation. Each emotion might find dramatic expression in this play or that, or at one point in a given story or another. Of course, such a varied rhetorical technique depends on the vocal virtuosity of the character voices that depict them and, as noted already, the regular members of the *Sewero* cast are past masters of such natural, true-to-life performances. A play-specific emotive "atmosphere" is created also by means of the manipulation of sound effects and the inclusion of the appropriate mood music or songs (sung, at times, by members of the cast themselves) to suit the overall dramatic situation as well as the current state of interpersonal relationships.

The sickening feeling of panic and horror that one experiences after committing a terrible deed that cannot be undone is powerfully evoked in the following selection from the play, "Wealth comes from God [alone]!" (*Chuma chimachokera kwa Mulungu*). A young man has gone to a witch-doctor in order to procure the magic needed to become wealthy. He drinks the required magical potion and is then given the awful instructions as to how he must activate this. One of the requirements is to sleep with his sister, but she later refuses because she is a Christian in deed, not only word. Now the man returns to the medicine man to see if he can "undo" the magical charge that is circulating, like a cancer, within his body, just waiting to be released when its lethal conditions have been satisfied.

(Setting: The man is in the witchdoctor's "office", pleading with him and his heartless wife, his "assistant", to reverse the effects of the magic that he had been administered. This pathetic conversation is nearing its cli-max—and an inevitable refusal: Malicious magic, once ingested, cannot be "disarmed" as it were! [D = the traditional doctor, W = his wife, M = the young man].)

D: I already told you that these matters require courage (*kulimba mtima* 'to be strong in the heart' – i.e., in order for the magic to operate properly). The fact that you have returned shows that your courage has failed (i.e., you have not been able to carry out the stipulated instructions). Now this [magic] is going to be a problem for you!

W: Eeh! (affirmation) That's true, you have failed—you have completely failed! You did not follow the instructions explicitly (*mndandanda wake*)! So all you can do is just get out of here and go home!

M: I tried! What can I do? Don't chase me away like this! What can I do now—what can I do?![53]

D: Yes (*Iyayi* – lit. 'No!'), I told you that these things (i.e., my magic—a euphe-mism) were going to trouble you—that if you waited two weeks—eeh! (affir-mation), you must not wait over two weeks (i.e., after you drank that potion)! No, you had just 'two or three days' (i.e., uttered in English for emphasis) before you were to return here (i.e., after completing the necessary tests). That was what you had to do!

M: Well how could I have returned [so soon]? My sister was giving me a lot of problems—to this very day she continues to trouble me (i.e., by refusing to give

---

[53] The tone and timbre of the young man's voice clearly reveals his agitated emotional state, which gets progressively worse as the play develops and his mental condition deteriorates due to worry, coupled with the poisonous magical potion that he drank. The repetitiveness of his words and his reiterated questions convey only part of his full feelings at this climactic juncture in the plot. This scene elicits a lot of pathos among any listening audience, who are lead to fear the worst for this poor fool, who was ready to risk his life in order to become wealthy.

in to my request to sleep with her). So what was I to do (*Nanga ndikadatani inenso*)?!

D: I told you that it is necessary to be courageous. You were not courageous, not at all! If she refused you, that simply means that you were not courageous enough! (i.e., the evil doctor may be implying here that the young man should have been bold enough to rape his own sister in order to satisfy the requirement.)

W: This fellow looked clever enough at the time—that he would obey [the instructions]. But now, well it's clear, there's nothing that he's done [right]! (*Koma ayi, ndithu, palibe chimene wapangapo ayi!*)[54]

M: Alright, tell me—alright, what can I do to avoid going mad (*kuti ndisapenge misala*)?!

W: Absolutely nothing! (*Palibeee!*)

D: Perhaps you wanted for us to try a different method (*tiyambirenso kapena*)?

M: Try again—how?? (*Kuyambirenso kotani?*)

D: To do something else, perhaps in that way... (i.e., some other drastic plan, for example, like killing his sister instead of sleeping with her!)

M: Now who could do that—for there were only three of us [in the family]: me, the oldest [son], my sister, and my young brother. Now I've already killed him (i.e., to satisfy one of the medicine's requirements), so what more can I do??

D: Well, that's too bad, and there's going to be trouble [for you] (*Basi! Ndiye zavuta pamenepa!*) because you've come [back too] late!

W: That's your problem (*Izotu n'zako*)! Many [clients] get rich right here—[like] I already told you, [gaining] 'farms', or perhaps 'rest houses' (*maresitihausi*)! It all came from this place!

M: So things won't happen (i.e., the magic won't work) if I perhaps go try somewhere else [and sleep with] someone else—maybe at some 'bar', I don't know, anywhere else?!![55]

D: I said that [it had to be] a close relative (*mbale wako*), not just anybody, no!

W: That's it, get out! (*Ndiye basi, tuluka!*) Go away—you are just wasting our time!

D: You'd better just go away!

W: Aah! (frustration) There are some other [clients] out there [waiting]; we now want to speak with them.

D: So some folks (i.e., like this young man here) want to make us out to be bad people, eh?!

W: Aah! (disgust) They simply want to degrade us right here [in our own office] (*Afuna kutilowetsa pansi ife panopa*)!!

(There is a scene change at this point: The young man goes back to try to persuade his sister to sleep with him—not so much to get rich now, but simply to save his life from that murderous magic working away within him [S = his sister, named "Dola"].)

M: Aaah! (fear and worry) What can I do—what can I do?! Shall I go mad? Dora, my [dear] sister, Dora, Dora, what have you done?! Mmmm (reflective), alright, let's see! Dora—Dora—hey Dora!

---

[54] The medicine man's wife typically performs an essential "support role"—encouraging clients when they first come, then arguing with them after they fail. Her words to the poor young man are harsher than those of her husband—sort of a "good cop—bad cop" routine in their dialogue together.

[55] The young man's desperation contrasts with the cruel wife's obdurate attitude towards him; she clearly despises him in his weakness and simply wants him out of their sight.

S: Eeeh! (affirmation) Well what is it? (*Bwanji kodi?*)

M: Say you, do you really want me to go mad?[56]

S: Iih! (shock) That's your business! (*zanu zimenezo!*)

M: Hey, will it really please you when you see me walking around naked (i.e., as madmen are wont to do)?!

S: Well, that's just how you'll have to walk around then! Did you not bring this all upon yourself with that witchcraft of yours? (*Simunaziputa dala ndi ufiti wanuwu?*)

M: Uuuh! (as if insulted) Whose witchcraft do you mean?

S: Aaah! (disgust) Did you ever see (i.e., hear about) a man sleeping with (*akucheza ndi* – 'chatting/conversing with', a euphemism) his own sister?!

M: Hey, I thought that after our father died I should be the one to help you out.[57]

S: Aaah! (disgust) How would you help me? Can someone help another in a [prohibited] way like that?!

M: There is time, Dora, there's still some time. Perhaps I will not go mad. So let's just do what we have to do, how about it? (*Tatiye tingopanga motero, eeeeh?* – i.e., let's sleep together to get rid of the curse)

S: Time for what? Who are you going to do it with (*Mupange ndi ndani moteromo?*)?

M: Why with you—you—you, Dora!!

S: Iih! (great repugnance) This foolishness of yours I will have none of! Get away from me, you are disgusting me! (*Tatiyeni uko mukundinyansa!*)[58]

M: Do I disgust you—I, your own brother?! Who do you have left here in the village?

S: Eeeh! (affirmation of her preceding utterance) [This is pure] witchcraft! (*ufitiwo!*)

M: I am left alone—I and you!

S: Aaah! (rejection of his line of argumentation)

M: Who's going to take care of you, Dora?

S: Aah! (denial) If we were really left alone (i.e., and you had first consulted me), then you wouldn't have gone and done such things!

M: Hey, Dora, please! (*Iwe, Dola, iweee!*)

S: Aah! (rejection) Perhaps (i.e., if I would agree to your request) you would just go and learn how to practice sorcery yourself! (*Bwenzi mukuphunzira ufiti inuyo*) Aaah! (no way!)

---

[56] The wretched young man tries to shift the blame for his foolish decision to engage in witchcraft and its ultimate punishment on to his innocent and upright sister. But he certainly arouses no sympathy among the radio audience. His situation is indeed pitiable, but he has chosen to put himself there and he must pay the ultimate price—a dramatic "case study" of warning to all listeners: Don't go there [to a traditional doctor] when you are in difficulties!

[57] First he blames her for his predicament, then he tries to convince her that he only did it to help support her; next he will try to move her to pity him and help him out.

[58] This feeling of revulsion over her brother's behavior contrasts sharply with his miserable situation and the terrors that he is beginning to experience, for which he blames everyone but himself.

M: Ooh! (I'm undone!) I'm damned, it's hopeless!! (*Kalanga! Koto!*) I'm damned, it's hopeless!! Do you really want me to go mad, Dora—should I go mad—Dora, do you want me to go mad!!!

S: Eeeh! (affirmation) Did you not go ahead and call this madness upon your own body? (*Nanga simunachita kuyiitana misalayo kuti ifike pathupi panupo?*)

M: You are speaking very resolutely (*molimba mtima*), Dola, and there's a hard look in your eyes (*m'maso muli gwa* – i.e., you will not give in to my appeal)!!

S: Absolutely right! (*Kwambiiri*)!

M: You are just talking [like this] because my father died![59]

S: Nooo, not at all! (*Aaayi, sizimenezo, ayi!*) It's just because of this sorcery that you've begun [to practice]!

M: Alright, we'll see about that! (*tiwonetsana* 'we are going to see each other' – i.e., to 'see' who will win out in this dispute between us) For there's still time, it's not yet up! (i.e., when the curse will take hold and he goes insane due to the un-defused magic within him) No, shall see about that!

S: Who are you going to see about that (*Muonetsana ndi ndani?* – a play on the idiom that her brother has just used) I am going to leave this village—you can remain alone with your witchcraft here!

M: Who's a witch?! Tell me, who is a witch?! (*Kodi iwe mfiti ndani?*) [If you had agreed to my request] you could be driving around in a motorcar—or perhaps you would be the owner of a maize grinding mill, or a 'store'!

S: A motorcar for what [purpose]?! (*Galimoto ya chiani?*) All this time have I needed to ride around in motorcars? (*Kale ponsepa ndimakwera magalimoto ineyo?!*) Aagh! (that's utter nonsense!)

M: I'm damned, it's hooopeless!! (*Kalanga! Kotooo!*) I am in terrible trouble!! (*Zandivuta ineee!*)

(A new scene opens. The young man is laughing and talking to himself—an indication of his emerging madness.)

M: (quiet laughter) Ehe-he-he-he-he! Hey you, you must not remain on my body! My, what a beautiful-looking fly this is! (*Koma nchencheyi njokongolatu*) (he laughs again) You'd (i.e., an unseen addressee) just love to eat it! My, what a beautiful-looking fly this is! Iya-ya-ya! (amazement) Here is my motorcar—let's drive away!! (*Iyo galimoto yanga, iyooo!*) Hey, there's my motorcar coming [to me] in the air (i.e., another big fly is landing upon him!) Yaaah! (excitement) Surely everyone will be amazed (*agoma* – i.e., at my good fortune), they will all be amazed! Iyaa! (joy) This is no joke! (*si masewera!*) Just look at my motorcar! And what's more, it's carrying my very own maize-grinding mill (*chigayo changa chija*)! Yaah, mmm, yaah! (overjoyed excitement)

Iiih! (surprise) What's up—who's this?! (*Kodinso, ndaninso?!*) Why it's you, O lice! (*Komanso, inu nsabwe!*) You should eat well now—you should eat me very well! (*Muzindidya bwinobwino!*) Aala! (watch out!) Why are you causing me to itch (*Mumandiyabwa bwanji*)?! You must just eat my blood, if you wish,

_____

[59] The young man is becoming irrational in his argument now. Here he claims that were his father still alive, he might have decided the dispute between the two in the brother's favor, which is most unlikely—unless he too were engaged in the practice of sorcery!

but don't make me itch, that's out! *Yaah!* (strong affirmation). What's this? (*Komatu?*) There in the distance, there they are coming, my friends are—those are my friends!!⁶⁰ *Eeetueeeh!* (verification—i.e., for sure!) Let me not complain, not at all! (*Osadandaula, iyayi!*) *Mm-mmm-mmm!* (with wonder) My friends—you are my very good friends, *yaah!* (affirmation)[61] But this world... *Aaah—aah, aah—aah, aah—aah!!* (amazement—he envisions something very strange) All these mountains—where do they come from?? There were no mountains here before! *Shyaa!* (i.e., that's bad!) Now where am I going to pass through—these mountains?! *Yeee!* (perplexity) *Aha-haah—haah!* (+ more undirected laughter; he is laughing pathetically to himself as the scene comes to a close).

This is a highly emotive, most plaintive scene, as we hear the young man get progressively more unstable as far as his mental condition is concerned. This is reflected in the dialogue as he moves from a futile effort to convince the medicine man (and his wife) to reverse the effects of his already administered magic, to a final attempt to convince his strong-willed sister to agree to his illicit request—and finally, to his wretched conversation with the biting insects that now populate his poor body and tantalize his deranged mind. The ups and downs of his fading hopes to make things right contrast with the resolute feelings and attitudes of those whom he is conversing with—the diabolical witchdoctor and his wife as well as his own sister, whose strong Christian convictions will not allow her to participate in her brother's sin, even if this results in his physical and mental downfall. These three short scenes are played (or "voiced") in an admirably realistic manner by the *Sewero* players involved. Indeed, it surely sounds as if they are actually experiencing these tragic emotions themselves. They thus entice their remote listening audience to sample such feelings as well—from diverse perspectives to be sure, depending on each one's current life circumstances, personal moral state, and spiritual well-being.

5.1.5 Dramatic action

"Drama" is another one of those qualities that may be viewed either in a general or a more specific way. The latter is the perspective of this section, that is, as another particular aspect of the artistic and rhetorical nature of *Sewero* plays, namely, their "dramatic" compositional structure. This is manifested in two special ways—that is, in a well-conceived and constructed "plot" (story-line), and second, by means of effective personal "characteri-

---

⁶⁰ The mentally unbalanced young man must see some human beings walking nearby—they are clearly different from the "friends" that now inhabit his body!
⁶¹ There does not seem to be any reply from his "friends"—so they could be a figment of his dislocated imagination. In any case, he's off on another subject, apparently becoming delusional now.

zation". This is not to claim that every play is "perfect" of course, especially the ones that have been contributed by outside groups (i.e., not the "resident" TWR troupe). But on average they all manifest a consistently high level of creative excellence and emotive appeal that would tend to influence the radio audience to give the current performance that they happen to be listening to the benefit of any doubt.

A narrative *plot* normally follows this general course of action or sequence of events: *initial situation* => *conflict* => *rising tension* => *climax* => *resolution* => "*coda*". The final element involves some pointed, Scriptural advice, reproof, or encouragement from one or more characters concerning the plain or implied "message" of the play. Most *Sewero* performances exhibit a more or less seamless movement in the action from one stage to another as the drama is developed to the crisis point where some explicit biblical instruction or Christian counseling is both necessary and applied as part of the resolution.

Fictitious, but life-like, characters then "play" the narrative through the dialogic action of drama. The appealing feature of the various character types that cross the *Sewero* stage is their naturalness and familiarity—"just like the folks we know in our home village or whom we have met at the local marketplace". There are several "stock personages" who tend to reappear in various guises in the plays, for example, the "strong Christian" (male or female, and usually *not* the local pastor!) who helps to identify the main spiritual problem that needs to be clarified and ultimately dealt with on the basis of the Word of God. There are also various types of "weak Christian" (e.g., the gossip, jealous spouse, church elder, religious syncretist) along with other typical roles and local personages (e.g., the traditional "doctor", polygamist, office "boss"), including also those "ordinary", everyday Christians who are facing some sort of trial, test, or challenge to their faith/life. An important aspect of the "realism" of the *Sewero* plays is the generally accurate "casting" of the different character voices, despite the relatively small corps of performers to call upon.

For a good example of this element of "dramatic action", let us briefly consider several prominent features of the play entitled "The Rich Man" (*Mwini-Chuma*), which is the *Sewero* team's powerful adaptation of Luke 16:19-31.[62] In order to provide a context for the comments that follow, I will begin with a synopsis of the complete play according to its plot sequence of six scenes (I-VI) of character dialogues, all but the second of which involve

[62] I discuss this play in detail in a paper (submitted for publication) presented at the Annual Congress of the New Testament Society of South Africa, meeting at the University of Natal (Pietermaritzburg) on April 23, 2003. It is entitled: "*Mwini-chuma* ('Owner-of-wealth'): A dramatic radio contextualization of the Lukan 'Rich-man' parable in Chinyanja".

just two interacting speaking voices. Each scene is set in Lilongwe, the capital city of Malawi, except for the last, which takes place on the hypothetical cosmic interface between heaven and hell.

I.   The play opens with a young girl, a street kid, who is trying her best to persuade the story's "villain", a rich man (RM) to give her just a small handout so that she can buy some food. He disparagingly refuses her persistent pleas for help, at the same time arrogantly bragging of his own great wealth and status in society. His harsh, insulting words finally chase the hungry little beggar away, while he walks on to a sumptuous banquet that he is giving for his sycophantic friends.

II.   This short scene, set in some first-class hotel banquet hall, provides a graphic contrast with the first, as we hear snatches of the RM and his adoring guests eating and drinking it up to their heart's content—and to the point of obvious excess. Again the RM brags obnoxiously as he, in god-like fashion, dispenses lavish gifts to his eager beneficiaries, even the very chairs that they are sitting upon!

III.   The RM rudely summons his fourth wife, Catherine, to the sitting room of their home and tells her to pack her belongings and leave. He obnoxiously informs her that he is immediately divorcing her because he has made it an arbitrary personal policy to stay with one woman for no longer than three years. So her time is now up! At first she thinks he's joking, but he soon convinces her in his characteristically offensive manner that she must get out of his mansion right away.

IV.   The RM goes out for a drive in his posh motorcar and sees a woman by the side of the road, waiting for public transportation. He offers her a lift, which she gladly accepts. His conceited small talk soon moves in the direction of a devious proposition: he wants her to divorce her husband and come with her children to live with him! However, she happens to be a solid Christian, and soon recognizing the direction that his conversation is taking, she begins to witness reprovingly to him in return. She tries to get him to repent of his immoral behavior, warning him of the judgment to come (citing several Bible passages in the process), and urging him to accept Jesus as his Savior. The RM now realizes his error and quickly tries to get this woman out of his life (and car!), while awkwardly parrying all her attempts to convict him of his wicked lifestyle.

V.   The RM drives along and, hoping to avoid the same mistake, picks up an obvious prostitute who is advertizing herself along the road. This young woman, only 17 years old, readily agrees to his proposal, which he boastfully promises to pay for her services at ten times her stated rate! The RM starts to fondle the girl along the way, and she worriedly warns him to watch out where he's driving. All of a sudden he loses control of his car and with a loud crash they smash into an oncoming vehicle. The accident is fatal, at least for both the occupants of RM's car.

VI. We hear the RM, now residing in hell, complain about his great suffering there. He cries out to "Father Abraham" for help—first to leave that place (a much greater favor than a little water!). Abraham reminds him of the corrupt, opulent lifestyle that he adopted while on earth and informs him that a great barrier now prevents him from getting out. The RM then asks that Abraham send someone with something to drink, but instead, Abraham reproves him for wasting all his worldly wealth with wicked living. The RM complains that no one warned him about this fiery place of punishment, but Abraham reminds him of that God-fearing woman who tried to witness to him and how he chased her away. Resigning himself to his horrible destiny, the RM requests that Abraham send someone to warn his wicked friends and relatives back home. Abraham refuses, saying that they have preachers and pastors to listen to. The man pleads again for his fellows with the excuse that they are impious rogues and thus won't pay any attention to ordinary humans. Abraham replies by citing the gist of Luke 16:31 and concludes with the judgment that the RM must now only worry about himself and the unending suffering that he cannot escape.

This play carries a very powerful impact in the Chinyanja language, prompting many listeners to write in requesting to hear it again. Christ's original parable resonates powerfully throughout the entire drama, being embellished with an idiomatic vernacular style, a familiar setting, and an interpersonal situation that is all too common in contemporary Malawi. Listeners are quickly led to empathize with the sequence of women who are so grievously wronged by the Rich Man, the obvious "villain" of this story— the little beggar girl, the wife whom he divorces, the lady he tries to seduce, and the prostitute whom he finally kills by his dangerous driving. His arrogant behavior is utterly disgusting and audience-alienating as well. That is a natural human reaction, but the key issue for each listener to decide is how far s/he wants to identify with the true "heroine" of the play, as adapted by the *Sewero* team from Christ's account in Luke (Scene IV). Here was an ordinary but honorable Christian lady, a loyal housewife and mother, who refused a rich man's clever advances with their tempting appeal to a life of luxury with him. Instead, ignoring any personal loss and putting herself at considerable risk, she was brave enough to testify boldly of her faith and to persist in her attempts to convince him of the need to repent of his sinful life and turn to Jesus.

As in the case of Christ's parable, so also most of the "action" of the *Sewero* story is verbal in nature. In the original text, there is really only a single verse which involves any significant physical activity, and even that is recounted in the passive voice after the two characters are dead (Lk. 16:22): Lazarus "was carried by the angels to Abraham's bosom"; the rich man simply "was buried". It is interesting to note that "Lazarus" does not have a role to play in the Chinyanja adaptation since he is not really in focus in Christ's parable either; rather, the spotlight is upon the rich man (RM). A rough comparison reveals the following structural relationships between the corresponding seven "scenes" of the play and the biblical "verses":

I ← Luke 16:20-21   II-III-IV-V ← 19 (22b)   VI ← 23-31

There is an obvious disproportion here: an asymmetrical "Lazarus" (a young female street beggar) is immediately introduced into the radio play and then, having served her dramatic purpose (namely, to initiate the negative portrayal of the RM), she is taken "off stage", so to speak, never to return. Most of this *Sewero* drama is then devoted to a tragic contextualization of Luke 16:19. The villainous *Mwini-chuma* is strongly personalized and placed in the capital city of Malawi, where he thoroughly (tragically?) condemns himself to hell by repeatedly engaging in actions that demonstrate that he has no regard either for God or for his fellow man. In fact, he has become his own god, interestingly enough, in a proud, selfish, and boastful manner that is very reminiscent of the "rich fool" parable of Luke 12:16-21.[63]

Although it is not given quite the prominence as in the two-part arrangement of original text, the final scene of the radio play (VI) clearly represents its emotive climax for these reasons: its textual position (natural end stress), non-worldly setting (heaven/hell), participants (the RM now in dialogue with the biblical Abraham), situation (a great role reversal for the RM), and special studio effects (the arresting "echoed" voice modulation). Several novel elements introduced into the conversation (see also below) also ensure that this spoken verbal aspect of dramatic "action" firmly captures the attention of the listening audience, and thus also reinforces the sobering message being conveyed. It is an implicit call to repentance for anyone who manifests attitudes and actions that are in any way similar to those that condemned the rich man to everlasting torment in hell.

The other prominent scene in the Chinyanja narrative adaptation is the middle one, which is also appropriate from a structural viewpoint. Scene IV, in which the RM tries to entice a Christian housewife on her way to the market, covers roughly 40% of the entire play in terms of verbal volume. This scene is also important because it includes all five of the explicit Scripture

---

[63] This correspondence with the former Lukan parable is explicitly reinforced (but only obliquely for the audience at this early stage in the story) in Scene III when the RM's soon-to-be ex-wife so designates him, twice in fact, in her disappointment and disgust over being divorced: "I knew that I should have thought about it more carefully because I am already your 4th wife. So you, husband, you are a *fool*—you are never, ever satisfied (*mukadali munjira zedi!* 'you are always on the way [to your destination]'). ... *Eeya!* [Indeed] but that might be the end of you, husband, this *foolishness* of yours!" The latter is an obvious case of plot anticipation, though the audience would not yet realize this.

texts that are utilized in the play—namely, by the woman in her efforts (a) to resist the temptation of the RM, and (b) to persuade him to repent and receive Christ. She warns him of a coming judgment, but he will hear none of it. His utter dismissal of her testimony at this juncture represents a crucial development in this contextualized plot (i.e. a proleptic "motivation") because it later leaves the RM without an excuse in his later appeal to Abraham (S-VI, see below).

Several other instances of dramatic foreshadowing are also built into the radio play's unfolding action, for example, both women whom the RM picks up in his car warn him about his inattentive, dangerous driving that may soon cause an accident.[64] Immediately after the second warning, that is exactly what happens. This violent crash (as evoked by sound effects coupled with the young prostitute's anguished screams) constitutes the most vividly conveyed "action scene" in the entire play. It also forms a graphic, albeit sorry contrast with the earlier, next most vibrant event, namely, the riotous party setting, where the RM is heard living it up with his friends (S-II). Here the impression of profligacy is conveyed by the background sounds of royal music, rather incongruously accompanied by the uneven commotion of a crowd of people, raucously laughing, shouting, cheering, clapping their hands, and ululating.[65]

A sharp contrast in emotive expression is dramatized at the very beginning and ending of this play upon the biblical parable. To begin with, two characters at opposite ends of the socio-economic scale collide in conversation (SK = street kid [i.e., "Lazarus"]; RM = rich man):[66]

> SK: Help, boss—boss, help! Don't pretend that you don't even see us at all!
> RM: Go away! Who is supposed to help you?
> SK: Why you, boss! If you help me, surely God will help you.
> RM: He has already helped me—I am very rich. So what do you know—nothing!
> SK: Just give me 20 Tambala (i.e., less than 1 cent), that's all, so I can buy a yellow bun.
> RM: Where are your parents? Your parents should help you! Why are they so primitive (*anatsalira kuti* 'where have they been left behind')? Perhaps it (i.e., your poverty) just runs in the family (*mwina ndi pachibale panu* 'perhaps it is on your relationship')!

---

[64] The Christian lady observes: "Right now the way you are driving this car, you could easily have an accident and die—then at which place would you arrive (*mukafikira kuti*)?" (S-IV). This is an understated adaptation of the stock evangelism question: If you were to die tonight, where would you go to spend eternity?

[65] This party "crowd" is here vocally represented by the other five members of the radio cast, who intermittently produce these different audio effects to suggest the group's riotous but also obsequious exclamations of thanksgiving as the RM is speaking in praise of his own beneficence.

[66] A few choice vernacular idioms are cited along with their literal back-translations (in single quote marks), just to add a little local color to these examples (for those who may be able to appreciate them).

SK: *E-eeh!* (an exclamation of shock at his harsh reply).

RM: Why should I help you—why should I give you anything?!

SK: OK then, I'll grab on to your jacket [i.e. hang on to you till you give me something]!

RM: Hey you! You're asking for trouble! (*undipangitsa ngozi-we* 'you'll cause me to have an accident'—i.e. I may lose my self control and give you a beating!).

Since there is no "narrator" to describe the different characters of this play, they must depict themselves in and by what they say. Throughout the drama then, the RM's own words characterize, incriminate, as well as convict him. They patently reveal what a supercilious, self-righteous, boastful, selfish, materialistic, and lecherous fellow he is. Nobody is spared his arrogant insults, not even his "friends", who do not complain lest they sever them-selves from his largesse, for example, at his banquet to himself (S-II).[67]

The drama's didactic message, which as usual occurs at its close (S-VI), must also be conveyed in direct speech. In this case, it is rather easy to follow the biblical parable fairly closely—naturally, with a bit of added dramatic embellishment! (see Lk. 16:24-26; RM = Rich Man, AB = Abraham):

RM: My life is being terribly punished by this fire! *Aaah!* (exclamation of dejection and disappointment) Will I ever get out of this place? Hey, Master Abraham! Hey, Master Abraham, help me! Help me to get out of this fiery place. Help me to get out—there's so much heat in here!

AB: Remember when you were alive on the earth. You had your chance then. But you threw your whole life away by doing wicked things. Besides, between me right here and you over there—well, it's just not possible, not even to put your big toe over, not at all! (*sichingafike chala poponda, ayi*).

RM: *Aaah* you! Well, if that's the way things are, how about someone coming here to give me something to drink? *Aaah!* I'm thirsty, veeery thirsty. Please Abraham, have mercy on me—give me some help!

AB: Just remember that God enlarged you (*adakulitsa*) with much wealth. And with that, instead of praising God, you just wasted it and threw it away. You followed the desires of your heart. So now there is nothing that you can expect but punishment. You had time on earth (i.e., to repent).

What a pitiable contrast in emotions we have at the opening and conclusion of this play to reflect the drastically changed dramatic situations of the central character—the Rich Man. The radio listeners may not be able to physically see what this entails (though their imagination will certainly suggest some likely scenarios), but the animated dialogue clearly conveys the

---

[67] This whole scene (based on Lk. 16:19b) may be an indirect ironic and critical reflection on the local "high society" (*apamwamba*), where wealthy "big people" (*akuluakulu*, whether new capitalists or ruling party politicians) always draw a crowd a sycophants who will do almost anything to stay in favor in order to gain personal material benefits.

intended message along with the biblical point to be learned—or rather, empathetically experienced.

5.1.6 Subdued humor

Most brands of humor automatically lead to the expression of some manner of emotion (see 5.1.5), but its purpose and effect is distinct enough to warrant our consideration as a special topic. Humorous subjects, treatments, outcomes, and sayings are an important aspect of many *Sewero* performances. Such carefully-placed, good natured, and nuanced wit—whether an extended comic overlay or a brief and pointed intrusion into an otherwise somber story—usually arises out of the current dramatic situation rather than as an actual verbal comment, though the highly colloquial participant dialogue does occasion some laughter too at times. Humor performs the important dramatic function of "lightening" an increasingly "heavy" emotional load as well as the underlying didactic message of a given play. Alternatively, a little light-heartedness often helps to reinforce a particular "point" that one of the characters is making or to strengthen her/his argument by thus seeming to de-emphasize it. Thus humor is not introduced haphazardly into a story, but normally (when successful and/or well motivated) it is injected where and when necessary for a particular communicative purpose, both in relation to the characters in dialogue—or more importantly, to influence the perception and reaction of the listening radio audience.

The notion of "subdued" (or "low-key") humor is of course debatable, depending on who is doing the evaluation and according to which criteria. My personal impression of the wit that is manifested within the *Sewero* corpus is that, though it tends to be always present, even pervasive in most texts, it is never allowed to dominate the drama or to divert attention from the more serious moral or theological issue that a given play seeks to convey. In other words the funny side of character speech never degenerates into what at least some members of the audience might regard as being rude or unruly—in short, over-the-top and out of place with regard to Christian drama.

While it may seem at first to the outside observer to be a relatively minor feature, humor is actually quite important, in drama as well as other types of African artistic discourse. Not only do laughable words, actions, or situations help attract and retain an audience, but more importantly, it is the expected way to "tell a story" in a local vernacular setting. Humor—sometimes subtle, sometimes comical, jocular, even risqué—is an essential element of traditional oral narrative performances—no matter how weighty the life topic that is being treated (see Wendland 1976:ii). In fact, a bit of wit is normally employed, either more or less in keeping with the context, as an essential device by most, popular and effective oral communicators (e.g., preachers) to ameliorate or provide some psychological relief from a particularly solemn theme or a weighty didactic or hortatory message. How suitable is humor in a religious discourse, especially where the Bible is itself used or referred to? That of course depends on the culture and the situation concerned; in central Africa, it is a vital aspect of virtually any communication, no matter how serious and somber, including at times, even funeral addresses.

In keeping with their popular, down-to-earth communications philosophy and purpose, the *Sewero* team usually manages to walk the narrow path between having too much and too little humor in their plays. It is the job of the program's producers to ensure that the story does not get out of hand or off the track by introducing elements that detract from the biblical message and Christian application that is at the heart of every drama. To this end, the use of humor is never deliberate or contrived; rather, it is allowed to flow naturally from either the current dialogue sequence or from the dramatic circumstances being depicted. In other words, frequently a smile or a laugh is elicited simply because of the colloquialness of the characters as they speak in vigorous vernacular interaction with each other, playing out their roles to the limit of their creative capacities. At other times, it is the specific situation in which the characters are or to which they refer that is humorous—perhaps ironic, satiric, even paradoxical. At times an obvious caricature is involved, for example, the "pastor" in the excerpt below who is so blind as to be willing to make a pact with the devil, as it were, in order to become more popular among his parishioners.

We have already seen many examples of *Sewero* wit in word. But it may be instructive to focus on this particular feature throughout a given selection, such as the following dialogue from the play entitled "Have you really been sent?!" (*Kodi mwatumidwadi?!*). In this portion the paradox of a pastor seeking and boasting about magical empowerment obtained from a traditional medicine man serves to foreground the point that no Christian is immune from such temptation: When problems multiply and build up to a personal or corporate crisis of some sort, witchcraft—either for or against—inevitably comes to mind. In this case, the ironic humor of the situation (the pastor speaking just like a syncretistic parishioner) acts like a deliberate form of "defamiliarization" to emphasize the opposite—that is, how such severe challenges really ought to be handled according to the Word of God.

(Setting: The present conversation, reproduced below in slightly abridged form, occurs near the middle of this drama about a local pastor seeking greater popularity with his flock. Various problems have arisen in the congregation, and the new pastor has not handled them very well; some influential leaders are now quite upset and have recently visited the pastor about these issues. For his part, the pastor, accompanied by his wife, has gone to seek help from a nearby medicine man since he apparently does not know what else to do! In this humorous scene we hear the animated conversation between the two after they have returned from an apparently successful visit with the medicine man. [P = the pastor, W = his wife].)

P: Well now, thank you very much, my [good] wife! (i.e., for accompanying me to go and see the medicine man for help; without her support, he may not have gone through with it!)

W: Certainly! (*Eeeeh!*)

P: So we've just returned from visiting the medicine man (*sing'anga*) there.[68]

W: That's right!

P: We ought to thank God very much who has so much concern for us in his heart (*anatitsimikizira kwambiri mumtima mwake*) (at this point she interrupts him in her excitement for being supplied with a supposed "cure")...

W: Yes (i.e., carry on).

P: ...that [he has helped us] in view of our troubles...

W: Mmmm! (mild affirmation)

P: ...as we keep on struggling...

W: Yes...

P: ...with those people who hate us here! (*otida kuno*)[69]

W: They hate us, they [most surely] hate us!

P: [But] God enlightened us [with this plan of] going to see that very medicine man!

W: That's for sure! (*Kwabasi!*)

P: And we must also thank the medicine man for his humble attitude... (*pod-zichepetsa kwake* – i.e., he probably did not gloat over the fact that the pastor was coming to get help from him—instead of preaching against his activities!)

W: Mmmm.

P: ...when he welcomed us so well with his whole heart (*ndi mtima umodzi* – i.e., with all sincerity, at least on the outside)...

W: For sure!

P: ...but also with a sad heart (*mtima wa chisoni*).

W: [Yes], with a sad heart!

P: It's very important, now that we've just come [home] here, that we do not forget everything that our father (*bamboo wathu*), that medicine man, [told us].[70]

W: [Whatever] he told us!

P: He explained [everything] to us.

---

[68] This sudden revelation (i.e., it has not been foreshadowed in the preceding dialogue) would come as a great shock to the members of the listening audience, most of whom are probably church-goers. "How could a pastor even think of doing such a thing? After all, it is his job to persuade us not to seek help from witchdoctors and diviners! And how could his wife agree to go along?!" It is not as if the leaders did not try to warn and encourage this pastoral couple either, for that was done in the scene just before the present one.

[69] Use of the verb 'hate' (*-da*) would immediately suggest to most people (but certainly not a man of God!) the hostile activity of witches or sorcerers.

[70] This is another shocking statement by the fallen pastor: He acknowledges that the traditional healer is his "father"—that is, a person with authority who is taking care of them in their time of need.

W: Most certainly [he did so]!

P: You remember that he said that as soon as we arrived [home], we must take some of that medicine—that stuff, the medicine in that little parcel you're holding (*m'kaphukusi akoko*).

W: Right.

P: I think I should put it into some water so that we can drink it.[71]

W: Yes.

P: The aim is (*kusonyeza kuti*) either tomorrow or the day after when we stand up to preach publicly (i.e., during a church meeting), we will speak words that are very powerful (*tilankhule mau mwamphamvu ndithu* – i.e., our preaching and teaching, or in this case also their "defense", will be most persuasive, in every respect)!

W: That's right!

P: So that our whole body will be filled with a fierce liquid (*madzi aukali*)!

W: Yes, very fierce!

P: Just like this liquid here!

W: Poison!

P: The liquid from a hawk (*Madzi a chiwomba-nkhanga*)![72]

W: [Pure] poison!

P: Eeyaah! (strong affirmation)

W: He prepared a medicinal powder [for us]! (*timankhwala taketi toperaperatu*)[73]

P: Yes, pour it in!

W: Right!

P: Eeh! (warning) That's enough, that's enough! (sound of drinking) Aaah! (I'm finished!)

W: So are we both supposed to drink this?

P: Eeh (mild affirmation), you too must drink as well (*iwenso tamwakonso*)!

W: (sound of drinking) Aaah! (she's finished too!)[74]

P: There now, the whole body is filled with much ferocity (*lidzala ukali kwambiri*)!

W: So much (*Kwambiri*)!

P: As a result, whenever I speak, instead of just seeing my body, people will see a most terrifying fire! (*azidzaona moto woopsa kwambiri!*)[75]

W: Fiiire! (*Moooto!*) (She certainly encourages his fantasy, for she fully believes it herself!)

P: Eyaa! (strong affirmation)

W: And they will greatly fear me too there! (*Ngakhale inetu akandiopatu kumeneko!*)

P: Aaah! (amazement) This is no joke for sure! (*Si masewera ayi!*)

W: (She laughs with glee at the prospect.)

---

[71] The pastor continues to use plural verb forms here (e.g., *timwe*), so it is apparent that he is applying the directions for these different magical devices not only to himself, but also his wife.

[72] This refers to some magical potion that was prepared from the bodily fluids of a dead hawk. Thus just like the hawk is known as being a fearsome bird of prey, so also anyone who drinks this potion will have their personality transformed into a similar fierce and awe-inspiring disposition!

[73] She uses the diminutive concordial prefix here (*t[i]-*), perhaps as a subtle way of euphemizing the prohibited substance that is being referred to.

[74] There appears to be a reversed allusion to the Fall story here, only this time the man takes the forbidden substance first, his wife second—following the lead of someone who should have known better!

[75] In other words, from now on the pastor's words will be so powerful and penetrating that no one will dare try to oppose, refute, or rebuke him (as happened in the recent past).

P: [Then] I will be speaking like a real pastor (i.e., with power, impact, appeal, and persuasion)!

W: And I like a [pastor's] wife!

P: Eyaa! (strong affirmation)

W: Yes, just like a pastor's wife!

P: Well now, remember that he also told us to apply this medicine by tattooing it into our bodies (*mankhwala awa titemere*).

W: Yes indeed, we need to tattoo ourselves—but we must do it in the evening.

P: Yes, this very evening, but [we must be] naked (*chambulanda*)![76]

W: Naked?

P: Naked—without wearing any clothes! (They both laugh.) My dear wife! (*Chemwali!*) We are laughing as if it's nice to be naked!

W: Iiih! (amazement) He has really helped us![77]

P: Aaaaah! (with great satisfaction)

W: He (i.e., the medicine man) is our very own father—our grandfather—we must not let him go (*tisamutaye* – i.e., we need to keep going to him for help)!

P: And I can say this with all fearlessness: God is [working] in that fellow! (*Mulungu ali mwa iye uja!*)

W: Truly God is [working] in that fellow!

P: That's for sure!

W: And we don't even know how [God] has ordained him [for such work] (*wamudzodza bwanji*)!

P: Did you see the people—all the people who were there?! (i.e., those who had gone to this medicine man for help)

W: Hiii! (amazement)

P: Being helped! (*Kuthandizika!*)

W: May the Lord be with him!

P: May he indeed be with him![78]

W: May [God] help him—may he direct him in his work!

P: 'Amen'! 'Amen'! 'Amen', God is great (*Mulungu ndi wamkulu*)!

W: Yesss, he's so great!

P: So then what was the next thing? You know what he said about this medicine.

W: Those little amulets there (*timphinjiri tili apoto*)?

P: Yes, he said that I must wear these things around my waist (i.e., underneath his clothes).

W: Eeeh. (affirmation)

P: You too have to wear some around yours.

W: That's right—me, two—and you, two! I was listening very carefully!

P: Now this string of yours [*kamkuzi kako* – i.e., for binding the medicine around the body]…

---

[76] All the familiar details of how to engage in sorcery are known to this couple; the more detail that they go into during this conversation only increases the humorous, but also horrible, irony of the situation for the listening audience. The wife is a little reluctant, however, but she quickly agrees, for to them the end certainly justifies the means.

[77] Now verbal irony further heightens that of their proposed actions: Their nakedness would only highlight (in the darkness) their foolish, unbiblical behavior—totally unbecoming of such supposed servants of the Scriptures! Again there are more humorous allusions to the Genesis Fall account.

[78] The adulation of this couple borders on blasphemy—they speak of the pagan medicine man as if he's the greatest prophet and healer of God.

W: Yes? (go on)

P: …you need to be strong and tie it onto your hand.

W: The twisted one there? (*Kopotapotako?*)

P: Eyaa! (strong affirmation)

W: Alright—alright!

P: So he said that we must cast this medicine here on our path.

W: The path that crosses where? (*Njira yodutsa pati?*)

P: The one that visitors must cross when the come to discuss that matter with us (i.e., the case that the leaders of the congregation had brought against him for neglecting his pastoral duties).

W: I see.

P: So that as soon as they arrive, they will be able to speak only nonsense (*mwachibwazibwazi* – an idiom) out of fear for me.

W: (she laughs) They will be defeated! (*Basi!*) [They will be] trembling before you *nje-nje-nje!* (an ideophone depicting someone who is shaking with fear).

P: Fierceness will be just dripping (*ndikulikitika*) from my mouth!

W: It's true!

P: So if we do that, the power of God will rest in our midst!

W: In the midst of both of us!

P: Don't raise your voice too loudly! (i.e., so that any passer by might overhear what they are discussing)

W: Both of us! (She speaks more softly now.)

P: That's right!

W: But there's also some [medicine] for putting under your tongue.

P: Ooooh, ya-ya-yaah! (i.e., recalling what he almost forgot)

W: Underneath your tongue (*Kutseri kwa lilime*)!

P: I almost forgot that!

W: That small amount of medicine that he put in here.

P: Ya-ya-ya! 'Thank-you!' (i.e., spoken in English for emphasis)

W: Here, this-this bit of reddish medicine…

P: Right-right!

W: …he said you must put in under your tongue so that wherever you go and speak…

P: [My] words…

W: …wherever you go…

P: …those very words, those very words…

W: at that very place…[79]

P: …those very words—will resound like thunder! (*ngati chivomezi!*)

W: …truly like the very thunder itself!

P: As a result [when my case is discussed again], inside they will all realize, "Aah! (remorse) This man is not guilty (*Munthuyu ndi wopanda chifukwa uyu*)!"[80]

W: Yes indeed, I'm telling you… (*Ndithu, ndipo inu*)

P: Whiiii! (i.e., the pressure will be over)

W: …God is good!

P: [We have] a body of flesh (*Thupi la nyama* – i.e., weak humanity, subject to trials and temptations)!

---

[79] In their excitement and joy, the pastor and his wife speak antiphonally here, one breaking into the speech of the other as they share this mysterious plan.

[80] The hoped-for verdict of the elders is foregrounded by being uttered in direct speech.

W: Yes indeed, [facing] many trials (*zosautsa*)!

P: You don't say!

W: It [the Word of God] says that we will enter into the kingdom of God with troubles (*zisautso*)![81]

P: Oh my—aah! (belabored) we, well for sure, we have encountered them!

W: Iiih! (in mock fear)

P: These problems, those—and still others, spiritual troubles (*auzimu awa*)!

W: Yes indeed!

P: No-no more, we're tired of them! And another thing…

W: Yes?

P: …we must surely thank this elder (*mkulu ameneyu*), this medicine man!

W: Iih! (amazement, i.e., at what he supposedly did for them) I'm telling you!

P: Because he has done his best to fight this war together with us in our lives!

W: It [the Word] says that God helps a person who helps himself![82]

P: 'Amen'!

W: He gives us a hand (*Amaikapo dzanja*)!

P: 'Amen'!

W: He comes through with his help (*Nangopyoletsa zithandizo*), and he just comes…

P: 'Amen! Praise the Lord!'[83]

W: …[with help] like the sort of things that we are doing here!

P: Yes, my wife, thank you very much indeed (i.e., for supporting me in this effort).

W: Yes, at first did you not refuse [this plan]?

P: Aaah! (with embarrassment) Well, ah, only out of ignorance.

W: So look now what we've gained!

P: Well, now isn't it true that… (she cuts him off)

W: Alright, but we can do that later. We've had a good talk, iiih! (surprise)—[we've] exhausted the subject (*kuchulutsa nkhani*)!

P: Aah! (with weariness) So how about first saying our prayers because…since it's already so late (*kwada kale*), we can just eat in the morning.

W: Should we just eat in the morning? (i.e., it would have been her job to prepare the evening meal, no small task)

P: Eeeh. (affirmation)

W: So you got filled with that [resolution to our problem], is that so?

P: Aaah, eeeh! (strong agreement)

W: (she laughs) Alright.

P: Let's close our eyes for prayer.

W: You go ahead and pray!

P: God our Father, we praise you for your good-heartedness (*chokoma mtima*)! In truth, our Lord, you have shown forth such great love for us…

W: Yes, so much!

P: …In truth, my God, you have looked upon our great problems…

W: Mmmm! (affirmation)

---

[81] Here we have a mis-placed application of Acts 14:22.

[82] This is a popular mis-attributed quote; the Bible says no such thing. If a genuine believer is "helped", it is God alone who does the helping—not man, let alone oneself!

[83] It sounds here like the wife is doing the preaching, and the pastor simply responds with the usual utterances.

P: ...You have agreed, Lord, to advise us in our spiritual lives (*miyoyo yathu ya uzimu*) that it was most necessary for us to go and find our parent (*kholo lathu –* an honorific reference), that medicine man. We thank you, our Lord, for being with us. When we sleep, our Lord, we ask that you would bless all the magic (*mizu –* 'roots', a metonym) that we have tattooed ourselves with in here—and all the other medicines, so that they might do their work in the right way...[84]

W: Yes, so true!

P: ...We pray these things, our Lord, in the name of Jesus Christ...

W: 'Alleluia'!

P: ...'Amen'!

W: 'Amen'!

So ends one of the strangest prayers and most amazing stories that many in the audience will ever have heard. How could a "Christian" pastor, and his wife, behave like that?! Humorous this portion of the drama is, for sure—and all audiences laugh when they hear it replayed. However, for most their laughter is in response to the absurd incongruity of the situation—that a man (and woman) of God could sink so low. This is humor with a stinger in the tail too, for they fully realize that if a minister could succumb to such a common temptation in the time of trouble, so could they. A serious warning thus rests just beneath the surface of the shocking situation being depicted with its rapidly moving dialogue: Take this message to heart, even as you laugh while it is being uttered!

5.1.7 External effects

This is another compound stylistic feature, consisting in the *Sewero* productions of any type of verbal or (usually) non-verbal device that is introduced to supplement the central narrative-dialogue progression of a given play. Since this dramatic resource was already described in section 1.3.2, and because it cannot really be illustrated on a silent page, I simply give a summary of what is possible to suggest something of the great diversity in usage that is manifested in these performances, both to enhance as well as to capitalize on the sound-sensitive medium of radio communication.

In the popular "Rich Man" (RM, *Mwini-chuma*) play (see 5.1.5) there are three main types of external audio effects that play a crucial role in the evocation of a suitable background for the intense verbal action that is taking place on the "stage" of the listeners' minds. These are—in order of importance for a typical *Sewero* presentation—the use of sound effects, thematic

---

[84] What a travesty of a prayer—as if he were praying for success to Satan himself, but in the name of God!

187

songs, and a program announcer, or story presenter. Each category performs a different sort of dramatic function:

(a) Sound effects

Three different types of sound effect are described (unfortunately not exemplified) below:

- *Musical motif*—This acts as an aural signal alluding to the RM's great wealth and also serves to specifically introduce two scenes: First there is a majestic orchestral piece that introduces his great banquet in celebration of himself (S-II); next we hear a modern pop instrumental tune that quietly plays in the background of his sitting room as he gets ready to chase his wife out of the house (S-III); finally, there is an allusion to a car cassette/CD player that he offers to turn on in an effort to impress the woman whom he has just picked up on the road (S-IV). Ironically, all this music is Western in style, undoubtedly also in origin, perhaps subtly suggesting the extent of the RM's alienation from his own traditional way of life and cultural value system.

- *Crash noise*—This loud and chilling audio device brings scene V to an obviously ominous end. It includes the young prostitute's terrified screams to suggest that there was a tragic loss of life involved (a fact immediately confirmed at the onset of S-VI). Coupled with our recall of both women's earlier explicit warnings, the crash clearly implies that the RM has foolishly killed himself as well as his passenger as a result of his inordinate lust and overweening pride.

- *Voice echo*—The RM and Abraham both speak throughout the final S-VI with a strong echo effect—the latter's being noticeably deeper and stronger. This conventional audio device evokes an after-life scenario and perhaps also suggests the extreme distance that separates the two speakers. This eerie, unsettling sound complements the overtones of seriousness and judgment which pervade the entire scene and brings the drama to a solemn, tragic close.

(b) Thematic songs

Popular Christian recorded songs are used to introduce and conclude the complete play. Both deal with the theme of judgment, which is prominent within the drama itself. The opening selection is more general, warning listeners of the need for repentance, for example: "Friends, right now is the time [to repent]—this present generation will not last long…" (the first line). The second and closing song is very appropriate for this tragedy; it specifically refers to the parable of Luke, hence also to the play just dramatized:

> Mother, woe is me, there was a lot of weeping there! (repeated)
> Just read Luke 16, verse 19 and ending at verse 31.
> So that king [i.e. the RM] died and was taken off to Gahena.
> Mother, woe is me, there was a lot of weeping there! (repeated)
> There was a poor man, Lazarus, but he knew Jehovah.

Typically, a great deal is left implicit in such musical renditions, but at least the gist of the story is presented to reinforce the point of its principal didactic message. The *Sewero* producers try their best to include such transitional Christian songs, whether traditional or modern in musical style, that reflect the day's play in some way, but it is not always possible to find a close match. In place of a vocal tune then, a pure instrumental melody may substitute on the borders of a play, or occasionally also internally at a major shift of scenes.

(c) Program Announcer

The program announcer (in this case, Mr. Nyongani Chirwa) normally introduces every play with some general exhortation for the audience to listen carefully to the forthcoming broadcast so that they can better benefit from it. Today he adds the semi-humorous personal appeal: "Don't leave me here by myself [at the station] lest I get lonely with nobody to visit with (*ndisungulumwa*)."

At the end of the day's drama the announcer usually has some regular closing remarks, e.g., "Well these events may seem like just a 'play' [to you], but in fact they are true!" Such words have obvious reference to the personal life-application that was rendered both explicitly and implicitly in the story. Often, if there is time (some plays are a bit longer than others), the announcer will elaborate to a certain extent on that application, adding his own word of encouragement to reinforce that of the performers. Here, for example, is what he had to say about the *Mwini-chuma* play:

> There are some people who long for the chance to live their lives again and to be like you [listeners]—to have this opportunity to hear the gospel and repent before it's too late. There will come a day, my brother, my sister, when the time for repentance like this passes one by (*idzadutsa*), so it would be better to demonstrate a good example while you are still alive. Wealth is a gift from heaven, but if we misuse it, it becomes a curse.

Every *Sewero* play is both informed and contextualized in particular by a judicious use of pertinent sound effects. We will note this also in the next chapter when considering the complete drama entitled "Do not hate one another" (*Musadane*). The original radio audience would hear, for example, the wheezes and coughs of an ailing AIDS-symptomatic father, the intoxicated (dagga?) threats of his son as he angrily confronts his innocent aunt with accusations of sorcery (for bewitching his father), the fierce barking of a little yard dog as he bravely tries to warn that young fellow away, and finally, at the close of this dramatic scene, the crashing sound of household goods being smashed to pieces as the boy vents his anger and suspicion upon the humble property of his aunt—an overt symbol of their now fractured interpersonal relationship.

All these sounds, as well as the various musical and choral insertions, serve to create a dynamic aural backdrop to the dialogic sequence that forms the backbone of every *Sewero* drama. Together they call to mind the mutually complementary imagery of familiar scenes and settings that offer a mental vision that automatically contextualizes the action and makes every play's didactic message that much more memorable.

5.1.8 Summary—Stylistic unity in diversity

Many different stylistic devices and techniques have been illustrated under the seven general categories described above, and certainly more compositional features could have been noted when moving through the various text samples. The main aim, however, has not been to focus on the details, but rather to demonstrate the overall impression that a given *Sewero* drama makes on the minds of its unseen audience. Admittedly, the preceding inventory of creative artistic forms is both partial and artificial because, as was pointed out in their individual descriptions, any given manifestation can usually be classified in more than one way or be further analyzed as consisting of several, more intricate devices in close combination. On the other hand, it is impressive to observe, even in silent print, how all these different features of dramatic radio dialogue have been employed in skillful, utilitarian harmony with one another to effect a pervasive narrative unity as well as a powerful thematic focus throughout a given sample selection.

The point of the preceding overview and exemplification then is not the preciseness, completeness, or correctness of my external categorization of elements, but rather to give a demonstration, admittedly imperfect, of the masterful manner in which these radio tales are put together. They are not merely "entertaining" narratives that exhibit "art for its own sake", nor are they, on the other hand, instances of typical preaching presented in the formal cloak of a play, that is, in the mouths of several different character voices. Rather, each drama manifests its own distinctive artistry with a particular aim, that is, as a composition in which the formal, creative means have been employed in order to infuse a captivating vernacular story with impact, appeal, dynamism, and appropriateness so that its biblically-founded message can have the intended spiritual effect (warning, reproof, instruction, encouragement, etc.) through the effectual working of the divine Paraclete. This concern for a definite persuasive impact will be further explored below through a consideration of the *Sewero* program's manifold rhetorical dimension.

5.2 Aspects of rhetorical argumentation

As just noted, the *Sewero* dramas embody *purposeful* art—that is, stylistic form (the manner of expression) employed in deliberate service of communicative function (the realization of meaning). Thus every play has a didactic point to make, and the dialogue is focused to display that particular aim or intention for the day. Each individual speech acts as an essential part in an extended rhetorical "argument" that is designed to persuade the audience to concur with the implicit or explicit Christian message being conveyed, whether for or against a certain moral or theological issue, attitude, controversy, belief, or behavior. If listeners happen to agree already with that particular "thesis" and its line of argumentation, then the objective is rather one of reinforcing the position from a biblical perspective, which is made clear by the selection of Scripture passages that are either cited or paraphrased, usually during a play's final resolution. This constitutes the "rhetoric" of performance—the skill of using language both effectively and excellently, that is, with impact as well as appeal. In this section we will explore several additional facets of this dynamic dimension of communication.

5.2.1 General communicative functions

A number of prominent communicative functions have been identified as being prevalent in didactic art. All of these have been amply illustrated in the various *Sewero* selections that have already been cited; more examples will follow in the excerpt below. The five principal aims may be briefly defined like this:

- *Expressive*: the speaker verbally manifests strongly felt emotions, attitudes, opinions, values, etc., as these relate to the current issue or crisis being discussed.

- *Imperative*: the speaker seeks to overtly change or modify the behavior (speech and actions) of listeners, that is, away from some undesirable pole and/or towards another option that s/he supports.

- *Informative*: the speaker intends to confirm, expand, or revise the thinking of an audience concerning some subject by providing them with specific elements of conceptual or referential meaning (exposition, explanation, clarification, definition, etc.).

- *Relational*: the speaker desires to establish, enhance, extend, or reinforce a harmonious interpersonal relationship with his/her addressees, thus promoting a feeling of social and/or religious "solidarity".

- *Aesthetic*: the speaker utilizes the artistic forms of his/her language (figurative language, rhythmic diction, phonic beauty, etc.) in order to augment the impact and appeal of his discourse, especially to enhance the effectiveness of one or more of the other speech functions.

These central functions are often manifested in conjunction with each other, that is, in a mutually complementary way with respect to a delimited discourse segment, e.g., a clause, sentence, paragraph, a larger sectional unit. Some communicative aims tend to be more prominent than others during the course of a distinct "speech event", each of which combines with another to comprise the complete drama. The *relational* function, for example, is normally found at the beginning or ending of a particular discourse or conversation; the *imperative* and *expressive* in areas of climax or culmination; and the *informative* to develop a certain argument or to provide certain essential background details. The *aesthetic* function then is utilized selectively throughout the dialogue to provide selected segments of emphasis or special appeal, that is, to highlight the main peak points of the play's verbal and psychological "action".

5.2.2 Speech-act analysis

The preceding speech functions are clearly quite general in nature; they thus serve to merely introduce one to a more thorough study of the rhetoric of artistic discourse. They may be complemented, especially in a dialogic text, by means of a "speech act analysis". According to this method of investigation, a discrete segment of oral or written discourse ("speech event") is viewed as being composed of a sequence of distinct "speech acts", which may be simple (singular), compound (conjoined), or complex (mixed) in nature. Normally the last type applies where literary works of a high standard are concerned. Every speech act in turn is composed of three elements: its particular purpose or intention (i.e., its "*illocution*"), the linguistic and literary forms in which it is expressed within a given language (i.e., the "*locution*"), and its actual outcome or contextual effect within the larger text (i.e., its "*perlocution*").

In this section on the rhetoric of artistic discourse, I am primarily interested in the different *illocutions* that a given dialogue exchange might reveal. These may be categorized into different categories for ease of reference, depending on the precise nature of the dramatic situation and the circumstances of the characters who happen to be speaking. Seven major classes of speech acts may be identified as summarized below (with typical illocutions given as examples); these overlap with the five functions listed earlier (see Wendland 1998:64-66):

- **Directives**: Speech acts (SAs) that are intended to modify the behavior of the listener(s) in some tangible way, e.g., to command, urge, preach, permit, refuse, prohibit, exhort, advise, etc.

- **Informatives**: SAs that seek either to reinforce the present cognitive state of the listener(s) or to modify/change this somehow, e.g., to declare, describe, predict, explain, etc.

- **Evaluatives**: SAs that express a particular personal judgment, assessment, criticism, attitude, or opinion of some sort, e.g., to rebuke, convict, condemn, certify, commend, praise, apologize, etc.

- **Expressives**: SAs that aim either to externalize the emotions of the speaker and/or to influence the emotive state of the listener(s), e.g., various types of exclamation and utterances that convey strong feelings, e.g., of joy, grief, anger, affection, frustration, hope, etc.

- **Commissives**: SAs that commit the speaker to some future course of action in relation to the listener(s), e.g., to offer, accept, promise, vow, pledge, guarantee, etc.

- **Interactives**: SAs that serve primarily to open, maintain, or close a complete text or speech event, e.g., the language of greetings, farewells, reciprocal ego-stroking, and ritual discourse (i.e., texts that give speakers/hearers positive feelings due to their importance and/or familiarity).

- **Performatives**: SAs that actually effect or institute the particular action or state which they refer to in relation to the addressees, e.g., bless, curse, baptize, marry, ordain, appoint, resign, etc.

The point here is not to overwhelm the reader with detail, but simply to suggest that our everyday discourse is often more complex in terms of communication than we realize, and this applies just as much to artistic oral or written composition. It is often helpful, therefore, to analyze a given text or transcript (oral text) at least superficially in terms of these speech acts in order to probe more deeply into *what* one speaker is actually saying to another, *how* s/he is expressing it, and *why*. This sort of an approach, for example, can reveal something of the rhetoric, or the persuasive force, of a particular line of argumentation.

An analysis of speech acts can by further supplemented and enhanced by exploring the *connotation* of certain utterances or speech clusters, that is, the specific feeling, attitude, opinion, or value that is conventionally associated with certain words and phrases. More sophisticated studies can go on to reveal the *presuppositions* that the speakers/hearers of a conversation assume (e.g., concerning traditional religious beliefs), as well as the many diverse threads of *intertextuality* (citations, allusions, echoes) that tie one utterance to another, whether these occur earlier within the same speech or in some completely different oral or written text. An entire conversation may be examined in this manner, and a topical and/or a relational outline can then be made of the major and minor communicative functions or the constituent speech acts. This enables the analyst to discern more fully and precisely both the rhetorical intent of the selection as well as its artistic manner of composition. While I cannot go into such detail in the present study, a more general annotation of the excerpt below indicates the potential utility of such research in revealing the rhetorical dynamics of a particular dialogue. This selection is taken from the play entitled, "If it had been you, what would you have done?" (*Mukadakhala inu, mukadatani?*), which is the *Sewero* team's partial (abbreviated), contextualized adaptation of the dramatic story of Job's trial and ultimate triumph through faith in God.[85]

> (Setting: We pick up this dialogue in the middle of Scene Two as the calamities continue to strike Job and his family. He remains steadfast in his trust that God has not forsaken him, but his wife suspects that jealous sorcerers are attacking them with their magic. She urges Job to take action in the traditional way—that is, to go to a diviner/medicine man to find out who it is that is troubling them and to protect their possessions with magical charms. A diversity of speech-acts are manifested during the course of their debate concerning the Christian's response to a situation of apparent arbitrary adversity; I have identified a number of the key examples in boldface type [J = Job, W = his wife, D = Job's daughter, S = a family servant].)
>
> J: God's word says that we will meet up with these sorts of [problems]
> W: Aah! But how was God's word there for us? (*adalikonso liti?* i.e., for protection or support; **denial, negative evaluation**).
> S: Aaah! (dejection) We have no maize, [and] the field of groundnuts, the whole place—all the flowers have begun to dry up and drop off. (**complaint**—indirectly against Job as she points out a little later)
> W: We were worried about having to till over there, and now this happens—something's amiss now, evil is around! (*chilipo-chilipo pamenepo, chilipo-chilipo!*)
> S: And I want to tell you this, madam (*Adona*), don't you remember...
> W: Yes?
> S: I told you (**warning**) that the boss here ought to do something (i.e., to protect our fields with magic).
> W: You (i.e., speaking to Job) heard all these things that your servant told you—he's very wise. You might even [consider] grabbing your grandchild to extend

---

85 This particular play deals only with the prologue and epilogue of the book of Job, that is, 1:1-2:13 + 42:7-17. Therefore Job's three "comforters," Elihu, and the Satan do not appear as characters at all. The validity of this "de-textualized" presentation of the drama may be debated (e.g., its effect on the overall "message" of the book); for the present, I am only concerned with the rhetorical features of the play as actually performed by the Sewero group.

194

the cattle pen (*kugwira kachidzukulu kupangira kholali*), or [to benefit] the maize milling business.[86] [If you had done so] we'd be so wealthy by now (*ndindindi!* –an ideophone denoting many-many items). [Yes, by now] we'd be so blessed, Father (my husband)—if it were not for this perseverance of yours (*khama laoli*—i.e., in continuing to trust in God's providence)! (**criticism, proposal**)

J: That will not happen (*Sizidzatheka!*)—how could I seek wealth and sacrifice a child?! Never! (**utter refusal**) Alright (speaking to the servant), I've heard you—you may go.

W: Iiih! (amazement) How your perseverance persists (*Angokhala a khama yawa*)! But now what can we do, [my] husband? What is it that is causing our possessions to pass away, what could it be? (**disapproval**) Wouldn't it be better to [magically] protect [our wealth] (*Si bola kutsirika*)?! (renewed **proposal**)

J: Nooo! When you protect [yourself like this], it doesn't mean that then…[all your troubles are over]. Tell me, all these people who protect themselves—has the rain fallen on all their gardens? (**argument** based on common experience: all the farmers suffered in the drought, not only Job)[87]

W: Aaah! (frustration over his line of reasoning here)

J: Tell me now, did the rain fall on the gardens of those who protected [them]? (The implied answer is "no!")

W: Then our cattle would not have died either! (an added aspect of her **argument** for being more magically proactive in this matter)

J: So [you mean to say that] the maize dried up in my fields alone? (negative answer implied)

W: Aah, well magical protection does help (*kutsirika kumatothandiza*), but you…aaah!

J: Alright, alright (i.e., let's stop this argument).

W: But you just cling to your Bible, nothing else! (*Koma baibulo gwagwagwa!* [ideophone] *Basi!*) (**criticism**—on a deeper, spiritual level now)

J: Yes, well is it not the Bible that leads us [in life]? It says, "In everything praise [God]"—that's what Jehovah (*Yehova*) expects [from us]. (**rebuttal**)

(Job's daughter comes to report that three of her siblings, two brothers and a sister, have died in different, but tragic circumstances. [I have omitted this material in the interest of space.])

W: Ihh-iiiigh! (cry of great grief)

J: What's happening to me here is just too much! (*Koma chandiona ine, sindizo!*) (**protest**)

---

[86] Job's wife here makes the awful suggestion that Job employ sorcery himself, involving the ritual murder of his own close relative, in this instance his own grandchild (!), in order to protect and promote their property. Such is the horror of traditional religious beliefs taken to their extreme, which due to their prevalence in religious and secular discourse alike would seem to be all to common an occurrence in society.

[87] This is the first major point in Job's rational argument to counter his wife's emotional appeals to seek "professional help" from traditional religious practitioners.

W: Old Man, now what did I tell you?! (*Madala, tere ndinati chiani?*) I keep saying that people are the cause [of this trouble] (*n'zamuanthu*), but you reject [that explanation], and so now I can't even mourn![88] (bitter **accusation**)

D: Mother, that's not all… (The daughter goes on to report yet another serious car accident involving one of her brothers.)

W: I will not weep—I will not weep—No, I will not weep!! (expression of **despair**)

J: Is he still alive?

W: Didn't I tell you that this was your responsibility (*pamutu panu* 'on your head'—i.e., to obtain the necessary magical protection against such disasters)?! Let me run to a medicine man, he can help us. As for me, I won't weep, Old Man, no I won't weep! (**blame, proposal**)

J: No—well, alright. Mmm, no indeed, I simply do not understand what Jehovah is doing to me! (*sindidziwa kuti koma Yehova wanditani?*)—or even to my children, as you are reporting… My, but noo!

W: You'd better change your story (*muzinena pang'ono-pang'ono*—'you must speak slowly/softly, i.e., instead of simply complaining to God, you had better do something concrete)!? (**accusation**—i.e., failure in fatherly duties, **order**) The children keep dying and you [do nothing but hold] your Bible in your hands! (*Ananso amwaliranso, Baibulo lili m'manja, eeeh!*)

J: Alright, but even if I start speaking in a different manner… (**deflection**—Job tries to sympathize with his wife without compromising his theological principles)

W: Iiih! (sorrow) What can I say?! (She is completely frustrated by his docile demeanor during this crisis.)

J: ..would the children return [then], would [our] maize return to the storage 'barns' (*mabalani*)??

W: What can I say—I used to think that it was a blessing to sleep with a believer (*ndi dalitso kugonana ndi munthu wopemphera*), but that's not true at all!! (**repudiation**—of the blessedness of their marriage!)[89]

J: Well, it's the Word of God that is able to calm our hearts down (*amatikhazikitsa mtima pansi*). (**profession** of faith)

W: Aaah! (i.e., how can you still say that!?)

J: Alright, I have heard the things [you have complained about]…

W: Iiiiih! Aaah-iiih! I will not weep! (she says this while she is weeping!)[90] (**remonstration**)

J: That is exactly how death is (*Malirowo ndi amenewowo!*)! God's Word testifies that we came into this world and we will return again to our home (i.e., in heaven). If that is how my children have died (i.e., as believers), that's alright—praised be the name of Jehovah![91]

W: Iiiiiihhh! (shock at his words of continued trust)

---

[88] Job's wife continues to claim that sorcery is the source of all their woes—and further now, Job himself is partly to blame because he has refused to resort to traditional means of protection.

[89] This is tantamount to a curse, or at least a request for a divorce! Job's wife seems to have reached the limit of her toleration now; something's got to give—either his faith in God, or her faithfulness to Job!

[90] This is a tremendously evocative scene, for all listeners can sympathize emotionally with the wife's great grief, and many too with her resolve to seek traditional help. The conflict of contradiction comes in that they also know that according to the Word of God which Job continues to cling to, he is in the right and his wife is wrong!

[91] This is an interesting contextualized paraphrase of Job 2:20. It is not just any death that is blessed, but only the passing of a believer, who returns then to the home of his Creator.

J: I know that God has his purpose [for this]. That's why in everything I thank Jehovah, yes, even though these things have happened. I know that my [heavenly] life has not been affected even though my [earthly] life here is most painful. Isn't it true that my help is found in Jehovah?! (reinforced **profession** of faith)

W: So your life is not painful? No, [if that were so], you'd allow me to go and find out who is the cause of all this trouble (*mwini chimoli* lit. 'owner of this sin'). I'd go to the medicine man so that these very matters, we would find out what it's all about (*zokhazi tikaone kuti n'chiani*). (**proposal**)

J: Noo! [Go] to the home of a medicine man and inquire there and you'll find out that the relatives of the medicine man himself have also died (i.e., he could not protect them either)! (**rebuttal**)[92]

W: Ih! I wish that I would have died! Shall I mourn my children—shall I mourn [our] cattle? I don't know what to weep for anymore! (expression of **despair**)

J: There—there now! (*Chabwino, ayi, chabwino!*) Alright, I know what I must do (prayer implied?). ... I will see what I can do. I'll fix [things], I'll make [things] right (*Ndikonza, ndilongosola*). But [I know that] Jehovah has his purpose for me... (expression of firm **faith**)

(A new Scene begins; some time has passed and the sufferings of Job and his family have gotten worse.)

J: (He is weeping and groaning as the scene opens.)

W: Is that weeping I hear? Why don't you just pray now? Why are you moaning? Take your Bible now and read it! Are these not real troubles now? All our things (possessions) are long gone. This very day these problems simply continue [as before]. Your mouth is completely dry and cracked with sores (*Kukamwa kwanyenyeka ndi tizilonda*)! What kind of good is there in that, huh?! (**derision**)

J: Nooo—[don't talk like that]! (**protest**)

W: Yes, and now you can't even wear shoes on these feet of yours—the cracks of your toes are full of sores (*unyawi khetekhete!*—ideophone)! Is this good?!

J: (groans)

W: My, what problems these are!

J: Please pour some water on my back here (*Tandithirani madziwo kumbuyoku*—i.e., to cool the pain of his sores and probably fever as well).

W: Ihh! (disgust) Now you start again with me about the water—instead of going to get some "medicine" [from the medicine man] to wash your back with! Why don't you make use of that?! (**insistence**)

J: Do you think that we only receive good things from Jehovah, mmh? (indirect **refusal** plus added **testimony**)[93]

W: Iiihh! (antipathy)

J: At times we do encounter difficult problems [in life].

W: Iih! But must they all come simultaneously like this with so many different [evil] 'designs' (*Zimangophatikiza chovuta madizayini-madizayini*)?! You mean that I must be here night and day with a cup in hand to pour water on your

---

[92]   This is the second major point in Job's rational argument to counter his wife's emotional appeals.

[93]   This is the third major point in Job's rational argument to counter his wife's emotional appeals; the God-fearing are not immune from life's trials and troubles.

body? How is it possible that you have not died by now?! (*Osangomwaliranga bwanji?*)[94] (indirect **imprecation**)

J: Don't talk like that!

W: It would have been better for you to die before you had encountered so many [problems] (*mukanafa pungwepungwe!*—ideophone)!

J: No indeed, when he [God] wants me to die, then I'll surely go! (*ndipita ndithu!*)

W: Iiihh! Well, just tell him to [let you die] because you are speaking out of the side of your lips now (*chifukwa chimene umanena pambali pamlomo*)! So simply blaspheme him (*momunyoza*) so that he gets angry at you (*akuphyere mtima* 'he gets hot in the heart at you') and takes you [in death/to heaven?]! (**proposal**)

J: Noo! That is talking like a fool (*chitsiru*)! (**reprimand**)

W: Aaaah! (anger at his rebuke) What impudence (*chibwanatu*)! I'll pour some water on you so I can then leave!

J: I cannot curse God so that I might die![95] (**dismissal**)

W: Aaaagh! (i.e., why not?!)

J: I sounds as if you've already found another place to stay (*Kukhala ngati inuyo mwapeza pena*)![96] (**accusation**)

W: Haah! (scorn) Me—"find another place"?? [Having experienced] a story like this (i.e., the loss of everything), could [a person] ever desire a family again?! (*Nkhani yache imeneyi ungafunenso banja?*)

(The conversation is interrupted and their son arrives with some more bad news: All the vehicles that they own have been destroyed in accidents and the goods they were carrying lost as well. They have nothing left. Job's wife now has had it—she says she is leaving him in the care of his paternal relatives. She feels that Job had refused all her advice about seeking help from the medicine man. He was very sick, but did not die; she could no longer help him in his state of living death—why should she die along with him?)

This excerpt from the *Sewero* group's adaptation of the Job story (at least a part of it) is an excellent illustration not only of their dynamic manner of contextualizing the Scriptures but also their expert rhetorical technique in traditional vernacular debating. Job's argument with his wife (or vice-versa) is a powerfully persuasive instance of idiomatic *repartee* in the Chinyanja language. The dialogue features an ever-changing recycling of the same basic set of speech acts (primarily directives, expressives, and evaluatives) along with their more specific illocutions—most notably, bitter recriminations and harsh demands on the part of Job's wife, countered by his persistent refutations and confident expressions of trust in Jehovah, his God. A

---

[94] These last words are equivalent to a curse (an interesting embellishment of the original account in Job 2:9)—Job's wife has reached the breaking point. She has concluded that she and her family have been bewitched along with her husband, the primary target, and she just wants it all to end.

[95] This adds a further contextualized perspective on Job 2:9—Job's wife urges him to curse God *so that* he might die (in response to God's anger over that act).

[96] Job takes her previous threat to "leave" as a threat to leave him (in his troubles) for another man. This is the first time that he displays any serious aggravation over her insulting speech and behavior towards him.

more detailed plotting of the diverse sequence of speaker intentions could be made, if needed, but the preceding overview is sufficient to demonstrate the complex artistry that enhances the intense argumentation of the two characters involved. This is a superb example of how well-played Christian drama can render the drama of Christianity in immediately relevant terms for a contemporary radio audience.

5.2.3 Assessment of "relevance" and rhetoric

I will conclude this chapter with a few comments regarding another method of cognitive and emotive analysis that may be employed to study and evaluate a given speech event or conversation from a somewhat different perspective. This is based on the so-called "principle of relevance" which maintains that good communicators endeavor to achieve a certain level of parity or balance between "efficiency" and "effectiveness" when composing a certain discourse, either orally or in writing (Gutt 1992:23-25).

Efficiency considers the relative complexity of the language that it used; in other words, a text should not be so difficult that it becomes unintelligible or too difficult to conceptually "process" for most members of the target audience. On the other hand, the discourse should not be too dull or simple either, lest people become bored or lose interest in what is being said. *Effectiveness* pertains to how helpful the text is in terms of its overall "communicative value"—that is, in realizing one or more of the speech functions (or set of illocutions) discussed above as these happen to relate to the hearer's (reader's) current sociolinguistic setting. In short, how beneficial is the speech act (or the event as a whole) either to the listener's state of mind or to the interpersonal situation that s/he is in? The more useful and valuable the discourse is, without being too complex or challenging to interpret, the more "effective", hence "relevant" it is—or vice-versa. The preceding example from Job was given to show how important these considerations are during verbal communication—especially when one is analyzing and assessing the practical relevance and importance of literary discourse, as utilized particularly in radio drama performances.

This and many other instances may be cited to demonstrate the extent to which the *Sewero* programs achieve a considerable measure of personal *relevance*—significance, appropriateness, applicability, etc.—during their broadcast presentation. The intense, closely interactive dialogue communicates *efficiently* in that it is generally quite natural in linguistic (dialectal) terms, appropriate to the sociocultural and dramatic situation, and clearly expressed or relatively easy to decode aurally with regard to its oral manner of articulation (assuming an ideal, static-free setting of reception). These plays are generally also highly *effective* in getting the desired message across to their target audience—that is, in the form of vernacular communication that has important implications for most people's understanding of Scripture and their Christian lifestyle too, whether this concerns them personally (or someone they know) or the religious fellowship of which they are a part.

The *Sewero* plays are also relevant on a secondary level in that they present some excellent examples of biblically-based, locally *contextualized* exhortation (admonition or encouragement) and instruction with particular regard to the confrontation of Holy Scripture with conflicting or antithetical African traditional religious beliefs and practices. At times, certain biblically aberrant doctrines of some so-called African Independent Churches (AICs) are dramatically critiqued, with selected passages of Scripture (conservatively interpreted) serving, as usual, as the recommended model to follow.[97] Prominent examples of the latter include (in the *Sewero* repertory) teachings on the authority of God's Word, the Trinity, the deity of Christ, the total corrupting influence of sin, the reality of hell, the bodily resurrection, and the certainty of the Lord's return for a final judgment of all people. In this sense then the *Sewero* plays also perform a minor *apologetic* function in their defense of a standard evangelical interpretation and application of the Scriptures.

To be sure, not all *Sewero* productions are equally effective or excellent in communicative terms. There is indeed a variable range that is manifested in terms of overall quality, e.g., certain examples that are stylistically substandard, poorly performed, rhetorically weak, overly moralistic, or theologically off the mark, either in part or throughout an entire play. But enough quality and consistency is manifested, especially on the part of performances by the resident TWR group of players, to warrant their recognition as being one of the most pervasively influential agents of Christian communication in all of south-central Africa. Such a positive critical evaluation may be further supported by presenting an entire *Sewero* drama for consideration (including the reader's personal enjoyment and edification), augmented by an accompanying set of more detailed expository and reflective comments (see chapter 6).

---

[97]   As noted in chapter four (4.4.3.1), the doctrinal stance of TWR (see Appendix C) acts as the general standard with regard to hermeneutical issues that pertain to the Scriptures.

6. Contronting the Occult: Anatomy of a Drama against the Diabolical

6.1 Orientation

The aim of this chapter is to present a detailed examination of a single out-standing *Sewero* production entitled *Musadane* "Do not hate each other!" This particular drama very well illustrates the pervasive influence that the indigenous occult has in society, even in the lives of professing "believers". The play also manifests a contemporary flavor in that the pervasively destructive influence of AIDS is introduced as an issue towards the end of the story in rather dramatic fashion. In addition to a brief structural and sty-listic analysis ("anatomy") of this play, I will also survey the apparent func-tion ("physiology") of some of the main compositional devices. My illus-trated overview is carried out by means of an English translation of the com-plete Chinyanja text transcription. Accompanying my translation is a selec-tive set of notes that call attention to certain important vernacular stylistic and rhetorical features as discussed in the preceding chapter.

My translation offers only a pale reflection of the original text, which is a dynamic oral performance that capitalizes on the full range of emotive expression possible in the human voice. The dynamic dialogue of the ver-nacular presentation also fails to find adequate representation in English, especially since it was not always fully captured in the Chinyanja transcrip-tion to begin with (due to various types of transmission-related interference as well as play-internal vocal overlapping). Nevertheless, this hollow shell of the complete audio recording, together with various types of annotation, is deemed better than a simple English summary of the play's plot, accompa-nied merely by my prosaic description of what is taking place in the original radio version.

The following translation provides a moderately idiomatic reproduction of the Chinyanja text. Interesting vernacular figures of speech and idioms are also supplied in parentheses in order to allow readers to savor a bit of the flavor of the local imagery, colloquial expressions, Bantu syntax, and color-ful diction. Parentheses are also used to provide shorter explanations about the actual language used or the sociocultural background of the original text. Longer comments regarding such issues are restricted to footnotes. Certain points of obscurity and uncertainty are also noted, as are special linguistic usages that cannot be duplicated adequately in my translation. Brackets are reserved for those aspects of semantic content, emotion, attitude, and other connotations that are clearly implied by a particular Chinyanja expression, e.g., ideophones and exclamations. Short English-based insertions into an utterance ("borrowings") are indicated by single quote marks, as are very literal English back-translations of Nyanja idioms. Each speaker is designated by an abbreviated reference that is given at the beginning of each scene. Every distinct segment of dialogue is set off as a separate paragraph in order to highlight as well as to distinguish the sequence of individual speakers. Longer speeches may also be divided into topically oriented paragraphs.

6.2 *Musadane* ("Do not hate one another!")

The entire play consists of six "scenes", each of which represents a shift in the physical setting (time, place) and cast of characters. The individual scene "boundaries" and transitions between them are plainly indicated within the production by a brief interval of rapid (recorded) drumming.

6.2.1 Summary

The six scenes that compose the play *Musadane* are first summarized below to give readers a brief plot-related orientation before the entire text is presented in translation.

I. An older man is very sick with severe coughing and diarrhea; he thinks that he is soon going to die. He tells his wife and elder sister about a strange and disturbing dream that he had—about a little creature that was chasing him with a spear. The man and his wife immediately suspect witchcraft and decide to take him to go and see a medicine man (*sing'anga*) for help. The man's sister, who is a strong Christian, tries to persuade them to go to the hospital for treatment instead. She even offers to arrange some transportation for them. But they both turn on her, accusing her of being the very witch who is trying to kill her brother! They chase her out of the house and prepare to go to the medicine man.

II. The sick man and his wife arrive at the medicine man's house. This "doctor" brags in typical fashion that he will soon discover the cause of the man's illness and cure him. The medicine man interrogates the man, focusing on the strange dream that he had (which he must have been told about in advance, not surprising in a small village setting). He says that this is a sure sign of witchcraft, against which he must be protected. Probing further, the medicine man plants the suggestion that it is the man's uncle and sister who are in fact the witches trying to kill him. He gives the sick man a strange magical ritual to carry out back at home and assures him that this will heal as well as protect him if he carefully follows these directions.

III. The sick man, who has obviously not recovered (even after observing the prescribed anti-witchcraft ritual), is complaining about the whole matter to his son. He says that his older sister, the young man's aunt, wants him to die so that she can gain possession of their house, which has a valuable corrugated metal roof. The son becomes furious and promises revenge. His mother only stokes up the hatred by complaining about where she will live with the children after her husband dies. The young man heads off to his aunt's house in a furious rage.

IV.   The angry young man reaches his aunt's house and raises a big ruckus there. He shouts insults at her, accusing her of witchcraft, and threatens to kill her if his father happens to die. The aunt tries her best to calm the boy down, insisting that she is the one who loves her brother the most. Her nephew, however, will not listen at all but, instead, becomes increasingly belligerent. He starts breaking up some of the household goods that are standing outside and says that next he is going to beat her up.

V.   The aunt and her daughter are surveying the damage that the young man did at their home. She cites several Bible passages in support of her decision not to try to defend herself or go to the police to press charges against her nephew. Forgiveness is the character of a Christian, she tells her daughter as they discuss what will happen now in the family after such a serious disruption in personal relations. Apparently, the only thing that prevented the nephew from doing greater damage was that he injured himself in the process and was forced to retire.

VI.   The sick man has partially recovered because his grandson came with an oxcart to bring him to the hospital, where he received treatment that alleviated his current symptoms. He is now discussing with his wife and their son the results of some blood tests that were taken, when his sister unexpectedly arrives to find out how he's doing. The man reveals that his illness is far worse than they suspected—he was found to be HIV-positive! He thinks that he will die immediately, but his sister reassures him that this is not necessarily the case; he can still live a productive life. The conversation turns to his life-style, past and future: He was living an immoral life before, but will now have to severely control his sexual appetites lest he pass on the HIV virus to others, his wife in particular. They discuss the wicked behavior that brought enmity to the family. The Christian lady testifies that it was her faith that brought her through the crisis and enabled her to forgive her brother's family. She now urges them to become believers themselves by renouncing witchcraft and receiving the forgiveness of Christ. The play ends with the sister publicly declaring her forgiveness of her brother's family and then leading them together in a joint confession of sins.

6.2.2 Translation

ANNOUNCER:

I have come again with our play for the week from your broadcasting house. I am Enos Kanduna and I welcome all you listeners wherever you might be at this time. My request again today is this: Let us remain together to listen to what I've brought you in the play for this week. Now don't forget, listeners, that in this program we always learn different things that concern our present life. So stay right there! But first—the title of our play: The title of this play is "Do not hate each other".

6.2.2.1 Scene I

[At the home of a sick man and his wife: MAN = the sick man, WIFE = his wife, SIST = the man's sister]

MAN:*Aagh-aagh!* (coughing) Nabanda! (more coughing)[1]

WIFE: What's wrong? *Iiih!* [i.e., exclamation of worry] My, but you are coughing a lot!

MAN: (more vigorous coughing)

WIFE:Oh my, these things [i.e., are serious]! *Iih-iih! Mmh!* [i.e., great worry]

MAN: As far as I'm concerned, I can see that I'm not going to live. The world hates me! (*dziko landida,* i.e., my problems are so great that I cannot escape.)

WIFE: *Iiih!* [shock] Don't talk like that!

MAN: Yes, it's true—it's [what] I am seeing…

WIFE: Don't say that!

MAN: Last night, while sleeping, I dreamed of a short little creature.

WIFE: *Aa-ah!* [surprise]

MAN: The short little creature was carrying a spear!

WIFE: *Iiih!* [surprise]

MAN: So it wanted to stab me, but I ran away.

WIFE: *E-eeeh!* [great shock]

MAN: Running, I just kept on running!

WIFE: *Iih-iih!* [suspense now]

MAN: That's it, then I woke up.

WIFE: *Iih!*

MAN: Next I heard a voice behind me saying, "*Aah!* [warning] So now it's all over because of that [i.e., what you just dreamed]. You will not live!"

WIFE: *Aah!* [you don't say]

MAN: I thought, *aah!* It must be true—because this diarrhea just does not stop at all!

WIFE: Well, that really is cause for concern.

MAN: Right, when I start purging [I don't stop]—for 'three hours'.

WIFE: That's for sure!

MAN: [I] purge, drink some water, purge [again]!

WIFE: It's as if it all comes out again [undigested]. You eat and [the food] just comes out without being ground up at all (*chosagaika chonse*)—pouring out in a watery rush (i.e., vividly depicted by the characteristic ideophone *fwanthu-fwanthu!*).[2]

MAN: There's no life left—no life left!

WIFE: *Iih-iih!* [worry] No, there's something out there (i.e., witchcraft) that people are doing. That short little fellow is around—he's right here!

MAN: That's right!

---

[1] The sick man addresses his wife in a rather formal, honorific manner, i.e., *Na-* (with reference to an adult female) + *-Banda* (her clan name). A more familiar form would be *(A)make* (Mother of) + the name of their last-born child, since they obviously had at least one son.

[2] Though rather graphic in its details, this exchange immediately invites the radio audience to participate in an everyday (unpleasant) occurrence that they must be very familiar with. They are thus able to easily identify with the characters and the situation that they are experiencing; this then will lead them just as surely into the main "argument" of the day's play.

WIFE: They are insulting us—and it's just terrible!

MAN: So that is why I am telling you, my Sister, when I leave (i.e., die), do not chase away this wife of mine. You see what she's doing for me—all the time she's right with me!

SIST:*Mhmm!* [agreed]

MAN: She's being troubled [with me]!

SIST: Certainly.

MAN: Very much troubled!

SIST: *Mhmm!*

MAN: When I start purging, she does all the work—even throughout the night!

SIST: *Mhmm!*

MAN: That's right!

SIST: For sure! I agree that this lady is very loving.[3]

MAN:*Mmmm*—that is so true! So now the way things are, what do you think about going to a medicine man?[4]

WIFE:Yes indeed, that is necessary—[let's go] to a medicine man!

MAN:Yes, a medicine man!

WIFE: Because when a person has dreams like that, it's better to go try out different medicine men (lit. *kumalimbikira kwa sing'anga* 'to work hard for a medicine man').

MAN:Right, for these [problems] are being caused by certain people *n'zamwaanthu!*—i.e., an allusive reference to witchcraft being practiced against him).

WIFE:For sure, these problems are being caused by certain people!

SIST:"By certain people"? No, don't talk like that. Don't rush off to some medicine man! Instead, go to the hospital. Because at the hospital- - (a mis-speak) Because when a person has severe diarrhea (*akatsegula m'mimba* 'if he has opened up in the bowels'),[5] what happens is that all the water drains from his body. So you go to the hospital there and let them help you. Perhaps they will give you some 'pills' (*mapilisi*) and they may add some water into your body (i.e., put you on a drip of replacement fluids). Now wouldn't that be much better? So go to the hospital—there they will give you some water.

MAN:*Aaah!* [i.e., disappointment] [You are] a child of Satan (*Satana*)!

WIFE:That's right—the devil (*mdierekezi*)!

SIST:No, that's not it at all—let's just go to the hospital!

MAN:No indeed, you [are] my Sister, no! (i.e., you ought to know better than that).

---

[3] The expression "this lady" (*maiyu*) may sound rather awkward in English, especially since the person being referred to is standing right there. However, this is an *honorific*, third-person mode of reference which is the required verbal etiquette whenever adults are speaking to or about each other. There are several different "levels" of social status, or formality, that may be indicated by such terminology (e.g., intimate, informal, formal, and regal), depending on who is speaking to whom on what occasion and under which circumstances. The *Sewero* players are very careful to observe such conversational norms in their various fictitious dialogues.

[4] In a traditional setting, this is where virtually every immediately inexplicable occurrence or action inevitably leads to—the "medicine man", or "diviner-doctor" (*sing'anga*). He is the common man's most credible "consultant" in such affairs.

[5] The third person pronominal reference is not marked for gender in Chinyanja; it can be either masculine or feminine. However, the default assumption is that a man is being referred to, unless the linguistic context or the non-verbal setting suggests otherwise. I will follow this convention in my translation, using the masculine pronoun for all indefinite and unspecified references.

WIFE: Do you really think that considering what he's been dreaming he ought to go to the hospital?

SIST:[You mean] that little person that he's been dreaming about?

WIFE:So do you think that if we go to the hospital with this matter, the doctors there will know what to do with this person? (i.e., whom he dreamed about).

SIST: No.

WIFE:So then we must go to a medicine man!

SIST:My friend (*achimwenewa* 'these friends of mine', i.e., my brother—honorific) thinks that he has been bewitched. So if a person thinks that he is bewitched, what happens is that he begins to dream about what he is thinking.

WIFE:Noo!

SIST:Don't you know that you dream about your thoughts (lit. *maloto ndi maganizo* 'dreams are thoughts')?

WIFE:No indeed, my In-law (*alamu*—honorific), don't talk like that!

SIST:Dreams are just dreams. This person (*amenewa* 'these [people]', i.e., her brother—honorific) was not bewitched at all, nor was anything else done to him!

WIFE:Here in the village people consider us to be fools now (i.e., because we are not going to see a medicine-man about this matter). Perhaps you are one of those who want this husband of mine to die! (i.e., a very dangerous accusation).

SIST:*Aaah!* [i.e., frustration] Just listen now to what I am telling you!

WIFE:My In-law, now you are adding some matters, that's for sure (*mukuonjezatu zinazi*—i.e., you are changing the subject from the real issue at hand).

SIST:That's absolutely right, until you will listen! (*inu mpakana pamenepo* 'you, right up to this very spot').

WIFE:*Aaagh!* [more frustration]

SIST:Let's just take my brother to the hospital. You can always go to the medicine man later [if you wish]. But first let's go to the hospital!

MAN:Go with whom—go with whom?!

SIST:Just listen—I'll drag you there myself! (*ndikukukokani*—i.e., a bit of hyperbole!) Let's just get going to the hospital!

MAN:How could you be a witch?!

WIFE:She's a witch!

MAN:She must leave—she must leave!

SIST:*Aaah!* [frustration] My brother, you will remember me! (i.e., what I have tried to do for you).

MAN:Get out—get out! (He begins to groan in anger.)

WIFE:You'd better go, my In-law, just go, that's all!

6.2.2.2 Scene II

[At the "office"/ house of a medicine man: MAN = the sick man, WIFE = wife, MEDI = medicine-man]

MAN:*Aaagh!* [i.e., expression of fatigue] Nabanda!

WIFE:Yes.

MAN:We've arrived—here we've arrived! (i.e., where help can be found).

WIFE:That's right.

206

MAN:Knock on the door, knock on the door. Announce that we're here! (lit. *chita zikomo* 'do/say thanks').

(There is the sound of knocking on a door.)

MEDI:Yes, alright—*ooh!* [that's enough knocking] Come in!

WIFE: *Mmmmh!* [OK]

MEDI:Truly, truly! *Eeya!* [to be sure] we left it open.[6]

WIFE:Alright.

MEDI:Truly, truly! (*ndithu, ndithu*)[7]

WIFE:*Eheeeee!* [that's good!]

MEDI:Well, we welcome you! (*Ayi, tikulandirani!*)

WIFE:*Eeee!* [i.e., thank you].

MEDI:Yes, judging by how you look here (*na mmene mukuonekeramu*—i.e., the sick man), you have arrived! (i.e., at the right place to get cured—a boastful assertion, typical of such "healers").

WIFE:That's good!

MEDI:You will recover (*Mwatha!* 'you are finished'—suggesting just the opposite in English!) Take heart! (*mtima m'malo!* '[let] the heart [return] to its place').

WIFE:That's good!

MEDI:*Eeeh!* [correct!]

MAN:You are *Sanza-muleka*, aren't you?

MEDI:*Kapha-gawani!* (i.e., the second part of his full "professional" name).

MAN:Thank you (i.e., for informing me).

MEDI:*Sanza-muleka Kapha-gawani!*[8]

MAN:*Aah!* [i.e., you don't say], thank you.

WIFE:(A nervous laugh)

MEDI:Right here! (i.e., is where you'll get the help you need).

WIFE:Yes, right here (i.e., she appreciates his confidence).

MAN:As for me, I don't feel well at all.

MEDI:You don't say! (*Inuyotu*—i.e., it's quite obvious that you are sick).

MAN:Yes, I don't feel very well.

MEDI:*Mmm!* [is that so!]

MAN:Diarrhea!

MEDI:Here at this place, change your attitude (*sinthani*), you've arrived! (i.e., where healing is found). You'll get better!

MAN:*Ooooh!* [surprise at such confidence]. Do you mean, that's it—I'm already cured?!

---

[6] The medicine man implies that his magic is so powerful that he fears no enemies; he can leave his door open (unlocked or unbarred) at night.

[7] The full repetitious ritual of conventional rural greetings is adhered to; no short cuts are taken in the normal *Sewero* dialogue. Thus a more complete illusion of reality—*verisimilitude*—is represented for the audience. This is exactly what they would expect to hear and say if a stranger came knocking at their door.

[8] This is a typical name for a well-known medicine man, an appellation which thus advertises his powers, here rather surprisingly, both to prevent witchcraft (*Sanza-muleke* 'vomit—cease your witchcraft', i.e., because of the magical potion that I have administered to you), and also to carry out sorcery on behalf of clients (*Kapha-gawani* 'kill [somebody] (i.e., through witchcraft)—share out the meat!' (i.e., the flesh of the bewitched person). Such allusions penetrate deeply into traditional occultic beliefs—thereby "detoxifying" them conceptually, as it were, by raising them to an explicit level where they are dealt with openly within the narrative framework of a given play.

MEDI:You are the very one! Perhaps I can tell (i.e., convince) you like this: Are you not the very one who was dreaming about some tiny little creature? (*kena-kake kakafupi*).[9]

MAN:That's right.

MEDI:It was holding a spear.

MAN:Yes, that's it—exactly, exactly!

MEDI:So do you mean to tell me that healing you can be any more difficult than that?! (*Tsono kuchira kukapose pamenepa?*)

MAN:That's what we want!

WIFE:Yes, it's what we want!

MEDI:Here is where *Sanza-muleke Kapha-gawani* [lives]! (i.e., He continues to brag.) Or in your language (i.e., the language of non-specialists, like he is)— *Masewera-siyani*.[10]

MAN:*Oooh!* [respectfully] (i.e., he is duly impressed by the boasts of this braggart.)

MEDI:*Sanza-muleke!* [that's me!]

WIFE:Right!

MEDI:I won't tolerate any "games" (*masewera*—i.e., a pun on his own name) around here!

MAN:*Oooh!* [let's get on with it]! So the one who caused this—do you know him?

MEDI:You're asking me?! (i.e., how could you even ask such a question?)

MAN:That's right.

MEDI:What could be the problem?! (*pagonanji* 'what is lying down here'—i.e., how could I fail?)

WIFE:*Iiih!* [i.e., wonder—she too is most impressed and awed by this wonderful medicine man.)

MEDI:What if I tell you about that little fellow of yours?

MAN:Go on—tell me! Explain it!

MEDI:For sure, before I say anything, there are two things that I must tell you (i.e., you'll have to choose now): [Either tell me], "I want him (i.e., the witch/sorcerer) to be healed (*machiritso*)—let's just let him live!" or "No, that person must be lost (*asowe*)!" (i.e., be put to death by the magic of the medicine man).[11]

MAN:But do you know him?

MEDI:There's no problem (*nkhani* 'story') for me to know him—but rather, for you to know him. Because I already know him!

WIFE:*Eeeh!* [affirmation] He says that he already knows that person!

MEDI:The short little fellow.

WIFE:That's him! He already knows him!

MAN:He must be my uncle!

WIFE:Right!

MAN:'Uncle'—that guy!

---

[9] It is not surprising that the medicine man already knew about the man's dream. After all, it was quite vivid and shocking, especially since the man was obviously sick; word about the dream's details would have spread quickly via the area's oral "grapevine". Such matters are not private, but available for public consumption, so that if necessary, a communal resolution may be sought.

[10] The proud "doctor" gives them another moniker whereby he praises himself and his magical powers: *Masewera-siyani* 'Leave your games!'—i.e., "don't mess with me!"

[11] The medicine-man continues to boast by asking his clients to choose how they want him to "handle" their problems—either by eliminating the witch/sorcerer or by rehabilitating him/her.

WIFE:Our 'uncle'—that's right, at our village the short person is 'uncle'!

MEDI:So you have an 'uncle', and perhaps there is someone else close [in relationship]—who did not want you to come here?!

WIFE:That's true.

MAN:Right—*mmm!* [he begins to think].

MEDI:Perhaps—tell me the truth now—perhaps it could be your sister?!

MAN:Didn't I tell you (i.e., my wife) that?!

WIFE:Yes, that's what you said.

MEDI:Is she not the one who told you to go to the hospital?[12]

MAN:She wanted to lead me (*kutsogoza*) [to my death]!

WIFE:You said it—it must be her!

MAN:(Now he weeps) Me—she wanted to lead me there! (*nkumanditsogoza*)

WIFE:Right!

MAN:She will know me! (*andidziwa*—i.e., that I will take vengeance upon her!)

WIFE:You always said that she had no character (*alibe khalidwe*)—no character!

MAN:She will know me!

MEDI:Since all your colleagues (i.e., patients who have come here previously) are gone (i.e., they've been healed)—now lady, I do want your husband to get well.

WIFE:Yes, alright!

MAN:Thank you, Chief! (*Mfumu*—i.e., an honorific term of address to this great "healer"!)

MEDI:What we have to do first of all...

MAN:Yes?

MEDI:Just take this.

MAN:*Oooh!* (i.e., he may be a bit surprised at the appearance of whatever the "doctor" is giving him.)

MEDI:So when you leave this place...

WIFE:Yes?

MEDI:...to go home... (In their anxiety to find out what to do, they keep interrupting the medicine man.)

WIFE:Yes?

MEDI:Your husband should enter the house.

WIFE:Alright.

MEDI:When he's inside the house, you must next take a garden hoe (*khasu*)...

WIFE:Alright.

MAN:Yes?

MEDI:You put it by the door.

WIFE:OK.

MEDI:Yes, here we go now: You take some water and you put this "medicine" (*mankhwalawo*, i.e., that I am giving you here) inside—right inside!

MAN:Yes, yesss!

MEDI:Right, then this big fellow here (*awa*)[13] must remove all his clothes at about 'six o'clock'.

---

[12] This is a very realistic dialogue sequence indeed; it closely mimics the "diagnostic" technique of the typical medicine man ("witch-doctor"). The good ones tend to be clever psychoanalysts: knowing the personal history and background of everybody in their area—personalities and interpersonal tensions—plus all the local crises that occur, great and small, they are able both to manipulate their "patients" into revealing their primary "suspects" in such cases of witchcraft/sorcery, and to proceed from there to make an educated guess as to the person(s) most likely to be "guilty" in the minds of their aggrieved clients.

WIFE:Right, 'six o'clock' in the evening...

MEDI:After he has taken off his clothes, he should be naked, completely bare! (*bulanda bwamufwa*—i.e., humorous expressions denoting buck-nakedness). That's right. Then he should go sit on that hoe.

MAN:I'll do it!

MEDI:Next when bathing him (i.e., with the previously prepared "medicinal" mixture), he must be sitting on that hoe![14]

MAN: I'll do it!

MEDI:Now when exiting from the house, he must do it backwards.[15]

MAN:Yes, I'll do it!

WIFE:Alright. (She too agrees to go along with this bizarre plan.)

MAN:I'll do it!

MEDI:They (i.e., the witches) won't leave you alone if you don't do this![16]

MAN:Yes, I'll do it! (This utterance has almost become a mantra by now.)

WIFE:Yes, indeed!

MAN:I'll do it! (His voice fades off into the distance.)

6.2.2.3 Scene III

[Back at the (still) sick man's home: MAN = the sick man, WIFE = his wife, SON = their son]

MAN:You have come, my son.

SON:*Mhmm!* [i.e., affirmative]

MAN:My son, my son, I'm leaving you! My son, I'm leaving you. The battle intensifies—the battle intensifies! (*nkhondo yakula* 'the battle has become great').

SON:Tell me about it, Dad (*madala* lit. 'a respected elderly man'—here, a very colloquial address).

MAN:It goes like this: I went to 'Doctor' *Sanza-muleke*.

SON:*Eeeh.* [OK].

MAN:So he gave me a lot of information—that these things (i.e., my sickness) are [originating] from certain people (i.e., witchcraft).[17] My sister, the one whom I

---

[13] This may be a (mock) respectful shift of reference to the man (the husband) from the second to the third person, as the medicine man's directions now get quite personal and potentially embarrassing. Again, these instructions are most natural—highly typical of some of the strange rituals that "patients" are called upon to perform in order to empower their medicine—to make it "work"!

[14] The directions are getting so personal here that the medicine man does not even mention who is to do the "bathing"—namely, the man's wife!

[15] "Backwards" –perhaps to shock any hovering witches so much by the nakedness that they won't dare come back to that house again. By 6:00 in the evening during the winter months, it will already be dark outside—but relatively cold too!

[16] *Sadzamuleka* 'they will not leave you'—perhaps another pun on the medicine man's name, *Sanza-muleke*. Such traditional practitioners characteristically speak very colloquial language—they tend to be verbal experts.

[17] Any discussion about witchcraft is normally conducted in a very cryptic manner—at least to the outsider. Cultural and relational "insiders", on the other hand, immediately know what is being referred to by such indirect language. Notice too how the medicine man is given much more credit that he deserves, thus enhancing his reputation in the community. Finally, we observe the "reason" given for the witch-

was born after (*uja amene ndaponda pamutu pake* 'the one whose head I stepped upon'), she wants to acquire this house of mine, which has a metal roof (i.e., made of corrugated metal sheets).

SON:You don't say—it is that 'Aunt'? (*anti aja*, i.e., who is the witch; a derogatory reference to her).

MAN:The very person!

SON:So you must die (*muduwe*) so that 'Aunt' can take the house—where then would we live? That will never happen—no way! (*mayazi!* i.e., a borrowed exclamative indicating complete rejection).

MAN:Calm down, my son.

SON:No way!

SON:So we are to become orphans?!

MAN:Just calm down.

SON:*Aaagh!* [i.e., anger]

MAN:We also went to another place (i.e., another medicine man)—we went to, what's his name, uh, 'Doctor Luke'. Now he said, well, it's 'uncle' (i.e., who is also bewitching me)—right, just like that![18]

SON:The very one—her 'uncle' (i.e., of the man's sister, who would also be his uncle too!)

MAN:That's right.

SON:I'm writing down the names of both of them (i.e., equivalent to a curse)! I will deal with them! (*ndithana nawo* 'I will be finished with them'—with an implication of a violent end).

WIFE:*liih!* [strong apprehension] That's no good—no good at all!

MAN:Now your comrade (*mnzako*—i.e., brother) went and made war (*anakachita nkhondo*) at 'uncle's' place (i.e., he destroyed some property there). He just went alone, without telling anyone about it. So the one who's left (i.e., to punish) is this sister of mine!

SON:Just let me deal with her—this sister of yours will be taken care of by me! I am going to cook her good (*ndiwaphika!*—i.e., teach her a lesson), and she'll know [me]! (*adziwanso*—i.e., why I am someone who should never be provoked).

MAN:My son, I'm leaving you—my son!

WIFE:*liih!* [fright] Well she's gone too far now (*afikaponsotu*—i.e., by practicing witchcraft)! Well, I never… (*koma ine* 'but I').

SON: Hey, Dad, don't worry (*musadandauleyi!* 'do not complain')! Dad, if you enter the grave, then somebody else is going to enter a grave, even that sister of yours! The very same day we will have two funerals (*tidzaika maliro awiri* 'we will bury two corpses')! [Or] You may enter on one day, and she will enter the very next day!

WIFE: So you will fix her then—really fix her?! (*kuwatema* 'to cut her up').

---

craft; its practice always has a purpose—namely, to somehow enhance the well-being of the witch or sorcerer.

[18] It is not surprising that the couple went to visit another medicine man, after *Sanza-muleke*. There are plenty of these fellows working the business these days, usually in competition with one another. Repeated failures of their implausible "cures" naturally lead people to shop around. The sad result is that, as in this case, the adverse social impact of witch-hunting is often multiplied. The couple may have forgotten about the "uncle" after their discussion with the first "doctor" since the man's sister was the most prominent suspect. "Dr. Luke", however, renewed the likelihood of the uncle's involvement in the affair.

MAN: My son, my son, my sister is trying to kill me—my sister wants to kill me![19]
SON: So she wants to kill my Dad, eh?! Does she want me to become an orphan then?!
WIFE: How will I take care of you in the village here? How will I ever take care of you? If I am left alone, how will I care for you (i.e., her sick husband)?!
SON: Just let me handle things! (*Ineyo ndithudi!* lit., 'it is I, I surely swear').
MAN: (He begins some more heavy coughing.)
SON: I swear, I will deal with her—and I'll never let her escape, no indeed, Mother!
MAN: No mercy! No mercy!
SON: No matter if I get jailed—no matter if I am executed!
WIFE:Only 'Jehovah' (*Yehova*) knows how I will ever care for these children of mine! (i.e., if my husband dies).
SON:So [she] wants to kill my Dad, does she?!
WIFE:How will I care for my children?!
SON:So [she] wants to kill my Dad, does she?! There's going to be war! (*tionetsana* 'we will show each other'—i.e., who is more powerful, a serious threat to injure/kill someone). I'm on my way over there!

6.2.2.4 Scene IV

[In the front yard of the aunt's house: AUNT = sister of the sick man, NEPH = his son, her nephew]

(The scene opens with a little dog barking furiously, as the Nephew approaches the yard.)[20]

NEPH:(He is shouting in rage:) We shall see now! *Aaah!* [anger] I'm telling you, if my Dad dies, there will be war! I'm going to cook you—[starting from] the head! Do you think that you can kill my Dad—bewitch my Dad?!

(The little dog interrupts with his incessant barking.)

NEPH:Let's get this war over with! I've come here so you can tell me why my Dad is sick. If he dies, I don't care, there'll be war! You are a killer! It's you, my aunt (*adzakhali*)—you are the one who is killing my Dad! Yes you—witch (*mfiti*)!
AUNT:Hey, is it you, brother (*achimwene*—i.e., a term of respect), who's speaking out there?
NEPH:That's right! Now whom do you think I'm talking to?! Just whom do you see here talking [to you] (i.e., this is very threatening talk, highly disrespectful to such an important relative).

---

[19] Observe the rising tension and personal passion here. Cases of witchcraft quickly excite the most intense emotions—especially because such practices always involve close relatives. What a horrible thing it is to see strong affections transformed into a correspondingly bitter animosity.

[20] This little dog keeps barking realistically in the background, sometimes becoming more intense as the young man becomes more threatening in his behavior. Special effects like these are simple, but contribute a great deal to evoke a certain scene in the minds of the audience, which is then mentally "localized" according to their own experience and physical setting.

AUNT:*Aaah!* [disturbed] Come here, you always come here to visit—so why don't you come closer?! (i.e., the tone of his voice and his physical stance make it readily apparent that some thing serious is wrong).

NEPH:No, today I cannot come close for a visit. I'm not in a visiting mood (*sindilinso mocheza*)! I might just cook you right here on the spot, yes indeed. That's what I'm saying, yes!

AUNT:Is that so? (*kodi!*) Well, just sit down and let's have a talk.

NEPH:No, I'm not going to sit down!

AUNT:*E-eeh!* [i.e., what's wrong?]

NEPH:If you are killing my Dad, then what about me?!

AUNT:Killing?—did some killers come [there]?!

NEPH:That's right! You have bewitched my Father (*abambo anga*—a more formal term now)! He went to a medicine-man and found out that you were the one who was witching him!

AUNT:*Aa-aagh!* [shock].

NEPH:My Father, at the moment, his life is uncertain. You are the one who wants me to become an orphan!

AUNT:Now you are telling me that some person... (he cuts her off.)

NEPH:But if my Dad dies, then I'm telling you, for sure you will also enter [the grave]! You will be buried the very same day!

AUNT:You are telling me now that his life is uncertain, while just yesterday I was over there in the evening. I left about 'nine o'clock'.

NEPH:So didn't you just want to finish him off?!

AUNT:*Oooh!* [how could you say that?] [You don't mean] to finish off the patient (*matendawa* 'this sickness, i.e., a metonym)?!

NEPH:Yes, you went there to finish him off (i.e., to cast a fatal magical spell on him).

AUNT:Say, your father and I were born together (i.e., of the same mother), so between you and I, which offspring ought to have the greater love [for him]?[21]

NEPH:I and my father who begat me!

AUNT:No, it is I because we were born of the same breast (*tabadwa bere limodzi*—i.e., the same mother, another metonym).[22]

NEPH:Maybe so, but I don't care. What I have come to tell you (i.e., his threat to retaliate if his father dies), I will not return to repeat it!

AUNT: *Iih!* [shock] But when there is a sick person at home, we all ought to get together to care for him!

NEPH:I will not return to repeat what I've said!

AUNT:*Iih!* No?

NEPH:I will not return to repeat what I've said! I have spoken![23]

AUNT:*Iih!* No? *Aaah!* [frustrated by his unwillingness to listen].

NEPH:No, in fact I'm ready right now to pick a fight with you (*kuchita ndeu*)! Right now I'm ready to start a whipping match (*kukwapulana*) with you! (He is

---

21 The consanguineal bond is considered to be stronger than the filial one.
22 The aunt gives her nephew a little lesson in interpersonal relations; in his rage he was ignoring some basic sociocultural facts, and this was clouding his judgment. So it goes with many witchcraft accusations.
23 The nephew knows that he is behaving badly—culturally in a very inappropriate manner. So he cannot give her any decent answer in reply; all he can do is angrily repeat himself. These dialogues capture human nature and behavior in a satirically critical way.

becoming more belligerent as he realizes that her replies are turning his case back upon himself!)

AUNT:Do you mean that you'll even start smashing up our chairs?![24]

NEPH:That's right—absolutely right!

AUNT:*Agh-agh-agh!* [dismay] Well go ahead and break [them], just break [them]!

NEPH:That's right—absolutely right, exactly! It's what you are used to doing! (i.e., an allusive reference to her practice of "destroying" people through witchcraft).

AUNT:Alright, brother, just go ahead and break [them]—break them up![25]

NEPH:Right—then it will be your turn!

AUNT:Yes, go on and break [them] up! But isn't it true that your parents sent you here to do this?![26] Just go ahead and break [them] up!

(There are the sounds of objects being broken up—various crashes and bangs!)

NEPH:Well you are the one who wanted to make me an orphan, that's right!

AUNT:OK, just break [things] up!

NEPH:Maybe I ought to just give you a punch—how about that?! Maybe I ought to punch you, right! Witchcraft—no more (*basi*)! Casting spells (*kutamba*)—no more! Let's have it out [today]! If my Dad dies, someone else will enter the grave! I am willing to die for my Dad. Let me be executed, that's OK! If I must be jailed, let me be jailed! No more spells! *Alaa!* (interjection, i.e., I'm completely fed up with you!) [So you want] me to become an orphan?! Can that make a person happy?! (*umasiye umasangalatsa?*) Witchcraft! Let's wage war with each other! Now is the right time for it! (*chaka chake ndi chino* 'this is its year', i.e., a metonymic idiom).

(The scene fades away with the sound of various things being broken up and smashed.)

6.2.2.5 Scene V

[In the front yard of the aunt's house: MOM = sister of the sick man, DAU = her daughter]

MOM:*A-a-a-aaah!* [i.e., great shock] All this property has been destroyed! (i.e., by her nephew).

DAU:You said it (*ndipo ino*), Mother! It has surely been destroyed!

MOM:So where did you flee to? (i.e., when the young man was ruining their things).

DAU:Me? I just went and hid under that big Baobob (*mulambe*) tree over there.

MOM:My, it was terrible! (*Koma abalee…*)

DAU:That's for sure. That big tree surely saved me, Mother, *eeeh!* [affirmation].

---

[24] The wooden chairs must have been sitting out in the front of the house. She tries a little humor (exaggeration) here, but of course he's too irate to respond normally. The irony is that her intended hyperbole is about to be transformed into reality by her enraged nephew.

[25] She perhaps hopes that as he exerts himself in breaking up her chairs, his rage and energy will diminish—that then there will be less danger of him doing physical harm as he was even now threatening (also in his next utterance).

[26] Perhaps she wants to shame him to realize the fact that he is only an errand boy, doing the dirty work for others.

MOM:*Ayi-yai-yai!* [emphatic negation] As for me, when I looked into his eyes and saw how red they were (*mmene anafiirira*—i.e., as if he were drunk or had smoked *dagga* [Indian hemp]), I knew that if I stood my ground here…

DAU:*Mmm!* [surely].

MOM:He could have injured us, especially when he started talking about punching me. I thought to myself, "For sure, now [I am in big trouble]!"

DAU:*I-iih!* [terrible].

MOM:This boy might even take out my teeth! But store-bought teeth are very expensive![27]

DAU:Absolutely!

MOM:It would be better for me now to run away because—"to flee is not to fear" (*sikuti kuthawa ndi kuopa, ayi*—i.e., a maxim that justifies her actions in allowing their property to get broken up).

DAU:No [it doesn't mean that].

MOM:I was only avoiding a fight (*ndeu*).

DAU:That's right!

MOM:Because [when you] worship (lit. 'pray'), your brothers see you (*kupempherakutu, abale amakuona*—i.e., fellow believers are always watching to see how you behave in public).

DAU:Right.

MOM:As you know, there in 'two Peter three'- -'two Peter two'- - (i.e., she has forgotten the precise location of the Bible passage that she wants to cite here).

DAU:'Two Timothy'…

MOM:That's right, 'two Timothy'…

DAU:'Two Timothy, verse twenty-four'.

MOM:It says, "The servant of God must not provoke quarrels."

DAU:*Eyaa!* [absolutely correct].

MOM:'Two Timothy, verse twenty-four' [continues] "and let [God's servant] be free with everyone."[28]

DAU:Right!

MOM:So after seeing that this fight has arrived at our very doorstep…

DAU:You said it!

MOM:[in the person of] the son of my brother…

DAU:*Mmm!* [correct].

MOM:We could have picked up our hoes and traded blows with him (*tizikhapana naye*)! Well, are we not more than one (*angapo*)?!

DAU:Right. [But] he [was] alone.

MOM:What would have happened?

DAU:You're right—what would have happened?

MOM:Would he have broken up all my furniture like this?!

DAU:Besides, he wanted to beat you up, but [instead] he hit the what…the wall (i.e., of the house)!

MOM:Thus he hurt himself on the hand.

DAU:The Lord surely punished that guy (*ameneyotu*)!

MOM:The Lord punishes, that's right. 'One Thessalonians verse fifteen' says, "Thank God!"[29]

---

27   Again, we have a little humor here to lighten the load of the plot and its lesson.
28   The Mother is quoting the older Chinyanja Bible translation here, *waulere*. The new version is *wachifundo*, 'merciful, kind', which is closer in meaning to the original Greek *eχ*□*)(*□❖ 'kind'.

215

DAU:Yesss!

MOM:Yes, just keep on praising God. Are they not saying that I am a witch? Well does a witch not know herself?

DAU:She knows that "I really am a witch!"

MOM:Yes, and that "I cast spells [of witchcraft]."

DAU:Correct!

MOM:So what if you do not realize that you go casting spells? (i.e., then you must not be a witch).[30]

DAU:*Mmm!* [right].

MOM:Well, anyway, 'Matthew five, verse twelve' says, "They will say many evil things about you"—beginning at 'verse eleven'.[31]

DAU:Right!

MOM:"If they say all kinds of evil things about you, rejoice, [for] your great reward is in heaven!"—especially (*bola*) if you do not do (i.e., say) such things.

DAU:*Ehee!* [correct]. That's true.

MOM:Well, [the story (i.e., the truth)] will become known. Righteousness cannot be hidden—[the story] will become known.

DAU:Mother, this furniture that he broke up is completely destroyed, so how will we replace it?

MOM:No, don't worry—God will restore [it].

DAU:*Ooh!* [is that so?]

MOM:Yes, well, what else can we do?

DAU:*Iiih!* [fear] Is this not the way things are…?

MOM:Well, does this not all belong to us—the things that the son of my brother…[destroyed]?

DAU:*Aaah!* [i.e., he did a terrible thing] So what [are we going to do]- - (She is interrupted.)

MOM:Now if I go and report [this matter] to the police, and they lock him up wounded like he is, would this not cause my brother a lot of worry (*nkhawa*)?

DAU:Right!

MOM:He would say, "Even while I'm so sick (*mkati mwa matenda* 'in the middle of a sickness'), my sister has caused my son to be jailed!"

DAU:That's true.

MOM:So if I really am not a witch, I should be free (i.e., kind) to all people.

DAU:*Eeeeh!* [correct].

---

[29]   The Mother appears to mix this passage up. 1 Thessalonians two (she did not mention the chapter), 16 (not 15) speaks about God taking vengeance upon the enemies of his people, which would apply to the first part of her utterance, not the latter, about "thanking" (the Chinyanja verb –*yamika* can also mean "praise").

[30]   Some might dispute this implication and would claim instead that certain witches (i.e., the necrophagous so-called "night witches", who have inherited this nefarious proclivity) are schizophrenic. When they are in their "right mind" (during the day), they do not realize that they are a completely different person at night.

[31]   Here the Mother realizes that she mentioned the wrong verse number at the beginning, so she corrects it here at the end of her utterance. She actually gets into "verse 12" in her next speech. As the *Sewero* players enter an "application" portion of their play, they have to be doubly conscious: Not only must they keep their plot moving along in a credible way, but they also need to insert certain pre-selected Bible passages into the dialogue at appropriate places. This requires a great deal of concentration to go along with the artistic freedom that they are already manipulating to make their didactic point.

216

MOM:I [must be] generous (*wa sadaka* 'a person of [the] feast/celebration', i.e., an idiom) to everyone, that's it (*basi*), completely open (*wabule*)!

DAU:But should we go and visit him?

MOM:He will be very ashamed—he won't come here to visit like he used to.

DAU:Right.

MOM:Whatever he wanted, he was free to take (*chimene afuna amatenga*).

DAU:Yes.

MOM:"Go and cook some food (*nsima* 'maize-meal porridge') for me" [he'd say], and we would do it, *aah!* [how things have changed!]. But now he will be too ashamed to come—but we would welcome him [if he did come].

DAU:Really?!

MOM:Yes, [we must] forgive our enemies.

DAU:Alright.

MOM:Do not get angry at them.

DAU:OK, it's true.

MOM:But why don't you just pick up all these things—these pieces of furniture around here.

DAU:Right.

MOM:When your Father comes, we'll explain it to him.

DAU:That's for sure!

MOM:If it's possible to repair [them], he will do it some other time.

DAU:Say, do you think that his mother sent him over to do this?

MOM:Well, they all [were involved]—his parents, including my own brother.

DAU:Yes, they must have sent him.

MOM:He could not have done all these things on his own.

DAU:No, he couldn't have.

MOM:Well, whatever—may the Lord help us to forgive; may he [also] forgive us!

DAU:Yes, that's right!

MOM:*Hooh!* [surprise] He's come back! (*atulukira* 'he has come out').

DAU:What's this world coming to?! (*Ndipo inu, dziko lapansi* 'And so you, the world').

MOM:That things should happen like this!

DAU:To be sure! *Mmh!* [affirmation].

6.2.2.6 Scene VI

[Back at the (still) sick man's home: MAN = the sick man, WIFE = his wife, SON = their son, SIST = the man's sister, VISI = a visitor]

MAN:For sure, Nabanda.

WIFE:*Mmm* [yes?].

MAN:I am most upset (*ndakhumudwa*).

WIFE:*Mmm* [about?].

MAN:Because according to the 'results' (*marezatsi*).

WIFE:'Resultses' (*maresultizi*—i.e., she wants to correct his "English").

MAN:'Result'—what did you say?

WIFE:'Resultses' (she repeats her "correction", then laughs lightly).[32]

---

[32] A little linguistic humor here lightens the onset of what is going to be a rather sad scene. It's a pity that much of this subtle, and often meaningful, verbal humor goes unnoticed on first listening to a *Sewero*

MAN:*Oooh* [I see now].

SON:No, Mother, *marezulti* [already] means many things (i.e., a plural form).[33]

WIFE:*Oooh* [I see] [it should be] 'results' (she laughs again, with a bit of embarrassment now).

MAN:[Concerning the results] I got while at the hospital, I see now that my sister must come here quickly—before I am finished off (*ndisanatsirizike*—i.e., a euphemism for death).

WIFE: *Mmm* [right], but...

MAN:Because of that rudeness behavior (*chipongwe*) we showed her...

WIFE:*Iiih!* [terrible!] [it was] a huge insult (*mwano*)!

MAN:Destroying her property!

WIFE:*Mmm!* [that's right].

MAN:(He begins weeping.) My Sister!

WIFE:No, do not weep, no, there now! But the way things are [between us], will she come after that great rudeness we showed her? Could she really come [over here]?

MAN:Well anyway, I am encouraged (*ndimasangalala* 'I am happy') [because] people who pray (*anthu opemphera*—i.e., genuine Christians) are good. No matter how badly you wrong them, they do not take revenge (*sakutengera*).

WIFE:As for me, I still doubt whether she can come over.

MAN:No, she is a faithful person (*okhulupirika*).

SON:Could that be her—the person who's coughing outside?

SIST:Hello there, excuse me, excuse me! (*Odi, zikomo-zikomo!*).

WIFE:*Eeeeh!* [we're here].

MAN:"If you happen to mention a lion, you'd better get ready to climb [up a tree]!" (*ukanena mkango, kwera m'mwamba!*—a proverb fitting this occasion, when a person whom you have been talking about suddenly appears on the scene).

WIFE:Yes, that's for sure!

MAN:Climb up then! (i.e., he extends the proverbial metaphor: get ready to welcome her!).

SIST:*Eeh!* [it's me] Excuse me, excuse me!

WIFE:*Eeeh!* [alright] You're welcome (*zikomo!*).[34]

SIST:(She enters the room.) *Eeh* [excuse me]—[it sounds like] coughing (*chifuwa*)!

WIFE:[This] coughing—*iiih!* [it's terrible!] Perhaps it is because of the wind (*mphepo*).

SIST:[And] dust (*fumbi*)!

WIFE:[Yes, the] dust.

MAN:*Iiih-iih!* [so sorry], my Sister!

SIST:*Iih!* [sorry], how are you, my Relative (*alamu*—i.e., my [sister]-in-law)?

WIFE:I'm OK (*moyo* 'life'), how about you, my Relative?

---

drama; these plays must really be listened to—carefully and repeatedly—to plumb the depths of their significance and import.

[33] Linguistically speaking, the son is correct: the Chinyanja noun prefix *ma-* on *marezulti* already indicates a plurality, "results"; her "correction" was in fact a double plural, *marezultizi* 'resultses'—i.e., both Chinyanja (at the beginning) and English (at the end). But of course such "loanwords" do not always follow logical lexical rules.

[34] It is the wife's role to welcome a visitor to the home. There is a reason for all of the seemingly redundant exclamations in this situation. Through the sound of one's voice, one is clearly recognized, even outside and/or at night.

SIST:Well, OK too, yes. And how have you arisen, my Brother? (*mwadzuka* [the regular morning greeting], *achimwene* 'brother', here used as a respectful form of address to her nephew).

SON:*Eeh!* [affirmation] [I'm] 'sharp' (*shapu*—i.e., just fine [slang]). How about you, 'Aunt'?

SIST:I have arisen (*tadzuka*—the normal response to a morning greeting). How about you, Brother (*achimwene*—i.e., her real brother now), how well have you arisen?[35]

MAN:*Aah!* [not so well]. I am just waiting for the time (*ndikuyembekezera nthawi*—i.e., to die), just awaiting the time!

SIST:Do not say, "waiting for the time,"—we do not [merely sit around and] wait for [this] time!

MAN:[But what about] the 'results'?

SIST:No, we don't wait around. When the Owner [of all things, *Mwini-wake*, i.e., God] has determined [them] (*wakonza*), then [they] are determined.

MAN:No, these are indeed 'results'. When we went to the doctor... (She now cuts him off.)

SIST:*Ooh!* [surprise] So you hurried off (*munathamangiranso* 'you also ran to') to the hospital then?!

MAN:*Mmmn!* [assent].

SIST:The day before yesterday?

MAN:*Mmmn!* [assent].

SIST:*Ohoo!* [critical surprise]. That time when I left [this place] then, you were completely refusing [to go to the hospital] (*mumakanakotu*)!

MAN:No, it was yesterday.

SIST:So did you go there right after I left, is that right?

MAN:So-and-so, I dunno who, came with an ox-cart (i.e., to collect and carry me there).

SIST:*Ooh!* [I see]. I met him, I met him! He said, "I'm on my way to see him [his sick grandfather]." He was on his ox-cart.

MAN:[It was] that grandson of ours (*mdzukulu wathuyi*), our grandson—that's right, the son of Chambwinja (i.e., he would be the son of either the sick man or his sister).

SIST:*Mmm* [I see].

MAN:He picked me up in his cart saying, "Hey, let's go, Father!" That's how I traveled there, *aah-yaiyaiya!* [surprise and disappointment] (i.e., I had a bitter-sweet experience there).

SIST:No (i.e., trying to counteract the negativity of his last exclamation), he did a good job! Diarrhea requires [the patient to be on] a 'drip' (*madripi a madzi* 'drips of water').

WIFE:*Mmmm!* [agreement],

---

[35] Notice how the sister/aunt greets each one of the persons whom she is visiting individually, in excellent traditional form. A less-skilled dramatic troupe would have been tempted to abbreviate all this verbal "tradition" in the interest of time—to get on to more "important issues". In an African setting, however, the establishment of such interpersonal relationships through dialogue exchanges such as this *is* the most important issue. No matter can be discussed before the discourse has thus laid the proper *phatic* foundation.

SIST:Perhaps they gave you some 'D-R-S' (i.e., "diarrhea replacement solution"), and what did they say? You must dilute that and drink it. The fluids (*madzi* 'water') are quickly restored in your body.[36]

WIFE:That's right!

SIST:And isn't it true that diarrhea also reduces [your] 'appetite'—when it's constant?

WIFE:Yes, that's true.

SIST:Yes, and so a person doesn't take [enough] food. [But] that water (i.e., the fluid replacement solution) helps to give the body some strength and prevents 'tracks' (*matakisi*)—wrinkles (*makwinya*) [in the skin], *eeeeh!* [affirmation], that for sure!

MAN:*Aaah!* [disagreement]—even with the bad diarrhea that I have? (*m'mene nditseguliramo* 'how I have opened up inside').

SIST:For sure, my Brother, just listen to me!

MAN:I have completely opened up! (*nditsegulira inemu*).

SIST:Now what I want to praise God for is the fact that he wants you to prepare yourself (*mukonzeke*—i.e., in terms of your past life-style as well as your destiny). Because if you had gone (i.e., died) with the hatred (*udani*) that you had in your heart, right now you'd be in hell (*gahena*)! But God wants that hatred to go because you only suspect that [this] disease came like this, perhaps through an 'injection' (*jakisoni*—i.e., a contaminated needle at a hospital or clinic), perhaps when you borrowed someone else's 'razor' (*lezala*—i.e., to shave with), or perhaps it could even be—since a person (especially a male!) [has] the body of an animal (*thupi la nyama*), completely misses the mark (*kuphophonya*—i.e., morally), that's right, and commits prostitution (*zachiwerewere*—i.e., she uses a strong term here, for she suspects this to be the case), *mmh!* [final affirmation]. Perhaps you thought, "Just this once!"—and you never did it again, like those who practice adultery (*zigololo zawo*) 'full time'. So you said, "Just once!" *Iiih!* [shock] Imitating others (*kalionera*) can get you sunk! (*ndikungoti chakwala!*—a dramatic ideophone depicting a loud splash into water). You might have met (*umatokumana*—i.e., been infected with, a euphemism) the beast (*chilombo*—i.e., the AIDS virus) in that way—it stung you! (*ga!*—i.e., another ideophone to intensify the imagery).[37]

WIFE:Perhaps this fellow (*iwowa*—i.e., her husband!) was cheating on me (*amandizembera* 'he was hiding himself from me')! Perhaps he was cheating on me, *aaah!* [disappointment].

SIST:No, my In-law (*alamu*)! I'm saying maybe a 'razor' [caused it], maybe our [method of giving an] 'injection'. Because you see, in the place where we live (*m'makomo muno* 'in our doorways'), if someone gets sick with a fever (*malungo*—a generic term referring to all flu-type illnesses), he simply gets stabbed (*kungobaitsa*) with an 'injection'. The [health] people around here don't sterilize [their] needles (*saphikatu jakisoni* 'they don't cook the injection'). They just stab one [person], then another. Some little beast (*kachilombo*—i.e., any virus, not necessarily AIDS now) exits from there and comes to enter here.

---

[36] Whenever possible, the *Sewero* team tries to educate their audience with regard to certain types of information of general value, especially health matters. Ignorance about sickness, disease, nutrition, and proper care for the body creates a fertile ground for witchcraft beliefs and accusations.

[37] This speech is an especially vivid and effective polemic against the sort of immoral behavior that keeps AIDS in business throughout the world.

That little beast really troubles the blood [of a person]! But now, since it (i.e., the virus, whatever) has been discovered [in the blood of my Brother], I praise God!

WIFE:*Mmm!* [alright].

MAN:Well, for sure now my [life] journey is finished (*ulendo watha*)! It's all ready [to come to an end]! (*wakonzeka kale*—i.e., he is very pessimistic).

SIST:Which journey?!

MAN:For sure, I've already begun the [final] journey—because of [those] 'results'!

SIST:Did you have another trip to take—to work (*kunchito*—i.e., another job to do yet)?

MAN:[I mean] the 'results' that they told me at the hospital.

WIFE:*Iiih!* [shock]. This too now—he is revealing everything! (i.e., normally one would not be so public about the negative results of any sort of testing).

SIST:*Iih!* [she is surprised by her in-law's reaction]. Why are these so bad? (*zofooketsa bwanji* 'how have they caused such weakness?']

MAN:Here it is now! (*basitu!*) They say that the plague has entered [my body] (*mliri wabwerawu*)!

SIST:*Aaah!* [sorrow]. *Oooh!* [sadness]. Is that what they said at the hospital?

MAN:Yes, that…I am dying!

WIFE:*Iyaa!* [grief]. Relatives…(i.e., what will I do?)

SIST:If they tell you 'HIV', it does not mean your [immediate] death, Brother, sorry!

WIFE:Sorry, he wants to annoy me now (*akhumudwitse ine*), aaah! [frustration].

MAN:(He starts weeping again.)

SIST:Nooo! Please quiet down! When they say that they have found you with 'HIV', it does not mean that your death is imminent, not at all.

VISI:They mean that 'AIDS' (*edzi*) has been planted [within you] like flowers.

SIST:*Aah!* [affirmation]. [Planted] sort of like a 'hedge' (*maheji*).[38]

VISI:That's it, that's it!

SON:I agree (*ayinso*), it doesn't mean that you are dying [right away]!

SIST:It's not that if they find out that you have it (i.e., you are HIV positive), you're dead, not at all! Rather, it's good [for you] that they discovered it so that you now know what to do (i.e., how to organize your life and behavior accordingly).

VISI:That's right!

SIST:You can live for many years yet—even up to ten (*olo teni* 'or ten'). You can live [as usual] farming, eating [the produce], rearing goats and seeing them breed. But just consider now your elder sister—the very 'sister' (*asisi*) whom you called a witch. [And consider] 'uncle'—the boy (i.e., your son) went and speared uncle's goat—that's right, [the goat of] your elder brother![39]

MAN:That's true—this one (his son) did so, he did so!

---

[38] The man's sister modifies the "flowers" simile to that of a "hedge"—AIDS does not just pop up within a person like flowers in a field; rather like an orderly hedge, there are rules that are broken to get it and rules to be followed in order to treat it.

[39] In this speech, the sister tries to get her HIV-infected brother to stop dwelling on himself and his own situation, wallowing in self pity. Rather, he should get back to the real world and begin facing the problems that his rash witchcraft accusations have caused in their own family. He has alienated the very ones who could give him the most support during his illness. She refers to herself indirectly in the third person, in order to render the conversation less "personal" in nature. It is an excellent psycho-therapeutic technique.

WIFE:He was terribly destructive (*waononga kwabasi*)!

SIST:On coming to our place there, he smashed pots, tables…

WIFE:*Iiih!* [shock]—even [your] pots?!

SIST:Even the tables, Mother! (*amayi*—honorific).

VISI:*Aaah!* [disgust]. But that, friends…[is going to far]!

SIST:Tables, even my layer hen—he twisted its neck (*anangopotokola*) and threw it down [dead]—smashing up [everything]!

VISI:*Iiih!* [shock]. Did he [accuse you] of witchcraft as well (*Kodi ufitinso*)?!⁴⁰

SIST:I had to run away and hide at the well (*kumadzi* 'at the water') with my last-born child.⁴¹

WIFE:*Iiih!* [shock]. My In-law, you even had to run away [from your own home]?!

SIST:He kept saying, "I'm going to beat you!" And I replied, "A servant of God must not fight!" What could I do? (*nditani?*)

WIFE:*Iiih!* [more shock at what happened]. I do declare (*koma inu* 'but you')…to have to do that [is unthinkable]!

SIST:Well, I did run away, but I knew that… (She is cut off.)

SON:Did you not tell me that Mr. Mbewe (*Ambewe*—the clan name of his aunt's husband) is the one who was bewitching this Father of mine (*Ababawa*—honorific term)?⁴²

WIFE:Nooo, *aaah!* [frustration], your Father here is the one who told us.

SIST:Now look here (*Koma tsono taonani*), if you had just rushed [to the hospital] to have some testing done, without first suspecting these what…these black arts (*zachikudazi*), no indeed [none of this would have happened]! We must always first rush for testing…

WIFE:*Eeeeh!* [strong affirmation].

SIST:So if we see that there [at the hospital] they say, "Everything is just fine!" (*zili bwinobwino*), then perhaps we can begin to suspect the things of Satan (*za Satanayo*—i.e., witchcraft/sorcery)!

WIFE:Right on! (*eeyah!*)

SIST:Furthermore, 'Jeremiah seventeen, verse five' says, "Cursed is he who boasts in his own strength, while his heart departs from Jehovah"!⁴³ So if a person gets sick and looks for a medicine man to help—you are cursed, and when you die, you will go to hell! Now is that good?!⁴⁴

WIFE:No, no!⁴⁵

MAN:I'm done with that (*ndaleka*)—I'll never go there again!

---

⁴⁰ This is a very ironic observation—and pointedly true. How much havoc witchcraft wreaks in society!

⁴¹ Observe the vivid details of these descriptive speeches—tables, pots, twisting the neck of a layer hen, hiding at (in?) a well; these are the features of "local color" that give life to a *Sewero* drama and enable it to be visualized on the "screen" of every listener's mind (see 5.3.1).

⁴² Mention of his aunt's husband is probably an indirect, euphemistic reference to her. The last personal term used in this utterance is not randomly chosen; rather, the alliterative euphony emphasizes what he is saying (…*Ambewe*…*Ababawa*).

⁴³ She alters the old literal translation here from the Hebraistic 'arm of flesh' to "my arm" (*mkono wa ine*—i.e., my strength, a metonym); see the new Chinyanja version *munthu wodalira munthu mnzake* 'a person who depends on his fellow man [person]'.

⁴⁴ The pronominal shift here, from a third to a second person singular reference (a device termed *enallage*), is typical of highly rhetorical speech—also in Hebrew prophetic discourse!

⁴⁵ The wife acts as the spokesperson for her sick husband here, lest he begin weeping again.

SIST:Here on earth, if you are troubled with sickness [and visit a medicine man], will you go to heaven? [No], you will go to hell and be troubled with fire—you alone, *eeeh!* [affirmation].[46]

WIFE:Nooo! (i.e., may it not happen).

MAN:I'll never go there again—I'll never go there again!

SIST:Listen (*inu!* 'you!')! 'John ten, verse ten' says, "A thief does not come except to steal, kill, and destroy." Whenever 'Satan' comes anywhere, he wants to destroy. He wanted to destroy our friendship (*chibale chathu* 'our relationship', a richer concept than in English)—so that we (i.e., my side of the family) would be angry (*okwiya*), that you would be angry, and so that you would die in your anger!

WIFE:*Eeeh!* [affirmation]—that's exactly right! (*ndipo apo*).

SIST:But today I praise heaven (*kumwamba*—i.e., God, a metonym) that he has helped you find [that you are] HIV [positive]. That does not mean death, my Brother—no, it is simply the sign of a disease![47]

MAN:You mean that I won't leave [right away] (*sin'choka*—i.e., a euphemism for death)?

SIST:Yes (i.e., no, you won't die immediately).

MAN:I won't leave? (i.e., he's not quite convinced, in the view of widespread popular belief).

SIST:No, you won't leave. But now what you have to do is to follow that advice they gave you at the hospital: Do not have sexual relations (*osakhalira limodzi* 'don't stay together as one') very often. *Eyaa!* [affirmation], and watch what you eat!

WIFE:*Oooh!* [surprise] (i.e., because of the personal nature of the preceding advice). [That concerns] this very house here! (*m'nyumbamuno*).

SIST:*Eyaa!* [affirmation]. Whatever they advised you there, you must carefully follow so that your children—during the next two or three years you're here—certainly you will be around (i.e., to help them out). We are talking about the matter of your making arrangements for their marriages (*muli kugwirizira zinkhoswe*), my Brother.[48]

WIFE:Is that really true?

SIST:But the most important thing is for you to stay (*kungokhala*—i.e., without sexual relations, a euphemism) in Jesus, that's it!

WIFE:You mean we just stay (*tizingokhala*) like that, finish?![49]

SIST:*Eeh!* [affirmation].

WIFE:Just staying like that?!

SIST:[By] completely devoting yourself (*kungodzipereka*) to 'Jesus' (*Yesu*).

---

[46] There is some wordplay here (i.e., the verb –*vutika* 'be troubled with') to heighten the contrast involved. The sister speaks rather hyperbolically here to emphasize her point.

[47] Many HIV+ patients in central Africa think just like the brother here and give up all hope; this advice is thus meant for them too!

[48] This would be a very strong motivation for him. His sister is trying to get him simply to focus on his responsibilities for the near future; however, she must not promise him too much (too long!) in this regard.

[49] Her sister-in-law means to say that a person's faith in and complete devotion to Jesus as Savior can help him/her to overcome the severest of obstacles, even the powerful attraction of sex. The man's wife, however, is not so sure about this proposal. In any case, the sister's initial expression (lit. 'to stay in Jesus') has a double meaning—that is, to "remain" strong in faith and also to "remain" without sexual relations in their home due to her husband's illness.

MAN:Then I won't die—then I won't die?!

SIST:Nooo! Absolutely, absolutely, absolutely not (*Iyayi, chachikulu, chachikulu, chachkulu!*—i.e., she wants to disabuse her brother of all superstition concerning his conversion). But 'Jesus' is the "Master-of-Creation" (*Mwini-chilengedwe*).[50]

MAN:Now nature is nature (*chilengedwe ndi chilengedwe*—i.e., a person cannot really control his/her deepest desires).

SIST:But when Jesus enters [a person], he enters completely, that's right; he will [help] 'control' one's nature.

WIFE:When you say, "Abstain" (*mupirira* 'you endure'), do you mean that we should just be looking at each other (*tizingoyang'anizana*—i.e., no sex at all, euphemism)?!

SIST:No, I'm saying that when both of you receive 'Jesus' as your Lord and Savior, Jesus is the one who will help you exercise 'control' just fine. The world's [method of] 'control' is faulty—that is, when they tell you just to, *aah* [pause], take 'socks' (*masokosi*—i.e., condoms!) and wear them. [But] perhaps they will break, who knows?

WIFE:*Eeeh!* [affirmation].

SIST:You yourselves have seen how things have gone wrong (*zakanikanso*—i.e., due to worldly ways, in particular, the immorality of her brother). Now [do you want to depend on] 'plastic' (*mapulasitiki*—i.e., condoms)? No indeed, Jesus alone will do!

WIFE: Alright!

SIST:And if you remain with Jesus, no matter how bad things get (*ziziwilima* 'they boil over'), when the 'signs' (*masayini*—i.e., that death is approaching), simply say, "Jesus, take me—let me rest there at your place!" (*ndikapume kwanuko*).

WIFE:Alright.

SIST:What happens when you remain with Jesus is that you have peace even during the time of sickness—you can have peace! Yes indeed, then when this Elder (*achikulirewo*—i.e., her brother, honorific) begins to get bad (*kuteketa* 'to split apart'—i.e., due to the complications that come with AIDS), no matter—you will just feel peace [inside], saying, "*Aah!* [it's enough!], [I'm] done! It would be better for me to start out on my journey now (*ndingonyamuka, basi*—i.e., depart this life), and be done with it!"[51] Your prayer will be to depart. If indeed a person suffers with this disease for 'four' years or so refusing death, he is also refusing this way (i.e., of repenting and becoming at peace with God). God wants him to admit [his sin], but he continues to refuse, saying, " No, I don't want [to die] [because] so-and-so has bewitched me!—[or] they have bewitched me!" (i.e., and thus I must first get revenge). God says, "No, do not leave with hatred! I want you [first] to get ready (i.e., through repentance). Then I'll take you." [But they keep on saying], "No, somebody bewitched me!"—leaving hatred *plop!* (*khu!*—i.e., an ideophone giving the sound of something sharply striking the ground) at the door! (i.e., of their house, a metaphor for their heart).

---

[50] There may well be another pun here in the expression "Master-of-Creation": Jesus controls life and death, including the time of a person's departure (which the man is so worried about), and he also helps one to control one's "nature" with reference to a person's greatest desires in life, including that of sex.

[51] The desire for direct speech is so prominent in Chinyanja dramatic discourse (see 5.1.1) that speakers often include snatches of it for emphasis within their own utterances, as we see exemplified here and elsewhere in this play.

WIFE:*liih!* [repugnance].

SIST:"Somebody has bewitched me [and his/her] 'secretary' (*sekilateri*—i.e., assistant) is so-and-so!" Nooo! There is no witchcraft at all! Since [your disease] has been discovered in this way, let us simply thank God. But we also have to pray very hard. Receive Jesus today—I want you both to receive Jesus as the Lord and Savior of your life!

MAN:I do need to receive him! So when I receive him, *eeya!* [strong affirmation]...so when I receive him, I am saved! How thankful I am too that the enmity between you and me... (his wife completes this utterance).

WIFE:It is completely finished!

SIST:Well, I also must say that I have forgiven you! The Lord has forgiven me of so many things— what has happened here is so little [in comparison]. *Eeeh!* [affirmation], let us forgive one another—and may [all] our sins be wiped away! (*afafanizidwe*).

MAN:But the [evil desires] of this nature of mine [remain], I'm not finished with them! And even though (*bola*) 'AIDS'...(i.e., I may still weaken and die)... [But at least] the enmity is gone—the enmity is gone!

SIST:No, as soon as you have received Jesus, you will be able to remain [celibate].

WIFE:Perhaps I should just leave—perhaps if I would leave [home]...

SIST:Nooo! Be still and just do what I say—to repent of your sins, that's right! And after you have repented, just see what Jesus will do [for you] (i.e., to help sort out their personal relationship in the home), *eeeh!* [affirmation]. Now kneel down, both of you, [for prayer].

MAN:Alright.

SIST:Both of you now confess the words that I am going to speak—just confess [them]!

WIFE:Let us make our confession now...

VISI:Please kneel down! Can anyone stop you from confessing [your sins] together! (i.e., not at all!).

CLOSING HYMN:

*SOLO:*I was a sinner, I was lost, [but] Jesus released me!
I was confused, I was bound, [but] Jesus redeemed me!

*CHORUS:*Today we are released, Jesus saw me!
From alcoholism Jesus delivered me, who would have seen me?![52]

ANNOUNCER:

Well, listeners, that's it for this week's play on the radio. The title of this play was "Do not hate one another!" The players were: Weles Banda, Yosafati Banda, Mexon Mulera, Mrs. Ligomeka, Mrs. Saidi, Mrs. Jairosi, and also Mrs. Ntambala. It may be that you were touched in a special way as you listened carefully to this play. Well if so, you can write us a letter to give us your thoughts. If you so wish, you may write to: The Producer,

---

[52] Each line of this song is repeated. The word "alcoholism" is literally *chipanda* 'a [traditional] drinking cup' i.e., for beer (metonymic usage).

Sewero (Drama), P.O. Box 52, Lilongwe, Malawi. Now the song that we heard [at the end] was sung by the Chicheka Family, and its title is "Jesus Saw Me." So indeed, we have come to the end of our *Sewero* program. Here at the radio [station], I, Enos Kanduna, say that if the Lord wills, why not meet me again next week!

6.3 Conclusion

A few final thoughts will bring this chapter to a close, first in a summary assessment of this play's overall technique in terms of style and content; second, in relation to some more general issues that pertain to the theological and hermeneutical significance of these Chinyanja vernacular radio dramas, with special reference to the several Scripture passages that have been incorporated into the dialogue.

6.3.1 Discussion and evaluation

Any valid evaluation of the preceding play (*Musadane* "Do not hate one another") should really be prepared by mother-tongue speakers/listeners on the basis of the original vernacular recording (including a good quality audio reproduction).[53] Despite the lack of this ideal, a number of provisional observations can be made concerning the annotated text-translation given above (assuming the general credibility of my notes). I need not go into details here, for that is up to every reader to do for him-/herself according to his/her impression of the play (form, content, message, impact, appeal, relevance), including its particular use of the several Scripture passages that were cited during the course of the story. I will simply offer a general assessment from my personal perspective.

All of the principal *stylistic features* surveyed in the preceding chapter are well represented:

- There is a constant flow of interactive *idiomatic dialogue* throughout the play, being dynamically as well as realistically articulated by all members of the cast, each in his or her own distinctive way according to the subject at hand and the particular character that s/he is verbally representing.

- The *rhetorical vigor* of the conversational sequence waxes and wanes in keeping with the prevailing dramatic tone and mood at the time, though on the whole it tended to be quite intense for the duration, as would be expected where witchcraft

---

[53] In a limited sort of way this criterion was addressed through a request to my student assistant, Mr. Pembeleka to choose what he felt was a very effective and well-performed play (he has listened and worked with the entire corpus). This was one of several plays that he selected from among them all.

accusations are involved and bitter enmity is continually simmering just below the surface of everyday life.

- A characteristic Malawian, true-to-life portrait in *local color* is also maintained by means of the precise, contextualized descriptions of the changing experiences and circumstances of the different personages, concerning for example, the sick man's original dream depiction, which sets all sorts of adverse suspicions alight in his mind; "Dr." *Sanza-muleke*'s self-revealing method of malady diagnosis and his innovative "prescription" for warding off the attacks of witches; and lastly, the popular but erroneous beliefs about AIDS that surface in the concluding scene.

- The play's *dramatic action* clearly reaches a peak along its physical, eventive plane of development in Scene IV when the sick man's son does some serious damage at his aunt's house; with respect to the psychological plane of argumentation, however, the climax occurs appropriately at the end in Scene VI, as the man's witch-craft-ridden family is gradually led to repent of the evil of their traditional religious perspective and to seek a new moral foundation and point of view through his sister's call to follow Christ.

- The drama's *emotive realism* patterns together with the varied advancement of its rhetorical dimension; a multiplicity of attitudes, feelings, and sentiments are strongly expressed in both words and non-verbal sounds, for example, by the sick man: fatalistic discouragement (over his prolonged, unexplained illness), bitter suspicion (when the likelihood of witchcraft points him towards possible culprits), joyful hope (when the medicine-man offers him a cure), vengeful anger (after his sister has been "confirmed" as the chief suspect), total dejection (over his HIV+ status), and penitent sorrow (when his sister is shown to be his best friend instead of his worst enemy).

- A certain *subdued humor* of both speech and situation recurs periodically in order to lighten the emotive load of a tragic theme and a high-strung dialogue progression—from the initial description of the man's relentless diarrhea to his sister's graphic description of the symptoms of AIDS at the end (intended to *de-familiarize* a terrible contemporary topic).

- Finally, we note the appearance of occasional, well-placed and expertly executed *audio effects*, human (e.g., paralinguistic modification of the voice, especially in the case of the sick man's emotively assorted utterances) as well as artificial (e.g., the little guard dog's protective barking at the opening of Scene IV and the jarring sounds of household goods being broken to bits, which bring this segment to an ominous close).

- The threat of witchcraft and sorcery, whether real (i.e., demonic forces) or perceived, accentuates certain aspects of a central African philosophy of life (3.1), while at the same time it leads people to ignore or downplay others. The principle of *synthesis* influences all those who are troubled, deprived, or afflicted to seek and to find suspicious connections of causality in the overtly unrelated events that occur in society (*experientialism*). For example, the simple fact that the sister had previously warned her brother to go immediately to the hospital, not to a medicine man, later makes her a prime suspect when the latter divines that sorcery is making him sick. Such self-centered apprehensions are reinforced by beliefs concerning the seen and unseen powers and potentates of *dynamism*, as established in the ancient hierarchy of *gradation* and demarcated in accordance with the variable, popularly-defined attitudes that pertain to the *circumscription* of personal authority, influence, and well-being in life This delicate balance of forces and interpersonal tensions which firmly locks the individual into a relationship with others in society (*humanism ⇔ communalism*), his own relatives in particular, is broken and great damage is done—physical, psychological, and spiritual. It is not surprising, then, that a cultural "misfit"—in this case, a strong Christian woman, who has completely repudiated the traditional religious world view—is "revealed" by her adversary, the medicine-man, to be that anti-social individual (the "witch/sorcerer") who is trying to enhance herself at the expense of those relationally closest to her in kinship terms. Indeed, it would not have taken much for this story to have had a completely different ending—from what it is, occasioned by a concerned boy coming to take his sick granddad to the hospital in an oxcart. So close this was then to becoming a full tragedy—one motivated by a belief and value system that views man, whether self or other(s), essentially as the creator or destroyer of his own destiny!

6.3.2 Significance

It is important to call attention to the significance of the "TransWorld Radio Drama Group" in furnishing an excellent model for Christian communication in central Africa. This non-clerical troupe is comprised of "ordinary" lay-persons, none of whom have had any extensive *formal* theological education (although two male members are engaged in a part-time evangelistic preaching ministry). In their radio performances, therefore, as well as in their inclusion of selected verses of Scripture, the team is able to provide a fresh, relatively non-conventional,[54] perspective on the sense and significance of the Word of God in relation to the lives of the many and diverse fictional, but realistic personages who people their plays.

The *Sewero* dramatic productions normally include some typical examples of creative "grassroots" vernacular theologizing. These may be larger or smaller in scope, ranging from the new "reading" of an entire biblical plot (as in the present case) to some insightful, contextualized use of a particular Bible passage. Such instances are helpful first of all to the widespread mem-

---

[54] All of the *Sewero* performers are regular church goers, however, and have therefore been influenced by the doctrines and interpretations of the particular denominations that they belong to (i.e. in general: non-Catholic, "evangelical" Protestant). On the other hand, they must work by compromise to agree among themselves with regard to how to interpret and present certain controversial theological or moral issues and Bible texts. As a rule, they are much more interested in portraying the various problems that pertain to life-related ethical matters than to become involved in hermeneutical affairs, which they would rather leave to the professional clergy (personal correspondence, a taped interview). For a much more "non-conventional" interpretation of the Bible, one would of course need to examine the sermons and teachings of "independent" evangelists and preachers/pastors of the so-called "African Instituted Churches" (see Mijoga 2001; Wendland 2000).

bers of the listening audience, who either are grappling with these same issues personally, or who know of others who are. So is the practice, as illustrated by a play's characters, of relating the Scriptures to the various crises and conundrums that arise in daily life. These localized interpretations and applications are also very enlightening for trained clergy, theologians, and Bible scholars who wish to learn more about the religious and spiritual matters that really matter to average Christians living in central Africa (their worries, troubles, trials, temptations, challenges, needs, desires, favorite verses, etc) and how they might be meaningfully confronted with the Word of God in the search for possible answers, solutions, instruction, correction, encouragement, and so forth. In short, the *Sewero* program illustrates an extremely attractive and artful didactic technique that is on display for the advice and edification of us all.

The following is a survey of how a diverse range of individual Bible passages were used, whether directly or indirectly, in the play "Do not hate one another":

- *2 Timothy 2:24*—This passage is cited by the aunt (Scene V) in a rather straightforward manner with reference to her aggrieved nephew who is threatening to do violence on her home premises. On the contrary, a "servant of God" (i.e., any serious Christian) must be kind, not quarrelsome.

- *1 Thessalonians 2:16*—This text is appropriately applied to the disabling accident that the aunt's nephew suffered during his destructive rampage, in effect preventing him from doing further damage. Thus God steps in to "punish" the enemies of his people.

- *Matthew 5:11-12*—Here is another rather straightforward usage. The aunt sees herself as a person who is falsely "accused and insulted" for the sake of Christ, i.e., her Christian testimony to her brother about the evils of witchcraft. She can also take comfort in the fact that "her reward in heaven is great". She makes an interesting little addition in this case—namely, that this "reward" will be given only to those who do not try to retaliate, which is a valid implication also in the original context.

- *Matthew 6:14*—This passage is referred to only by implication, that is, the need for "forgiving" one's enemies. In the present story this applies of course to the aunt in relation to her brother's family, who have caused her all kinds of grief based on the belief that she has bewitched her brother. At the end of Scene V, the aunt again mentions the importance of forgiveness and asks God to help her to do this, even as he has forgiven her—an obvious allusion to the Lord's Prayer.

- *Jeremiah 17:5*—This verse is cited in its entirety by the aunt (Scene VI) as part of her effort to lead her brother away from his dependence on traditional religious beliefs. People who turn to medicine-men for help on earth, she says, have turned from the Lord and are therefore "cursed". She extends this "curse" to being sent to hell ("gehena") if one dies in such a destructive faith.

- *John 10:10a*—The aunt continues her "brotherly" appeal by quoting the first half of this passage. She now gives him a more personal, "African" motivation for ceasing from his trust in witchcraft. Such beliefs, she claims, are only used by the Devil to cause anger and hatred among friends, as has happened in their family. Her implication is that the only way to end such enmity is to reject all adherence to an occult faith and practice.

- *John 8:36*—After the "law", the sick man's aunt turns to the "gospel" in urging her brother to allow Jesus to give him protection, peace of mind, and "freedom even in times of sickness". This text is not quoted, but again, is directly alluded to in her life-and-death argument with a loved one.

- *1 John 1:9*—At the close of the play (Scene VI), the aunt alludes to yet another Johannine passage as she asks that her brother's family all kneel down—to "confess your sins". This could simply be a formal practice (along with its verbal formula) of the church that she (the cast member) belongs to, but the ultimate reference is biblical. The same might be said of the expression "receive" Jesus, which she had used earlier in this climactic conversation (see John 5:43-44).

- The *Sewero* group thus perceptively and persuasively handles the Scriptures to scratch where it really itches in their society and culture. However, they try to apply their corrective, minatory, didactic, or hortatory pressure gently and in such a way that the principal offenders, whether secular or "religious", are caught off guard, like David by Nathan's pathetic pastoral parable. Thus the guilty (a group that includes just about all of us) are initially enticed by the narrative excitement, dynamic artistry, and contemporary realism of a given drama so that they are led to listen to the message before they realize what is happening—that one of the characters in the story is actually impersonating them, to a greater or lesser extent. The implied criticism (rebuke or condemnation, as the case may be) cannot be avoided or ignored. Serious Christians, on the other hand, are strongly encouraged by identifying with one of the play's admirable character(s) to "go out and do likewise" (Lk 10:37). Such relevant (efficient and effective) techniques of religious communication need to be studied and compared with other recorded examples so that a comprehensive bank of theological "case studies" can be collected and made available to others for their instruction and a possible local adaptation in other parts of Africa.

7. The Future of Christian Vernacular Radio Drama: *Masewero* in the New Millennium

7.1 Developing the communicative potential of *masewero* –locally "contextualized" biblical-Christian messages

The crucial subject of local adaptation and application was introduced in section 4.4.3, but its importance for encouraging the development of a locally relevant, "Africanized" biblical interpretation (*hermeneutics*) and practice is such that it bears further consideration here in my concluding chapter. I will discuss several additional aspects of this essential contextualization process with reference to biblical *theology* in general and more specifically to its associated *pedagogy*—that is, the manner in which theological content may be imparted to the masses. My consideration of audience education will be extended also to the subject of *apologetics*, for here too these appealing radio dramas serve an underlying, but important communicative function. My point is that the *Sewero* dramatic format coupled with the mass-medium of radio provides an excellent means of both instructing and empowering a large lay audience for Christian witness as well as defense, particularly with regard to the culturally sensitive issues that are automatically involved with the beliefs and practices of the traditional religious occult. It would be difficult to duplicate this artistic effectiveness in any other way, given the local sociological setting and available resources, both human and financial.

As was pointed out in chapter 4, the communicative setting under consideration (rural southeastern Africa) is one that is still very "oral-aural" (non-literacy based) in character. It may be generally described as a varied and variable complex of the following significant features (see Primrose, cited in Sundersingh 2001:110):

- The people devote much time to interpersonal, face-to-face, interactive (i.e., dialogic, not monologic) communication.

- This interaction involves the whole body, indeed one's entire personality, including meaningful facial expressions, gestures, body movements, and paralinguistic vocal modifications.

- Such communication is always communal in nature; those who may not be directly involved in the dialogue are nevertheless always reacting and contributing to the conversation in one way or another, verbally or non-verbally.

- These discussions are not about abstract or generalized topics; rather they are typically very concrete, specific, and life-related in style, content, and implication.

- This is communication that demands reciprocal time, effort, and a commitment to "saving face" (i.e., avoiding the giving and taking of personal "shame") where sensitive, difficult, important, and/or controversial topics are being discussed.

- "Religious" topics are not treated as an extraordinary, "sacred" subject; while God, the ancestors, magic, or witchcraft may be the focus of attention, they are always related to the everyday occurrences and experiences of human life, and conversely, they may be integrated into the discussion of any "secular" discourse.

- The dialogue is frank (though there be various degrees of allusion and indirection), informal and idiomatic, enriched by nonverbal elements, and colored by different forms of oral artistry, e.g., local imagery and figurative language, hyperbole or bombastic flourishes, rhetorical devices, repetition, phonological patterning and punning, poetry, proverbial utterances, colloquial diction, and/or enigma—as dictated by the occasion, the audience, and the purpose of the conversation.

These seven different characteristics (not an exhaustive listing) were abundantly described and demonstrated in the exemplified analysis of chapter 5 as well as in the complete play of chapter 6, which clearly overviewed and illustrated the typical verbal style of the *Sewero* performances.

A number of text-based examples of *Sewero* grass-roots contextualizing were given in summary form in chapter 4 (section 4.3.2). Another representative selection will be surveyed in this section as it pertains to theology, pedagogy, apologetics, and hermeneutics. This provides another concrete illustration of how this all-lay (non-cleric) production team subtly and artfully introduces or highlights such potentially controversial issues and then deals with them in a dynamic, creative, interactive manner. This is a flexible and fluid method of "natural" or "local" application whereby the particular problem, temptation, crisis, or challenge is integrated within a dramatic situation and a familiar sociocultural setting by a staff that is completely at home in this fictitious but realistic narrative environment. The issue can thus be easily experienced vicariously and personally reacted to as the play unfolds and almost unobtrusively conveys its message.

I will first consider selected aspects concerning four major areas of application that a typical *Sewero* drama offers religious communicators.

7.1.1 Theology

A potentially large and diverse audience may be reached on a regular basis via these weekly radio broadcasts. The *Sewero* program generates a great deal of individual listener feedback as well as an unknown (but presumably significant) amount of subsequent discussion concerning key theological and practical issues of immediate import to the Christian community. The question of how to stimulate, interact with, and benefit from these widely distributed and informal local deliberations needs to be further considered (see, for example, West on the principles and procedures of "contextual Bible study"; 1993, 1995; Wendland 2000:ch. 5). The possibility of general as well as specific "benefit" is perhaps most important outcome, especially with regard to better understanding the various uses, needs, and goals of Scripture use in various settings, e.g., in the home, at school, in different church bodies, on the job, and in many other settings of public interaction. Clearly some follow-up research is needed in order to more adequately assess what is going on in terms of the personal impact and application of the *Sewero* program with respect to home-grown moral and religious thinking and behavior.

As an example of the great potential in this field, we might summarize several prominent features that are manifested in the popular play "Rich Man" (*Mwini-chuma*; see 5.1.5). First of all, the character of "Lazarus" is not given a leading role at all, which is in keeping with his relative lack of prominence in the actual biblical account of Luke 16:19-31. Instead, the dramatic spotlight focuses completely on the pride, greed, and immoral actions of the urban Rich Man (RM). This negative portrayal is intensified by the depiction of his treatment of the various women that enter his life—a young female street beggar, the man's browbeaten third wife, a righteous housewife on her way to the market, and finally a teen-aged prostitute plying her trade along the road. Second, in the play's long medial scene the RM is confronted by the persistent and urgent Christian testimony of the housewife after he attempts to proposition her in his car. He ultimately rejects her bold witness and offer to lead him to repentance, but the fact that he has thus been duly warned by the Word of the Lord is made abundantly clear to all radio listeners, who thereby act as silent witnesses against him. This dramatic twist represents an important Malawian contextualization of the Lukan account, which has in effect become "parable-ized" in Chinyanja for the current *Sewero* audience—people who know of many such "rich men" in their society who behave just like the fellow characterized in this radio rendition.

It is important to note that the RM is not condemned to hell due to his ignorance; he ends up in torment there because of his impudent refusal to listen to good advice (which is also the moral of many a traditional Nyanja folktale). There is an additional twofold implied audience obligation that this development entails: Christians must not be afraid to testify of their faith and to reprove wicked conduct, wherever and whenever it manifests itself; the ungodly, on the other hand, and those who are living in sin must listen for dear life when they have been reproached. Later, during his pathetic dialogue with "Father Abraham," the RM reveals the principal reason why he is condemned, along with the former wealthy friends whom he requests a special messenger for: they despise and disregard both the Bible and also its commissioned messengers. The crucial warning of Abraham therefore applies just as acutely today (Lk. 16:31). Finally, the dreadful plight of women in every sector of contemporary African society is sympathetically highlighted as the play progresses: How long will they continue to be abused by the bestial behavior of men—whether the traditionally submissive wife at home, the prostitute who thinks that she must be such in order to live, or even "anywoman" innocently going about her everyday business, who can fall prey to a roving male at just about any time and place.[1] A theology without praxis is religion without a reality, and the *Sewero* team emphasizes this crucial distinction in one play after another.

7.1.2 Pedagogy

The final observation above leads us into the second major area of potential influence as far as the *Sewero* dramatic productions are concerned. It is not only the religious content (theology) of these plays that needs to be further studied and stimulated, but the same thing applies, perhaps even more so, in the matter of their didactic style as well—that is, as *case-studies* which model effective teaching technique. Is it possible, for example, to duplicate this dramatic mode of interpersonal instruction (pedagogy) in other areas of Christian communication? Alternatively, to what extent and in which respects can these *Sewero* plays be utilized as individual illustrations in some specific field of applied theological or missiological studies? It is clear that this vital, essentially *inductive* (non-propositional, derivational, experiential) manner of presenting contextualized "*narrative-oriented* theology" as abundantly manifested in the *Sewero* corpus is highly effective for teaching and learning in an oral/aural-based society, for this is the traditional, well-known way of doing things (see Wendland 1998c; Bradt 1997; Healy & Sybertz 1996). Perhaps a little more background regarding this important subject may help to highlight its key points of contemporary relevance.

The relationship between the case-study approach to teaching/learning and the so-called "inductive" method of reasoning is not difficult to discern (see Wendland 2000:ch. 2). The former is simply a sub-type of the latter.

---

[1] An application to the raging AIDS crisis in Africa could readily be made here. That is not done in this particular play (as in others) because the didactic freight of the drama is already pretty heavy. Mixing in the AIDS issue could well dilute or diffuse the intended message with a consequent loss of impact and specific relevance.

Induction typically proceeds from the analysis of a set of specific facts which are life-related and culture-specific to a general conclusion that is based on those facts and which, in turn, may be applied to a large number of similar situations. It works from the known to the unknown, from the familiar to the unfamiliar, from individual instances to an inclusive category, from a problem to its solution. The inductive process focuses upon concrete personal examples, analogies, anecdotes, contrasts, images, figures, details— evidence which tends to appeal to one's feelings and senses, his imagination and personal experience. The threefold objective is to develop on this familiar foundation a natural conclusion (based on the indigenous "logic" of the society concerned), a generalized principle of thought or behavior, or a directive for action (e.g., exhortation, admonition, warning, prohibition, etc.). For this reason, particularly in literary contexts, learning-teaching by induction is often set within a narrative framework, one which manifests a great deal of participant interaction in the form of dialogue, as diverse positions and possibilities are progressively explored and evaluated. A *Sewero* play is by its very nature an outstanding example of this method.

The inductive mode of education and exhortation is strongly audience- and experience-orientated, and this is one of the primary reasons for both its appeal and its effectiveness in promoting sound teaching as well as better learning. It begins where people are at—with their understanding, assumptions, point of view, needs, wants, values, goals, opinions, fears, deficiencies, abilities—and works out from there in order to encourage a deeper level of understanding with regard to some significant human problem or crisis, hence embodying a greater potential for personal improvement. The typically dialogic procedure greatly stimulates audience interaction (verbal, at times even physical) and involvement (emotive and volitional as well as cognitive) along the way. This takes place as the diverse facts being considered are sorted out, categorized, and organized so as to derive an agreeable and satisfying conclusion or consensus at the end. The latter may then be applied in a practical way toward solving one of life's mysteries, difficulties, or deficiencies—particularly as this concerns one's deeply-held religious beliefs and practices. Such problem-solving activity has, to a certain significant degree, to be carried out by each participant by him/herself; otherwise the impact of the exercise is diminished and its benefits correspondingly reduced. However, in an African context (for one example, as opposed to a Western setting), however, it may be more natural for the individual to effectively learn by active participation within a group discussion situation.

Such a didactic scenario is very much encouraged by dialogues that constitute a *Sewero* play. First of all, the radio audience may participate *vicariously* in the life experience of any of the characters being portrayed in a given drama—ideally with the Christian "hero" for the day, namely, the person who most forcefully enunciates the play's main biblical truth or lesson. Second, teaching is effected subsequently, as the plot and purpose of any performance is perhaps debated and evaluated by the listening audience, who will learn even more in terms of both quantity and quality through this practice of reflective drama criticism.

Certainly learning by induction is no stranger to Africa, or to many other predominantly oral-aural societies throughout the world. Despite the rapid progress being made in technological development, economic diversification, political pluralism, and literacy-based education, an ancient system of communication known as "oral tradition" still plays a prominent role in popular African social culture, in both urban and rural settings. This traditional manner of message transmission—or better, dramatization—generally encompasses a broad range of predominantly artistic-didactic genres, such as, proverbs, riddles, myths, legends, historical records, folktales, praise poems, songs of all sorts as well as those verbal forms that are primarily utilitarian in function, for example, prayers, formulae of divination, magical incantations, curses, initiation instructions, and official pronouncements at social and religious ceremonies (see Wendland 1979:ch. 8).

Although each of these popular forms of oral discourse is quite distinct, they all tend to have several noteworthy inductive features in common. One is that they are firmly rooted in human experience (including a people's ethnic history, or "tribal tradition") as well as the ecological and environmental features that characterize the physical surroundings of the society concerned. The content of such *experiential*, culture-preserving and promoting literature is thus quite familiar to the masses to begin with. It is easier then for them to identify with the participants and situations that are presented and hence also to meaningfully relate to the specific problem or need that is being addressed.

Secondly, these literary types are highly *participatory* in presentation. In other words, the audience either has a formal role to play in their performance (e.g., a riddle, responsive narrative, or song chorus), or they are encouraged to make an informal spontaneous verbal contribution to the proceedings (e.g., at an initiation ceremony or a judicial debate). This helps to ensure that most, if not all, listeners become themselves personally involved both physically and mentally with the composition of the message, whether old or new, which consequently makes a greater and more lasting impression upon them.

Finally, the forms of oral tradition are clearly *functional* in nature, that is, they are motivated by and intended to accomplish certain communicative objectives in the particular sociocultural setting in which they are performed. Among such purposes, the didactic element is perhaps the most important since it appears to be manifested to a greater or lesser degree on just about every occasion. Participants either learn for the first time (if they are younger) or they reinforce in their own thinking and behavior some of the chief moral and ethical tenets of their society through the means of their oral lore. Yet by virtue of the equally prominent aesthetic and social dimension of such literature, this instructional component is subdued, downplayed, and frequently even completely disguised. Participants, whether young or old, are acculturated into the key beliefs, mores, customs, and behavioral standards, of the group even as they are fully engaged in an enjoyable communal endeavor. Education is not perceived, therefore, as being an activity that is somehow esoteric, restrictive, oppressive, unproductive, tiring, or just plain boring—not if one can have fun while one is doing it!

As a didactic exercise, the case-study method is hard to surpass in effectiveness for achieving its stated objectives. However, it works best (in an African setting) when utilized in conjunction with other didactic modes and means of communication as part of a larger inductive emphasis within a course curriculum, one that favors, for example: oral (or written) instruction by the dialogic, question-answer with examples method, rather than by concentrated lectures (no matter how "logically" or "systematically" these may be organized); periodic joint, as opposed to individual, homework/research assignments and class presentations; frequent sessions involving interdisciplinary "team"-teaching (for expatriates, definitely with a national co-worker); instruction (if possible) in a common vernacular language to encourage and check up on the correct transmission of key theological terms, concepts, and applications; participation in some form of Bible translation work (e.g., reviewing a draft for accuracy); and frequent oral-visual evaluation (by cassette tape or video) of student performance in sermon delivery, teaching style, evangelistic witness, and various pastoral acts (e.g., visiting the sick).

While a case-study method, one that makes use of selected *Sewero* plays, may not be appropriate or successful for use in all of the subjects that need to be covered in a given theological curriculum, for example (e.g., dogmatics), it can certainly be of assistance in many areas of instruction, whether formal or informal in nature (e.g., ethical, or applied, theology). A set of *Sewero* dramas (ideally presented in their original audio version, but more likely as a printed translation) could easily form the basis for a case-study course in African traditional religion (ATR), as follows:

    (a)   present a chosen play right up to its point of dramatic "resolution";

(b) debate the various possibilities for dealing with the problems presented   by the plot as well as the different moral and spiritual issues involved;

(c) give the play's actual resolution and denouement as originally presented;

(d) discuss and evaluate (c), with suggestions for improvement and/or alternative solutions.

In an African "high-context" society (see 4.4.2) the audience is usually quite familiar with the pertinent sociocultural setting and thus can immediately "stage" it imaginatively in their minds, thus providing an environment in which the ethical or theological message can be further developed and dramatized. The question then is whether the *Sewero* corpus, if made widely available in both audio cassette and printed translation formats, might be utilized more often or fully also in both formal (pastoral) and informal (lay-leadership) theological training programs, for example, to offer "case studies" of controversial issues or demonstrations of pastoral praxis in action (e.g., an evangelism visit, sick call, funerary consolation, disciplinary rebuke, an apologetic argument with a gainsayer, or a personal counseling session). Clearly these "plays" have a lot more to offer the church in Africa (and elsewhere) than their wholesome entertainment value.

7.1.3 Apologetics

The role of the *Serwero* group's artistic, dramatically-presented "defense" (or "apology") of the basic tenets of Protestant Christianity has already been touched upon (see 4.4.3.2). Apologetics may be taught and studied either as a subject in its own right or as a particular branch of Christian theology or pedagogy. In any case, these plays impart an evangelical (at times "semi-pentecostal") biblical perspective on various controversial issues in contemporary Malawi, thus taking a relatively conservative theological stance on such matters in keeping with the doctrinal position of TWR (see Appendix B). In the great majority of cases this defensive, at times polemical viewpoint is adopted, whether more overtly or implicitly in any given play, over against the contra-Scriptural beliefs and practices of traditional African religion, like those of the occult which I have chosen to focus on in the present study (i.e., witchcraft, sorcery, the use of magical substances, divination, and spiritism).

It happens much less frequently, but on occasion some prominent contentious teaching or ritual of one or another of the many Malawian "independent churches" is critiqued in dialogue through a given play's plot, that is, in comparison with a more traditional ecclesiastical position on the matter, for example, the practice of polygamy; healing the sick through an appeal to the ancestors; forecasting God's will by means of dreams or "prophetic" divination; the selection and veneration of church leaders (e.g., how this is carried out); the origin, nature, and results of saving "conversion" (e.g., is it of God or of man?); recognizing the deity of Christ (often denied) or the innate nature of humanity (is it essentially good or evil?); and, not surprisingly, the personality and various manifestations of the Holy Spirit among believers. It is interesting to note that the team's apologetic strategy of instruction in relation to the teachings of Scripture does not extend to other non-Christian religions that practice their faith in Malawi, such as, Islam, Hinduism, or to a much lesser extent, Buddhism. These religions are, by and large, not even mentioned at all, no doubt in order to preserve peace in the nation.

There is one common thread in the *Sewero* team's treatment of all such areas of dispute and controversy—namely, the use of explicit Scripture to settle the issue, one way or the other. Generally, there is no ambiguity or uncertainty over the main matter in question at the end, whether a crucial belief, some focal activity, or both, are involved. As was periodically illustrated in the actual excerpts from plays throughout chapters 4-6, specific Bible passages are normally cited or alluded to by one or more of the leading characters during the post-climax denouement of a given play. Such quotations or indirect references may occur at some earlier point too, whenever the central topic of a given drama is being contested, or in the build-up to the key moment of crisis in the lives of the chief character(s), but more often these passages are reserved for the final climactic portion, perhaps so that they make more of an impression upon listeners.

I would conclude that the *Sewero* group's chosen thespian technique, as far as this concerns their practice of biblical apologetics, could offer a variable range of illustrations and options that might be evaluated in terms of their individual and corporate rhetorical effectiveness and textual fidelity. Alternatively, depending on the drama concerned, the team's method might well serve as a model that demonstrates one possible way of confronting wrong with right in respect to a particular trial, trouble, or test of one's personal faith. In either case (the "Rich-Man" play gives an example of both; see 5.1.5), the members of just about any group of believers might benefit from a closer text study (whether in print or via an audio version) and subsequent interactive discussion.

To be more specific, these plays would be especially relevant, hence beneficial, to people who are concerned about more fully exploring the contextualized dimension of their faith, ranging from a teen-aged Bible-study fellowship to a class of seminary students. They all would learn that, in contrast to the prevailing philosophy in much of Western Christianity in these post-modern times, there are certain disciples who do care to "eagerly…examine the Scriptures" (Acts 17:11-12) in order to learn, by example, how to more effectively discern error from truth (as they come to biblically differentiate the two) as this is manifested in their own sociocultural setting. They would also have a bank of illustrations that demonstrate how ordinary Christians can publicly stand up for their faith—no matter what the situation, no matter what the consequences (Acts 17:13-15).

7.1.4 Hermeneutics: Exegesis or "Epigesis"?

There is an important question that arises as one carefully considers the content, intent, and method that is manifested in and through the *Sewero* corpus: Where do such local "readings" and contextualized interpretations, as so expertly and effectively practiced by this Nyanja drama group, fit into the overall hermeneutical process that is set in motion when people engage the Scriptures? Does it make any difference at all—either to the dramatic team, to their radio audience, or to biblical scholars and interpreters in general? My query arises, perhaps too obviously, from a Western viewpoint, but it does have wider implications, in Africa too, because the underlying issue is one that seriously concerns and has been actively addressed by the producing editors of the Sewero program in consultation with the players themselves (as recorded in my personal interviews with them).

This perspective, which undoubtedly also reflects my teaching experience as a Bible translation consultant and seminary instructor, envisions a rather conventional ("non-postmodern") two-phase hermeneutical procedure. The principal focus and guiding norm for this interactive process is the biblical (Hebrew/Greek) text as it closely relates, first of all, to its own Ancient Near Eastern (Palestinian) sociocultural and religious context and, second, to the current vernacular setting of oral, written, audio, and/or video communication. There is a certain developmental flow here that may be diagrammed, very simply, as shown below:

Aspects of critical hermeneutical engagement with the biblical text

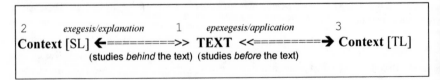

2 *exegesis/explanation* 1 *epexegesis/application* 3
Context [SL] ⬅==========>> **TEXT** <<==========➡ **Context [TL]**
(studies *behind* the text) (studies *before* the text)

The older theoretical viewpoint is that the hermeneutical process is undertaken in stages, that is, initially considering the conceptual area (or cognitive "horizon") of 1 ➔ 2 (*exegesis*), and subsequently that of 1 ➔ 3 (*epigesis*).[2] However, more recent communication studies have correctly pointed out the fact that the ethnically diverse interpreters of the biblical text (1) always perceive things from the perspective and within the mental framework of their own cultural context and sociological situation, including its prevailing world view and value system (3). Similarly, the original writers were just as strongly affected by their own communicative setting (2), including a general conception of their intended audience and the circumstances of reception, when they composed their various historical, pastoral, and prophetic works.

In actual effect, then, the practice of hermeneutics turns out to be quite circular, or interactive (call it "dialogic" or "conversational"; see Draper 2002:13), as one interpretive operation invariably influences and is also influenced by another in an ongoing alternating and overlapping progression. A set of protocols, priorities, and norms must therefore be agreed upon if the results of any analysis and/or exposition are to be made reviewable or "testable" by others and evaluated accordingly.[3] This theoretical stance would also suggest that any particular reading of a biblical text must be approached from two distinct perspectives, which invariably impinge upon and influence one another.

To be specific, interpretation may be carried out exegetically with a focus upon the original co-text and context, and/or epigetically in relation to the current sociocultural setting of the target audience. *Exegesis* applies various historical, linguistic, literary, social-scientific, etc. studies to the original document in order to determine what it may have (most probably) meant to its primary receptors (hearers/readers), that is, its intended "*sense.*" *Epigesis* utilizes these and other scholarly disciplines in order to effect a present day communication of certain aspects of the "*significance*" of that same biblical text via one or more media to a very different contemporary target group. The outcome of any act of interpretation, i.e. "meaning," can be viewed as the combination of both of these sub-processes (explanation + application),

---

[2] "*Epi*-gesis"—that is, applied studies which are based "upon" (𝔐𝔒𝔛) a prior, comprehensive examination (*exegesis*) of the biblical text within its overall, original setting of communication, no matter how suppositional the latter might be due our lack of adequate knowledge concerning the initial event.
[3] For some contemporary interpreters, on the other hand, such issues are not of immediate concern or relevance, and different methods of qualitative assessment are therefore established.

and the end result may be judged to be more or less successful, relatively and contextually speaking, with respect to either or both of them.[4]

One can therefore choose to emphasize either sense or significance in one's analysis of a certain passage or text of Scripture, recognizing of course their interactive relationship. I prefer to adopt a certain procedural priority during the overall hermeneutical operation, namely, to seek the sense *before* the significance of the text at hand. In other words, the initial aim of interpretation, that is, understanding a biblical text would be to analyze and explain its contextually-based "original" meaning. All contemporary applications—practical inferences, translations, compositional transformations, and various medium-sensitive communicative re-presentations—then flow from and with reference to that. In short, I would always begin with exegesis and move from there to epigesis.[5]

To give one example, the Sewero group's imaginative expansion of the Lukan "Rich-Man" parable (5.1.5) to include, for example, the housewife's passionate testimony to RM and Abraham's later reference to this fateful discussion, would need to be clearly distinguished in any subsequent review or assessment of the play as a Malawian applicative usage. It does not fall within the scope of a valid interpretive, or exegetical, meaning because there is no actual biblical text to base it on, whether explicitly or implicitly. In other words, such a contextualization deals primarily with the significance of the original parable for Christians in Africa, whether practicing or not, and others who live in the present day world. This would certainly overlap with, since it is derived from, a complete exposition of the passage (via a vernacular translation) in the light of how it would have been understood and the impact that it would have made when Christ first told it, as represented by Luke.

The producers of the Sewero program do endeavor to maintain a definite standard of hermeneutical responsibility, or legitimacy, with regard to interpretation during the composition and performance of their dramas. That is to

---

[4]   In this section I am using the terminology, but not the definitions of Hirsch (1967:8; see Vanhoozer 1998: *passim*, and Ryken 2002:chs. 4-5). Draper (2002:16-17) employs the terms "contextualization" and "distantiation" in a roughly comparable way to my "epigesis" and "exegesis" respectively. He also adds a third procedure to the hermeneutical mix, namely, "appropriation", which is the "process of 'owning' the Word, of accepting the meaning I have discovered in my own context and community and taking responsibility for it" (2002:78). I find this to be a helpful, even necessary, perspective but one that actually derives from or is based upon the prior activity of distantiation (epigesis).

[5]   Many would not wish to be so dogmatic about our hermeneutical activity: "It does not really matter where one starts, whether one starts with reconstruction, interpretation or context" (Draper 2002:16), although he does prefer to "give priority to the context of the reader". I favor the procedural priority stated above (with an initial emphasis on investigating the context of the biblical text) simply on the basis of my own teaching preference, but I recognize that other methods may be equally, if not more valid and effective.

say, they closely monitor the production process to ensure that the players remain within a certain credible as well as acceptable framework of biblical exegesis. This happens either when they create the plot and purpose of a play or, more specifically, when they employ selected passages of Scripture within it, e.g. the Christian lady's minatorial usage of the notion of "judgment" when citing Hebrews 9:27 to her rich but iniquitous tempter.[6]

My point in making the preceding distinction is that there appears to exist nowadays a disturbingly high level of involuntary ignorance or passive unawareness concerning the basic facts of Scripture, with regard to both the recorded text as well as its situational context. This appears to be generally true, not only in Africa, but throughout the world. Despite all the sophisticated new study tools being developed and made available, most people still do not have access to these or know how to use them efficiently (in some cases being prohibited from doing so by church officials!). Even many pastors and preachers, whether speaking in a local congregation or via radio and television, do not seem to make much use of the available educative resources (e.g. study Bibles, hypertext computer programs, audiocassette guides, CD information banks) in order to enrich and expand the informative or didactic quality of their presentations. Practical, situation governed biblical instruction should therefore be a high priority during any sort of message-enhancing effort, no matter what the medium and mode of message transmission.

One must not go overboard of course and risk turning the vibrant verbal message of creative communicators into some dry, academic-sounding but practically irrelevant discourse. On the other hand, people should be enabled intellectually through every available means so that they gain not only a fuller understand of the Scriptures, but also the critical capacity to discern the essential difference between the sense and significance of any given biblical text, regardless of the form and format in which it is presented (e.g., homiletical, pedagogical, dramatic, musical, audiovisual, etc.). They then need to be trained also to assess the relative value and effectiveness of either aspect with reference to any current communication activity involving God's

---

[6] This hermeneutical framework is also governed to a considerable degree by the evangelical doctrinal position of TransWorld Radio, as set forth in their "mission statement" (www.twr.org). Thus local program directors seek to ensure that the content of their various productions, including the *Sewero* plays, does not explicitly violate these principles. On the other hand, a biblically-based performance such as we have in the *Mwini-chuma* play might be enhanced or enriched conceptually through a greater utilization of some of the interesting sociocultural and religious features that are found within the original text itself, for example, the ritual significance of the dogs licking the sores of Lazarus, the retributive notions associated with *hades*, the importance of Abraham in Jewish eschatological thought, or indeed, the symbolic relevance of Lazarus being situated 'at Abraham's bosom'.

Word. This pressing pedagogical challenge leads to several suggestions and specific proposals in my concluding section.

7.1.5 A dramatized vernacular example of applied theology, pedagogy, apologetics, and hermeneutics

The following example is given to illustrate, admittedly in a somewhat subjective manner, how the various interests, concerns, and applications of a locally contextualized biblical theology (THE), pedagogy (PED), apologetics (APO), and hermeneutics (HER) merge together and interact during the performance of a typical *Sewero* play—*Kodi mwaiwala?* "Have you forgotten?" Several prominent instances of each dimension, which normally co-occurs with another, are noted in the dialogue where they are footnoted for further explanation. This overview, along with the preceding discussion, lays the groundwork in my concluding section for an informal critical evaluation of the program, including several suggestions for possible modifications and new developments.

> (Setting: We pick up this concluding dialogue in the final scene of the play, which presents the climax and resolution of the drama. The theological problem being discussed concerns the customs regarding reverence/worship (??) of the ancestral spirits at the time of a major (elderly adult) funeral. The leading character, a strong Christian woman [W] who lives in town, is supported by her husband [H] as they both take a stand of opposition to their rural relatives, primarily her maternal uncle [U], who wish to perform a rite of remembrance for her late mother, who became a Christian shortly before she passed away. [additional voices: B = the Woman's brother, who lives an urban life in South Africa, E = another village elder, N = the elder's niece, L = a lady of the village])[7]
>
> W: Yes, indeed, Uncle, that is what the matter is all about (i.e., her dispute with him over the matter of the funeral ritual which is in the latter stages of preparation).
> U: Yaah! (enthusiasm) Let all of us relatives (i.e., gathered here on the village common) clap our hands (*tiwombe m'manja* – as a sign of reverence and welcome)—let them (the ancestors) return again! (There is the sound of clapping hands.)
> E: (Let us) give the spirits a hearty hand!
> L: You (spirits) are welcome!
> U: es indeed (*Iyaai!* lit. 'No'), I'm so happy because you have heard us (i.e., our prayers)!
> L: That's right!
> U: So as you have heard in town, Mother (*Akaka* lit. 'respected sibling'—here, his niece), things are not going well here (in the village).
> L: For sure!

---

[7] We note here the "crowded stage," typical of a narrative climax, but uncommon in the *Sewero* corpus.

U: The spirits of your aunt who has left us (*anatisiya* – i.e., died), as well as all the other spirits of our ancestors... (They expect a traditional sacrifice of reverent celebration.)

L: Right!

U: Well, we know, aah, we are not able to manage this business on our own (*tachepa nazo* 'we are too small for them' – i.e., to raise enough money to prepare an adequate feast of propitiation).

W: I see.

U: It was necessary for all relatives—(including) my sister (*mlongo* – an honorific term, actually his niece)—(living) in town to come. She must help us with some advice (*nzeru*, but actually some needed funds), so thank-you, thank-you, thank-you! (*zikomo!* – i.e., for coming to be here with us).

L: Yes, thank you very much for coming. You have done us a favor by coming—I was getting very disappointed (*ndimakhumudwa* – i.e., since you had not visited us for some time).

W: 'Uncle' (*Onkel*), Uncle—you do not want to listen! Do you (really) hear me? You, Uncle, you do not listen because last year I came with the body (*maliro* 'funeral') of our Mother (*amayi* – honorific, actually her aunt, his sister). At that time I told you that when I sent her to the hospital, I told my fellow worshipers (*anzanga opemphera* – i.e., to help stay with her during her critical illness) to do this: "If you travel with Mother along a different path (i.e., not the path of recovery)—that one, the one to the village (*chiani-chiani wakumudzi* – i.e., a euphemism for death), well..." I told the friends I worship with and they spoke with Mother (i.e., they witnessed to her), and she confessed her sins—she repented, left them (sins), and allowed Jesus to begin to rule in her life so that, while she remained alive, Mother would be singing hymns about God—only [songs like] those![8]

H: That's for sure (*Kwa basi*)!

W: The Bible was always right next to her, and Mother was reading it.

H: All the time (*Kwambiri*)!

W: My husband (*Apongozi awo*) here is [my] witness (*mboni*).

H: For sure, for sure!

W: She reached the point (i.e., during a visit) where she would begin (with the request), "Pray for me. I want prayers to be near me all the time (*azikhala pafupi-pafupi ndi ine*). Now I see that heaven is really open (*kumwamba ndithu kwatseguka*) and my house [there]!"[9] We would keep telling her, "Please do not frighten the children (*Musaopseze ana* – i.e., with this talk of her death), don't frighten them!" But I knew that Mother would not live long—(and) she died (*ananyamuka* 'she departed' – euphemism). But the Lord loved her and was kind to her and was merciful to her.

---

[8]   PED: Before she begins her argument, the Woman must create a sufficient historical context for her later rebuke of her Uncle for continuing to adhere to traditional religious rites. This takes the form of an indirect, narrative "testimony", namely, that provided by the account of her Mother's conversion before she died.

[9]   PED: The deathbed testimony of a respected elder would carry great impact; close relatives would disregard such crucial instructions at their peril. This is a highly effective and powerful argument strategy. THE: This revelation of course reflects the story of Stephen's death (Acts 7:55-56), with great implicit rhetorical impact.

Now when I came here [to the village] with the body (corpse), accompanied by my friends and singing hymns, you stopped the singing. [You said] "Hey, you must not sing (Christian songs)! Eeh! Just let us sing the ones that we know (*ife tiimba zathu zimene tikuzidziwa* – i.e., traditional religious songs)." But I said, "When a person repents (*walapa*), s/he is a 'Christian' (*Mkhristu*)—s/he has been 'Christianized' (*wakhristuka* – i.e., been converted), s/he has been changed in the heart (*watembenuka mtima*)."[10] So because of the grace (*chisomo*) that was given to me [by God] and due to the perseverance (*khama*) of my friends, we kept on singing hymns of God, and we completed the burial of Mother in peace (i.e., with no more disruptions by the "traditionalists") by the grace of the Lord.

So this very day, right after her child (i.e., the nephew of the deceased, younger Brother of the leading Woman) has arrived from his journey [from town], instead of telling him what has happened concerning how the gospel (*uthenga* 'message') has been preached throughout this village, people are "converted" to (a concern over) the death of Mother.[11] Consequently, you are telling him that Mother's spirit is visiting you (*akumakubwererani inu*). Why should Mother come to visit you, not me, her firstborn child?!

H: That's right! (*Eeti!*)

W: Or [she might have visited] her in-law here (*mpongozi wao uyu*), the one who used to arrange to transport her to the hospital by means of an expensive car![12]

H: I would (often have to) go with her at night.

W: So then, why should her spirit first come to visit you?! Tell me! (*Eeeh!*)

U: Hey you! You will soon die! The madness of the ancestral spirits will bind you (*misala ya mizimu ikumanga*)!

W: 'Uncle', I am not even going to give you a chance to convince me!

U: What sort of foolish words are these?! (*Mau opusa ngati amenewo?!*)

W: You...no, not at all! (*ayii-ayi!*)

L: 'Sister' (*Asisi* – i.e., the Woman) is very contentious—we know how troublesome she can be.

W: Will all of you please quiet down (*Inu takhalani chete*)! I suffered with you last year (i.e., when Mother died)—[my] maize meal was completely consumed, aah! (*chimanga chinatheratu* – i.e., she spent much of her personal resources to help fund the funeral arrangements in the village.)[13] The gentleman here (*abambo awa* – i.e., her brother—honorific reference), a good-hearted person (*munthu wokoma mtima*), helped us too, by bringing three bags of maize for you

---

10   THE: The Woman here defines what Christian "conversion" consists in.

11   APO: The debate over the continuing influence of traditional religion in the village begins here. There is a bitter irony in the Woman's words: Instead of being converted by the gospel message, these people have been "converted" to a conventional mind-set with regard to the ongoing malevolent influence of the dead upon the living.

12   PED: The Woman teaches her rural relatives that even according to their traditional beliefs, there was something wrong with their reasoning: The Mother's spirit, if it had really wanted a commemorative celebration to be held, would have revealed this requirement to its closest (in-life) relative (meaning herself), or to a person who had helped her during her final helpless period of life (namely, the Woman and her Husband).

13   PED: Again, the Woman utilizes an historical context to lay the groundwork for her later argument. Her point is that she, her husband, and her brother contributed by far the most to her mother's funeral; without their help it could not have taken place at all, let alone in an honorable way. Therefore, she had a right to say how it would be conducted—namely, in a Christian, not a traditional religious manner.

246

to eat here in the village—at another time, two bags more. (Remember, you [Uncle] said) "You arrived just in the nick of time! (*Si umu mwafikamo!*) I've spent (*ndagona* 'I have slept') three days without eating anything (*osadya—ndi njala* 'not eating—it is hunger!*)—my children are troubling me [about that]!"[14] You have harvested a good crop (because) I tried my best to buy each one of you (family members) a bag of 'fertilizer' (*kathumba ka feteleza* – lit. 'little bag', a self-depreciating expression)—each one a bag (*kathumba-kathumba*)— so that you would not starve. Yes indeed, I also bought you seed maize (*chimanga cha mbeu*) so you could plant it well (*bwinobwino*) in the hopes of a better harvest the following year (*kuti chaka cham'mawa tione zina* 'so that we might see something different next year').

Now (*Lero* lit. 'Today') we see, for sure God has given you—you have harvested [plenty]. Have you forgotten [this fact] so quickly (*msangamsanga*)?![15] Thus you are saying, "(This person must contribute to the ancestral celebration) so many baskets [of maize]—that person, so many baskets (*uyu madengu akuti*)." (Then you plan to) soak the maize [in water] with spouted millet (*chimera* – i.e., as a fermenting agent) so that in 'two weeks' (*tuu wikisi*) you can drink beer [in honor of the spirits]! You want to wander around in the dirt here (*muzikhala mukumaingitsira m'madothi panopa* – i.e., a pejorative, idiomatic reference to traditional dances in honor of the ancestors)—just destroying this maize![16]

U: Do the spirits and I drink beer together? (*Inetu ndi mizimu timakamwa mowawo?*)

W: It's as if you have become one of the spirits! (*Mizimu mungakhale inuyo!*)[17]

U: You young people (*Anyamata inu* – lit. 'You young men', i.e., the younger generation which does not respect the customs and traditions of the past), I'm telling you—this is bad luck! (*tsoka* – i.e., the ancestors will punish them for their impiety!)

W: Aaah! (disgust), what are you saying! (*Koma inuuu!*)

---

[14] APO: Her Uncle's own words, here cited by quotation for emphasis, strengthen her case against him. Without her assistance, even he and his family would have been in serious trouble. Friends and relatives coming to attend the funeral were eating them out of house and home since apparently they were also living under famine conditions at the time. Therefore, Uncle owed her!—at the very least, to allow her to arrange the funeral rites as she wished, that is, in a Christian manner.

[15] THE: The Woman here combines her pedagogical and apologetic arguments with a theological one: God—the God whom she worships, of the Bible—is the One who saved them, so now how can they think about abandoning him for a traditional perspective and practice? Their behavior smacks of pure ingratitude! In this respect too the hermeneutical factor (HER) comes into play: The Woman is interpreting the historical facts of their recent life-threatening experience in this light of the biblical teaching of the gracious providence of God for his people—with the implication that they in turn ought to be faithful to him in their lives and worship.

[16] APO/PED: The Woman here introduces an economic dimension to her developing argument: The money/maize meal that the people are wasting in order to celebrate the spirits could have been used to support their families in some way. What a waste of limited resources!

[17] APO: The Uncle and his niece trade arguments: He wants her to believe that the villagers are simply engaging in a harmless ceremony of remembrance; she, on the other hand, claims that by participating in such traditional rites, people become one with those whom they are in effect worshiping. Her argument at this point is reminiscent of Paul's in 1 Cor. 10:18-22, but it is doubtful that many in the radio audience would have detected this allusion.

U: If you refuse [to give me] these things (i.e., money/goods for the sacrifice and feast), then don't even think about giving them to me in future—how can you refuse what I'm telling you (i.e., as your elder close relative)?!

W: You will have misfortune (*tsoka*), I'm telling you Uncle, if you fail to listen! If you fail to repent, you will die for sure (*mufatu!*), 'I'm telling you!' (spoken in English for emphasis)![18]

U: Just tell me you people: What can I do to the spirits (*mizimoyo ndiyichita chiani* – i.e., either to overpower or defend myself against them)?!

H: Noooo! Spirits from where (*mizimu yakuti*)?! The Word of God tells us that when a person dies, he's dead, that's it (*kuti munthu akafa, wafa, zatha*)!! There's no coming back to interact [with us] again (*palibe kubwereranso kugwirizananso, ayi*). You can't just come and go like that![19]

W: 'Luke' 16:26 does tell us that there's a chasm (*pompho*) there—a chasm right at that place! Where the spirits [dwell] there is another chasm.[20]

H: Mother (*Amayi* – i.e., his wife), what they do... (a broken utterance) The devil (*Mdierekezi* 'Slanderer')—his work involves those things (i.e., contra-biblical beliefs). So if you have ideas like that (i.e., concerning the influence of the ancestors), you'd better just get rid of them (*muwakhazike pansi* lit. 'set them down') because 'Satan' clings to (*amakakamira*) such things—to twist up (*kumakukupotozani*) your thoughts so that you think they're real (i.e., the truth).[21]

U: Noo!

H: So now about that idea of preparing a *sadaka* (remembrance) feast for the spirits, why don't you just save that maize that God has given you—do not let it be used for beer![22]

U: No, that would be a real insult (*chipongwe chimenecho*)!

W: 'Galatians six verse 21' says (i.e., she mispronounces the text, which should in fact be 5:21)...

U: That's an insult!

W: ...It says that anyone who gets drunk (*woledzera*) and all your beer-drinking buddies (*antchezo amene muchezera nawo pamowa*), you will not enter into heaven—Galatians![23]

U: You think that you have come to refute me (*mudzapala pakamwa* lit. 'you will come and scrape my mouth')?? The spirits have come this morning—they have come this morning, I met with them (*ndakomana nayo*).

L: Aah, it's true, and they're troubling us, they're causing us to suffer!!

---

[18] THE: The wages of sin (impenitence in this context) is death. The Woman's apologetic argument (APO) now becomes deadly personal.

[19] PED/APO: The Husband now enters the debate and instructs his in-laws about the nature of death (and the afterlife). Furthermore, he implies that the ancestors really have no power over the living nor do they have the capacity to return to the world that they have left. That is both a sobering as well as a comforting ontological fact.

[20] THE/HER: The "pit" of separation/demarcation referred to in the Lazarus parable is here applied to the Bantu "Sheol" of the spirits; it is a powerful piece of local contextualization.

[21] THE/APO/PED: The Husband presses his argument now to forge a connection between traditional religious beliefs and Satanic deception. The main problem is that it goes unrecognized for what it is.

[22] PED: Again the economic argument is appealed to: Save your food to feed your families, not to get drunk on in the misguided notion that you are thereby honoring the ancestors and protecting yourselves from their anger.

[23] APO: Spirit worship is evil on its own, but worse, it leads people into the sin of drunkenness.

248

W: And I am telling you that... those spirits at the time of [your] famine (i.e., last year), where were they? They did not come![24]

U: You were not farming with us, so...(i.e., how could you know what really happened or not?)

W: Now your "Father" (*Atati* – i.e., nephew in-law, her husband) here you keep on denying (what he's telling you)!

U: Aaagh! (frustration over her resistance)

W: Those ideas of yours come to you at night (i.e., in your dreams). Those spirits, if there are spirits...(i.e., a broken utterance) After Mother repented and died, should her spirit not have come to request beer from me (i.e., as her closest living relative when she passed away)??[25]

U: [They] do not want beer—what is that, what are you saying?? (i.e., his niece's arguments are frustrating him as he begins to suspect that she may have a point.)

W: The insult that you are giving me [concerning] the spirit of my Mother![26]

U: What do you mean (*Ukuti chiani*)?!

W: It (i.e., her spirit) is at the chest of Abraham at this very moment—that's how you are insulting me (i.e., by claiming that her Mother's spirit is still here on earth)![27]

U: What now?! A "spirit of beer"—what is that?! (i.e., her argument has thoroughly confused him now.)

W: Where is *your* mother—why does *she* not come to you?![28]

U: Noo—noo!

W: Yes!

B: So you are saying that [these beliefs] about the spirits are from Satan??

W: That's right! 'Leviticus (i.e., Deuteronomy) 18, verse 9' up to '14'—'Leviticus 18'...

U: I could go out and hang myself! (*Nditha kudzimangirira!*)

W: Noo, don't say that!!

H: No, do not talk like that, 'Uncle', [that's the way] to hell (*gahena*)! Yes, come back from there (i.e., such thinking)!

L: Yes—reject (*asiyeni* lit. 'leave them!') these [ideas], they come from 'town' (*ndi akutauni* – i.e., modern, tradition-breaking concepts)! Leave them (*asiyeni*) [these people] be! (i.e., do not listen to them).

W: Hell—but you [Uncle] are from hell (*ndi wakugahena* – i.e., destined for fire) if you die without repentance (*mukafa wosalapa*)![29]

---

[24] PED/HER: The Woman tries to teach her relatives how to critically "interpret" the facts of life: Did the people ever stop to ask themselves why the spirits only showed up at the time of a good harvest? Certainly, it did not pay for them to appear during a famine! Her reasoning evinces a moderately sarcastic tone.

[25] PED/HER: She continues with another "natural" argument—one based on common experiential sense.

[26] APO: She reverses her Uncle's complaint about insults—*she* is the one who is being insulted in this matter involving her faith as well as her departed Mother.

[27] THE/HER/APO: The Lazarus model is interpreted more or less literally as it is applied to the case at hand; furthermore, her case carries more weight since she has more to lose if it is wrong, that is, if her Mother is not really in heavenly glory, as she believes.

[28] PED/APO: Here the Woman applies another ironic reversal—a turning of the tables—to lead her Uncle to see the illogicality of his position: Instead of her mother, it is his own mother who should be visiting him in his dreams!

H: Leave them, leave them (*asiyeni*)! If he (lit. 'they'—honorific) wants to die, let him leave—let him die! OK, he can go away (*apite*). But we are telling you that between the living and the dead there is no movement (*palibe kuyenderana*)![30]

W: What good (*chilungamo* 'uprightness') would it do (i.e., if people refuse to repent in life, how can they in death)??

H: The business (*nkhani* 'news') of ancestral spirits is not true at all—it's a lie, a doing of the Devil![31]

W: And [your] maize...

H: It [ATR] confuses people's thinking (*kupotoza* 'twist' *maganizo a wanthu*), but it also destroys your property (*katundu wanu* – i.e., when you sacrifice your food and spend money on ritual)!

W: This maize [that you have harvested]—you simply destroy![32]

H: The little maize (*kachimanga* – i.e., a diminuative) that you have troubled yourselves to gather (*munapezako*, lit. 'you found'), now you are simply destroying (i.e., wasting) when you brew beer (for the ancestors)—Nooo! (*Iyaaii!*)

W: And so you return [to the situation where] you just persecute yourselves (*mudzidzazunzikira*) [over the matter of] maize![33]

H: What you need to do here, the first step (*gawo loyamba* lit. 'the first part') now is to take the maize that you have harvested—which you want to use so that you can brew beer—and go give that to 'church' (*chalichi*). Let that be your harvest offering (*masika*) to thank God![34]

W: Eeeh! (affirmation)

H: Go and thank God! (*Kathokozeni Mulungu!*)

W: Yes, [take] one carrying basket full up (*mbu!* – ideophone) and go make an offering [to church]!

H: Don't get involved with these things (*osati zimenezo* – i.e., traditional worship), nooo!

W: But you [want to] offer one basket to Satan—was Satan the one who gave you the rain?[35]

---

[29] HER/APO: In an effective, poetic expression of vernacular rhetoric (note the rhyme, rhythm, repetition, and parallelism), both the Woman and her Husband (in the next speech) echo the preceding Lady's utterance as they urge their Uncle not to 'leave' or 'reject' what they have been telling him. That would mean condemnation ('Gahenna') in the Judgment of God.

[30] THE/HER: The contrast between biblical belief and traditional religion is highlighted here: The ancestral spirits are thought to have regular interaction with their living relatives; on the contrary, says the Husband, after death there is absolutely no contact at all—and no change of state is possible. It is a shocking, but sincere warning and a strong appeal for repentance.

[31] PED/APO: The 'instruction' about traditional religion and 'defense' of the biblical position is now stated as bluntly as it could be; there can be no compromise, no mixing of world-views (syncretism)!

[32] PED: The economic argument is reiterated: Why waste your meager possessions on activities that profit you absolutely nothing?!

[33] APO/PED: The Woman reduces the traditionalist's position to absurdity: The people waste their food on useless offerings, then they must starve because they lack food—is this not a case of self-persecution as well as self-delusion?!

[34] PED/THE: Now the Christian couple begins a positive approach in their practical, didactic apologetic (APO): Instead of the ancestors, God—the God of the Bible—ought to be first in mind. He is the Creator and Preserver of all people; he gives people their crops and so he needs to be appropriately thanked.

[35] PED/APO: Another aspect of the couple's argument against the absurd (*reducio ad absurdam*): Everyone present would shudder in shock over the connotation and implication of this accusation. Surely Satan, also from a traditional religious perspective, could never be regarded as a Rain-Giver; so how could the people even think of offering their harvest to him—or to his agents, the demons (1 Cor. 1:20)?!

H: But Satan is wily (*wochenjera*)—he wants only to destroy. His [*modus oper-andi*] is to steal (*kwache ndi kuba*), to kill, and to destroy! Thus for this reason [we say] that when a person steals, he wants to destroy. He [Satan] wants to destroy you, and I do not want these things to happen to you!!

W: These children (i.e., apparently several of her own in the audience), when they were with me in town (when they were young), they were very good (i.e., prac-ticing Christians). You see now, they have been destroyed (i.e., by traditional beliefs)![36]

L: But now if we stop practicing these things (i.e., traditional customs), will it not happen that the spirits will visit us [with troubles] more frequently?? (*sindiye kuti mizimuyi izibwerabwera?*)

W: No, they will not return!

H: The spirits of whom? Whose spirits are you talking about?

N: [Do you mean that if] we pray [now] (i.e., in a Christian manner), they won't return?

H: Whose spirit would come? Why would they come at all?[37]

W: Say you—you were a very good [Christian] (i.e., speaking to the Elder's Niece, perhaps someone her own age) when we [lived] together. How is it that you have backslidden (*wabwereranji*) to speak about [and fear] the spirits?!

H: What is necessary now, what is really needed, is for a person to become estab-lished upon (*ndikukhazikika pa*) the Word of God—the Word of God that comes through Jesus. Your protection (*chitetezo chanu*) is in Jesus![38]

W: In Jesus—not in the spirits—your protection [is found]!

H: When the spirits come, what do they look like—how do they appear those spir-its? They are just dreams, nothing more! (*maloto basi!*) Aaagh! (disparage-ment)[39]

W: [They are merely] the invention (*maganizo* lit. 'thoughts') of human beings.

H: You may dream of a huge person—that's it, you start fearing your own dream!

N: They grabbed (*inamugwira* – i.e., possessed) this fellow (not identified) and he began jumping all around (*kumangodumpha*) and then went unconscious (*ata-komoka*).

W: Nooo! You've forgotten that even while he was away at school the spirits would come to this fellow (*inamubwerera iyeyu*).[40]

H: Furthermore, my In-law (*alamu*), these are pagan affairs (*izi n'zachikunja* lit. 'these things are on the outside')! We must not be giving our money to perform

---

[36] PED: The Woman here personalizes her argument: Her own children, brought up in town as believ-ers, have become syncretistic in their faith upon their return to live in the village. Her Uncle has "destroyed" them in this respect—a serious accusation indeed because in a traditional matrilineal society, they would be regarded as his children!

[37] PED: The Husband again draws attention to the illogical, contra-intuitive nature of traditional reli-gious beliefs and practices: No personality or purpose can be concretely identified in their alleged activi-ties.

[38] PED/THE: Here another positive solution is proposed: Study God's Word, build a foundation for faith there, and Christ will offer his peace—and protection (as promised in the Word).

[39] PED/APO: Another argument from experience is offered: Spirits are unseen, so how do people really demonstrate their existence—or even distinguish their manifestation from ordinary dreams?

[40] PED/APO: An apparent counter example (namely, someone who witnessed a person who had seem-ingly been possessed by spirits) is itself countered by a little history: The young man involved used such "possession" experiences in order to get out of homework or attendance at his classes.

a remembrance ceremony (*sadaka*). Those are traditional matters (*zachimidzi* lit. 'village-related things')—pagan matters!

B: Aah! (disgust) 'From the darkness' (i.e., English insertion)! Oooh! (disappointment)

H: 'I can't do that!' (English) Christians cannot get in the habit of [supporting what] some people might request. [For example], "Ah (deference), perhaps you could help us with some money—only that if you do not [want to] attend [the ceremony]." No, 'we don't have to participate in those things.' (English) They are pagan affairs![41]

B: So we must not waste our money on the ancestors?

H: Let the spirits do their own farming (*ikalime yokha*)—let them find their own money and beer, let them drink it over there (i.e., wherever they happen to be)?[42]

W: Do not give this money to them (i.e., to the celebration organizers)—buy them some [needed] clothing instead!

B: Oooh! (recognition), 'okay'.

W: Because they will use it for their spirits if you give them any money!

H: 'Don't leave them any money!' (English)

B: 'Alright, I will buy them some food—food or clothes.' (English)

H: 'Yes, food, but not cash' (English)—they would only use it to buy beer![43]

7.2 A critical evaluation of *Sewero* productions

In this section, I offer an informal note of positively motivated criticism in the form of a personal as well as a group response to the *Sewero* program. This is based on my own experience of these dramatic productions over the years and also on a little questionnaire that I prepared for the purpose of gaining a more concrete external response to this exceptional (non-usual) form of Christian didactic communication.

7.2.1 Audience opinions

One crucial requirement applies with respect to any mass-medium presentation, whether religious or secular, and that is the need for a sufficient amount of systematic, contextualized target audience testing (see Sundersingh 2001:ch.13; Sogaard 1993:ch.7; 2001:chs.10-12, 34, for suggestions). This

---

[41] PED: The Husband cites a little "case study" to illustrate how to go about refusing requests for money and goods destined for use in traditional religious ceremonies.

[42] APO/HER: The irony here is obvious—but it is more than that. There is an implicit counter-hermeneutic engaged within the framework of the traditional belief system. If the ancestors do exist, right here with us on earth, then why do they not support and entertain themselves, without burdening their living relatives?!

[43] PED/APO: The play ("Have you forgotten?") concludes on a practical note—a repetition of the appeal for listeners to manage their limited resources well, that is, not spending them on unhelpful, unhealthful activities (e.g., the excessive beer drinking associated with such remembrance ceremonies). One prominent underlying motive that encourages such practices is also repudiated, namely, as an excuse to engage in such an alcoholic binge.

must be research that is geared specifically to evaluate the *Sewero* show, not merely radio broadcasts in general, or even the Chinyanja corpus of programs that is currently being broadcast via TR. What do particular listener group segments (e.g., youth, middle-aged men/women, the elderly, non-/church goers, Protestants, Catholics, Pentecostals, etc.) think of this production in its various aspects (e.g., opinions concerning the style, message, format, potential applications, etc.). What reasons do people give for their diverse comments and criticisms? What suggestions for possible modification can either individuals or groups put forward to the producers? These might apply, for example, to certain theological and moral issues discussed or positions taken in the plays, or to the team's dramatic techniques perhaps, that might raise questions of an exegetical, theological, ecclesiastical, and/or practical nature. Any such program, whether more artistic or more didactic in nature, is only as good, or effective/relevant, as the degree to which it achieves its basic communicative objectives.

In this section I summarize the results of the audience questionnaire noted above (a copy of which is found in Appendix C). The questions were asked with regard to the play whose conclusion was presented (in translation) above, namely, *Kodi mwaiwala?* ("Have you forgotten?"— 7.1.5). This condensed response will hopefully give at least a tentative idea of the indispensable *emic* (insider's) critical perspective on these plays, as distinct from, but not necessarily different from my own *etic* (outsider's) opinion, which is expressed in the next section. This modest sampling project, though very inadequate (due to the small number of respondents and relatively informal method of carrying it out),[44] at least provides one possible model to consider when planning further, more intensive and extensive research programs of this nature. It is obvious too that these feedback procedures need to be adapted for non-literates, especially hearers in the case of radio, e.g., through the use of a cassette recorder. Another option, given the local technology and finance, would be a time for phone-in responses in urban areas, perhaps conducted immediately after a *Sewero* drama has been broadcast (Sogaard 2001:4/2).

The student respondents all enjoyed the play "Have you forgotten" (including its opening and closing topically-related songs), especially the mother-tongue speakers, which is not surprising (e.g., "the Chichewa was very beautiful!"). They gave various reasons for their enthusiastic assess-

---

[44] My time allocated for this project expired before I could carry out my intended wider audience survey. Therefore, I was only able to get an individualized written response from the 12 members of my seminary African Traditional Religion (ATR) class. The opinions of this section therefore represent a rather small and incomplete sample of audience opinion. All of these students know Chinyanja but only 6 are mother tongue speakers, so this fact too may have also skewed the results to a certain degree.

ment: "radio is a good way to teach about the Bible because in our culture we are good at listening"; "hearing this story was better than reading it in a book"; "the play is full of African tradition, which is part of our life and very interesting for us"; "it gives good advice to Christians, like not wasting their time and money on useless customs of the past" and helping us "to defend Bible teachings from those of ATR, such as the continual need to brew beer for the ancestors"; "it shows us how to use Bible passages step by step to support the plot of a [narrative] play"; "[the play] expressed my emotion as an African because this is what happens in day to day life in our villages."[45] Even the use of interspersed English phrases by one of the characters (the uncle who lived in town) was appreciated because "this sounds very natural to me," that is, with respect to how people actually speak Chinyanja in such mixed-language, town and country situations.

Several criticisms were duly noted as well: "the speeches were spoken too fast to follow at times"; "some words were difficult for me to understand"; "the recording was not always clear enough to hear properly"; and "the story was not long enough" (presumably, to make its didactic point). On the other hand, the student responses also indicated several points where the questionnaire itself needs clarification and improvement. For example, instead of giving a compositional critique to explain what the respondent "did not like" about the play, several replied in terms of their reaction to non-Christian characters in the play whose behavior they did not like. Several persons identified the village "uncle" as an instance of this (a double "villain") because he not only promoted non-Scriptural religious practices within the community but whose speech also revealed the result of inebriation, a harbinger of a worse cognitive state to come. Along these same lines, one student noted that the practice of drunkenness was not dealt with sufficiently during the play's final argument section. This was not the main issue, of course, but he felt that the subject should have been considered at greater length since it is such a big socio-religious problem. Finally, one perceptive commentator noted that the uncle's behavior in wanting to "brew beer for the spirits" would be somewhat more motivated, narratively speaking, if he had been allegedly "troubled by the spirits" (through some earlier

---

[45] Several other key topics that were suggested for future *Sewero* production include: traditional spousal "cleansing" rituals at the time of a funeral; the practice of polygamy, both official and covert; proper versus improper marriage customs; the tying of protective charms on infants and small children; proper stewardship practices, such as field offerings, to support church work instead of the dead ancestors; the prominent influence of "medicine (wo)men" in supporting the belief and practice of ancient ancestral religion; drug abuse, both traditional (i.e., "Indian hemp") and Western; problems relating to family planning.

misfortune, a dream, divination, etc.), hence provoking such an active propitiatory response on his part.

While most respondents appreciated the use of the several Scripture passages that the play made reference to, several pointed out the fact that two of the passages were wrongly cited, that is, Galatians 5:21 (referred to as 6:21) against drunkenness and Deuteronomy (given as Leviticus) 18:9-14 against occult practices. Seminary students, of course, should be able to pick out and correct such errors; however, this is a more serious problem for ordinary listeners. One student felt that the Christians were a little "too argumentative" when presenting their case in public. Another pointed out a difficulty that arose due to the unusually large cast of (vocal) characters in this particular play: it was hard in a few places to distinguish who actually was speaking. He went on to make a good suggestion for improvement in this respect: Have a "narrator," or each of the characters using their own "voice," clearly identify which person and role they play at the very beginning of the drama. Finally, one student proposed that a narrator's part at the close of the story would also be helpful, namely, to highlight the importance and relevance of the play's principal topic—the practice of ancestral veneration.

All of the students said that they would be willing to pay a basic cost fee of 10,000 *kwacha* (approximately $2.00) to purchase a cassette tape recording of the *Kodi mwaiwala?* drama. It is one thing to praise such a performance—but would one be prepared to pay for it as well in order to share the message with others? One student specifically mentioned that he wanted a copy to go and immediately play for his wife back at home. Another suggested that such tapes would be most helpful to have available in a congregational cassette library so that they could be used as models and resource material to stimulate Bible study group discussions or at an annual "camp meeting" retreat: "Through them we can learn about the familiar cultural mistakes that we make each and every day"—"in too many situations of life the old ancestral customs crowd out our Christianity!"

7.2.2 Personal suggestions

In this section I will call attention to several salient implications of my study as they concern the *Sewero* program in particular and the possibilities of Christian radio drama in general as a tool for promoting a greater understanding of the Scriptures and a fuller application of their relevance to contemporary life in east-central Africa. These thoughts do not set forth a comprehensive, all-inclusive vision of the potential of this radio resource, but are offered merely as my own personal reflections to encourage a greater effort to develop this artistic, expressive, and educational endeavor in the field of religion. Most of these recommended developments, it should be noted, have significant financial implications in terms of the funds necessary to implement them.

7.2.2.1 Regarding the "hardware" of production

"Hardware" refers to various aspects of the technological means of message transmission, in this case, radio broadcasting. One of the greatest limiting factors in the case of shortwave is the relatively poor quality of the audio signal that many in the wider Chinyanja-speaking "catchment" area are forced to listen to. This technical or physical deficiency acts as a serious barrier to stimulating and maintaining the impression of vocal immediacy, naturalness, personality, and presence which stands as the greatest advantage of the radio medium of communication. One obvious solution then would be to increase the power of the SW transmitter that beams the program (and others) to the central African region, including especially the countries surrounding Malawi, i.e., Zambia and Mozambique, where large numbers of Chinyanja speakers reside. More feasible perhaps would be to expand the number of FM stations that broadcast the *Sewero* program, as has been done in Malawi. Even a primarily English-medium station like the popular *Radio Christian Voice* in Lusaka, Zambia, for example, might be willing—even pleased—to air such a dramatic show in the vernacular, one that happens also to be a lingua franca for many local listeners.

Another type of hardware problem that could be improved is the provision of better studio and recording equipment. As was noted in section 2.5, the *Sewero* team must work under professional conditions which, while certainly adequate, are nevertheless not completely satisfactory with respect to the studio facilities that are available to them, that is, considering the size of the group as well as the close and complex nature of their dramatic interaction during any given performance session. The matter of equipment applies also to recording machines, microphones, and other supporting gear needed to gather appropriate background noises, special audio effects, musical interludes, and Christian hymns or contemporary songs that play such an important auxiliary part in any program as an integrated whole.

7.2.2.2 Regarding the "software" of performance

The term "software" refers to the dynamic and diverse human dimension of a *Sewero* production. In my opinion, not much can be done to enhance the actual "dramatic" compositional and performance aspect of these plays. But with regard to the "Christian" (ideological) component, perhaps some additional theological and biblical training for the producers as well as the players would be helpful both as a motivation and a stimulus to probe pertinent Scriptural truths to greater depth. This might best be done by means of annual (or semi-annual) study workshops, which could be offered for 1-2 weeks at a time in a concentrated format, but located right in the Lilongwe area (to make it possible for all players to attend without much difficulty).

The purpose of such an educational, personal-growth program would be to provide more Scriptural depth, balance, and diversity in the weekly presentation, just to keep the dramas fresh, relevant, and covering the "whole counsel of God" as set forth in his Word, including a larger number of key theological topics. In addition, one might seek to develop a somewhat more "substantial" and challenging (though not necessarily a longer) exposition of the Bible passages that are utilized in the closing section of "resolution"—as long as this does not defuse or "spoil" the players' enthusiasm and spontaneity! Instead of single isolated passages, a longer Scripture text could be explored in relation to the main problem or topic at hand. If the dramatic situation presents itself, a greater measure of background knowledge concerning the Ancient Near Eastern sociocultural setting might also be incorporated into the dialogue in a natural, unobtrusive way, e.g., as part of a Bible study session that includes several of the characters. Such didactic insertions would enable listeners to better understand and appreciate theological and moral issues that pertain to the main theme of a particular play as well as the application of particular passages in the "moral" portion at a play's concluding "resolution".

A related pedagogical aim would involve making more effective use of the program *announcer*. Some speakers in the past have not done very much in this role, serving basically only to open and close the program in general, but providing little or no specific comment or evaluation concerning the day's play. To take this function a step further, it would perhaps be helpful at times to allow this "official" voice more time at the end of a play to review the main theological and moral points that have just been dramatized and to elaborate a bit more with regard to their implications for the contemporary church in Malawi (Africa). One does not have to overdo it in this respect, but just to ensure that the didactic element of the program receives due attention at the very end of the broadcast. On the other hand, the occasional use of a play-internal, third-person, "objective" *narrator* might be considered. In addition to introducing some variation in the dramatic format, this device would allow for stories with more complex characterizations and plots to be presented since everything would not have to be conveyed by means of interpersonal dialogue or private soliloquies. This would also provide a natural means of introducing relevant biblical background information into a given play.

It might be possible also to set aside some program time—most likely after the close of the day's *Sewero* play—for the producer/presenter to interact in a meaningful way with listener letter *feedback*, e.g., their suggestions, criticisms, and especially questions on some of the key issues that have been dramatized either during the just completed play or on previous occasions. This sort of an "interactive" conclusion (or introduction) would serve to give more of a substantial "voice" to the audience, which is such a vital aspect of traditional oral narrative performances and most radio broadcasts as well. Such audience interaction could also be extended by researchers who would go out to record the comments and criticisms of regular listeners who are not literate. This sort of "field feedback" could also be used as a basis or forum for discussion, either as a short part of the *Sewero* time itself, or better perhaps, reserved for presentation as a separate program in conjunction with the drama itself. Listeners might be asked to respond, for example, to the resolution of a particular play: did they agree with how it was handled; could they suggest another way, or different passages that would apply to the situation, and so forth.

In closing this section, I might call attention to another, a personal sort of "human" need, namely, on behalf of the *Sewero* players themselves. They would be greatly encouraged in their unique ministry if it were possible to grant them a more substantial financial "honorarium". This would allow the members more time and freedom to devote to various areas of personal growth, e.g., biblical studies, as well as preparing for their most demanding form of artistic evangelism work.

7.3 Prognosis: What is the future of Christian vernacular radio drama?

> Ultimately the challenge [for radio] is not the technology but the programming. To attract listeners, hold their interest and draw them into a relationship with Jesus Christ—either directly or indirectly—it needs to be contemporary, contextual and engage their interest. If these conditions are applied to our Christian broadcasts we will continue to see people's lives impacted for the Gospel through faith in Christ [by the power of the Holy Spirit] (Gray & Murphy, "The Unlikely Missionary", p.22; material in brackets added).

How may the preceding quotation be applied specifically to the *Sewero* radio drama program? Do the designated criteria still apply to a production that is over a decade old? In my personal experience, the *Sewero* plays continue to attract listeners, hold their interest, speak directly to their everyday relationship with Christ, and remain contemporary as well as contextual in nature.[46] But I may be biased in my judgment; therefore, a thorough evaluation through listener field surveys needs to be made. Proposed changes in content, format, and purpose need to come from the target audience of regular listeners themselves.

The ever-changing needs of the Christian (and non-Christian) community, coupled with the rapid advances in communication technology that are an everyday part of our age, would suggest that only the near future can be reasonably envisaged for solid planning purposes. But careful research must investigate the key variables with regard to possible new resources, trends, barriers, and challenges posed by important advances that are occurring in the world's information storage capacity and transmission structures. But it is indeed necessary to broach such issues and to engage in this sort of creative speculation and strategic planning if Christian communicators hope to remain current. They must always stay in tune with their social setting and potential audience if they wish to keep in step with cultural, technological, and religious developments that are likely to affect their program production at any time within the next year or the coming decade (e.g., the rise of militant Islam in Africa, perhaps also via the airwaves as well).

7.3.1 Radio drama in general

So what is the likely future of radio broadcasting in our modern, technological age, where, despite all the advances in communication, certain societies and cultures seem to be becoming increasingly estranged in relation to others (e.g., the "haves" versus the "have nots")? How viable/practical will this venerable mass medium continue to be? In short, it would seem that radio has a definite potential for at least the next decade or so. It remains a vital mode of mass communication in Africa and even for special, niche purposes in the Western world (an opinion supported by a recent *Newsweek* article as well as a nationwide survey on radio use in South Africa).[47] There seems to be a definite shift in popularity from SW to FM radio, which the planners of TWR seem to have taken note of. Internet as well as satellite transmission will greatly increase the potential audience, at least for those who are eco-

---

[46] At least this was true until April 2003 when the *Sewero* program had to be suspended (hopefully only temporarily) due to financial constraints currently being experienced by its sponsors, the TransWorld Radio Christian communications network.

[47] See "A Little Space Music," in *Newsweek* November 12, 2001, pp. 67-68. As UBS Media Consultant Viggo Sogaard observes: "Radio is a very good medium for Bible communication in a world where so many people are not reading, and, as we are formatting these programmes specifically for the medium, we will get a very large audience" (*UBS World Report* 365, December 2000, p. 9).

nomically advantaged. Radio drama as a distinct genre of artistic expression appears to have a bright future: It is very popular in Africa, relatively easy to produce and inexpensive, as well as being a highly effective, "personal" (vocal) means of confronting audiences with issues that may be difficult to discuss by other public means—notably the dark mysteries of the occult!

7.3.2 The Sewero program in particular

How long can the *Sewero* program continue in its present form (assuming that it will be resumed in the near future); has any timetable been established to determine when it will come to an end? This is a management decision, of course, but it is one that needs to be made on the basis of adequate audience research and the current level of concrete support (e.g., in the form of sponsorship of one or more shows).[48] There would certainly seem to be an ongoing need for this type of a dynamic, dramatic format to present practical Christian theology, apologetics, and education to a wide rural constituency, many of whom may not have a ready or easy access to such information, either now or in the near future. Perhaps new players can gradually be brought in to take over from experienced colleagues—after learning by personal experience and apprenticeship from the veteran resident experts, and also by carefully studying (critiquing) recorded copies of previous broadcasts to study how they have been "played." Some possible future topics for dramatization on the *Sewero* program include the following: "retold" popular Bible stories (paraphrased, perhaps with additional dialogue, and expanded), transculturized Gospel parables, "Christianized" folktales, both ancient and modern, culturally adapted Christian "classics," e.g., *The Screwtape Letters* and others books by C.S. Lewis.

7.3.3 Adaptations to different media and modes of presentation

The following is an unordered summary listing of some other potential avenues of communication that it may prove beneficial to pursue in response to the *Sewero* stimulus and model that has been so successful already in its established rural (plus lower income urban) audience niche.

TWR might consider the production of another dramatic series of plays in imitation of the *Sewero* program, but this one in English, as spoken in the

---

[48]   In view of the recent suspension of the *Sewero* program due to financial constraints, it has become evident that outside sponsorship is necessary in order to support the production of such non-affiliated programs, ones that in effect serve the entire Christian community. Since the *Sewero* troupe is not in a position to promote their own ministry, it behooves some established communication organization to undertake such a PR and funding operation on their behalf. It is hoped that the present monograph might also serve as a positive motivation toward this end.

localized national "Malawian dialect." This program would be aimed at a more sophisticated urban audience, one whose sociocultural, economic, and religious situation is significantly, though not entirely, different from that of the current broadcast.

As noted in section 1.5, there could easily be a development or extension of the *Sewero* plays into a *cassette* ministry which would enable the frequent "rebroadcast" of the most requested plays, plus those dealing with key topics that need to be heard again (e.g., on AIDS, care for orphans, "street kids," and other "vulnerable people"). This would make a variety of themes and crucial issues available to a different audience and perhaps also for a different purpose, such as a follow-up discussion on the current relevance of a given drama. A production of this nature could be accompanied by the provision of written (or oral/cassette) *study guides*, composed on various levels for different readership groups, to help review and apply a particular tape/lesson/issue. The use of audio cassettes can compensate for some of the major deficiencies of the radio mass-medium (see Sundersingh 2001:69-74, 113-115; Sogaard 2001:ch.5; 1993:ch.9). When used in a structured (regular meeting time and place) group format with a discussion leader or facilitator, the *Sewero* program might serve as a very productive stimulus for both Bible study and contextualized Christian application (Sundersingh ibid.:114). I need not say more about this vision of encouraging local interactive Bible study groups, which has been well articulated for some time by others in this region of Africa (e.g. West 1993, 1999).

The publication of a book of *Sewero* plays (transcribed, edited, and stylistically adapted for the medium of print), either with or without accompanying English translations, but including introductions and possibly also extensive expository annotation, might be another viable experiment. Associated workshops could then be organized that would use the *Sewero* program as the focus of attention for evaluation by interested groups of Christian pastors and educators who wish to add a dynamic new mode of communication to their ministries, especially to the younger generation. The aim would be to demonstrate how a given play might be utilized so as to serve as stimulation for group discussion, interaction, planning, and resource development.

The *Sewero* program might be used also as a concrete *model* to follow, whether as is or in some adapted form, using the medium of one of the other major Bantu languages in the region. If the broadcast is popular in Chinyanja, why not also in Chibemba, Chitonga, Silozi, or Chishona too? The *Sewero* production team might even serve as informal instructors or advisers for other drama groups, which could be brought in to observe their techniques and to interview them for further advice.

More radio productions patterned after traditional oral-aural genres and vernacular verbal styles need to be developed, including, for example, such widespread artistic forms as folktales, myths, legends, histories, ritual pageants, proverbs, riddles, prayers, and poetry, sung or recited, of all sorts. Local African languages would be the medium of choice for, as was stressed throughout our survey of *Sewero* plays, this is what gives these performances their dynamic life and vitality. Virtually all of the vibrant idiomacity of the dialogues would be washed out if they were composed in English—along with much of the meaning and impact which happen to be culturally conditioned to the linguistic mode of communication. Employing local languages would also promote a greater use of indigenous stylistic techniques and conceptual categories (including cultural symbols and key terms that trigger important social norms and values), which when introduced in a foreign language, often sound awkward and ill-fitting. More important than the issue of literary form, however, is that of conceptual content, and here too there is little doubt that the use of African languages will encourage a certain frankness and freedom of expression that would facilitate the development of indigenous modes and methods of theological expression as well as a certain perspective on the biblical text that could stimulate new insights and creative applications.

Various types of popular musical (song) rendition have already pointed out some of the prospects and procedures here in terms of local composition, production, and publication (marketing, distribution, etc). The aim is not to slavishly (or even partially) imitate the standard mass-media program "brands" of the West, which are already being broadcast on a large scale in Africa, but to work harder to tap more indigenous styles and models of message transmission. The audio channel of communication is already a very highly developed sensory resource in all local societies, so why can this not be capitalized on to a much greater degree in the strategy planning sessions of churches, organizations, and agencies that are commissioned with this task?

Finally, as was also proposed earlier, more interaction on the national and inter-national level should be sponsored so that the available resources in a particular area might be stored in some sort of electronic, internet-accessible database and then shared by others who are engaged in a similar communicative activity. Due to the financial cost of such a venture, however, it would most likely have to be undertaken by some established institution or agency, for example, by the theological department of some

African university or a Christian radio station. The field of vernacular Christian rhetoric, pedagogy, apologetics, etc in relation to creative art on the one hand and biblical theology on the other needs to be much more thoroughly and aggressively investigated, promoted, and popularized by every means and medium possible. Only then will this dimension of the dynamic African church begin to get adequately recognized as well as utilized for the common good of the continent as a whole.

These are merely my personal suggestions of course; the most likely candidates among them would need to be fleshed out and tested with regard to both their validity and applicability. The preceding ideas may also be augmented in several different directions. Today's Christian communicators are limited only by the bounds of their imagination, vision, and determination to widely "broadcast" the Word of God—both Law and Gospel—as creatively and consummately as the Chinyanja *Sewero* drama troupe have demonstrated now for a period of so many years together.

> Let's sit together here—I've brought you some good things [to listen to].
> Don't leave me all by myself now—lest I become lonely!

(From the opening announcement of the *Mwini-chuma* play.)

These words were originally directed of course towards the *Sewero* radio audience. But the overt appeal applies also to studies like the one presented in this monograph. What difference will/can it make? Certainly not very much if the writer is left alone with his results—all his accumulated data, examples, interpretations, assessments, etc.—interesting and entertaining though these may be in certain respects. Just as "one head does not raise the roof (of a traditional hut)" (*mutu umodzi susenza denga*), so also substantial and lasting encouragement and support for various (semi-)traditional modes and media of conveying the drama of Christianity in the African vernacular will not come from one study on its own, or even several of them, operating in isolation from each other. Rather, all these "heads" put be put together somehow by some coordinating agency (or agencies) for the common good with respect to communicating the Word of God that they all hold in common as the ultimate source and norm for their faith and life.

BIBLIOGRAPHY

(The following texts are especially helpful resources with regard to the various subjects touched upon in this monograph; it includes all references that are cited in the body of this book.)

Bradt, Kevin M. 1997. *Story as a way of knowing.* Kansas City, MO: Sheed & Ward.

Calloud, Jean. 1976. *Structural analysis of narrative.* Philadelphia, PA: Fortress Press.

Chakanza, J.C. 2000. *Wisdom of the people: 2000 Chinyanja proverbs* (Kachere Book No. 13). Blantyre, Malawi: CLAIM.

Chimombo, Steve. 1988. *Malawian Oral Literature.* Zomba: Centre for Social Research (Malawi Institute of Education).

Douglas, Mary. 1966. *Purity and danger: An analysis of the concepts of pollution and taboo.* Boston: Ark.

Draper, J. 2002. "Reading the Bible as conversation: A theory and methodology for contextual interpretation of the Bible in Africa." *Grace and Truth* 19/2, 12-24.

Fernando, Keith. 1999. *The triumph of Christ in African perspective: A study of demonology and redemption in the African context.* Carlisle, UK: Paternoster Press.

Fiedler, Klaus, Paul Gundani, and Hilary Mijoga (eds). 1998. *Theology cooked in an African pot.* Special volume of the *ATISCA Bulletin* 5/6 (Association of Theological Institutions in Southern and Central Africa).

Finnegan, Ruth. 1992. *Oral poetry: Its nature, significance and social context.* Bloomington: Indiana University Press.

Gutt, Ernst-August. 1992. *Relevance theory: A guide to successful communication in translation.* Dallas: SIL.

Gwengwe, John W. 1970. *Kukula ndi mwambo* [Growing up with tradition]. Limbe: Malawi Publications and Literature Bureau.

Healey, Joseph and Donald Sybertz. 1996. *Towards an African narrative theology.* Nairobi: Paulines Publications Africa.

Hesselgrave, David J. 1991. *Communicating Christ cross-culturally: An introduction to missionary communication* (2nd ed). Grand Rapids, MI: Zondervan.

Hiebert, Paul G. 1982. "The flaw of the excluded middle." *Missiology* 10:1, 35-47.

Hirsch, E. D.1967. *Validity in interpretation*. New Haven and London: Yale University Press.

Kalilombe, Patrick A. 1980. "An outline of Chewa traditional religion." *Africa Theological Journal* 9:2, 39-51.

_____. 1999. *Doing theology at the grassroots: Theological essays from Malawi* (Kachere Book No.7). Blantyre, Malawi: CLAIM.

Klem, Herbert V. 1982. *Oral communication of the Scriptures: Insights from African oral art.* Pasadena, CA: Wm. Carey Library.

Kombo, Kisilu. 2003. "Witchcraft: A living vice in Africa." *Africa Journal of Evangelical Theology* 22:1, 73-85.

Kumakanga, Stevenson L. 1975. *Nzeru Zakale* (Ancient Wisdom). Blantyre: Dzuka Publishing.

* Malina, B. J. & Rohrbaugh, R. L. 1992. Social-science commentary on the synoptic gospels.

* Minneapolis: Fortress.

Marwick, Max. 1965. *Sorcery in its social setting: A study of the Northern Rhodesian Cewa.* Manchester: Manchester University Press.

McLuhan, Marshall. 1987 (1964). *Understanding media: The extensions of man.* London: Ark.

Mitchell, Jolyon P. 1999. *Visually Speaking: Radio and the Renaissance of Preaching.* Louisville, KY: Westminster/John Knox Press.

Mojola, Aloo O. 1990. "The traditional religious universe of the Luo of Kenya: A preliminary study." In Stine and Wendland (eds), q.v., 154-174.

Mytton, Graham. 1978. "Language and the media in Zambia." In Ohannesian & Kashoki (eds.), q.v., 207-227.

Ngulube, Naboth. 1989. *Some aspects of growing up in Zambia*. Lusaka: Nalinga Consultancy/Sol-Consult A/S Limited.

Nyirongo, Lenard. 1997. *The gods of Africa or the God of the Bible: The snares of African traditional religion in biblical perspective* (Brochures of the Institute for Reformational Studies, No. 70). Potschefstroom: Potschefstroom University for Christian Higher Education.

_____. 1999. *Dealing with darkness: A Christian novel on the confrontation with African witchcraft* (Brochures of the Institute for Reformational Studies, No. 72). Potschefstroom: Potschefstroom University for Christian Higher Education.

Ohannesian, Sirarpi and Kashoki, Mubanga (eds). 1978. *Language in Zambia*. London: International African Institute.

Okpewho, Isidore. 1992. *African oral literature: Backgrounds, character, and continuity.* Bloomington: Indiana University Press.

Ong, Walter. 1967. *The presence of the word.* New Haven and London: Yale University Press.

_____. 1982. *Orality and literacy: The technologizing of the word.* London & New York: Methuen.

Patte, Daniel. 1976. *What is structural exegesis?* Philadelphia, PA: Fortress Press.

Ryken, Leland. 2002. *The Word of God in English: Criteria for excellence in Bible translation.* Wheaton, IL: Crossway Books.

Schoffeleers, Matthew. 1997. *Religion and the dramatization of life: Spirit beliefs and rituals in southern and central Malawi* (Kachere Monograph No.5). Blantyre, Malawi: CLAIM.

Smith, Donald K. 1992. *Creating understanding: A handbook for Christian communication across cultural landscapes.* Grand Rapids, MI: Zondervan.

Søgaard, Viggo B. 1991. *Audio Scriptures handbook*. Reading, ENG: United Bible Societies.

_____. 1993. Media in church and mission: Communicating the gospel. Pasadena, CA: Wm. Carey Library.

_____ (ed). 2001. *Communicating Scriptures: The Bible in audio and video formats*. Reading, ENG: United Bible Societies.

Sundersingh, Julian. 2001. *Audio-based translation: Communicating biblical Scriptures to non-literate people*. New York and Bangalore: United Bible Societies and SAIACS Press.

Tarr, Del. 1994. *Double image: Biblical insights from African parables*. New York: Paulist Press.

Van Breugel, J.W.M. 2001. *Chewa Traditional Religion* (Kachere Monograph No.13). Blantyre, Malawi: CLAIM.

Vanhoozer, K. 1998. *Is there a meaning in this text?* Grand Rapids: Zondervan.

Wendland, Ernst R. 1974. *Nthano za kwa Kawaza* ("Folktales from Chief Kawaza's Land"). Lusaka: Zambia Language Group.

_____. 1979. *Stylistic form and communicative function in the Nyanja radio narratives of Julius Chongo* (PhD dissertation, University of Wisconsin, USA). Ann Arbor, MI: UMI Dissertation Services – www.il.proquest.com.

_____. 1989. "Julius Chongo's adaptation of Nyanja *nthano* to the radio." In Philip Noss (ed.), "The Ancestors' Beads," a special issue of *CrossCurrent* 2:3-4, 25-32.

_____. 1990. "Traditional central African religion." In Philip C. Stine and Ernst R. Wendland (eds), *Bridging the gap: African traditional religion and Bible translation*. Reading, UK and New York: United Bible Societies, 1-129.

_____. 1991. " 'Who do people say that I am?'—Contextualizing Christology in Africa." *Africa Journal of Evangelical Theology* 10:2, 13-32.

_____. 1992. "*UFITI*—Foundation of an indigenous philosophy of misfortune: The socioreligious implications of witchcraft and sorcery in a central African setting." In *Research in the Social Scientific Study of Religion*, vol. 4. Greenwich, CT: JAI Press. 209-243.

_____. 1998a. Buku Loyera: *An introduction to the new Chichewa Bible translation* (Kachere Monograph No. 6). Blantyre: Christian Literature Association in Malawi (CLAIM).

_____. 1998b. " 'Dear children' versus the 'antichrists': The rhetoric of reassurance in First John." *Journal of Translation and Textlinguistics* 11, 40-84.

_____. 1998c. "A 'case-study' approach to theological education in Africa." *Africa Journal of Evangelical Theology* 17:1, 41-57.

_____. 2000. *Preaching that grabs the heart: A rhetorical-stylistic study of the Chichewa revival sermons of Shadrack Wame* (Kachere Monograph No. 11). Blantyre: CLAIM.

_____. 2002. " 'Theologizing' in Bible translation, with special reference to study notes in Chichewa." *The Bible Translator* 53:3, 316-330.

_____ and Salimo Hachibamba. 2000. "A central African perspective on contextualizing the Ephesian potentates, principalities, and powers." *Missionalia* XXVIII:3, 341-363.

West, Gerald O. 1993. *Contextual Bible study.* Petermaritzburg, RSA: Cluster Publications.

_____. 1995. *Biblical hermeneutics of liberation: Modes of reading the Bible in the South African context* (2nd ed). Maryknoll, NY: Orbis Books.

Winter, Ralph D (ed). 2000. "Crossing boundaries: Radio is bringing the gospel to the unreached" (special issue). *Mission Frontiers* 22:5.

APPENDICES

Appendix A: A paper presented by TWR National Director for Malawi, Mr. Patrick Semphere

(Note: the original copy of this paper has been lightly edited in view of its inclusion here.)

EAM SCHOOL OF EVANGELISM

THEME: Proclaiming Christ to the Nations

OBJECTIVE: To Equip And Encourage The ChurchIn Malawi To The Task Of Evangelism And Discipleship.

PRESENTATION ON TRANS WORLD RADIO

PREAMBLE

We appreciate the vision of Billy Graham Evangelistic Association and indeed EAM for this crucial conference on evangelism. I am always amazed that God with all His capability to evangelise without using us (see capability to convict men of sin without the preaching of the gospel) should rely on us:

"As the Father sent me, so send I you".

"Therefore GO and make disciples of all nations…"

"And this gospel of the Kingdom will be preached in the whole world as a testimony to all nations, and then the end will come".

Last February, I was part of a team of 21 Malawians who attended *Prescription for Hope* conference on HIV/AIDS organised by the Samaritan Purse & the Billy Graham Evangelistic Association. The challenge I brought from the conference was: "If Jesus was walking the streets of our nations, would he have responded to the HIV/AIDS crisis the way we are doing?"

And here they come again, determined to ensure that Malawi does not have any excuses for not accomplishing our task. It is in this connection that I appreciate this invitation to share with you the mandate of Trans World Radio Malawi and how, in our little corner, we are striving to "proclaim Christ to the nations".

BACKGROUND

Trans World Radio is an international Christian broadcasting ministry that has been proclaiming the Good News of God's unfailing love and everlasting forgiveness for nearly five decades. We were founded in 1952 by Dr. Paul E. Freed, who had attended a special missions conference four years earlier in Switzerland and thought he was going to be a missionary to Spain. His country focus was right, but God would redirect his method. Instead of telling people one-on-one and face-to-face, Dr. Freed was led of God to consider radio as the means of telling people about Jesus.

Our first programs were aired to Spain in February, 1954, in Spanish and English from a small transmitter in Tangier, Morocco. From that humble beginning, TWR has expanded to a weekly broadcast schedule of more than 1,800 hours of Christian programming from 13 primary super-power transmitting sites and by satellite. Broadcasts are also aired via more than 2,300 local stations. Listeners in over 160 countries can hear God's Word taught in more than 180 languages and dialects. The impact has been incredible. Today, over 1.5 million letters, faxes, e-mails, and phone messages are received each year, describing how God has used the broadcasts to change lives forever.

From Brazil...
"I have been your listener since 1993, when I chanced upon your program. I listened regularly for some time, then forgot about it for awhile. Later, when I was put into prison in 1998, I started listening, again by chance, and in a superficial way, for I did not know the 'truth that frees.' About two months ago, I committed my life to Jesus Christ, and today, seek to live according to the Word of God. Since then, not one day goes by that I don't enjoy the wonderful teachings of your program. I intend to become an evangelist. I find that the broadcast is very interesting, and I have learned so much."

Some of the programs TWR airs are produced by our staff to meet the unique needs of the people living in those regions of the world. But most programs are translated and adapted for other broadcasters–ministries such as Thru the Bible Radio, Insight for Living, the International Mission Board, and the Billy Graham Evangelistic Association.

TWR's new international president, David Tucker was in the country (Malawi) two weeks ago and he briefed us of the strides TWR is making to expand into as many languages as possible–so that even more men, women, and children can hear the Gospel. We're utilizing teamwork to fulfill that goal, and we're members of the World by Radio project, along with Back to the Bible, FEBC, FEBA, Galcom International, HCJB, IBRA Radio, SIM, and Words of HOPE.

AFRICA

Broadcasts from TWR's two locations on the continent of Africa target all of sub-Saharan Africa, with a potential audience of 700 million people. Broadcasts originating from Swaziland go out over the airwaves via a 50,000-watt MW* transmitter, one 50,000-watt shortwave, three 100,000-watt shortwave transmitters, and three 200-watt FM transmitters. TWR also broadcasts over 500,000-watt and 250,000-watt shortwave transmitters from the TWR Relay station near Johannesburg, South Africa.

Trans World Radio-Africa operates a satellite network to distribute Christian programming to local radio stations throughout the continent. Programs are sent from our studios in Pretoria, South Africa, to an uplink center, which sends the programs to Intelsat Satellite 602 and PAS4. Programs can then be received by any radio station in sub-Saharan Africa with a consumer satellite dish and receiver. The first radio stations to receive these programs are located in Malawi, Tanzania, and South Africa.

LANGUAGES

Trans World Radio is broadcasting in more than 55 languages from Swaziland and from Johannesburg: Afrikaans, Amharic, Arabic, Bambara, Bemba, Borana, Chichewa, Chokwe, English, Ewe, French, Fulani, German, Hausa, Igbo, Juba Arabic, Kanuri, KiKongo, Kimbundu, Kimwani, KiRundi, Kunama, Lingala, Lomwe, Luchazi, Lunyaneka, Makhuwa, Malagasy, Mooré, Ndau, Ndebele, Nupe, Oromo-Borana, Oromo-Wellega, Pedi, Portuguese, Sena, Shangaan, Shona, Shuwa Arabic, siswati, Somali, Songhai, Sotho, Swahili, Tigre, Tigrinya, Tswa, Tswana, Tumbuka, Twi, Umbundu, Yao, Yoruba, and Zulu.

PARTNERS

Trans World Radio offices are located in Kenya, Burundi, Côte d'Ivoire, Malawi, Zimbabwe, South Africa, Mozambique, Swaziland, and Angola. Several cooperating studios also work with Trans World Radio in the region. TWR-Africa has partner organizations in Ethiopia and Nigeria.

MALAWI

In Malawi, TWR has been operational for the past 17 years, largely on shortwave. Programs have been produced in Malawi and sent to Manzini Swaziland where they have been aired. After nearly ten years of preparation, two years ago marked a milestone in the work of TWR Malawi as the Malawi government granted us an FM license for what is now known as Blantyre FM on 89.1 mHz. The station is currently covering Blantyre and most of the southern region, about 150km. We thank God that this license allows us to expand countrywide. Already the Malawi Communication Regulator Authority has given us 2 additional frequencies allowing us to expand to the central region in the next two months. Transmitting equipment has already arrived in the country—

We're currently looking for funds to buy 8 more transmitters for expansion work to the northern region of Malawi!

Range of programming:

Gospel is core
HIV/AIDS
Family Enrichment
Food security
Youth counselling.

Is anyone benefiting from these programs?

A LISTENER FROM KASUNGU, MALAWI, WRITES:

"I am a woman of 32 years old and I was working with a certain non-governmental organisation here in Kasungu as a Cashier. I used to steal cash from the money that I was keeping for the organisation though I have been a churchgoer for many years but without Christ. One day I tuned to Trans World Radio and I heard a preacher preaching the Gospel that touched my heart and I made a decision to accept Jesus as my Saviour. Right now I am a changed Christian because of the wonderful message that I heard on this Lovely Radio Station."

"I was imprisoned for three months for stealing my uncle's money while he was away. While in Police custody a friend came to see me who told me what he heard when he tuned to Trans World Radio, Manzini Swaziland. One of the things he told me was about the new life one receives when one accepts Jesus to be Lord and Saviour of one's life. Right now I am a changed person and I like listening to Trans World Radio."

Could be a member of your church—benefiting from TWR ministry!!

YOUR ROLE:

Prayer

Participation in ministry activities

Financial support, e.g., expansion of Fm

This is not begging, but a sincere call for partnership, for "this gospel of the kingdom…"

Appendix B: TWR Mission Statement and Specifics of Ministry

Mission statement

The purpose of Trans World Radio is to assist the Church to fulfill the command of Jesus Christ to make disciples of all peoples, and to do so by using and making available mass media to:

➤ proclaim the Good News about Jesus to as many people as possible
➤ instruct believers in biblical doctrine and daily Christ-like living
➤ model our message through our corporate and cooperative relationships.

we believe:

1. In one Holy, Almighty God, eternally existing in three persons, the Father, the Son and the Holy Spirit, co-eternal in being, co-identical in nature, co-equal in power and glory, each with distinct personal

attributes, but without division of nature, essence or being.
Biblical Reference: Deuteronomy 6:4, Matthew 28:19, John 1:1-2, II Corinthians 13:14, Philippians 2:6

2. In the verbal and plenary inspiration of the Old and New Testaments; that they are infallible, inerrant in the original writings, and the final authority for faith and life.
Biblical Reference: II Timothy 3:16, II Peter 1:20-21, Matthew 5:18, John 16:12- 13

3. That the Lord Jesus Christ, the eternal Son of God, without ceasing to be God, became man by the Holy Spirit and virgin birth; that he lived a sinless life on earth; that he died at Calvary as a satisfactory substitutionary sacrifice for sinners; that his body was buried in and arose from the tomb; that he ascended to Heaven and was glorified as a man at God's right hand; that He is coming again for His own and then to set up His Kingdom.
Biblical Reference: John 1:1, Matthew 1:20-23, II Corinthians 5:21, Hebrews 1:3, Hebrews 10:12, John 16: 7-11, Matthew 19:28, Matthew 25:31, II Timothy 2:8

4. That the Holy Spirit is a divine person who convicts the world of sin, of righteousness and of judgement; that He is that supernatural agent in regeneration by whom all believers are baptized into the body of Christ; that he indwells and seals them until the day of redemption. He is the divine teacher and helper who guides believers into all truth; it is the privilege of all believers to be filled with the spirit.
Biblical Reference: John 16:7-15, 1 Corinthians 12:13, II Corinthians 1:22, Ephesians 1:13

5. That God created man in His own image and in the state of innocence. Through Adam's transgression "sin entered the world, and death through sin;" and consequently, mankind inherited a corrupt nature, being born in sin and under condemnation. As soon as men are capable of moral action, they become actual transgressors in thought, word and deed.
Biblical Reference: Genesis 1:26-27, Romans 5:12, Romans 3:23, I John 1:8, Ephesians 2:3

6. That salvation is a gift of God brought to men by grace and received only through personal repentance for sin and faith in the person and the finished work and atoning blood of Jesus Christ.
Biblical Reference: Ephesians 1:7, 2:1-10, John 1:12

7. In the bodily resurrection of all men, the saved to eternal life and the unsaved to everlasting punishment. That the souls of the redeemed

are, at death absent from the body and present with the Lord where, in conscious bliss they await the first resurrection when spirit, soul, and body are reunited to be glorified forever with the Lord.

Biblical Reference: Revelation 20, Acts 24:25, John 5:28-29, Luke 16:19-31, II Corinthians 5:8, I Thessalonians 4:14-17, I John 3:2

8. That the church universal is a spiritual organism composed of the regenerated who are baptized into that body by the Holy Spirit at the time of the new birth and that the local church, the visible manifestation of the body, has the responsibility to provide for the fellowship and edification of believers and to propagate the Gospel into the world.

Biblical Reference: Acts 2, I Corinthians 12:13, Ephesians 5:27, Mark 16:15

TransWorld Radio is...

- *a global ministry.* TWR is the most far-reaching Christian radio network in the world. Each week, TWR broadcasts more than 1,800 hours of Gospel programs in over 180 languages and dialects from 13 super-power transmitting sites and by satellite. It also airs programs via more than 2,300 local stations and transmitters. TWR is on the air in more languages than BBC, Voice of America, China Radio International, and Voice of Russia combined.

- *an experienced ministry.* TWR has been broadcasting the Gospel since 1954 and continues to demonstrate global leadership, vision, and commitment in missionary radio.

- *a partnering ministry.* TWR teams with national organizations in more than 40 countries. An international staff of over 1,000 cooperate with Christian broadcasters, program producers, mission agencies, local churches, and individuals to declare the Gospel.

- *a proclaiming ministry.* TWR is bringing the message of God's love and light to those desperately searching for help and hope, particularly in seemingly impenetrable places where missionaries are unable to serve.

- *a discipling ministry.* TWR's solid Bible-teaching programs build the Body of Christ by cultivating the faith of new believers and helping Christians to daily put into practice God's Word in all areas of life.

- *a training ministry.* TWR equips church members to become better leaders and coaches pastors to proclaim the Good News of Jesus Christ even more effectively.

- *a pioneering ministry.* TWR's broadcasts help establish new Bible-believing churches on nearly every continent.

- *a high-tech ministry.* TWR is taking advantage of emerging, sophisticated technology to reach people within the 10/40 Window and other strategic areas throughout the world.

- *a connecting ministry.* TWR receives more than million letters each year from listeners in more than 160 countries. Wherever and whenever possible, staff members provide substantial listener follow-up via mail, e-mail, and personal visits.

- *a trustworthy ministry.* TWR adheres to meticulous standards of responsible stewardship and integrity set by the Evangelical Council of Financial Accountability. And since we air programs by respected evangelical leaders, TWR is broadcasting Truth that you can believe in.

Appendix C: Samples of analysis forms

I. Analysis sheet for *Chinyanja Christian Radio Drama (Sewero)*

(Use an additional page if necessary to complete all the following points.)

Play *Reference Number*(s): Your Initials: _____

Has this play been [tick]: TRANSCRIBED [   ] – TRANSLATED [   ]

1. Give any *Performance Details* (name of drama group, date of broadcast, place of performance):

2. On the back of this sheet, write an *English SUMMARY* of this play:
(What was the story about; who were the main characters and what did they do—the main events?)

3. What was the *principal lesson* or Christian teaching of this play?

4. How would you rate or "grade" this play:

excellent [   ], *good* [   ], *fair* [   ], *poor* [   ]?

   Why do you say so (give *reasons*, e.g. what insight or instruction did it give you)?

5. List all the *Bible* texts that are used and briefly summarize their *chief application*.

[Note whether they are quoted *exactly* (Q) or just *summarized* (S), with (+) or without (-) an explicit reference]

a)_____

b)_____

c)_____

d)_____

6. Was *African Traditional Religion* (*za ufiti, matsenga, kulodza, mankhwala, maula, mizimu, ziwanda, zolaula, ndi zina zotere*) referred to in this play? If so, summarize the various points or references:

7. Do you think that any *false doctrine or practice* (contrary to Scripture) is being encouraged or supported by this play? If so, tell what this is.

[NOTE: On the copy of each Chichewa transcription, circle in red ink any examples that you can find of the following: Ideophones, Idioms, Figures of Speech, Proverbs, Dramatic/Forceful Language. Be sure to give English explanations for these, where possible, in the paper margins.]

II. QUESTIONNAIRE for recording one's personal reactions to a *Sewero* program: (Available also in Chinyanja)

Title of play presented: _____

Date and Time: _____

Place and occasion: _____

Name of tester: _____ Person tested: _____

1. What is your general opinion of this *Sewero* play? Did you enjoy it or not, and why?

2. Mention two (or more) specific things that you liked about this presentation:

3. Was there anything in particular that you did *not* like about the presentation? Explain what this was:

4. Were there parts of the play that you did not understand well? If so, mention them:

5. What do you think of the Chinyanja language that was spoken—easy to understand, difficult to follow at times, very beautiful, too quickly spoken, or what? Mention any idioms that you may remember.

6. How did you like the opening and closing songs—did they fit the theme of the day's play? Explain:

What about the transitional music or drumming—how effective was that?

7. Did the background sound effects help you to visualize the events of the story in your mind? Explain:

Which sound(s) do you remember best and why?

8. What was the main point or teaching or admonition of this play?

9. How clearly and convincingly was this teaching expressed?

Could this idea have been conveyed in a better way? If so, suggest how.

10. Were the Bible passages used in a convincing way? Explain your answer.

11. Which was the most believable character (person) and why do you say so?

12. Was any character not realistic or natural? Tell why you think so.

13. Are there any other suggestions that you can make that could improve the presentation of this play?

14. Which topics would you like to see dramatized in this manner?

15. Do you listen to the *Sewero* program on TWR? How regularly? If not, why?

16. Do you think that Christians should listen to this program? If so, why—and what ages are best suited for such a presentation?

17. Would you buy a cassette tape containing two of these plays? If so, would you pay K10,000 ($2.50) for this? If not, why?

18. Could cassette tapes of this program be used in your own Christian congregation or worship group? If so, in which way(s)?

19. Do you have any other comments to make about these *Sewero* plays? Please express your opinion openly with as much detail as possible.

Appendix D: Annotated translation of a sample *Sewero* sermon "testimony"

- (Setting: We are at the last funeral rites of a young man who was killed by his elder brother by sorcery—that is, in order to gain the magical power that was intended to enrich the latter. Ironically, this surviving brother [B] now has the responsibility of making all the arrangements for his brother's funeral rites. In this scene, the elder brother introduces the village pastor [P] who preaches a short sermonette for those who have gathered at the graveyard, and then offers a prayer of protection after the body has been committed to the ground.)

(The scene opens with the mixed sounds of traditional mourning, but rather more subdued since this is a "Christian" funeral.)

E: Attention! (*Iyayi!*) Thank you very much, you elders (*akulu-akulu* – 'big-big ones', honorific term to include all those present)! Thank you very much, elders, thank you very much (i.e., this is intended to function as a call to attention, or simply to quiet down)—that you have allowed me to speak with you here at the graveyard (*kumanda*).
(The sound of mourning gradually diminishes.)

E: As for me, as I mentioned back at the village, I am not the right person (*munthu woyenera*) to speak at all (i.e., the radio audience realizes the *irony* of these words, uttered by a murderer at the grave of his victim)—I ought not be speaking here (i.e., it should really be his uncle, the *mwini-mbumba* 'owner of the clan'). This person who has left us (*Uyu wapitayu* – a *euphemism*), I repeat, was my very own younger brother (*mng'ono wanga weniweni*). Everywhere I would go, I would depend on him [for help]. As you see me standing here, well, the one who was providing for me (*ine panopa kuvala* lit. 'me right her to clothe'— *metaphor*).

But now he has left us. Brothers, brothers, thank you very much for your help [in mourning]. Thanks to all of you who have come. I do not have much to say. Indeed, I am most blessed (*Moti ndadala kwabasi!* – i.e., that so many of you have come, an honor to the family and the deceased). He has left 'six' children—five plus one (i.e., the traditional Chinyanja method of counting is given after the English borrowing)—how can I help them? Well, you allowed me to speak here at the grave. That is what I have to say. But I am sorrowful (*ndili ndi chisoni*), I am sorrowful, I am sorrowful! But Yahweh (*Chauta*) himself, the Almighty (*Mphambe*), the Creator (*Namalenga*), the Rain-Giver (*Chisumphi* – the 4th in a series of vernacular *praise names* for the Supreme Deity) knows this (i.e., how mournful I am; how I want to help the survivors). Thank you!

(The sounds of women mourning resume.)

P: Sorry (*Pepani*) all relatives, sorry all you survivors, sorry all you important people (*mafumu* lit. 'chiefs'—honorific) who have come to this place (i.e., a typical, formulaic introduction to a funeral discourse). Aaah! (chagrin) This is a very difficult time. For this reason, as I told you back at the village… I realize that some of you have joined us along the way [to the graveyard]. …so now I want to give you a summary of what I preached there:

I just want to tell you that this death, as it has happened here, does not mean that [one's] life is at an end, no indeed. Death is a 'transfer' (English)—we begin another, a new life. Now our [departed] brother, [as] I explained earlier [at the village], made a very good choice (*chisankho chabwino*), and so he prepared his way in advance. He knew Jesus to be his Savior (*Mpulumutsi*).

(The sound of mourning in the background increases in volume.)

Sorry, all you mourners, sorry—listen to me, sorry! Listen to me because Jesus is the Way. Our Lord Jesus himself speaks in 'John 14:6', saying: "I am the Way (*njira*), the Truth (*choonadi*), and the Life (*moyo*). No one comes to the Father (*Atate*), except through me!" Yes indeed! (*Eeya!*) If a person desires to go to heaven, the way is when he knows Jesus well (*adziwana ndi Yesu*). If we get separated from Jesus, things will go badly (*zatisautsa* lit. 'they have caused us to suffer'). We can be members of a church—but not for that reason. At [your] funeral, we may sing songs for you, but there in heaven it will be too tight for you (i.e., to enter inside)! (*kumwambako zidzakuthinani*)[1]

You who are alive, who are right here this afternoon, when we bury the body of our friend, you ought to look at your own life and change [it]. Are you looking at Jesus? Have you allowed this Jesus to be your Savior (*Mpulumutsi*)? Because, for sure, death can come at any time. This brother of ours was not sick for a long time at all.[2] For that reason [we see that] it can find you suddenly at any time at all. Where will you have reached (i.e., in your Christian life) when it finds you? But Jesus is ready right now today to receive you, so that when you die [down] here, you may go to be with him in glory (*ku ulemerero*) forever.

Remember the words of the Lord Jesus which he explained there in John. He said, "I am going to heaven to prepare a place for you there. So when it's ready I will come again"—his purpose is that you should be together with him there. My brother, if you refuse that place, what's going to happen? Because, if you refuse [to go] there, the place where you're going to arrive is in hell (*gahena*)—

---

[1]   Nominal "Christians" often think that simply being the member of some church, or having lots of songs sung at your [big] funeral, are sure signs that a person is "saved". On the contrary, says the Pastor, such people are going to be to fat to enter—or they will fail to pass God's last judgment. This figurative expression functions like a euphemism, to depreciate the horror of eternal separation from God and the faithful.

[2]   The unexpected, sudden death of a relatively young person always raises suspicions of sorcery or witchcraft.

in eternal punishment (*chionongeko chosatha*)! For that reason, while you are alive, you are able to become acquainted with Jesus.

As you well know, our [departed] friend's life gave an example (*chitsanzo*) that he really knew Jesus as his Savior. Even during his [personal] testimony when he would preach (i.e., as a lay leader in the congregation), he explained about the day when Jesus shed [his] blood (*adataya mwazi*) and repaired his (i.e., the man's) life (*ndi kukonza moyo wake*) and changed it to become completely new (*kuusanduliza kukhala watsopano*). That is why we are alive—and this message we are preaching to you who are living (i.e., spiritually). You who do not repent (*Osalapanu*) will not be going there (i.e., to heaven) because you are not listening to this [message of] salvation (*chipulumutso*). Jesus Christ is your Savior!

My friends, this is a good time [to repent] because then when you die here [on earth] you will be received in heaven. So while we are alive is when we really need to get our lives prepared. That is why I beg every one of you to examine his/her life individually (*payekha-payekha*) and ask yourself whether Jesus is in his life or whether he has not yet entered inside (*mukadalibemo*). So may the Lord help you when you make that choice to permit Jesus to enter your life. May he strengthen you and be with you along the journey to heaven![3]

Let us close our eyes and pray!

Father, in the name of Jesus I want to praise you very much this afternoon for the unexpected (*msonkhano wadzidzidzi*) gathering that you prepared for us right here. [Your] purpose was that this man, or this woman, or this mother, or perhaps someone who has never been to a gathering like this—might come to this place. Lord, since you have spoken by your Word that she/he might fully prepare their way, for you, Jesus, are the way—I want to thank you for that!

For that reason I [also] pray that you would convict every heart (*tsutsani moyo uli wonse*)—every stubborn heart (*moyo wa makani*), anyone who is stubborn at any time at all. But right now, Lord, I pray [that you would] convict that heart and repair that heart so that it might recognize the salvation that is in you, Jesus. Remove that evil heart from within them and replace it with a new heart of [soft] flesh (*ndikuikamo mtima watsopano wa mnofu*)!

And now, O Lord, I want to "inoculate" this place (*nditsirike malo ano*), for I know that when such things happen (i.e., a sudden death), he comes here with his messengers to play and to disturb things (*kumadzasewera ndi kudzasok-*

---

3   This Preacher's manner of sermonizing follows a simple, standard popular Evangelical model that features a "decision theology" approach which emphasizes one's personal decision and a subsequent radically changed life-style that is manifested when one becomes a Christian believer. Unfortunately, he does not spend a great time explaining and applying his chosen biblical text (John 14:6) in its original text and co-text (cp. Wendland 2000:chap. 6). His following prayer, however, is much more overtly contextualized in the light of the prevailing traditional religious beliefs and practices of Nyanja society, the occult in particular.

oneza).[4] For that reason I protect this place in the name of Jesus. I sprinkle the blood of Jesus Christ on this whole place (i.e., the gravesite) so that if anyone wants to come and disturb it (i.e., by means of occult religious practices)—perhaps even to obtain their magical charms (*zizimba zawo* – e.g., by removing some key body parts) in order to do foolish things (*zopusa* – i.e., to practice witchcraft, *ufiti*), I hereby repudiate [them] and innoculate [this place] in the name of Jesus!

For this reason, Lord Jesus, [we ask you to] do your wondrous work [here] (*muchite chodabwitsa*), as you always do for [us], [and] protect us all together (*katichinjirizeni pamodzi*) all the while as we leave this place to return home, to the funeral house (*siwa*). Lord, I pray that you would be in our midst and strengthen us—especially all the mourners (*anamalira onse*) we leave them in your hands. Comfort them most mightily (*Muwatonthoze komanso kwakukulu*) so that they might know you Jesus Christ (i.e., through this personal experience) as their [source of] salvation. Do these things, O our God, even as [we] await the fulfillment of your Word (*poyembekezera mau anu*). In the name of Jesus we have prayed—'Amen'!

Appendix E: Translation of part of an interview with Josophat Banda[5]—On the threat of witchcraft in Christian congregations

Aaah (with regret), these days, or we might say ever since long ago, this problem of witchcraft (*ufiti*) has been very great indeed in the churches, especially those that do not teach very well about the power (*mphamvu*) that is in the blood (*mwazi*) of Jesus Christ. For those who do not know this, it is difficult to say that they do not fear witchcraft, and it is difficult for them to remain steadfast in the [Christian] faith (*okhazikika m'chikhulupiriro*). This is because if there is anything that can hinder Christianity here on earth it is

---

[4]   The Pastor here takes the place of the traditional medicine man (*sing'anga*) whose job it is to supernaturally "protect" a new gravesite from the malicious activities of witches (*mfiti*). Although "Satan" may seem to play the role of the witch in this conception, the latter is probably also in mind—that is, as an agent ("messenger") of the former, the principal Enemy. This performative act of protection is ritually "sealed", as it were, with the figurative "blood" of Christ, i.e., by the power of his death on the cross for the believer whose body now lies beneath the ground.

[5]   Rev. Josophat Banda is the chief playwright of the *Sewero* troupe. In this interview he spoke to me about his dramatic work as well as his evangelistic-revivalistic ministry, which is his chief occupation. His words are a clear indication that the stories about witchcraft that the team composes and performs are not fictional—they come from everyday life.

witchcraft. [Witches/sorcerers] can frighten a person, perhaps by causing [mysterious] fires to appear (*kumuyatsira moto*) in different places, so that if that person does not know the power of Jesus Christ at that moment, s/he may be tempted to go to a medicine man (*sing'anga*). Is it not true that a person desires help if one night when sleeping he suddenly realizes that he is somewhere outside [the house] (i.e., having been mystically "transported" there by the action of sorcery)!?

I recall that one day I arose early in the morning to go somewhere and I met a certain lady who asked me, "Pastor, would you help me with some 'lessons' (*malesoni*) about witchcraft? I have a problem in that my son every night when we go to bed—in the morning when I get up I find him outside. Every morning I find that he is outside the house! Sometimes I notice blood on his mouth (i.e., a sure sign that the boy has been engaged in the practice of witchcraft during the night.) I immediately realized that I have a serious problem, so I quickly went to a medicine man—I went there fast! But this problem has not ended [so what can I do?]!" So I told her, "Aah, you simply trouble yourself [for nothing]. A medicine man cannot help [you]. The only one who can help is Jesus Christ, namely, when you know and receive him.

The other thing that causes people to remain weak (*ofooka* – i.e., in their faith-life) is that, for our part, we teachers do not preach the real truth (*choonadi cheni-cheni*) or sow the words of faith (*kusolera mau achikhulu-piriro*), which is able to free them. If we do not teach them, it becomes difficult for a person who seeks help—and that is when he may go to medicine men. It is for this reason that 'Isaiah 3, verse 12' says, "My people are being destroyed because of those who are leading them!"

This is indeed a problem, but [the activity of] witches in [Christian] congregations and other areas is an even more terrible trouble. As a result, many people are being oppressed, even though it is a hidden affair (*nkhani yobisika*). Yes, this is a huge problem. I recall that I went to preach somewhere, we call the place *Mvera* ('Listen!'), and I preached at a certain church. When I had finished, a certain gentleman [came up and] said, "Aah (discouragement), I would like you to help me, but I will find (visit) you [some other time]." After that, he left the place and went home. When he arrived—now it took no time at all (*sadatenge nthawi*)—I think that he made use of magic (*matsenga*), perhaps he flew (*mwina adauluka* – i.e., making use of a magical "airplane" derived from the practice of witchcraft). So it did not take long—I would say, just '15 minutes' (English)—and he was there, even though it was very far away.

The next morning he came to see me and said, "I want you to help me because I have been worshiping (*ndikupemphera* lit. 'I am praying') for many years and am even the secretary (*mlembi*) of the congregation. But my problem is this..." And then he gave me a very black little pouch (*kasaka kakuda kwambiri*) and took out a long bottle (*kabotolo kakatali*)—in length about like this—really black! (*ka bii* – ideophone) Then he said, "Don't put your hand in here! (*m'menemumu musagwire*) And when you are praying, never touch this!" But I said, "In the name of Jesus I will touch it!"

So after I prayed, I grabbed it in the name of Jesus. I opened it up—[my] but (*koma*) inside there were some very black items that seemed like they were rotten, very bad indeed! (*zoipa kambiri!*) So I asked him, "What is this?!" He replied, "This is magic (*mankhwala*). When you hear about a 'calabash' (*supa*), well, here's one! So as far as I'm concerned, there's nobody who can play around with me!" (*sangandiseweretse ayi!*) I said, "Well today I am telling you that someone—Jesus Christ—will play with you! We are going to take and burn these things up (*tiocha*)!" So we went and smashed [them] all up (*tidaphwanya*).

So those people (i.e., the family and friends of the former sorcerer) came to the Lord. [They asked], "How is it possible that you burned [it all] up—will you not go mad?! (*moti basi simupenga?*)" [I said], "Well, since the time of [our church] gathering yesterday right until this morning I have not gone mad." So there was a lot of magical items that the people [in the area] brought to be burned—about 'three-quarters' of the people of the 'church' where I had preached came along with problems about this witchcraft business (*mavuto a zanyangazi*) to repent [and confess], "We were cutting these incisions [for magical protection] (*timatemera mphini*). We were doing this—we were doing that (*timatere—timatere*)." There were about '40-50' [people] in all. Thus if the 'church' has a sin like this—[involving] '40-50' [people]—that's about the whole church! That's the problem of witchcraft—for many 'churches' it is a terrible problem.

We are really explaining to people about witchcraft through these plays, which affect many people (*zimakhudza kwabasi*). [The *Sewero* players] focus on [the subject of] witchcraft, preaching—but especially by showing [in the plays themselves]. In many places, when I go for a [church] meeting (*msonkhano*), I announce in the 'microphone' (English), "We are beginning a meeting today and will be here for three days. If there are any witches (*mfiti*) in the village here, you'd better not come and try to practice it (*musadzidzatamba*)—[for] you are fools (*zitsiru*)!" We are doing this in many places [in Malawi] as God is our witness.

There was one elder whom I had married in Dedza, and he was a witch. Once when I was preaching with the 'microphone', saying that, "If you practice witchcraft (*ngati umadziwa kutamba*), there's no fool like you—you are a fool of fools (*chitsiru cha zitsiru zonse*)! See if you can do anything to us (*utipeze* lit. 'may you find us')—we're here today, and tomorrow, and the day after that (i.e., an open challenge to all "witches" in the crowd to try their worst!)." So [this man] came, but his manner of coming (*kabweredwe kake*) was very strange. He looked like he had been in a [car] accident (*adavulala*). He came and told us, "I came [to practice witchcraft]..." But what I saw was that he had changed into a what-you-call... (*adasanduka ujeni*).

(Rev. Banda interrupts his account at this point to interject a word of explanation.) There is witchcraft (*ufiti*), magic (*matsenga*), and sorcery (*nyanga*). There are these three types of [malicious] people.

[This fellow] had changed into a bird and came [to the meeting] by means of magic, but when he arrived, he was felled (*adadzagwa* – i.e., by a supernatural power greater than his).[6] That morning he made his testimony [to me] about what he had experienced (*zimene adaziona* lit. 'what he saw'). [He was] praising the Lord so I brought him [to the worship meeting] to make a great public testimony. In this way we are able to preach and to insult them (i.e., any witches that happen to be present), as we have been doing.

Aaah! (disgust) most of the time witches are fools—people who are ashamed (*amanyazi*) and afraid (*amantha*). You see this when we publicly expose them (*tikamayalutsa pagulu*). They do not say a word, and they are ashamed, saying [to themselves], "If I stand up, they'll say I'm a witch!" The same for sorcery (*nyanga*)—hidden knowledge—"If I say anything, they will call me a sorcerer!" What these people do is simply keep [their secret], saying [to themselves], "As soon as those people have gone to sleep, then we'll see [what will happen to them]!" During the day they cannot speak [like this] since they know how they must practice their magic.

Now for their repentance (*kulapa kwawo*): When they come at night [to bewitch people], they see the power [of Christ] and how we rebuke (*tanyoza*)—we rebuke—we rebuke [them]! So when we go to sleep, we know what to do, saying (i.e., praying), "O Lord, you know that we have done what we could (*tachita izi-izi*), and now we are going to sleep. We protect (*tikutsirika*) this house by the blood of our Lord Jesus!" So we pray for a wall of fire (*linga la moto*)—a wall of fire—that it would stand between us [and those witches] by faith. So when those people come with the intention of biting us (*adzatiluma* – i.e., to bewitch us), they could get seriously injured (*atha kuvulala*), and that is what has happened in many places. [For

---

[6]   In a traditional occult setting, a potent and experienced medicine man (*sing'anga*) is believed to have the magical power to "fell" (*gwetsa*) the attack "aircraft" (*ndege*) of a witch. In this case, the man of God appears to possess similar protective power, which he accesses from Christ through prayer. Indeed, the dividing line is not always very clear, and the power "source" might just as easily be demonic as divine.

example], there was a certain man at Nkhoma, Chimphire Village, who died; he had come [to the meeting] through the magic of his witchcraft (*m'njira ya matsenga*).

We also preached at a [worship] meeting where there was a dense thicket (*nkhalango*) close by. Frequently witches would perform their bewitchment rites (*kumatamba*) at that place. When '7 o'clock' arrived (i.e., p.m.—the time of the worship service) we learned that many people were afraid to come since they had to pass by that thicket. When we heard that report, we went over there and announced that at that thicket where the people feared to go we would say a prayer: "Today, if any witch comes, may he die on the spot! And if it is your will, let me testify (*ndithirire umboni*) [by saying], 'If you practice witchcraft, if you know how to fly [the witch's night craft], let's see if you can find us here. Right here is the house where we intend to sleep! But if you cannot find us, then you are indeed a fool!'"

Now there was a certain man in the village there who possessed some gremlins (*ndondocha*). So he came that night by way of his magical flight (*m'njira youlukira*)—right there at the place where we said we'd be sleeping. However, he fell [out of the sky] (*adagwa*) on his airplane (*ndege*). God showed us a bird that wanted to land, but instead it fell down (i.e., as a visible sign of the foiled attack of witchcraft). So the next morning—it was Saturday because the meeting began Friday night—we announced that a certain person (i.e., the witch) had been injured when he "crashed" with his plane. We said, "If you know that it was you [who fell], come and repent!" But 'at that time' (English) he did not want to come and submit or to explain; he just stayed where he was.

At the end of the week we returned here to Lilongwe (i.e., where this interview was being recorded) [and stayed three days]—'Monday', 'Tuesday', 'Wednesday'. Now that fellow told his family, "I caught this illness that I have at church (*matenda anga ano ndawatengera ku chalichi*). So go call that pastor who was preaching there so he can help me!" Unfortunately, his people arrived only to find that I had already left to go and preach someplace else. That man died—it was on the 'first of January, 1996' (English). He died without repenting (*osalapa*)!

Indeed, when we travel, we assure Christians that they can find power and sufficient protection in Jesus Christ. "If you receive him and remain with him, faithful, and also remain with the Holy Spirit, for sure you will have a victorious life (*moyo wa chigonjetso*). But there is one problem that we have—which is to reach many places. It's difficult because traveling is hard. But that's how we do our preaching, and it is the way of preaching to people by showing them a play. It is a powerful way because we are performing in the very village where the witches may reside. When people see that nothing happens to us, they begin to trust us, saying, "Truly, these people... the power of God is really here! (*mphamvu ya Mulungu ilipodi*)!" Some say this and others say that (*suja amanena izi, amanena izi* – i.e., predicting a disaster for the evangelists), but nothing happened at all!" So if even the witches are afraid, that's it—all their fear retreats and [finally] is finished. (*mantha aja amabwerera ndipo amatha!*)

In order for us to be effective (*Kuti tichite zogwirika*), we must know what we are saying about medicine men and witches, and we know [about] them because of our preaching. For example, in many places where we preach about the power of Jesus Christ, perhaps there is someone present who's a witch. Then perhaps God calls him through his grace, and he comes and explains, "As for my problem [of witchcraft], I was doing such and such (*ndinkachita chakuti*)." So after he has explained (i.e., confessed), then we help him. [Later we ask], "What about these things? How do you do them? And how do you start out [being a witch/sorcerer]?" For this reason, with these very hands I have burned a witch's airplane (*ndege ya mfiti*). And I snatched many more (*ndidaigwiragwiraponso*), not only at one place, but at many. Therefore, when I describe witchcraft (i.e., in a *Sewero* play), I am able to explain exactly what they do, how they begin to bewitch, and what happens when they change their appearance. I know very well about all this because of the people whom I preached to, after they repented (i.e., and told me their diabolical tales).

Appendix F: A Comparison with Medieval Miracle-Mystery Plays

In this appendix we will turn back the pages of history to medieval times in order to consider a partially corresponding analogy to the *Sewero* dramatic productions:

For many centuries in the early (Western) Christian era drama was vigorously opposed by the church due to its apparent promotion of pagan thought and practice. By the end of the first millennium,[7] however, short dramatic pieces were gradually being introduced into the liturgy by the priests and monks, with a particular emphasis upon the passion story and Christ's resurrection. The great significance of this artistic-didactic development is concisely summarized by the church historian Philip Schaff:

> An important aid to popular religion was furnished by the sacred drama which was fostered by the clergy and at first performed in churches, or in the church precincts. It was in some measure a mediaeval substitute for the sermon and the Sunday-school (1907:869).

As time went on, more and more segments of the gospel story and well-known Old Testament events were being dramatized for the purposes of religious instruction—and no doubt also to attract a crowd. This led to the later development of several relatively long and elaborate "cycles" of biblical history, which were composed within and attached to a particular parish or area of ecclesiastical influence.[8] Dialogues based on Scripture (originally, still largely in Latin!) were introduced, thus providing people with no direct contact with the Word of God at least some knowledge of selected Bible content.

The high point of religious drama in England and Germany was generally reached during the 15th century. By this time the business of production and acting had been turned over to gifted lay people, while the preferred settings of performance had shifted to the public squares and streets (Schaff 1910:736). This was genuine folk art and, at the same time popular religion, for these homespun miracle-mystery plays were enjoyed by all segments of society—rich and poor, prince and peasant alike. The repertory of themes treated became quite extensive as well, eventually covering the gamut of Scriptures, from Adam's fall to some rather vividly embellished portrayals of Revelation's graphic visions. Unfortunately, as the topical scope widened and the plays' popularity increased, so also the manner of treatment correspondingly changed. Thus the original intention, stemming from a strong religious and educational motivation, began to be overshadowed by the desire merely to please and entertain the fickle masses. More and more imaginative facets were introduced into biblically based accounts, and a subdued, subtle humor gradually gave way to burlesque, buffoonery, and the farcical:

---

[7] It is interesting to note that "mediaeval drama had its first literary expression in the six short plays [celebrating martyrdom and celibacy] of Hroswitha, a *nun* belonging to the Saxon convent of Gandersheim, who died about 980" (Schaff 1907:870; cf. Cross & Livingstone 1974:425).

[8] These dramatic plays are variously termed (in English): "mysteries", "miracle plays", or "moralities". There were four English cycles of miracle plays: York, Chester, Coventry, and Wakefield; the first dates back to 1360 and contains about 50 plays (Schaff 1910:737).

288

These elements were furnished by Judas, the Jews, and the devil, who were made the butts of ridicule. Judas was paid in bad coin. The devil acted a double part. He tempts Eve by his flatteries… But he is as frequently represented as the stupid bungler. He was the mediaeval clown, the dupe of devices excelling his own shrewdness… His mishaps were the subject of infinite merriment (Schaff 1907:873).[9]

As the secular began to overtake what was sacred in many (not all) of these productions, certain quarters of the church again became more vocal in their opposition to this form of religious art. Nevertheless, it could still be said that for many years, up to and including part of the 16th century, "the [common] people found in [these miracle and mystery plays] an element of instruction which, perhaps, the priest did not impart" (Schaff 1910:736). Their gradual demise at that time coincided with two major concurrent movements, one spiritual, the other profane—namely, the rise of the Reformation and the growth of purely secular theatre in Europe.[10]

There are, along with the obvious differences, a number of important similarities that link medieval religious drama and the modern Chinyanja *Sewero* radio plays. Foremost among these is their central communicative function—that is, to offer a popular means of biblical *instruction* to the masses, a large majority of whom still do not have a ready access to God's Word (nowadays, the main barrier is literacy). The message is presented in a vividly idiomatic, interesting and attractive, at times humorous, dramatic form, and it normally deals with contemporary moral issues that the people are seriously concerned with or eagerly want to learn more about. Especially moving and memorable depictions easily enter into the living vernacular "oral tradition" where their particular instruction, warning, or correction continues to circulate widely and to promote their didactic influence within the "public domain". Christian lay people are again in the vanguard of the essential composition and drama production process. They are thus able to provide in many instances what amounts to a distinct, non-conventional (or relatively "un-dogmatic") perspective on the interpretation of some of the key themes, issues, and actual passages of Scripture as well as their contextualized local application to the current crises and challenges of today's African society. Thus the *Sewero* plays, just like their medieval counterparts,

---

[9]   In keeping with the lamentable prejudices of these times, biblical women too were often portrayed in a crude, unflattering manner. In the popular Noah's Flood play, for example, the patriarch's wife "alone held out and scolded while the others worked…[and as] they were about the set sail…still she resisted entreaty, and all hands were called to join together 'and fetch her in'" (Schaff 1910:737-738). As an outstanding instance of excessive burlesque, one might cite "the feast of the Ass—*festum asinorum*—[in which] the beast that Balaam rode was the chief *dramatis persona*" (Schaff 1907:875).

[10]   Since that time, publicly performed religious drama has not been very popular in Western Christianity, with several important exceptions—for example, T S Eliot's *Murder in the Cathedral*, and the gospel "Passion Play" performed every decade since 1634 at Oberammergau in Bavaria.

offer many contemporary applications of an ancient popular dramatic method that has now been coupled with a modern mode of message delivery to encourage creative theological and moral communication in the primary vernacular of south-central Africa.

Cross, F L and Livingstone, E A, eds. 1974. *The Oxford Dictionary of the Christian Church* (2nd ed.). Oxford: Oxford University Press.

Schaff, P 1907. *History of the Christian Church* (Vol. V: "The Middle Ages"). Grand Rapids: Eerdmans.

Schaff, P 1910. *History of the Christian Church* (Vol. VI: "The Middle Ages"). Grand Rapids: Eerdmans.

INDEX

A

291

Printed in the United States
58266LVS00002B/463-471